The Anglo-Saxon Way of Death

Burial Rites in Early England

SAM LUCY

SUTTON PUBLISHING

First published in the United Kingdom in 2000 by
Sutton Publishing Limited · Phoenix Mill
Thrupp · Stroud · Gloucestershire · GL5 2BU

Copyright © Sam Lucy, 2000

All rights reserved. No part of this publication may be reproduced, stored in a retrieval system, or transmitted, in any form or by any means, electronic, mechanical, photocopying, recording or otherwise, without the prior permission of the publisher and copyright holder.

Sam Lucy hereby asserts the moral right to be identified as the author of this work.

British Library Cataloguing in Publication Data
A catalogue record for this book is available from the British Library.

ISBN 0-7509-2103-X

Typeset in 10/12 pt Sabon.
Typesetting and origination by
Sutton Publishing Limited.
Printed and bound in England by
J.H. Haynes & Co. Ltd, Sparkford.

Contents

Acknowledgements   v

1   ANGLO-SAXON CEMETERIES: AN INTRODUCTION   1
What is an Anglo-Saxon Cemetery? 1   A Short History of Anglo-Saxon Cemeteries 5   From Invasion to Ideology: Changing Perspectives in Anglo-Saxon Cemetery Research 14

2   DATING BURIALS AND GRAVE-GOODS IN ANGLO-SAXON CEMETERIES   16
How are Burials Dated? 16   Jewellery and Dress Ornaments 25   Weaponry 47   Vessels and Other Grave-goods 51   The Meanings of Things 63

3   INHUMATION BURIAL PRACTICE   65
Introduction 65   Interpreting Skeletal Remains 65   Pre- and Post-mortem Burial Rites 75   Variations in Skeletal Position 78   Multiple Burials 82   Variations in Costume and Related Grave Furnishings 83   Other Variations in Burial Practice 95   Variations in Grave Structure 97   Interpreting Variations in Burial Rites 103

4   CREMATION BURIAL PRACTICE   104
Introduction 104   The Cremation Process 104   Cremation Pyres 106   Interpreting Cremated Skeletal Remains 106   Cremation Grave-goods 108   Animal Remains as Grave Offerings 112   Interpreting Cremation Urns and Containers 113   Interpreting Variations in Grave Structure 116   Interpreting Variations in Cremation Burial Rites 119

5   STUDYING CEMETERIES   123
Introduction 123   The Landscape Context of Cemeteries 124   Cemetery Layout 130   Cemetery Composition 139   Burning and Burying the Dead: Cremation and Inhumation 140   Cemeteries Through Space 146   Cemeteries Through Time 149   The Living and the Dead: Cemeteries and Settlements 152

CONTENTS

6 FROM MIGRATION TO INVASION — 155
The Impact of the Historians, 1800–1900 155   Tracing the Conquest Through Pots and Brooches, 1850–2000 163   Relating Artefacts to Identities 173

7 DEVELOPING ALTERNATIVES — 174
Debating Culture-history and Rethinking Ethnicity 174   Tracing the Conversion 181   Conclusions 184

Bibliography — 187
Index — 205

Acknowledgements

I would like to thank the following for supplying me with information on unpublished sites and material: Tim Reynolds (Cambridgeshire County Council), Roy Canham (Wiltshire County Archaeologist), Colin Pendleton and John Newman (Suffolk County Council), Alison Tinniswood (Hertfordshire County Council), Tim Grubb (Gloucestershire County Council), Bruce Howard (Hampshire County Council), David Motkin (Wight Heritage), Paul Cuming (Kent County Council), Mark Bennet (Lincolnshire County Council), Edwin Rose (Norfolk Landscape Archaeology), Susan Freebrey (Northamptonshire County Council), Virginia Baddeley (Nottinghamshire County Council), Emma Jones (Warwickshire County Council), Victoria Buteux (Worcestershire County Council), D.H. Evans (Humber Archaeology Partnership), Linda Smith (North Yorkshire County Council), Richard Knox (Leicestershire County Council), A.M. Myres (Derbyshire County Council) and Jonathon Last (Hertfordshire Archaeological Trust).

Nick Stoodley, Dominic Powlesland and Andrew Reynolds supplied me with unpublished data from their fieldwork and excavations, for which I am extremely grateful, while the following gave permission to cite from their unpublished theses: Becky Gowland, Geoff Harrison, Tania Dickinson and Catherine Mortimer. Phil Howard provided much-needed assistance with the computer-generated maps, John Naylor with the computer database, Trevor Woods with the photography, and I would also like to thank Sudeshna Guha (Cambridge University Museum of Archaeology and Anthropology) and Kenneth Penn (Norfolk Landscape Archaeology) for their help in obtaining photographs, and John Collis (University of Sheffield), Martin Carver (University of York) and Charlotte Roberts (University of Durham) for supplying me with illustrations. Most especially, my thanks are due to Yvonne Beadnell, to whom all the original artwork is acknowledged.

I am also most grateful for the constructive comments made by Catherine Hills (University of Cambridge), Martin Carver (University of York), and Geoff Harrison and Becky Gowland (both University of Durham) on a draft version of this book. All errors, however, remain my own. Finally, I would like to thank all those people with whom I have discussed material and ideas, and all those who have offered encouragement, especially the very patient Rupert Harding and Sarah Cook of Sutton Publishing. Last of all, special thanks go to my husband Mark, for not complaining (too much) when I spent most of Christmas and New Year 1999 with my computer rather than him.

ONE

ANGLO-SAXON CEMETERIES: AN INTRODUCTION

WHAT IS AN ANGLO-SAXON CEMETERY?

In the fifth century AD new burial practices started to appear in the eastern half of Britain (**Fig. 1.1**). These different ways of burying the dead included cremating the deceased on a funeral pyre, rather than burying them straight in the ground, as had been the usual practice for around two centuries in the preceding Roman period. The cremated ashes were collected off the pyre and placed inside a (sometimes elaborately decorated) pottery urn which was then deposited in a pit, often with grave offerings in the form of combs, tweezers and other cosmetic items, and occasionally the remains of clothing (brooches, for example) that the dead person had been wearing when cremated. The existing methods of burial were not entirely replaced though. Indeed, burying the dead unburnt was by far the most popular mode of burial, certainly by the sixth century. Here too, the dead were often buried fully clothed (identified again by the remains of metalwork and occasionally by preserved textiles which archaeologists find in the graves). They were frequently given other offerings – joints of meat, and pottery or metal vessels that presumably contained portions of food or drink. A number of these unburnt burials (or inhumations) were accompanied by items of weaponry, such as spears, shields and swords (**Fig. 1.2**).

What brought about these alterations in burial rites? In the decades following the withdrawal of Roman control from lowland Britain in the early fifth century, major changes were seen in where and how people lived, and especially in how they buried their dead. That the dead were often buried with grave-goods, and were also sometimes cremated, suggests that non-Christian burial rites were in use, marking a major shift away from the official religion of the late Roman Empire. Late Roman Christian cemeteries such as Poundbury in Dorset (Farwell & Molleson 1993) are characterised by largely unfurnished burial, with the bodies laid out in the grave so that heads were consistently placed at the west end. Their locations were different too: burial within the walls of Roman towns and cities was forbidden by law, so cemeteries were often placed by the side of major roads leading into centres of population (known as 'extra-mural' cemeteries, literally outside the walls).

Cemeteries of the fifth and sixth centuries AD in eastern Britain differed from these earlier places of burial, and also from contemporary rites in western and northern Britain (which maintained a tradition of west–east unfurnished burial, cf. Alcock 1992; James 1992) quite

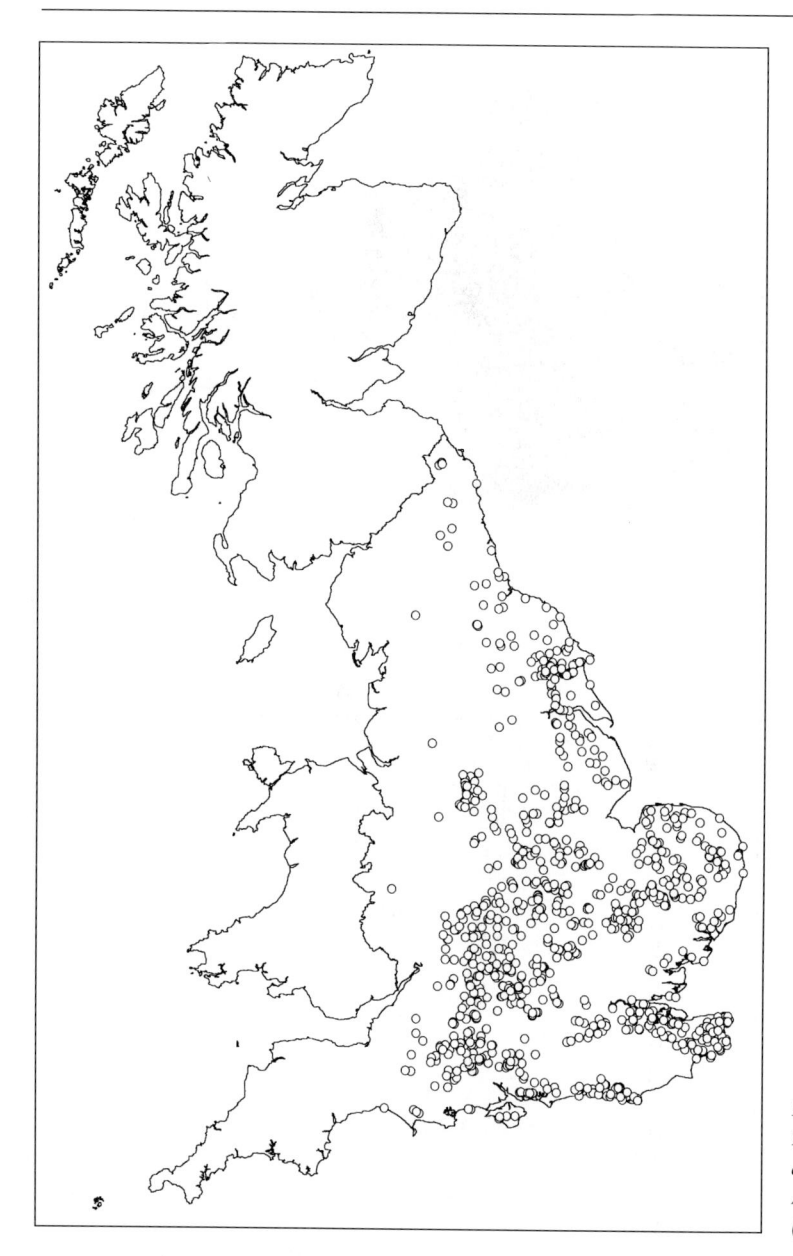

Fig. 1.1. Map of the British Isles, showing the distribution of all furnished Anglo-Saxon cemeteries. (Author)

markedly. Although some of these Anglo-Saxon cemeteries did position the dead so their heads were largely pointing in one direction, variability was more common. These cemeteries are often found away from the Roman towns, often in quite rural locations. There is obviously a link here with where people were living at the time: Roman Britain had a substantial urban population, whereas 'living in towns' was not a major feature of settlement in the following centuries. The people of the fifth and sixth centuries lived in wooden houses in small- to medium-sized settlements, ranging from the five to seven

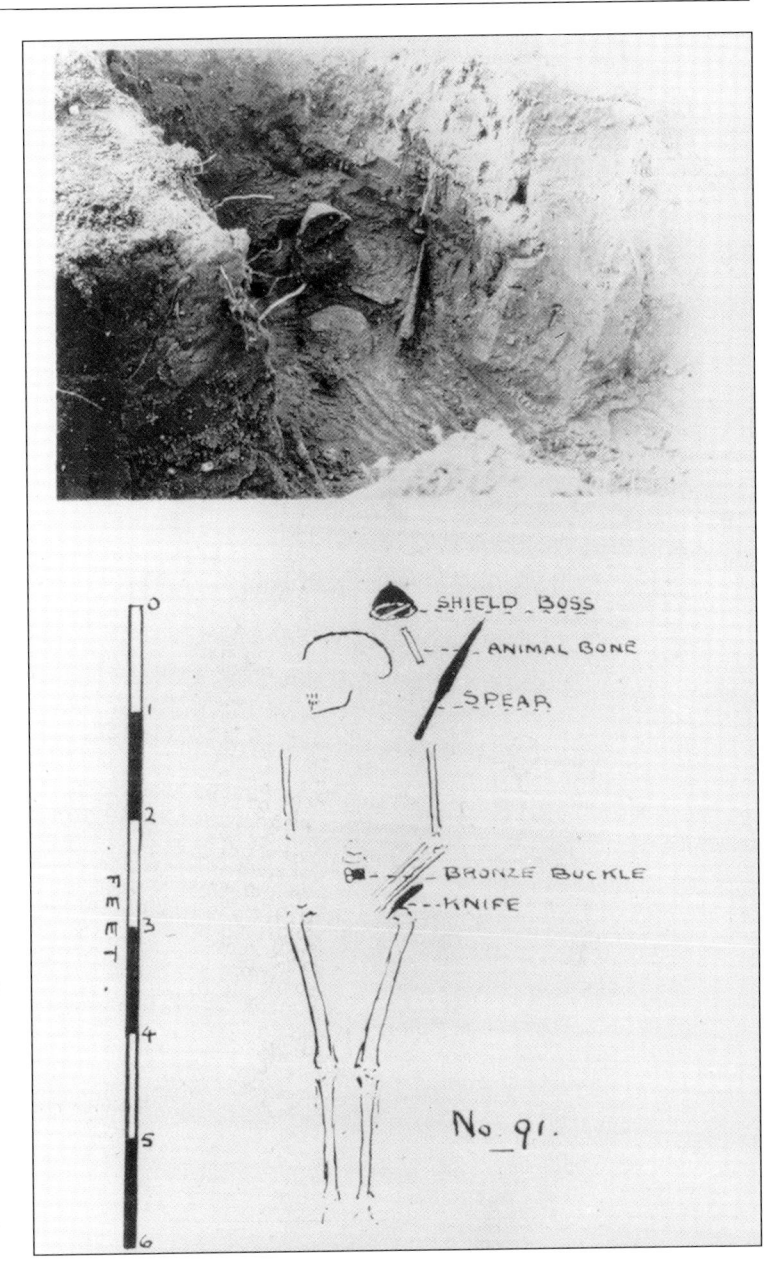

Fig. 1.2. An early excavation by Tom Lethbridge of G91 at Holywell Row, accompanied by the preliminary plan of the grave. (Copyright Cambridge University Museum of Archaeology and Anthropology, Acc. No. LS 44872.)

farmsteads of West Stow in Suffolk (West 1985), to the more village-like appearance of West Heslerton in North Yorkshire (Powlesland 1997a). The shift to furnished burial, in particular the burial of weapons (another practice banned under Roman law), and the use of cremation suggest that major changes in society were afoot. What caused these changes?

It is often assumed that these new burial rites were brought to Britain by immigrants from across the North Sea during the fifth and sixth centuries AD, and several features of these new rites do indeed imply links with continental Europe in this period. Inhumation burial with weapons, especially, was not generally seen in Britain during the Roman period, but is evidenced in northern Gaul (that part of the Roman Empire which is now northern France and Belgium) in the latter years of the fourth century AD (Böhme 1974; James 1988: 45–51), though occasional cremations with weapons are found in northern Germany outside the empire before this. Some of the brooch and pottery forms also find close parallels in contemporary cemeteries on the other side of the North Sea, especially in the area which is now north-west Germany. Cremation itself was the predominant rite throughout the third and fourth centuries AD in northern Germany. As will be explained in Chapter Seven of this book, however, these similarities do not mean that we can infer that everyone buried in an 'Anglo-Saxon cemetery' was, in fact, an 'Anglo-Saxon' – an immigrant from northern Europe. The immediately post-Roman period in Britain, and indeed in the whole of Europe, was a time when identities were in an extreme state of flux, generated by the fading power of the Roman Empire, when charismatic leaders could gather strong bands of followers around them and gain control of often extensive tracts of territory. Their territories later derived their names from the elite groups – France after the Franks, England after the Angles. Just because we know from early documentary sources that most of what is now England was comprised of Anglian and Saxon kingdoms by the seventh century AD, we cannot infer from this that all the people living in these kingdoms were descended from migrants of two centuries before. When the term Anglo-Saxon is used in this book, it is as a descriptive shorthand for the type of cemetery under discussion – furnished cemeteries of the fifth to early eighth centuries AD – and it is not intended to convey any ethnic connotations. The story of how these cemeteries came to be seen as graves of immigrants is, however, an extremely interesting one, which sheds much light on how early archaeologists approached their evidence. Chapter Six explores this story in detail, while Chapter Seven argues that many of the assumptions involved, especially about the relationship of burial rites with what we now call 'ethnic identity', are highly questionable. Given that the origins of 'The English' are often traced back to the people buried in these cemeteries, these questions are important ones.

Another period of radical change in the burial rite can be seen towards the end of the sixth century AD, coinciding fairly closely with the first Christian missions from Gaul into eastern Britain. (This period of furnished burial is often termed the 'Final Phase'.) The arrival of St Augustine in Canterbury in AD 597 at the behest of the Frankish princess Bertha, wife of King Aethelbert of Kent, indicates the sort of high-level contacts that existed between the elites of the newly emerging kingdoms. The changes visible in the burial rites of the last three or four decades of the sixth century and the early decades of the seventh century, with different grave-goods starting to be used and different burial practices employed, indicate other kinds of influence. The raising of earthen barrows over graves came into wider use around this time, while weapon shapes changed and jewellery became more 'refined'. The large florid brooches and brightly coloured bead strings of the early and mid-sixth century came to be replaced by delicate gold and garnet jewellery, silver pendants and rings. The so-called 'princely' graves at Sutton Hoo (Suffolk), where the ship burial in mound 1 was famously excavated in 1939 on the eve of the Second World War, and Benty Grange (Derbyshire), with its copper helmet topped by a figurine of a boar, both belong to this new series of barrow burials, and are assumed to reflect these emerging aristocracies who seem to have had vast resources and wealth at their disposal, to judge from their grave offerings. Although such burials and other contemporary cemeteries are probably not Christian, they are evidence for close contacts with the continental Christian kingdoms at this time. These later sixth- and seventh-century burial rites in eastern Britain are not just tied in to the Frankish sphere, however, for they also show strong links with contemporary Scandinavian practice, for example in the use of ship burial and the raising of large barrows at Sutton Hoo. These rites are paralleled by sites in Scandinavia such as Vendel and Valsgärde, and the forms of the weapons and art styles used at these two sites are also closely linked. Moreover, the material culture from Sutton Hoo evidences a wide range of contacts from across Europe and into northern Africa. What lay behind these widespread contacts? Why did people at this time feel the need to borrow traditions and use artefacts from such far-flung places as Egypt and eastern Sweden in their burial rituals? Investigating such issues can help to shed light on the role that the burial rite played in the societies of eastern Britain at this time.

In the course of the seventh and eighth centuries the use of furnished inhumation gradually died out in Britain. While this has been linked to the strengthening of Christian ideology and belief, it is clear from looking at the Frankish burial rites of the sixth century that there was no immediate contradiction between Christianity and the use of grave-goods. Indeed, the church never banned grave-goods; other reasons must be sought for this further change in burial practices.

It is clear that burial evidence in eastern Britain in the fifth to eighth centuries represents a range of contacts and influences from various parts of Scandinavia and continental Europe. Ideas about how these influences made their way to Britain have been subject to scholarly (and not so scholarly) debate for the better part of two hundred years. While these ideas will be outlined and explored further in Chapters Six and Seven, it is instructive to look at the origins of these debates, when physical remains were first starting to be identified as 'Anglo-Saxon' (i.e. dating to this period in British history). The next section will take a look at the early archaeologists working in this area, showing how they came to correctly identify and date the remains of their excavations, and at standards of excavation and recording from that time to the present.

A Short History of Anglo-Saxon Cemeteries

Discovering and recording the Anglo-Saxons

Traces of Anglo-Saxon cemeteries have been noted from as early as the twelfth century, if Roger of Wendover's *Chronicle* account of the excavation of mounds at Redbourne in Hertfordshire by monks in search of the bones of St Amphibalus is to be believed (Meaney 1964: 104–5). A more secure description comes from the seventeenth century in a pamphlet by Sir Thomas Browne on cremation urns found in Norfolk, entitled *Hydriotaphia, Urn Buriall* (an illustration shows them to be of Anglo-Saxon date, though Browne believed them to be Roman): 'In a Field of old Walsingham not many months past were digged up between forty and fifty urnes, deposited in a dry and sandy soil, not a yard deep, not far from one another . . . some containing two pounds of bones, distinguishable in skulls, ribs, jaws, thigh-bones, and teeth, with fresh impressions of their combustion' (Browne 1658, 1966 edn: 10, see Schnapp 1996: 196–8). However, the accolade of being the first excavators of Anglo-Saxon cemeteries should really go to two Kentish gentlemen clerics, first the Revd Bryan Faussett (who excavated sites such as Gilton, Kingston Down and Sibertswold, all in Kent, between 1759 and 1773), and then Captain (later Revd) James Douglas (who carried out his excavations at sites such as Chatham Lines and Greenwich Park from 1779 to 1793). Kent is one of the areas with many barrow cemeteries of the late sixth, seventh and even eighth centuries AD, and it was the standing mounds that first attracted antiquarian attention. As a boy of ten, Faussett had been present at some even earlier excavations into the barrow cemetery at Chartham Down in 1730, and it may have been this which prompted his life interest in these sites, to the extent that he explored the same site himself in 1764 and 1773 (Smith 1908: 369–70). Ironically, though, the first excavation recorded by Faussett was at a site being destroyed through sand extraction in a quarry at Gilton, Ash, in 1759 (Hawkes 1990: 1–2). Such accidental discoveries tended not to be marked on the surface, and considerable destruction of the remains often took place unless the discovery was brought to the attention of local interested parties. The description by Bryan Faussett of these first excavations at Gilton makes this point vividly:

> The miller and his companion immediately produced two ladders and as many spades; and with these began to delve in a very rough manner into the sand rock in an horizontal manner, as if they had designed to have made an oven . . . I found, in short, that this method of proceedings would not do; but that if the grave did chance to contain anything curious, it must, most likely, be lost and overlooked. I therefore advised them to desist, and advised them to rather open the ground above, till they should get down to the skeleton, and then carefully to examine the bottom of the grave. This advice . . . they did not at first at all relish; but after a little persuasion and a little brandy (without which nothing, in such cases as the present, can be done effectually), they very cheerfully approved and very contentedly followed, so that in a very short time they got to the skeleton, I mean to what remained of it. (Faussett 1856: 2)

Faussett returned to Gilton the following year with his own labourers, and excavated forty-nine graves in two days (**Fig. 1.3**). He went on to excavate over 750 graves, mostly in the later barrow cemeteries of Kent, between increasingly painful attacks of gout, before his death in 1776. As well as excavating burials under small barrows (**Fig. 1.4**), he also developed a sort of 'probe' which enabled him to find graves under a flat ground surface. Despite this apparent haste of excavation, he recorded each grave in his field notebooks, even noting anatomical details, with knowledge presumably gained from his studies at Oxford (Hawkes 1990: 2–3), though he identified the remains as those of 'Romans Britonized' and 'Britons Romanized'. The results of Faussett's excavations were left in manuscript form, and were first published by Charles Roach Smith in 1856, who added a minimal commentary, as *Inventorium Sepulchrale*.

ANGLO-SAXON CEMETERIES: AN INTRODUCTION

Fig. 1.3. Etching showing the site of early excavations by Faussett in the sand-quarry at Gilton, Kent. (Reproduced from Faussett 1856: 1.)

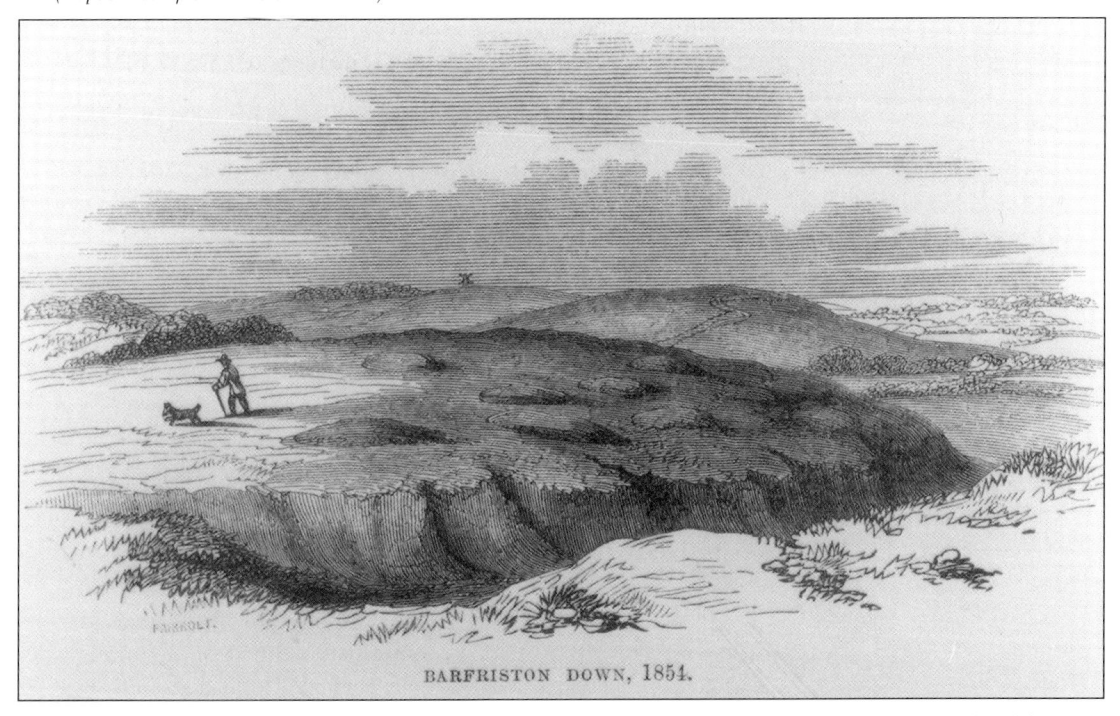

Fig. 1.4. Etching showing the then extant seventh-century barrows on Barfriston Down, Kent. (Reproduced from Faussett 1856: 135.)

7

The Revd James Douglas, a trained surveyor who later took up a post as curate at Chiddingfold (Hawkes 1990: 16), was the first person to identify artefacts as Anglo-Saxon, publishing his Kentish excavations of 1779 to 1793 (along with some sketches of material from the Faussett collection) as *Nenia Britannica* (1793). He offered the following proof of their dating:

> The discovery of coins, the workmanship of the relics, arms, and nature of the burial places, either considered externally or internally, shows them to belong to a people in a state of peace, and in general possession of the country. Their situation near villages of Saxon names, their numbers proportioned to a small clan of people existing at a particular area, afford the critical evidence of their owners. They are scattered all over Britain in places which the Saxons occupied, and are not discovered in the parts of Wales which they had not subdued. (Douglas 1793: 177, cited by Baldwin Brown 1915: 124–5)

This opinion of the date of the remains did not, however, become widespread for several decades.

Both Faussett and Douglas recorded their excavations to a remarkably high standard for their day, noting which artefacts were found in which grave, and often how the body was arranged, and where the goods were placed. Douglas, moreover, had recognised the importance of topographical plans and illustrations of sections through barrows (Rhodes 1990: 27). Unfortunately, more common in other areas of the country was the destruction of graves without adequate (or any) recording, and the dispersal of any grave-goods found. It was only really from the middle of the nineteenth century that these sites received anything very much in the way of systematic excavation, and even then standards across the country varied widely. For example, an account of barrow-digging in Cambridgeshire in 1874 was recorded as follows: 'Three urns, the smallest very nice . . . They were found in Stoney Hill with the skelitons and other things. I shall want ten shillings for the urns. I have got four heads two are Pretty good and two are broaken and some Leg bones I have got a Bullick face with the horns on it Perfect' (cited in Laing & Laing 1979: 5).

The British Archaeological Association (BAA), founded in 1843 by Roach Smith and Thomas Wright, another keen Anglo-Saxon scholar, was the first body to actively encourage the excavation and recording of sites under threat. The decision to found this association was prompted by their exasperation at the Society of Antiquaries' failure to do anything about the increasing amount of destruction being caused to archaeological sites by the large-scale railway building and road improvements of the mid-nineteenth century. The BAA had its first opportunity to act when plans for a reservoir in Greenwich Park were announced, which involved the destruction of barrows, several of which had been excavated by Douglas. The subsequent controversy reached the House of Commons and generated correspondence in *The Times* (Rhodes 1990: 32–3). The first British Archaeological Association Congress was held in Canterbury in 1844, and served to boost the popularity of Anglo-Saxon archaeology with participation of nearly 200, full press coverage and 'dancing until midnight' (ibid.: 33). On the second day, the entire congress was taken to Breach Down, where Lord Conyngham, the president of the association, had already excavated. On that day, he had arranged for eight barrows to be opened in public view (ibid.: 34). The Faussett collection, containing artefacts from his excavations of several decades before, was also visited during the congress, and amazed many of the participants with the evident 'skill and taste of Saxon workmen' (Wright 1845).

A great deal of effort, however, was to be put into persuading the national authorities of the value and importance of Anglo-Saxon antiquities. Roach Smith in particular was incensed by the refusal of the Trustees of the British Museum to purchase the Faussett collection when it was offered to them following Faussett's grandson's death in 1853. In his introduction to *Inventorium Sepulchrale* he wrote: 'not only does the Government begin with gathering the monuments, ancient and modern, of all foreign countries, but it ends there also. Our national antiquities are not even made subservient and placed in the lowest grade; they are altogether unrecognised and ignored' (Faussett 1856: x). This refusal of the British Museum also meant that material excavated by William Wylie at Fairford went to the Ashmolean in Oxford, while the finds from Akerman's excavations in Oxfordshire and Gloucestershire were donated instead to Liverpool, where the Faussett collection had been bought for the nation and displayed in its own museum by the goldsmith and collector of antiquities Joseph Mayer, who also financed the publication of *Inventorium Sepulchrale* (MacGregor 1998: 130–2). The British Museum eventually founded a new department dedicated to British Antiquities in 1866, with Roach Smith's own collection (for which he accepted £2,000 rather than the £3,000 it had been valued at, in order to keep the collection together) forming the basis of it, and it soon developed an international reputation under the keepership of A.W. Franks (ibid.: 135–6).

In the following decades archaeology became widely popular nationally among the educated classes, as illustrated by the formation of numerous local archaeological and ethnological societies at this time, and by the large crowds which often used to attend barrow openings. Indeed, barrow excavations were often planned as entertainment for the field-outings of these local societies, such as those carried out by the Yorkshire Antiquarian Club in 1849 and 1853 around Aldro, Acklam and Riggs (Marsden 1974: 96). The heyday of such excavations was in the years 1840 to 1870 (ibid.: 94) and, again, standards varied widely. Some openings were not reported at all, while others were published with lavish illustrations in the pages of journals such as *Archaeologia* and the *Antiquaries Journal*.

Even into this century, there have been many instances of the unrecorded and unplanned destruction of sites. Myres (1937: 318 n3), for instance, noted angrily that:

> During the past year . . . the site of a Saxon cemetery in Yorkshire has been obliterated by mechanical scoops employed by a Government department in constructing an aerodrome. The use of these tools renders scientific record of discoveries impossible, and without such record the historical value of the few objects that survive destruction by the scoop is gone for ever. Historical opinion would not tolerate the destruction of other classes of documents by a Government department: why should archaeological documents be an exception.

The situation has now changed, especially in the last decade with the introduction of Planning Policy Guideline 16 (otherwise known as PPG16), which requires the site of any building or development work to undergo an archaeological evaluation, designed to identify any remains at risk. Several large cemeteries have been located and excavated (with funding from the developers of the sites) as a result (although competitive tendering for contracts may turn out to have an adverse effect on publication of such sites). Also having an impact very recently are the new guidelines on treasure trove, which require reporting of all finds of metalwork to the authorities (previously only gold and silver objects were covered by the legislation). The vast quantity of finds now being reported by farmers and especially metal-detectorists to local museums and archaeological offices is, however, making clear the extent of destruction of cemetery sites by modern agricultural methods such as deep ploughing, especially in areas with much arable farming such as Norfolk (Helen Geake pers. comm). Once artefacts have reached the topsoil where they can be spotted by eye or by a metal-detector, the contexts from which they come are already in the process of being destroyed.

Telling Romans from Anglo-Saxons

Despite their unusual quality of recording for the time, the results of Faussett's first 'modern' excavations in the Anglo-Saxon cemeteries of Kent were to confuse the antiquarian world for almost a century. By chance, in some early diggings at Crundale in 1757 and 1759, Faussett had discovered an Anglo-Saxon cemetery sited in the same place as an earlier Roman cemetery. Faussett, quite naturally, believed that as most of the objects found were clearly Roman, all the burials on that spot were of Roman date too (Faussett 1856: 177–98; Baldwin Brown 1915: 731). As many of the Anglo-Saxon cemeteries that he was later to excavate also contained Roman coins as grave-goods, he never acted on his slight suspicion that they were, in fact, of later date (Hawkes 1990: 4). It was not until the middle of the nineteenth century that this mis-dating of the later sites was finally overturned, although Douglas was to lay down the basis for this. In *Nenia Britannica* he demonstrated clearly how a single source, such as a coin in a grave, could be used to date not only that grave (such as a grave at Gilton, which had to be later than the coin of Justinian (527–65) it contained), but also, by extension, other graves containing similar assemblages but lacking coins (Rhodes 1990: 27). His achievements, however, were largely ignored by his contemporaries. It was not until the mid-nineteenth century that archaeologists started to accept that the grave-goods dated from the three centuries after the Roman period (before this, for example, shield-bosses tended to be identified as 'Roman helmets').

Indeed, it was Charles Roach Smith, once again, who brought this matter to the fore. In 1843 he published an article demonstrating that the hand-made urns with stamped decoration often found in the cemeteries were in fact fifth to sixth century in date (as suggested in 1793 by Douglas) and not Roman (as suggested by other antiquarians), basing his argument on their association with weapons and shield-bosses (Rhodes 1990: 48; Roach Smith 1850b: 33–48). In 1847 he showed that bossed urns (pots with raised areas on the surface) and several other forms were also of this date (Rhodes 1990: 49). After the publication of John Yonge Akerman's *An Archaeological Index to the Remains of Antiquity in the Celtic, Romano-British and Anglo-Saxon Periods* in 1847, the matter was largely settled – these cemeteries, and the majority of the artefacts within them, were of fifth-, sixth- and seventh-century date (Rhodes 1990: 49). Roach Smith's careful observations of where objects were found within graves also allowed him to infer their correct nature, demonstrating, for example, that graves were sometimes accompanied by a bucket (with the wood staves having decayed away from the bronze bindings), rather than a crown, as the excavators had assumed (Rhodes 1990: 50). From this point on, the way was clear for archaeologists such as E.T. Leeds, Nils Åberg and J.N.L. Myres to develop their typologies and associated chronologies (often based on similar artefacts in continental cemeteries which were dated by coins). Indeed, many of the dating schemes still in use today rest on the foundations laid down by these early archaeologists, as will be made clear in the following chapter.

Telling Angles and Saxons from Jutes

Until the late 1840s the vast majority of published Anglo-Saxon material was from Kent. With the growing recognition, excavation and publication of cemeteries in other parts of the country, it soon became evident, especially to Roach Smith, that there was considerable regional variation. In a series of papers, he noted the distinctiveness of Kentish buckles (Roach Smith 1861: 143), the distribution of cruciform brooches in East Anglia and the Midlands (Roach Smith 1852a: 166), and the concentration of saucer brooches in the Upper Thames valley (Rhodes 1990: 53). At an early date Roach Smith (1850b: 88–9) linked these now-evident regional variations in brooch styles and other artefact types to the Venerable Bede's eighth-century account of Jutish, Saxon and Anglian territories in his *Ecclesiastical History of the English People* (I, 15), such that the Kentish material was linked with the Jutes, the saucer brooches with the Saxons and cruciform brooches with the Anglian areas (see Chapters Five and Six for more detail).

Wright expanded on this in *The Celt, the Roman and the Saxon* (1852), explaining in detail the differences between the artefacts of the three apparent tribal groups (Rhodes 1990: 54). Roach Smith was also one of the first scholars to promote the study of the British material in comparison with similar artefacts from the continent. He had noted several similarities between artefacts found in Britain and those being excavated in Frankish cemeteries near Dieppe, publishing his observations in the journal that he had founded, *Collectanea Antiqua* (Roach Smith 1852a), and even arguing that some of the graves in Kent could be of Frankish migrants (Roach Smith 1860: 135).

J.M. Kemble (brother of the famous stage actress Fanny Kemble) built on this work by demonstrating the similarities between British and German material of this period. During a visit to Hanover museum he noted similarities between the funerary urns of the two areas (**Fig. 1.5**), concluding that 'the urns of the "Old Saxon" and those of the "Anglo-Saxon", are in truth identical . . . The bones are those whose tongue we speak, whose blood flows in our veins' (1856: 280). Kemble thought that by the comparison of such urns 'we are brought . . . many steps nearer to our forefathers on the banks of the Elbe and its tributary rivers, and we can henceforth use indifferently the discoveries of Englishmen and North Germans for the elucidation of our national treasures' (1863: 230). With these observations, he was able to convince his German contemporaries that the urns in their museums should be regarded as Saxon, rather than Slavonic, as they had thought them (Rhodes 1990: 49). The influential work of these men was to be further built on in the first few decades of the twentieth century.

Fig. 1.5. An illustration of cremation urns from Stade-on-the-Elbe. (Reproduced from Kemble 1856: pl. XXII.)

Webster (1986: 123) has identified three different approaches to archaeology in the period 1900–1945: the historical approach, exemplified by E.T. Leeds, who tried to understand historical events and ethnic divisions through the analysis of artefacts; the typological approach, such as Åberg's (1926), which attempted to construct chronological frameworks for the art styles; and the collections approach, such as that of Baldwin Brown (1915), and the county surveys carried out by R.A. Smith for various volumes of the Victoria County Histories between 1900 and 1926, collating vast bodies of material.

E.T. Leeds started his career as Assistant Keeper at the Ashmolean Museum in Oxford in 1908. As the Keeper's interests lay elsewhere, the north European and British work in the museum was left to Leeds, and one of his tasks was to catalogue the 'Dark Age' part of Sir John Evans' collection, which his son Arthur had donated. His research into Anglo-Saxon and 'Teutonic' remains was synthesised in 1913 in *The Archaeology of the Anglo-Saxon Settlements*. More than forty years later it could still be said that this work had transformed early Anglo-Saxon archaeology, 'giving it its continental background, showing for the first time how the material was to be studied and interpreted, and raising in acute form the questions of the validity and limitations of the surviving literary sources. It made the masses of archaeological material intelligible for the first time. All work done since on pagan-period grave-goods has been done under its shadow or in working out or modifying its conclusions' (Bruce-Mitford & Harden 1956: xiii). After the First World War Leeds had helped to refound the Oxford University Archaeology Society, which conducted excavations at the first Anglo-Saxon village site to be found, Sutton Courtenay, as well as many other sites of different periods. In 1928 he became Keeper of the Ashmolean until his retirement in 1945. It was in 1945 that he published his massive survey of the 'minor' brooch types, most especially the small-long brooches, complete with distribution maps, on which many later arguments were to be based (ibid.: x–xiv).

Nils Åberg was a Swedish archaeologist who attempted, in *The Anglo-Saxons in England* (1926), to lay a firm chronological basis for the English material by tying it in to the continental and Scandinavian typological and chronological sequences. This was a work of vast scope, covering a wide range of different artefact types, and outlining their distributions, parallels and development. It is perhaps indicative of the increasing amount of material available for study that, aside from these few men working in the early decades of the twentieth century, such detailed coverage of all the available material, and synthesis and interpretation of it, remains extremely rare.

More common is the pattern of archaeologists spending their entire academic career pursuing a single artefact type. J.N.L. Myres, for example, devoted his whole life to the study of early Anglo-Saxon pottery. Although an historian by training (gaining firsts from Oxford in Greats in 1924 and Modern History in 1926), Myres developed an enthusiasm for archaeology, joining the archaeology society founded by E.T. Leeds in 1919, and becoming its president in 1923. He participated in a few excavations on Roman sites before the demands of his lectureship in modern history at Oxford meant he eventually had to give up this branch of archaeology. In 1931 he was asked to contribute to R.B. Collingwood's *Roman Britain*, and in his survey of the archaeological evidence for Anglo-Saxon settlement he saw the lack of any systematic study of the pottery (Collingwood & Myres 1936). He thus 'sallied forth into the unknown'. As a lecturer after the Second World War and then as the Librarian of the Bodleian (a post he held from 1948 to 1965), he used his spare time to compile *A Corpus of Pagan Anglo-Saxon Pottery*, eventually published in 1977, and wrote his major synthetic work *Anglo-Saxon Pottery and the Settlement of England* (1969) (Taylor 1991).

Myres (1937: 317) made a telling comment on the relationship between history and archaeology in the 1930s when he said: 'I make no apology for introducing the archaeological material into an historical discussion, nor for deliberately treating it as relevant to the present purpose.' Myres saw archaeology as having the potential to throw light on 'the main questions outstanding in this period – the character and distribution of the earliest settlements, the continental provenance of the invaders, the fate of Romano-British institutions and population' (ibid.: 320). These questions can be seen as central to Anglo-Saxon studies for the next fifty years, especially in the work of two central researchers in this field, Sonia Chadwick (later Chadwick Hawkes after her marriage to the prehistorian Christopher Hawkes), and Vera Evison. Both were active excavators of cemeteries – Hawkes at Winnall and Finglesham, Evison at Great Chesterford, Alton and Dover Buckland among others, and also experts on various aspects of material culture, from which they tried to write histories of the political developments of the fifth to seventh centuries (cf. Hawkes & Dunning 1961; Evison 1965). Both were influential in putting forward new explanatory mechanisms for the Saxon 'take-over', especially in the form of Germanic soldiers (*laeti* and *foederati*, although Hawkes saw the prime movers as coming from north Germany and southern Scandinavia, while Evison saw them primarily as Frankish).

Anglo-Saxon archaeology in the 1950s, 1960s and 1970s continued in much the same way as it had in previous decades, with a few notable exceptions. Throughout this period, the same emphasis on the importance of chronology and typology for answering historical questions is apparent in research (Hunter Blair 1977: 27; Wilson 1960: 29). For example, Christopher Hawkes was interested in the ethnic affiliations of the Kentish settlers, relying on the accepted historical frameworks – 'it seems best, really, to believe what we are told. The Saxons came in 443' (1956: 94), – and identifying these ethnic groupings through the grave-goods. The questions asked were still concerned with the date and progress of the barbarian incursions, and increasing consideration of their impact on the native inhabitants, which manifested itself in an increase of interest in 'late Celtic' archaeology (e.g. Alcock 1971; Ashe 1968; Morris 1973). This should be seen in the context of a wider tradition of popular Arthurian literature (for example Sutcliff 1959, 1979, 1981; White 1958).

Yet, the traditional historical frameworks were still in place. In 1974 Hawkes saw Anglo-Saxon archaeology as entering a fruitful area of enquiry, 'with historians and place-name specialists joining archaeologists in seeking a fuller understanding of the direction and character of the Germanic people's landtakings, the nature and development of their settlements and economy, their society, and their relations with surviving late Roman institutions and peoples' (1974: 408). Cemetery studies seemed, however, to stagnate slightly in the 1960s and 1970s. As Meaney & Hawkes (1970: v) commented: 'Recent years have not seen the study of cemetery evidence progress as it should, mainly because attention has been concentrated on the need for research on settlement sites, and there have been insufficient people working in the field to cope with both adequately. Cemeteries seem in any case to have gone out of fashion.' Some of the reasons for this evident lack of enthusiasm for the field among many specialists can perhaps be inferred from comments made by Hope-Taylor, the excavator of the palace site at Yeavering, a few years later: 'our so-called Anglo-Saxon archaeology is today still blinkered by antiquarian pre-occupation with grave-goods. Every year we see Anglo-Saxon cemeteries used as convenient quarries to provide raw material for the perpetuation of an habitual and unquestioning academic activity (itself not without a curiously ritual aspect). The Anglo-Saxon cemetery in Britain has never been studied as a complete phenomenon, as the deeply revealing local entity it certainly is' (Hope-Taylor 1977: 262).

From Invasion to Ideology:
Changing Perspectives in Anglo-Saxon Cemetery Research

From this brief survey of the careers of some of the most influential researchers in Anglo-Saxon cemetery studies, it is plain that, although the typologies have sometimes been disputed and the chronological frameworks shifted slightly back and forth, there has been a remarkable uniformity in the approach to archaeological evidence. Imported goods are seen as a direct reflection of immigrant people, and the archaeological evidence is interpreted largely in line with the accepted historical frameworks (see Chapter Six for a deeper investigation into these approaches). This is starting to change, however. The increasing application of scientific methods to Anglo-Saxon archaeology is starting to offer alternatives to the typological approach, as is the improvement in recording, which means that correlations with grave-good assemblages are easier to carry out (i.e. one can look at which objects are actually buried together, rather than assuming that they are later or earlier than one another on the basis of form or decoration, which is a notoriously subjective process). The use of information technology is also starting to make the manipulation of the very large data sets from modern cemetery excavations easier, and to promote different sorts of analysis which can reveal detailed and complex patterning.

New theoretical models are also starting to be applied to this more detailed understanding of the material. For much of the past two centuries, Anglo-Saxon cemetery evidence has been interpreted in a very 'common-sense' way. If a grave was found with weapons, for example, the person interred was assumed to have been a warrior in life. A burial with jewellery, similarly, was assumed to be a woman, often of some rank, as burials without any goods at all were often interpreted as slaves (see Lucy 1997). There were widely held assumptions, too, about the origins of these burial rites. Based largely on a single documentary source, Bede's *Ecclesiastical History*, both historians and archaeologists have assumed that this form of furnished burial is inherently 'Germanic', and therefore that a person buried with grave-goods in one of these cemeteries was either a migrant from northern Europe or the descendant of such a migrant. As will be explained in Chapter Six, these assumptions were based on historical models, elaborated on in the eighteenth and nineteenth centuries, which saw the inhabitants of Britain being wiped out, or driven into Wales and Cornwall, in the early years following the Roman withdrawal. Such views can be challenged, however, from within both history and archaeology, and more recent models for understanding the fifth and sixth centuries will be outlined in Chapter Seven. This last chapter will also look at ideas which have been used to explain the change in grave-goods and burial practices in the later sixth century, and the shift to unfurnished inhumation in the course of the seventh and eighth centuries.

Before looking at changing interpretations, however, the evidence itself must first be examined. In the next chapter, methods for dating both burials and grave-goods will be outlined, and the main types of those grave-goods are described and discussed. Chapter Three will then survey the evidence for the inhumation burial rite, Chapter Four will look at the cremation burial rite, and Chapter Five will look at the structure and layout of cemeteries as a whole, and at why they were placed where they were.

Almost two-and-a-half centuries after the initial investigations, archaeologists are still refining their knowledge of the nature and extent of furnished burials of the fifth to eighth centuries AD. Discoveries of new sites are still being made, challenging long-held beliefs, and new interpretations are continually being put forward. This book hopes to chart these changing ideas about a type of site which has been used heavily in the writing of the history of the 'English', and to describe the nature and extent of these sites and some of the intriguing burial rites used within them.

Two

Dating Burials and Grave-Goods in Anglo-Saxon Cemeteries

Before anything meaningful can be said about the nature of the evidence for early Anglo-Saxon cemeteries and their variations both across the country and over time, it is first important to understand how archaeologists are able to say, for example, that a burial dates to the earlier sixth century rather than to the later seventh. This chapter will look at methods for dating burials in general, before looking at the main classes of grave-goods – jewellery and dress-ornaments, weaponry, vessels and other items – in terms of how they can be dated and how they were used. This will form the basis on which changing patterns of use and distribution can be assessed in the following three chapters.

How are Burials Dated?

A burial represents a single event in time, with the simultaneous deposition of the body and any associated grave-goods. The nature of this evidence means we can be sure that any grave-goods found co-existed in time with the person buried – later goods could only make their way into the grave through the agency of another person, such as a grave-robber, or by other disturbance, such as burrowing animals. Thus, where we have a selection of grave-goods within a single grave, we can be reasonably sure that they are broadly contemporary in terms of use, though they may of course include very old objects among them. Unfortunately, for much of the history of excavation of Anglo-Saxon cemeteries such associations have not been reliably recorded. For example, it was not always noted which grave-goods came from which grave (or even, sometimes, from which cemetery). Thus for many workers in this field the basic material has been lacking in context, and they have been forced to try to date the material on purely typological grounds, arranging them by apparent stylistic order. This is why much of the attention of Anglo-Saxon archaeologists has been directed towards the metalwork, especially brooch types, for it is these which seem to undergo the most rapid changes, and thus seem to be more amenable to organisation into typological (and thus chronological) sequences. One must be careful, however: assigning a date of manufacture to a brooch need not give any indication as to the date when that brooch came to be deposited in a grave. A collection of burial-goods (an assemblage), if consistent in date, can give more certain grounds for dating, although they could still all be old objects at the time of burial. Dating the skeleton itself, using scientific methods, is a more reliable guide to date of burial, although this has its own problems and limitations. The next section will outline typological methods first, and the various decorative schemes and assumptions on which they rest, before looking at other ways of ordering and dating burials, such as stratigraphic or scientific methods.

Typological methods: attempts to date objects

Principles   There are, of course, some major assumptions which archaeologists make when they start to construct typologies of artefacts (i.e. deciding which forms come before or after others in a developmental sequence). Many of these assumptions rest on modern opinions about how things develop over time. As early as 1913 Leeds was setting out the principles of comparative dating of artefacts. He argued that in a large number of objects of one type there was an evolutionary process by which they developed, both in form and decoration (1913: 28); in practice, this often meant that they started simple and became more complex. Leeds thought that the graves of Anglo-Saxon men were not of much use, as they retained their equipment of spear, shield, knife and belt-fittings throughout the period. Fortunately, however, even 'in these early times the subservience of the feminine mind to the dictates of fashion is clearly perceptible, more especially in that most distinctive article of feminine attire – even far back in prehistoric times – the fibula or brooch' (ibid.: 29), hence his reliance on brooch types as a source of information (see, for example, his paper 'The distribution of the Anglo-Saxon saucer brooch in relation to the Battle of Bedford, AD 571' (1912)). Leeds also relied on the historical frameworks to date the start of this evolutionary process, using Bede's mid-fifth-century dating of the *adventus Saxonum* ('the coming of the Saxons') as a starting point for Anglo-Saxon material in England (Dickinson 1980: 11). If an object had parallels on the continent, it had to date to a time after AD 450. Unfortunately, these typologies remain the basis for much classificatory work, to the extent that several papers in a recent volume on computer seriation (Palm & Pind 1992, Stilborg 1992) still took this date as the starting point for several material culture sequences, even though the factual basis of Bede's dating has been heavily criticised in the last two decades (cf. Sims-Williams 1983).

Myres (1937: 318–19) offered a more critical view of methods for dating artefacts from graves:

> . . . faced with this large and somewhat chaotic mass of loot from graves, often excavated at a time when too little importance was attached to keeping separate the objects belonging to each body, or under conditions which rendered careful recording impossible, archaeologists have been compelled to arrange its different constituent groups on typological rather than strictly chronological lines. And while all would agree that a typological sequence frequently implies an evolution over a period of time, it is but rarely possible to speak with confidence of the speed of that evolution or to relate it directly, as the historian demands . . . to the passing even of centuries and decades, still less of individual years.

In this paper, which contained a justification for his life-long work on Anglo-Saxon pottery, he made some pertinent comments about the reliability with which certain artefacts can be used for dating: 'attention has hitherto been largely concentrated on the brooches and other metalwork, objects which in most periods are regarded as unusually difficult both to date accurately themselves and to use as dating evidence for associated finds, because the very durability and intrinsic value of the individual pieces tend to keep them in use over a great number of years' (ibid.: 320). Despite these critical comments, Myres was to use historical arguments in his dating of the pottery. He saw the great cremation cemeteries coming into use at the end of the fourth century AD (in his phase of 'overlap and controlled settlement') (Myres 1969: 63, 74). He also relied on some dubious cultural stereotypes in his work, assuming, for example, that 'barbarian' peoples should have exuberantly decorated pottery – which was partly why he based his classifications on decorative schemes (Richards 1987: 24–7). Thus, when discussing 'Romano-Saxon' pottery with triangular groupings of dimples, he noted: 'It is not a normal decorative motif in the Anglo-Saxon homelands in the late fourth century, yet the whole scheme of decoration is certainly Teutonic rather than Romano-British' (Myres 1959: 8). Myres saw Roman potters catering to the tastes of Germanic customers, yet the ornament used on this wheel-thrown pottery comprised dimples and round bosses of the sort that were already found on Roman pottery, glass and metal vessels (Hills 1979: 308–9).

Hills (ibid.: 326) has pointed out some of the flaws in these typological arguments: 'The emphasis on typology has led to a corresponding concentration on chronology, since the inevitable tendency is to arrange material in a sequence and then to assume that this has a chronological significance.' However, differential use of material may instead represent differences of status or origin, or different uptakes of new fashions. Moreover, the date of manufacture may not correspond with the date of burial – the 'heirloom' factor (ibid.). There are additional problems when it comes to attempting to assign absolute dates to the typological development of British material. As Scull & Bayliss (1999: 39) have recently reminded us, this is heavily reliant on the use of continental coin-dated chronologies (which may bear little relation to the span of use of the British material). From this perspective, the arguments about how quickly or slowly material becomes adopted are exacerbated. More encouraging are some recently developed techniques which employ computing and scientific methodology to put these dating schemes on to a more secure footing. These will be outlined below, after looking at the main traditional methods for assigning an object to a place in a typological sequence: the use of decoration and of form.

Decoration There is a range of decoration used on the metal objects found in Anglo-Saxon graves, and this has long been taken as an indication of the date of manufacture. Åberg (1926: 158–9) for instance, drawing on a background of continental scholarship, divided Anglo-Saxon ornament into three consecutive phases: Phase 1 with spiral ornament (also known as Nydam Style, after the late fourth-century boat deposit from a bog in south-east Jutland, which included some artefacts decorated with this geometric ornament); Phase II, with Salin Style I animal ornament (characterised by the decorative technique of chip-carving and the use of crouching animals as motifs); and Phase III, with Salin Style II animal ornament (characterised by elongated and intertwining, almost snake-like, animals) and interlacing (**Fig. 2.1**). He saw these as running in sequence, but thought

Fig. 2.1. (a) Example of Style I decoration (after Bakka 1958: fig. 8); (b) example of Style II decoration (after Laing & Laing 1996: 69).

they had elastic limits. Åberg (1926: 161–3) also identified another style, characterised by detailed ornament (often using shallow chip-carving) and naturalistic representations of animals (animals of provincial Roman style often executed in relief, as on the famous Sarre Quoit Brooch), which occupied a more indefinite position in his sequence. While there have been various attempts to rename and reclassify these styles (see, for example, Hawkes' arguments for Jutish Style A and B (Hawkes 1961) and Kendrick's Helmet and Ribbon styles (Kendrick 1934)), Salin's styles, first published in 1904 in his *Die altgermanische Thierornamentik* are still the predominant method of classification.

There has, however, been much debate about the dating and historical significance of all these art styles. Åberg's naturalistic animal style came to be known (following Bakka 1958) as the Quoit Brooch Style (after the characteristic brooch type on which it is often found). While Åberg (1926) and Leeds (1936) saw it as having little to do with the development of later styles, Sonia Chadwick Hawkes argued in an influential article (1961) for the Quoit Brooch Style to be renamed Jutish Style A, since she regarded it as a style that evolved after the Germanic settlement of the south of England, being a product of Germanic craftsmen. She also argued that it should be seen as the direct predecessor of Style I in Britain, standing at the beginning of the development of Germanic zoomorphic ornament (ibid.: 69–70). The most influential part of her argument was the identification of the style on a series of belt-fittings from early Anglo-Saxon cemeteries, such as the Mucking belt-set from grave 117 (see also Böhme 1986; Welch 1992).

In contrast, Haseloff (1974: 5) saw the Quoit Brooch Style as a short-lived and insular British development, drawing its inspiration from late Roman provincial chip-carved bronzes, in the first half of the fifth century, thus running parallel with the Scandinavian development of the Nydam Style. Evison (1968) viewed the buckle decorated in Quoit Brooch Style found in G117 at Mucking in a similar way, seeing the developed decoration on a late Roman form of buckle as indicative of insular development. However, because Evison believed that 'Romano-British bronze workers of the late fourth century do not seem to have produced any work which would make credible a sudden blossoming into works of inventive and technical merit on these lines', she placed the responsibility for the formation of this style on to the migration of Frankish craftsmen from Gaul (ibid.: 240), suggesting that they were made for *foederati* invited in (as per the historical sources) in the early fifth century (ibid.: 241). Likewise, Welch (1992: 273) sees artefacts decorated in Quoit Brooch Style (both brooches and belt equipment) as items issued by British 'tyrants' (in imitation of Roman practice) for use by the (male) leaders of the Saxon federates. There still seems to be no consensus over the origins of this style (although all seem to accept British manufacture for it), but it should be noted that objects decorated in this way seem largely to have been buried in the sixth century, by comparison with their associated goods (Hawkes 1961: 30), something which Welch (1992: 273) explains by arguing the early Saxons 'bequeathed these brooches to their women'.

There are problems with such scenarios. Harrison (1997: 22) makes the pertinent criticism that only single examples are known of Leeds' quoit brooch types A and C, and only two of his type B – remarkably small numbers given that the style was defined from these artefacts, and through which it has been largely debated. Hawkes lists only twenty items in Quoit Brooch Style in her corpus, yet Ager (1985: 18) sees it as filling the 'stylistic void' between the first Germanic mercenaries and the beginning of Style I in England (Harrison 1997: 22). In addition, Harrison notes that Leeds' quoit brooches of type D (which are more numerous) lack the characteristic animal ornament found on types A, B and C, and may in fact be earlier rather than later (ibid.: 23). The central issue here – the problem of inferring the ethnicity of the population (and via this, the answers to historical problems) through the characteristics of their associated material culture – will be discussed further in Chapters Six and Seven. As Hills (1979: 308) has said, 'While there may be little doubt that there were soldiers of Germanic origin in late Roman Britain or that some of these were mercenaries, it is doubtful whether much of the metalwork which has been used to demonstrate their presence does so in fact.'

It used to be thought that Style I was sixth century in date, and that it was replaced by Style II at the end of that century. Haseloff (1974) demonstrated that Salin Style I was ultimately derived from late Roman metalwork, via the Nydam style of geometric chip-carved ornament. He identified the progressive disintegration and degeneration of the border animals found on late Roman strap-ends and buckle-plates, until they appeared as stylised representations on south Scandinavian brooches and belt-fittings of the fifth century. The use of 'chip-carved' wax models to create this Style I ornament served to exaggerate the already disjointed appearance of the animals (Hills 1979: 322). Haseloff (1974, 1981) has thus argued for seeing the origins of Style I ornament in the second half of the fifth century, rather than the beginning of the sixth (although he puts forward a rather alarming picture of Roman provincial craftsmen being forcibly taken back to Germanic territories after raids, and set to work for new masters). Meanwhile Speake (1986: 204) has put forward a strong case for the probability that, outside Kent, Style I persisted into the seventh century. We are thus left with a picture of regional diversity in the use of these decorative styles, and no longer have a clear-cut picture of development.

The idea of the replacement of Style I by Style II in the mid- to late sixth century depended partly on the theory that Style II had developed under Mediterranean influence, with the sinuous snakes/ribbons being associated with Coptic or Byzantine plait or interlace patterns, and being transmitted to northern Europe by the Lombards – the Lombards did not cross the Alps into Italy until 569, and therefore Style II had to post-date this (Hills 1979: 323). Other origins are now largely accepted for it, with East Anglian traditions of Style II deriving from Scandinavia, while Kentish versions are more related to Frankish decorative sequences (Speake 1980: 34, Høilund Nielsen 1999). It has also been argued, however, that the differences between Styles I and II may be one of technique: whereas the chip-carving used for Style I results in disjointed forms, the filigree (narrow strips of twisted gold wire, soldered on to a base – see Avent 1975: 17 for a full description) often employed in Style II lends itself to sinuous forms (Hills 1979: 323–4). Some regions, such as Kent for example, seem to have a greater preference for Style II, leading Hills (and later Speake) to suggest a great degree of overlap for the two styles, rather than immediate replacement: 'Perhaps poorer people bought brooches made in simpler, older fashions decorated with Style I for a long time after more sophisticated jewellers had turned to Style II' (Hills 1979: 324). The beginnings of Style II ornament are now thought to be earlier, perhaps as early as the mid-sixth century or even before (Hines 1999a: 65), although others, such as Helen Geake (1997), argue for the introduction of Style II to England around AD 600. Høilund Nielsen (1999) sees a more symbolic reason behind the adoption of Style II ornamentation from both the Scandinavian and Frankish areas, interpreting it as an attempt by elite families to signal their descent or affiliation with elites in what may have been seen by the later sixth century as the 'parent country'.

Form Artefacts can be grouped and then arranged into sequences on the basis of their perceived similarity or difference of form. As will be outlined below in the discussions of individual types, these groupings are often rather subjective, and based on the presence or absence of features which may or may not have been at the forefront of the maker's mind. The ordering of these groups is also heavily reliant on evolutionary assumptions about how objects should develop over time, so that, for example, they are often seen as starting small and simple and becoming larger and more elaborate. While this may, in fact, hold in some cases, it is not universally valid. Rather than rely on these assumptions, recent work has been exploring alternative methods of arranging objects into date sequence, which relate more to how they are used, and their combinations with other artefacts, rather than trying to date them by their nature alone.

Stratigraphic and cross-dating methods

Stratigraphy is one of the cornerstones of archaeology – by working out, through careful excavation, which layers in a vertical sequence were laid down first, and which were later, relative dates can be assigned to the contents of those layers. If a layer containing a brooch, for example, sits above a layer containing a comb, we can say with absolute certainty that the brooch was deposited later than the comb. Although this does not necessarily mean that the two acts of deposition were separated by any great length of time, or that the brooch was manufactured later that the comb (for it could have been worn for years before being deposited), with a number of such relationships patterns can start to build up. If, say, certain brooch types were always found in later deposits than other brooch types, there are reasonable grounds for arguing that the bulk of production was later too.

Unfortunately, the users of Anglo-Saxon cemeteries seem to have had rather an aversion

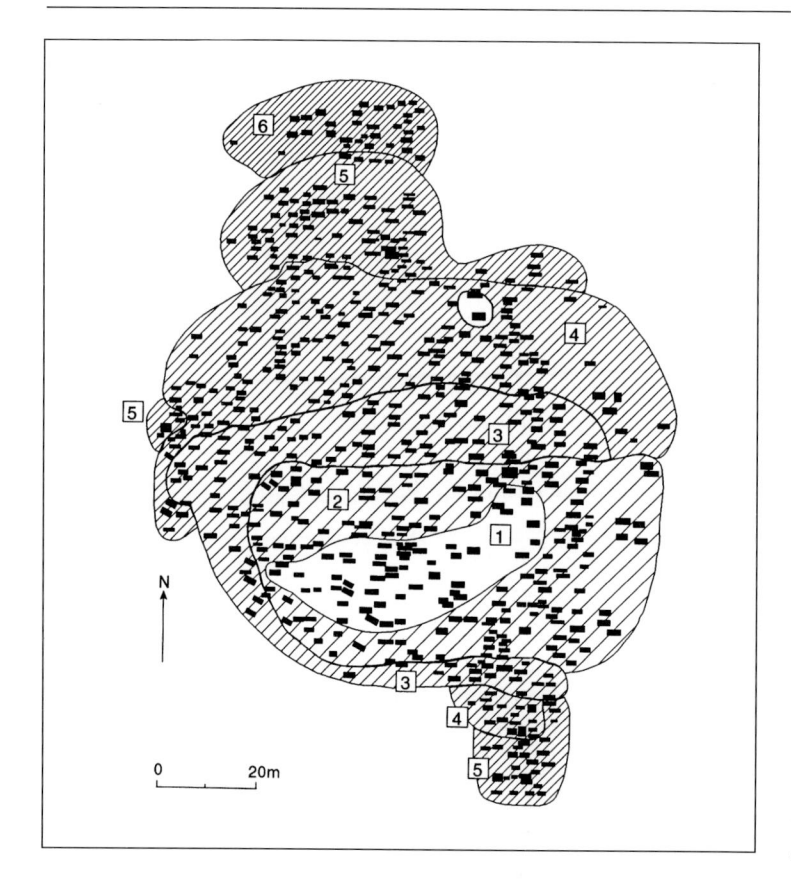

Fig. 2.2. An example of horizontal stratigraphy within the German cemetery of Stadt Dillingen an der Donau (after Fehring 1991: fig. 13).

to inter-cutting graves, to the extent that many archaeologists believe the graves must have been marked in some way. Only rarely do we find burials in a stratigraphic sequence, where one grave pit cuts into another one; instead, burials spread out, often over quite wide areas. Some attempts have been made to use horizontal stratigraphy (**Fig. 2.2**), on the assumption that burial starts in one area of the cemetery and spreads out from it (as has been seen in some continental cemeteries), but this has been largely unsuccessful in Britain, where various parts of cemeteries seem to have been in use at the same time (leading to suggestions of 'family burial plots' in some cases).

Instead, the grave-goods are usually relied upon. There are a number of methods of arranging associated goods in sequence. Geake (1997: 7) has described the two types of seriation which are used in archaeology: **frequency seriation** where, on the assumption that certain artefacts start rare, become more popular, and then decline, 'battleship curves' for artefact types are produced which can put them in relative order; and **occurrence seriation** where no assumptions are made as to this development, but instead the finds associations themselves are used to order the artefact type. The latter is the more useful for Anglo-Saxon assemblages. A table is drawn up with the assemblages (usually by grave number) along one axis and the find types along the other. This table is then sorted (which can be done by hand, but is much quicker and easier by computer) so that a diagonal appears which is assumed to reflect change through time. This can also be done with the attributes of the artefacts themselves, if the changing nature of that object is to be mapped.

Thus, use of computer (occurrence) seriation can place objects (and therefore the graves containing them) into a general order, based on the assumption that gradual changes in the style of those objects occur (Kjeld Jensen & Høilund Nielsen 1997: 37). However, Hines (1992: 81) points out that the differences between computer seriation and traditional typology are not as radical as one might think. In order to carry out a seriation, artefacts still have to be grouped into types first (thus, brooch types would still have to be distinguished, so as to be able to list the find types). He also points out the fact that demonstrating that objects are different in form is not the same as demonstrating that they are different in terms of their absolute chronologies (ibid.: 82). Groups using completely different assemblages could still appear on a seriation as if one follows on from the other, when they are in fact contemporary.

Correspondence analysis (popular in Scandinavia, but not yet in Britain) can be used to produce a seriated matrix of finds combinations (in other words, it can sort a group of graves into an order based on, for example, which brooch types they contain; or it can sort a group of brooches into an order based on which stylistic attributes they display). The results of this analysis are presented as a scattergram of points arranged in relation to two axes – if the points form a perfect parabola, then the seriation is near perfect (and continuous), and it can be assumed that the brooch types (in both cases) are changing gradually over time. On this basis chronological dates can be attached (Høilund Nielsen 1997: 75). The points can, however, cluster, indicating that something more complex is going on, such as the use of different brooch types by contemporary social groups, and the method will therefore offer little information with regard to dating. The assumptions which rest behind this method are that the types used should change quickly, and that they should be uniform over the area being analysed. While this is thoroughly valid for some areas, for example Iron Age Denmark, applications of this approach to English cemetery material have produced unsatisfactory results (see, for example, Stilborg 1992; Palm & Pind 1992), as there is a great deal of regional (and also local) variation, while at the same time many grave-good types remain in use for a long time (Høilund Nielsen 1997: 77). The problems of regional variation could be overcome by analysing single cemeteries (see Ravn 1998, who has produced some interesting results for Spong Hill), rather than amalgamated groups of burials, but this often leads to very small sample sizes (Høilund Nielsen 1997: 77–8). As Høilund Nielsen stated: 'To be able to establish firm and detailed chronologies, it is therefore necessary to eliminate the influence from regional variation and social groups' (ibid.: 94). Unfortunately, such variation seems to be the most important and interesting factor in the early Anglo-Saxon burial rite, and can tell us a great deal about the active uses of material culture in this period. A final possibility for dating later graves comes when they are associated with coins (Rigold 1974) – these can give a *terminus post quem* (i.e. a date after which the burial must have been made) for the burial with which they are associated, such as various late seventh-century graves from Dover Buckland (Evison 1987: 136; see Welch 1999: 32).

Scientific methods

Scientific analysis of metalwork has made a large contribution to the field, suggesting some possible alternative ways of approaching this material. An analysis of sixth- and seventh-century Anglo-Saxon gold objects in the Ashmolean Museum substantiated the hypothesis that certain types of jewellery were made from melted-down coinage, and with the existing knowledge of debasement of Merovingian and Anglo-Saxon coinage was able to give rough dating estimates for these artefacts (Brown & Schweizer 1973). A more recent comparison of the metal composition of great square-headed brooches alongside more traditional formal and decorative analysis has shown the potential of this approach. Although these brooches were characterised by the diversity of their metal content (supporting the idea that they were manufactured from existing 'scrap' metal), there were a few instances where two brooches appeared to have been made from the same source. Comparison of such brooches suggested that the traditional method of typology (based on art-historical principles) works on some occasions, but also casts doubt on some traditional dating principles, such as that more 'degenerate' styles of ornamentation are necessarily later in date (Brownsword & Hines 1993). A similar approach has investigated the possibility of stamp-linking metal artefacts (Mortimer & Stoney 1996). Stamps made with tools are recorded using silicon rubber peels and then examined under an electron-scanning microscope to look for similarities. A study of forty-five objects from the Edix Hill cemetery at Barrington in Cambridgeshire managed to identify the same stamps being used on brooch pairs from the same grave, suggesting that wider application of this technique has the potential to identify other manufacturing links between different graves, and even different cemeteries. Presumably, if objects are this close in manufacture, they should be close in date.

Until very recently radiocarbon dating was not precise enough to offer assistance in resolving dating issues in Anglo-Saxon cemetery studies. However, the development of high-precision radiocarbon dating, in conjunction with mathematical modelling, is now potentially able to give date ranges of less than fifty years at high degrees of probability (95 per cent) for the first half of the fifth century, and the late sixth to early eighth centuries (Scull & Bayliss 1999: 39). This high degree of accuracy is the result of rapid changes in the atmospheric concentrations of carbon during these years. The potential offered by this approach is emphasised by the case study on which Scull & Bayliss have been developing these methods: the late cemetery at Buttermarket, Ipswich. One grave in particular, 4152, contained a penny of Offa, giving it a *terminus post quem* of AD 792. However, the skeleton was securely radiocarbon dated to the first half of the seventh century. As this grave contained the only evidence for burial on this site continuing into the eighth century, this discrepancy was of great interest; in fact, it was accepted that the penny was either intrusive or had been accidentally substituted during post-excavation work. Such a conclusion could never have been made without such scientific dating, and the interpretation of the history of early Ipswich would have remained based on a false premise.

There are thus a number of approaches which are now available to archaeologists working on early Anglo-Saxon chronologies. While none is perfect, being limited in terms of either date, material or accuracy, they offer a way to test at least some of the established chronologies (which, as seen above, are often heavily reliant on assumptions about the nature of artefact change, or on historical and ethnic assumptions about the routes and manner of their introduction). The rest of this chapter will look at the various grave-good types which are commonly (and not so commonly) found in cemeteries, with regard to their ability to date the burial with which they are associated, and the ways in which they were used.

Jewellery and Dress Ornaments

A major change in dress fashion took place in the late sixth or early seventh century, with the wearing of pairs of brooches and the use of multi-coloured (polychrome) bead strings becoming less common, although single brooches of certain types and strings of single-colour (monochrome) beads remained. Other forms of beads and pendants, such as amethyst and metal beads, and gold and garnet pendants, became more popular. Within these two major traditions (which I shall term 'early' for the fifth and sixth centuries, and 'late' for the very late sixth, seventh and early eighth centuries), there is, however, much variation, especially in the former, which is characterised by a wide range of brooch forms and other artefacts. This early tradition usually involved wearing brooches in pairs at the shoulders, from which Owen-Crocker (1986: 25–64) has argued for the wearing of a *'peplos*-type' gown, an untailored tubular garment which had the front and back clasped together by the brooches (**Fig. 2.3**). Beads seem usually not to have been worn as complete necklaces but rather to have been arranged in festoons between these two brooches. Sometimes a third, central, brooch is found, which Owen-Crocker suggests may perhaps have fastened the gown to a sleeved undergarment which would have been worn in cold weather, although it may also have secured a cloak. This costume also featured elaboration of the waist with a belt or girdle to which was often attached a range of items such as a knife, a bag, 'latch-lifters' (a simple form of key), and the probably symbolic 'girdle-hangers'. In some areas the long-sleeved undergarment seems to have been fastened at the cuffs with sleeve-clasps (also called wrist-clasps). There also seems to have been some regional costume traditions, especially in the sixth century, where some brooch and other artefact types differ between the putative Anglian, Saxon and Kentish areas (although Chapter Five will demonstrate that these overlap to a greater or lesser extent in some areas).

In the later tradition, a different dress type seems to be present, as this regional differentiation largely disappears. From the later sixth century, only single brooches tend to be found, and these are predominantly of circular form. New artefact types include decorated pins held together by small chains ('linked pins'), which acted as dress fastenings, different types of beads and necklaces (with increasing use of pendants), and other items such as the small bronze circular 'work-boxes' which were fastened to the waist (Geake 1997; Owen-Crocker 1986: 85–106).

For the beginner one of the most confusing aspects of early Anglo-Saxon archaeology is the plethora of brooch forms, with their associated terminology, especially in the fifth and sixth centuries when brooches are at their most varied. Being confronted with a mass of

Fig. 2.3. The construction and wearing of a 'peplos'-type gown (after Owen-Crocker 1984: figs 26–7).

terms such as 'cross-pattée small-long brooch' or 'Leeds Type A1 great square-headed brooch' with little explanation can put off even the most interested student. A further problem is that for much of the history of early Anglo-Saxon archaeology the brooch forms have been used to try to answer historical questions, based on assumptions about their dating and origins, and so even the most basic of typological work becomes embroiled in these debates. The classifications often provide, however, a convenient shorthand for describing the details of the type of artefact (even though their datings are sometimes challenged), and thus the following sections will discuss the various types of grave-goods, giving details of the chronological and typological schemes which have been proposed for them, and discussing their use in more detail. The 'long' brooch forms (those based around the bow brooch form, with the spring-coil attachment lying behind the headplate, the pin-catch behind the footplate, and the pin running down the length of the brooch) will be discussed first, followed by the circular brooch forms, and then the other jewellery-associated artefacts.

Long brooch forms

A **cruciform brooch** (Fig. 2.4) has a head-plate with three knobs, a bow and an animal head terminal (Mortimer 1990: 45). Åberg (1926: 32–3) classified cruciform brooches into five types: I with full-round knobs; II with half-round knobs, a foot without lappets, animal heads with half-round nostrils, free or grown together below; III with half-round knobs, a foot without lappets, animal heads with scroll-shaped nostrils; IV with a foot with lappets; and V with knobs and nose-parts greatly changed and animal ornament. This series is obviously based on the assumption, outlined above, that brooch forms should start simple, and become more complex, for this series starts with the small plain brooches, and ends in the large 'florid' types (Hills 1979: 315–16, see also Leeds 1945 and Leeds & Pocock 1971 for further subdivisions). Leeds & Pocock (1971: 13–14) dated types I and II to the fifth and early sixth centuries, type III to the sixth century, type IV to the mid- to later sixth century and the development of florid cruciforms (type V) to the later sixth and early seventh centuries, originating in East Anglia or south Cambridgeshire and spreading rapidly to the east Midlands. The dating of the early brooches, especially, was dependent on the historical framework, with Åberg (1926: 32), for example, placing the English development of cruciforms 'from the time of the invasion until the end of the 6th century, or possibly even longer'. Reichstein (1975) also studied these brooches (except the florid types), dividing them into four stages: *ältere*, *jüngere* (together equal to Åberg Group 1), *späte* (= Åberg Group 2) and *späteste* (= Åberg Group 3) on a typological basis. (He was unable to use type combinations and cemetery analysis as he had for the Scandinavian and continental material (Høilund Nielsen 1997: 79).)

Catherine Mortimer, in her as yet unpublished thesis (1990), has proposed a new classification. Types A and B are found both on the continent and in Britain, while Types C, D and Z are essentially English, without continental or Scandinavian parallels (1990: 47–108). Very simply, those of Type A are small brooches with simple, unexpanded foot forms; they have top-knobs with a circular cross-section, and are plain or very simply decorated. Those of Type B are similar, but with an expanded headplate, semi-circular or flattened top-knobs and simple animal-head foot forms. This foot area is found expanded in Type C, lappets are added in Type D, and Type Z consist of zoomorphic forms with decoration at the knobs, lappets and foot. Interestingly, she notes that Type A brooches, which date from the early fifth century on the continent, are often heavily worn and/or mended when found in Anglo-Saxon cemeteries, with a few even showing traces of being sown on to clothes after the pin had broken, suggesting that these early brooches were often old when buried (1990: 110–11). Several of these brooches could easily have been made on the continent (ibid.: 158). Moreover, these early brooches also share technical attributes with continental examples, strengthening this argument (Mortimer 1999: 85). Some of these early brooches are found in Kent, and Hawkes (1982: 70) sees early

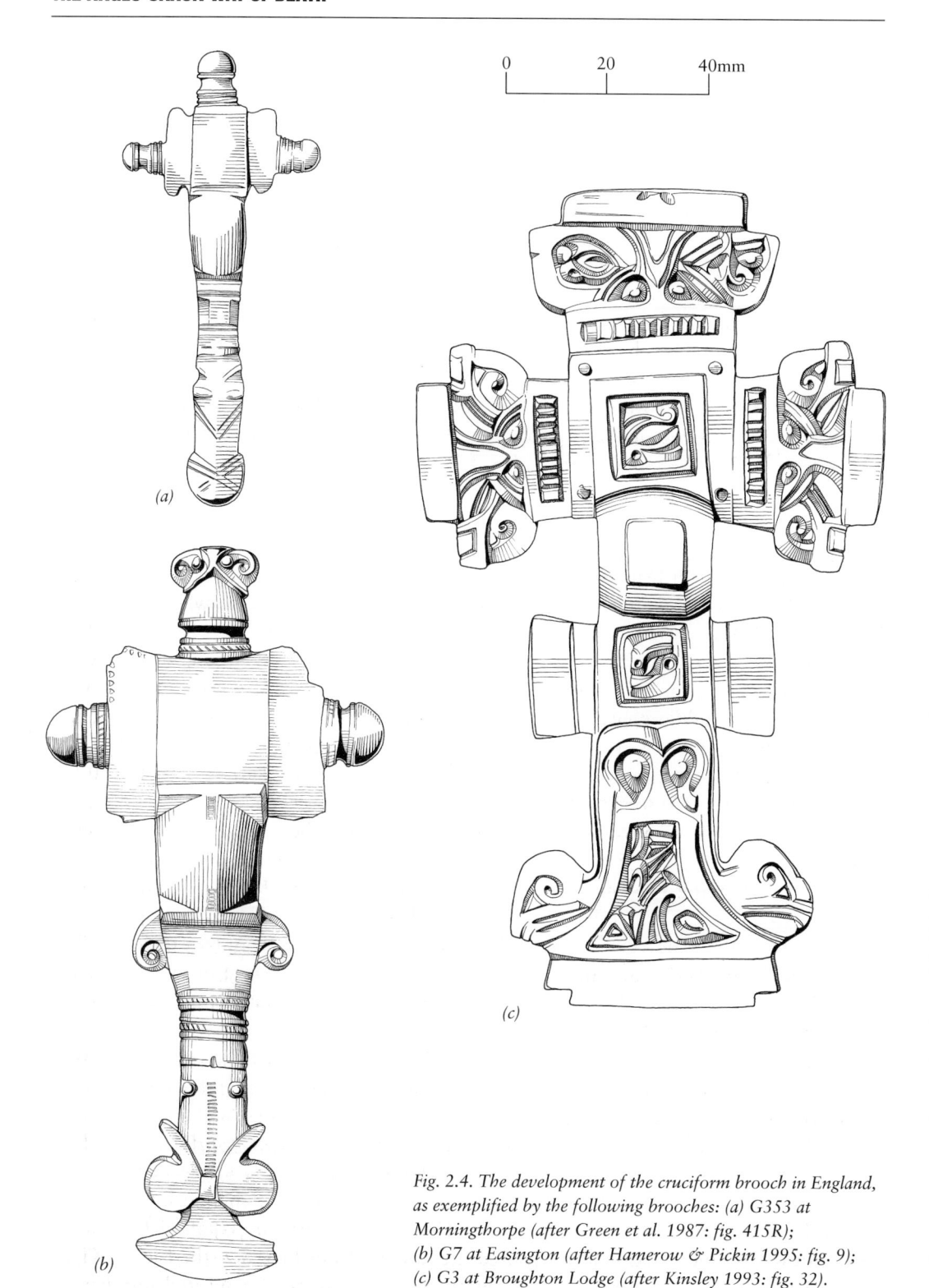

Fig. 2.4. The development of the cruciform brooch in England, as exemplified by the following brooches: (a) G353 at Morningthorpe (after Green et al. 1987: fig. 415R); (b) G7 at Easington (after Hamerow & Pickin 1995: fig. 9); (c) G3 at Broughton Lodge (after Kinsley 1993: fig. 32).

cruciform brooches as attesting Jutish origins at Beakesbourne, Howletts, Bifrons and Sarre (all in Kent), with the earliest examples being brought over in the mid-fifth century. Cruciform brooches are therefore dated only by continental parallels, by assumed development from those parallels and by the goods with which they are found associated in graves.

The **Anglo-Saxon (non-Kentish) square-headed brooch** (Fig. 2.5a+b) was classified and discussed by Leeds (1949). It comprises three elements: a rectangular headplate, an arched bow, and a lozenge- or diamond-shaped footplate. Leeds (ibid.: 5) classified them by the form of the footplate, with his Type A having an undivided foot, Type B having a divided foot (i.e. with a bar, or other stylistic division running vertically down the centre of the footplate), and Type C with a 'cruciform' foot (i.e. a foot type that would usually be seen on a cruciform brooch – it was not cross-shaped). He saw Type A as having a source in the Rhineland (ibid.: 33), to the extent that the brooch (of Type A1) from grave G3 at Finglesham, Kent, was thought to come from the same workshop as an example from the cemetery at Engers in Germany (ibid.: 7). Thus Type A was thought to begin in the later fifth century, Type B to date largely to the sixth century and Type C to the seventh (ibid.: 120–1).

Hines (1984: 110–98) also divided these brooches into three chronological phases, on the basis of changes in features rather than consistently by association with other grave-good types. He disagreed with the importance Leeds (1949) placed on whether the foot was divided or not, instead describing twenty-two groupings of these brooches, each of which he saw as more or less linked by common characteristics. These groupings were seen as divisible into three phases: an early phase with a small set of brooches which were individualistic, a middle phase with a larger set of brooches, some of which were quite similar to others, and a latest phase characterised as an attempt at 'mass production' (Hines 1984: 180). He gives these date ranges of c. 500–520 for Phase 1, c. 510–550 for Phase 2 and c. 530–570 for Phase 3 (ibid.: 197). In a more recent study (Hines 1997), he expands this classification to twenty-five groupings. He sees the earliest Phase 1 brooches as products of a current of southern Scandinavian influence in southern and eastern England (overlapping to some extent with that producing the Kentish square-headed brooches – see below). This influence continues in Phase 2 brooches, but in that phase and later there is a clear tendency for Anglo-Saxon brooches of this type to find their parallels in increasingly northerly parts of Scandinavia, especially the west coast of Norway (ibid.: 232), although these English brooches are not of Norwegian manufacture, with one or two possible exceptions (ibid.: 233).

The smaller **Kentish square-headed brooches** (Fig. 2.5c) are generally seen to display a different trajectory from those in the rest of the country. Åberg (1926: 74–86) distinguished them from the types found in Anglian areas by their decoration, form and frequent use of garnets (he also noted the small sub-set which have a circular ornamented disc mounted on the bow). In contrast with the non-Kentish examples which tend to have a divided foot and little animal ornament, the zoomorphic design on the footplates of the Kentish brooches is not broken up (Laing & Laing 1996: 27). They were studied by Leigh (1980) in an unpublished PhD thesis. Around a hundred are known, from Kent and the Isle of Wight (Leigh 1990: 108), and they are thought to be the product of a limited number of

THE ANGLO-SAXON WAY OF DEATH

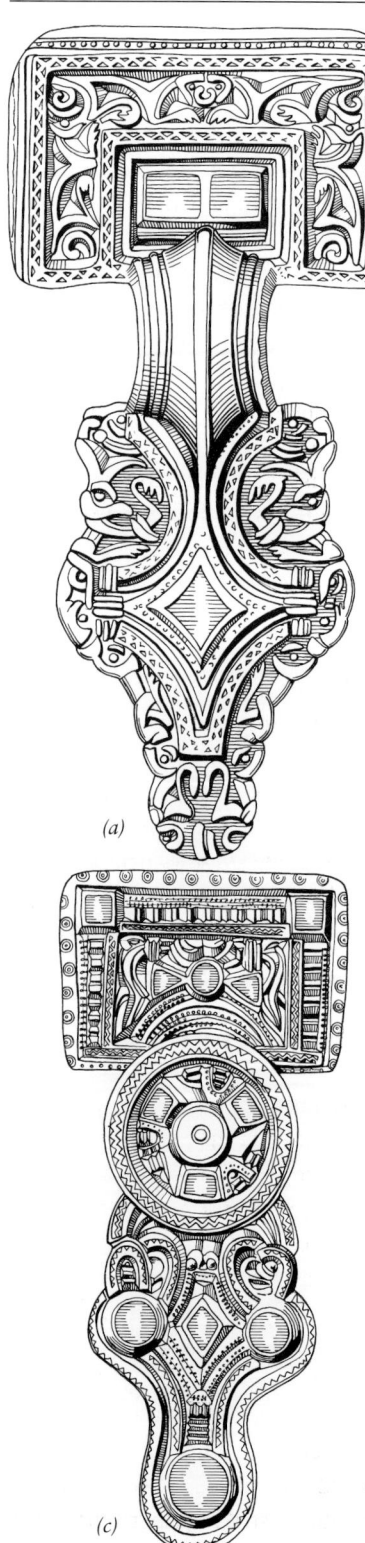

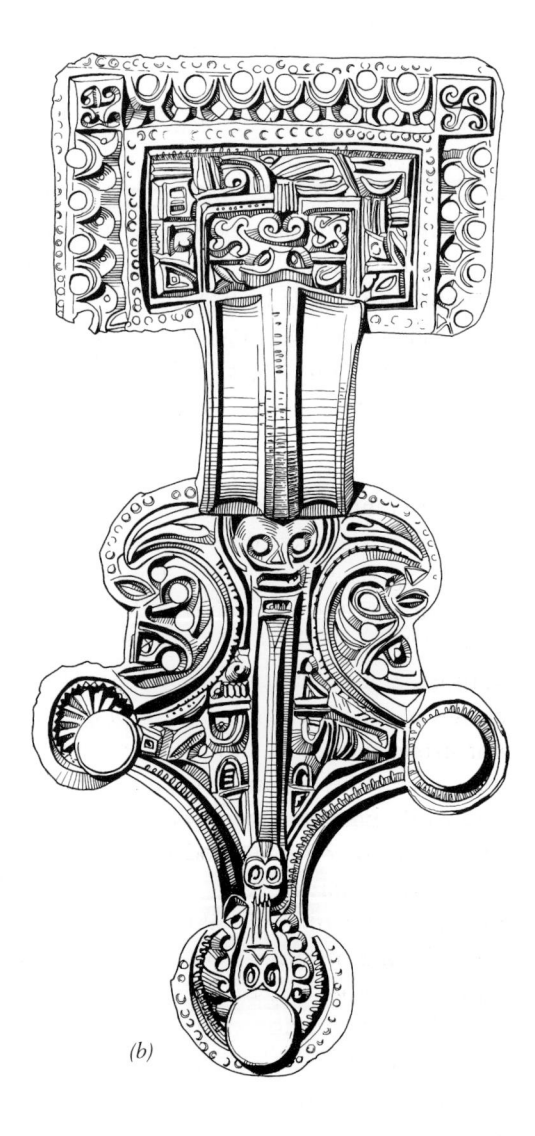

Fig. 2.5. The different forms of square-headed brooch: (a) Leeds Type A, example from Milton-next-Sittingbourne, Kent (after Smith 1923: fig. 56); (b) Leeds Type B, example from grave A11 at Beckford (after Evison & Hill 1996: fig. 11); (c) Kentish example from Dover Buckland (after Evison 1987: fig. 64).

workshops (and possibly even of a single one – Leigh 1990: 114). Some seem to carry the earliest examples of Style I decoration and these are thought to have been imported from Jutland in the last two decades of the fifth century (Laing & Laing 1996: 27). These Kentish brooches may also have stimulated and influenced production of some of the non-Kentish types (Dickinson 1976: 153), a suggestion that is supported by a few finds outside Kent and the Isle of Wight, such as the eight in the Upper Thames region cited by Dickinson (ibid.: 172), which were very small and crudely made of gilt-bronze. Very recently Parfitt & Brugmann (1997: 35) have distinguished two main types within the Kentish tradition: a 'Jutish–Kentish' group resembling Scandinavian great square-headed brooches in size and style; and a 'Kentish–continental' group, which are mostly smaller and have simpler geometric and animal style art designs, and sometimes garnet settings.

The whole area of the classification of square-headed brooches has been the subject of an unpublished PhD by Brooks (1994). She critiques the basis on which both Hines (1984) and Leigh (1980) distinguish Kentish brooches from non-Kentish and their approaches to constructing chronologies (1994: 43–4), arguing that they both use subjective methods, rather than objectively defining classificatory features. Brooks then uses a variety of statistical tests to identify different classes of square-headed brooch, without making *a priori* assumptions as to their date on the basis of form or decoration. She suggests that two different types of brooch can be distinguished, on the basis of size rather than decoration, splitting off brooches over 7.8 cm long from shorter ones. While her classes largely agree with those of Hines, she also notes that there does seem to be a true difference between brooches with a divided footplate (Leeds' Class A) and those without (Leeds' Class B) (Brooks 1994: 121–58). She does not, however, unlike these earlier authors, think that changes in decoration are an adequate basis to suggest how these classes relate to each other chronologically, and notes that the contextual associations are not strong enough to do this either, although she allows that linking groups by tool-marks may offer some potential in starting to arrange these groups into date order (ibid.: 167). Her work must serve as a warning that current methods of ordering artefacts by date are often based on dubious models and assumptions, especially as she shows how many of the seemingly separate chronologies for different types of metalwork are, in fact, interdependent (ibid.: 85–90).

Small-long brooches (Fig. 2.6), as the name suggests, are small bow brooches, which may be cheaper copies of or substitutes for the larger cruciforms and square-headed brooches. Decoration on them consists of moulded ribs, facets and stamps, and they probably date from the late fifth century at the earliest (Dickinson 1976: 174–5, although Drinkall & Foreman (1998: 254) cite an early fifth-century example from Shakenoak, Oxon). They are often worn in pairs at the shoulders, sometimes with an additional large brooch, perhaps securing a cloak, between them (Hills 1979: 320). Leeds (1945) divided them into five types: four were classified by the shape of the headplate – trefoil, cross pattée, cross potent (these last two rather confusing terms derived from heraldry) and square (which includes those with a 'horned' headplate) – and the fifth by its lozenge-shaped foot. Åberg (1926: 56–61) had, however, identified them as a single group: 'Long brooches with triangular or shovel-shaped foot'. His Fig. 92 shows the whole range of brooches which Leeds goes on to classify into types. Leeds noted a striking distribution for

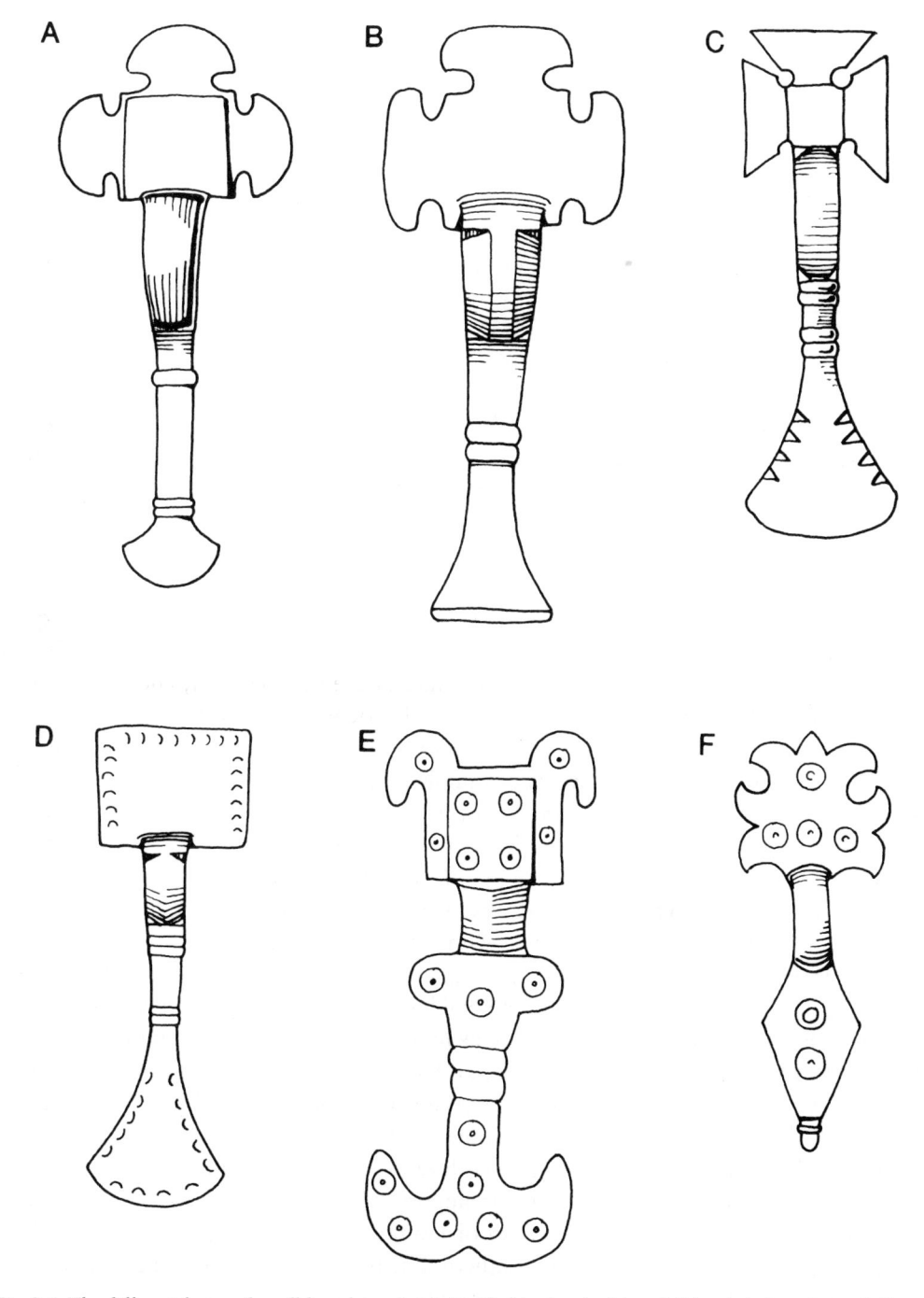

Fig. 2.6. The different forms of small-long brooch, as classified by Leeds: (a) trefoil-headed, from Stapenhill, Staffs. (after Leeds 1945: fig. 4c); (b) cross-potent, from Darlington (after Leeds 1945: fig. 8c); (c) cross-pattée, from Linton Heath G94 (after Leeds 1945: fig. 13b); (d) square-head (plain), from East Shefford (after Leeds 1945: fig. 18d); (e) square-head (panelled) from Holywell Row G37 (after Leeds 1945: fig. 22g); (f) brooch with lozenge foot from Barrington A (after Leeds 1945: fig. 23h). Scale 1:1.

this type of brooch, with a strong clustering in the mid-Anglian region, and most examples being found to the north and west of the Icknield Way. He was also struck by the lack of parallel forms on the continent, as these brooches were 'so much a feature of English Anglo-Saxondom' (1945: 5).

The other types of long brooch found in early Anglo-Saxon cemeteries tend to be imports, or based closely on them (**Fig. 2.7**). **Equal-armed brooches** have a headplate that is the same as the footplate. The 'classic' examples, such as those from Haslingfield and Little Wilbraham (both in Cambridgeshire), have exact parallels in north-west Germany, and were seen by Leeds (1913: 91) as denoting 'the presence of settlers belonging to a tribe which had emigrated from Hanover', who had entered Britain from the east, to judge by the distribution. Böhme (1974) distinguished five types: (1) the Seraing Verform (simple, with no chip-carving); (2) the Sahlenberg type (with projecting animal heads on the inner sides of the head and foot); (3) the Wehden type (usually silver, with a wavy border on the edges); (4) the Dösemoor type (large with animal borders); and (5) the Nesse type (like the Dösemoor type, but with an animal border on the outer, as well as the inner, edges of the head and foot). To judge by their associations, they were generally buried in the second half of the fifth century (Evison 1981: 130–4). Although the majority of examples in England seem to be imports, some may be imitations (ibid.: 135). There are also other sorts of equal-armed brooch. Hines (1984: 253–9) discusses the small group of equal-armed brooches with trapezoidal headplates, all of which are found in East Anglia. Where dateable, their contexts seem to be of the first half of the sixth century, and they seem to show considerable parallels with a number of brooches from Norway, which Hines suggests could be the source for their inspiration (although he notes a considerable gap between the date of the latest Norwegian examples and the earliest English ones).

Other apparently early imported brooch forms include supporting-arm brooches, radiate brooches and bird brooches, all of which are reasonably rare. Böhme (1974) classifies the **supporting-arm** brooch (also known as the *Stützarmfibel*), which has a flat bow and two lugs on the headplate, into the Mahndorf type (with the 'arm' or headplate 25–30mm wide), the Perlberg type (12–22mm), and a type with a trapezoid foot (Evison 1981: 128). These appear to be imports from the north German regions, as do the very small number of *tutulus* **brooches** found in Anglo-Saxon graves. Resembling an elongated shield-boss in miniature, these were uniformly old when buried, for example the two late fourth-century fragments found in a probably early fifth-century grave at Abingdon (Dickinson 1976: 183–4). **Radiate brooches** have a semi-circular headplate with an odd number (usually five or seven) of decorated knobs or roundels attached. Some of these brooches have bow and foot of uniform width, while others have bulging or lozenge-shaped footplates. To judge by their continental distribution, they appear to be imports from the Frankish areas and middle European areas (Åberg 1926: 92–3). Also of Frankish origin or inspiration are the **bird brooches**, which show a predominantly southern distribution in Anglo-Saxon cemeteries.

These long brooch types, therefore, date predominantly to the fifth and sixth centuries. Some are found solely as imports, such as the *tutulus* brooches and the 'classic' equal-armed brooches, while others, such as cruciform brooches and square-headed brooches, are based on continental or Scandinavian forms, but undergo a process of insular development in the later fifth and sixth centuries.

THE ANGLO-SAXON WAY OF DEATH

Fig. 2.7. Different forms of imported brooch: (a) supporting-arm brooch from Kempston (after Smith 1923: fig. 80); (b) equal-armed brooch from Kempston (ibid. fig. 81); (c) bird brooch from Mill Hill Deal G25A (after Parfitt & Brugmann 1997: fig. 29); (d) radiate brooch from Mill Hill Deal G25B (ibid.: fig. 30). Scale 1:1.

Round brooch forms (Fig. 2.8)

Disc brooches are round, cast, copper alloy brooches, often with an ornamented surface. Unusually uniform in size, with most having diameters within the range of 26mm to 45mm and close to a mean of 36mm, they employ random designs built up from simple elements, such as incisions and punched stamps, which are applied after casting and before the 'tinning' with white metal which is often observed (Dickinson 1976: 118–19; 1979: 39–41). The other grave-goods with which they are associated suggest burial between AD 450 and AD 550 for the majority (Dickinson 1979: 42). Leeds (1945) noted that there were no north European prototypes for this type of brooch, and suggested that they might

Fig. 2.8. Different forms of round brooch: (a) applied brooch from Beckford grave B55 (after Evison & Hill 1996: fig. 28); (b) saucer brooch from Alton G12 (after Evison 1988: fig. 26); (c) button brooch from Dover Buckland G48 (after Evison 1987: fig. 27.1); (d) disc brooch from Broughton Lodge G35 (after Kinsley 1993: fig. 55). Scale 1:1.

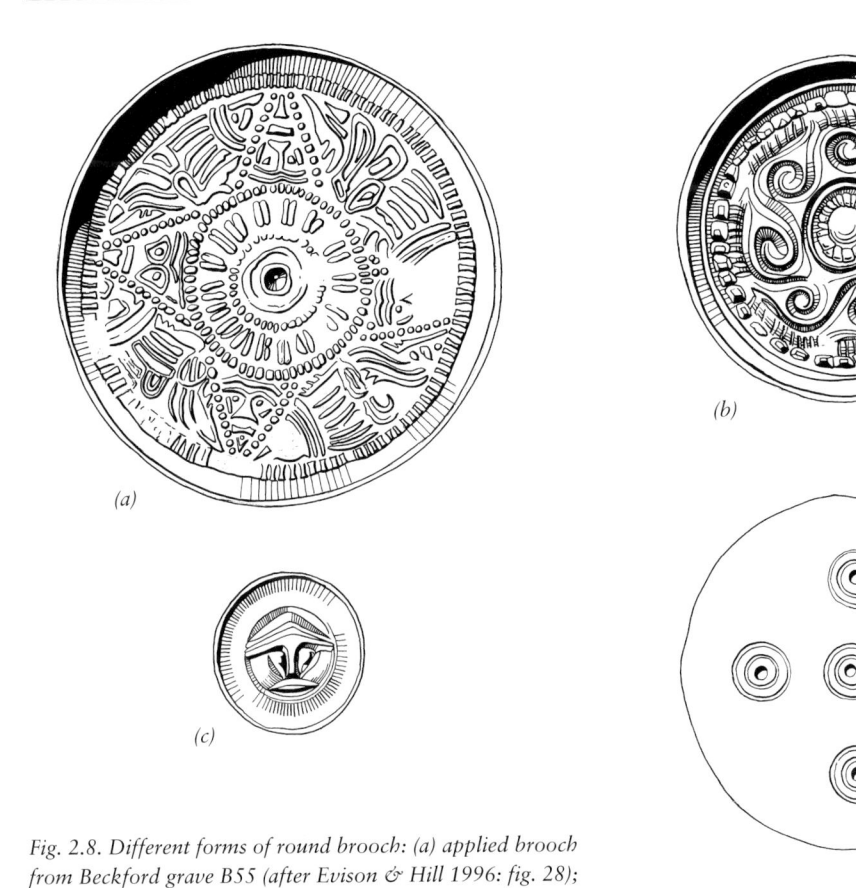

have evolved from Romano-British forms. Dickinson (1979: 48) agreed with the lack of prototypes, pointing out that although there are comparable examples on the continent, these are either contemporary with the British examples or later than them. Moreover, the techniques used to make and ornament these disc brooches are rooted in late Roman metalworking traditions, for example the use of stamps, nicked edges and rough casting (ibid.: 51). She suggested (1976: 118), based on their concentration in the Upper Thames region, that this may have been a major production centre. She also divided these brooches, on the basis of decoration, into seven main groupings, but these are difficult to distinguish chronologically (1976: 123–34).

Although Åberg saw **applied saucer brooches** as having a relatively late development in the latter half of the sixth century – a date based on stylistic considerations (1926: 23) – applied brooches do in fact begin to be made earlier than cast saucer brooches. The applied forms have a repoussé decorated foil mounted on to a backplate, and a separate strip could be fitted as a rim (Dickinson 1993a: 11, 13). Although they start early, perhaps before the mid-fifth century in Britain (Evison 1978: 100), they also have a relatively long life, as large applied brooches with Style I decoration are found through the sixth century (ibid.: 88). Often they have lost their decorated foil and sometimes their rim by the time of excavation (Dickinson 1976: 100–1), meaning that schemes classifying them on the basis of ornament, such as Dickinson's division into three major groupings (ibid.: 101–13), will necessarily exclude many of the known examples.

Dickinson supports the view put forward by Böhme (1974: 28; 1986: 531) that **cast appliqués** were developed at the same time, or soon after, applied foil saucer brooches, in the later fourth or early fifth century, and continued being made until the middle of the fifth century (Dickinson 1991: 52). Cast appliqués are only found singly (either on the shoulder, paired with another brooch, or as a central ornament on a dress or cloak) (Dickinson 1991: 60). **Cast saucer brooches**, however, were worn in pairs, one at either shoulder, and are thus assumed to have fastened a peplos-type dress, although rare instances of saucer brooches found below the waist may suggest the wearing of an open-fronted shift. They are found with females, the vast majority of whom were in late adolescence or adulthood (Dickinson 1993a: 38).

The cast version was developed from the applied saucer brooch, with an average diameter of 40–45mm, though they range from 24mm to 82mm (Dickinson 1993a: 13–14). They have a range of decorative motifs, on which basis Dickinson (1976: 50–99) classified them into eighteen groups. Brooches which can be dated as later by their associations have great variety of decoration, with geometric designs generally preceding those based on animal ornament (Dickinson 1993a: 23). Like other brooch forms, cast saucer brooches get noticeably larger, over 60mm in diameter, in the later sixth century (ibid.: 34). The brooches are cast from a range of copper alloys, with varying proportions of tin and zinc. An initial model of wood, bone or wax was covered in clay to form a two-piece mould, into which the molten alloy was then poured; almost certainly the mould was then broken to extract the brooch (ibid.: 34–5). Analysis of the copper alloys indicates that two very similar brooches could be made from different batches of metal, while a single batch could produce two very different brooches (ibid.: 36). While Chadwick (1907: 75) saw saucer brooches as probably of British origin, as he only knew of examples from this country, Åberg (1926: 16) agreed with Leeds (1912) that cast saucer brooches had probably originated on the continent but later developed entirely within England. He noted their different distribution when compared with cruciform brooches, and suggested that this supported the idea that saucer brooches were Saxon, whereas cruciforms were Anglian (ibid.: 18).

Resembling miniature saucer brooches, with an average diameter of 15–20mm (Dickinson 1993a: 13), **button brooches** have a round human face motif, or occasionally simple crouching animals on their lower surface (Dickinson 1976: 143), and were dated by Åberg to the middle and later half of the sixth century (1926: 27–8). Both Dickinson (1991: 55, n38) and Welch (1986) would put them earlier, though, from the later fifth to the mid-sixth century (although not as early as Evison (1981: 137) who would put virtually the whole series into the fifth century). They have been classified into twelve groups, mainly on the basis of ornament, by Avent & Evison (1982) who see them as a Saxon product, evolving either in north-west Germany, in the Elbe–Weser triangle, or in Britain. Welch (1986), however, inferred a different origin, linking the use of button brooches to sleeve-clasps on the basis of two graves. The first, from Erdsten in Norway, contained a woman with a row of sleeve-clasps running down her front, fastening a garment, and in the second, G62 at Alfriston, four button brooches were used in the same way. Welch also argued that the button brooch may have been inspired by Scandinavian clasp buttons with face masks. Whatever their origins, Dickinson (1976: 148) saw their regional distributions as suggesting production in a number of workshops in this country.

Annular brooches (Fig. 2.9a) (also called ring-brooches in older reports) are the most common brooch type in 'Anglian' areas of Britain, although they do not derive from any obvious continental origin (Hills 1979: 316). They also exhibit a great deal of variation: along with what are now known as quoit and certain penannular forms (types a to d – see below), Leeds (1945) divided them into Type e, which are flat in section and do not have notches or a stop for the pin; Type f, which are narrow, half-round or oval in section; and Type g, which are large, flat examples. Hines, however, has criticised Leeds' division into types 'because they fail to reflect the enormous range of variety of form found in this large body of material and . . . oppose definitive elements that occur together' (Hines 1984: 260). The vast majority are of bronze, but iron, silver, lead and bone examples have also been found (ibid.: 261; Drinkall & Foreman 1998: 258), and decoration largely consists of incised lines running across the ring and various punched impressions (Drinkall & Foreman 1998: 255). It seems to be one of the few brooch forms which carries on in use from the sixth into the seventh century, especially in the case of small delicate examples and those which make use of silver and garnet settings (ibid.: 263). With a start date probably in the late fifth century, they thus remain in use for a long time. Hines disputes Leeds' arguments for a 'native' British origin for these brooches. While he concedes that these simple brooches could have been invented independently, he does note a number of parallels in Denmark and on Bornholm among objects which were used as buckles or belt-fasteners (Hines 1984: 266–7), concluding that the 'sources and history of the annular brooch in Anglian England remain largely obscure' (ibid.: 269). There seems to be a regional distinction between narrow-banded types which are found in eastern and northern regions, and broad-band annulars, which occur predominantly in south and south-eastern England (Cook & Dacre 1985: 77).

Resembling annular brooches in size but with a slightly different appearance, **swastika brooches** are a type of openwork disc brooch (Fig. 2.9b), with irregular slots (and sometimes T-shapes in the case of 'cognate' forms) cut through the disc so that the remaining metal represents a swastika (Leeds 1945: 52). Also seemingly related to annular forms are **penannular brooches**, which have a break in the ring (Fig. 2.9c). Fowler (1960) put forward a classification for simple penannular brooches, mainly on the basis of the elaboration of the terminal ends of the ring, with types A–E being Iron Age and Romano-British, while types F–H belonged largely to the late- and post-Roman period. In a later article (Fowler 1963) she distinguished her types G1.1–4 (with a predominantly western British distribution) from types G1.5–8, having a ribbed or plain hoop with single dot or plain terminal decoration (with a more easterly distribution). Where types G1.5–8 have

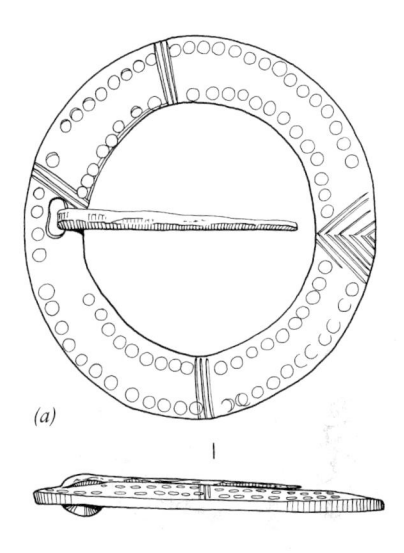

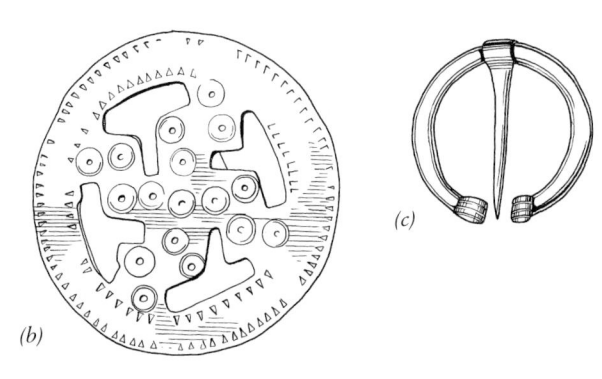

Fig. 2.9. Different forms of ring brooch: (a) annular brooch from Sewerby G15 (after Hirst 1985: fig. 37); (b) swastika brooch from Beckford grave A9 (after Evison & Hill 1996: fig. 10); (c) penannular brooch from Sleaford (after Fowler 1963: fig. 6.8). Scale 1:1.

datable associations in Anglo-Saxon graves, they are of the sixth century and were used to fasten a dress at the shoulders (Dickinson 1982: 51–3). Type C is the only other one to be used in this fashion (Dickinson 1976: 139). Examples of Iron Age and Roman types have been found in Anglo-Saxon graves, but they are generally included in purse collections or have been transformed into another object, such as a bracelet (Dickinson 1976: 139). Leeds (1936: 3) saw this brooch type dating back to pre-Roman times in Britain and persisting throughout the Roman period, so that 'its appearance in English graves bears witness to the survival of a native substratum in Anglo-Saxon culture', to the extent that he thought some of the examples might actually be of Roman date (1945: 44). Leeds also saw the penannular as the origin of the annular brooch, via the quoit brooch (1936: 3; 1945: 46), and Dickinson (1976: 142) agreed.

Quoit brooches are annular-like brooches, with a broad flat metal band and a pin hinged on the inner edge, with a notch cut opposite (though not all the way through the width of the band) for the pin to pass through (Ager 1985). Leeds saw the classic quoit brooch as a combination of penannular and flat annular forms which he dated to the late fourth or early fifth century (the 'fur' on the animals being a Gallo-Roman technique of this date), thus pre-dating the invasions (1936: 3–7). Type a is represented by a single brooch, the penannular from Alfriston which has Quoit Brooch Style decoration. Type b consists of two examples, the outstanding brooch from Sarre with its distinctive decoration and animals in relief, and the fragmentary brooch from Howletts, while Type c comprises a single example, also from Howletts (Harrison 1997: 75). Brooches of Type d, reclassified as simple quoit brooches by Ager (1985), are more numerous, as well as being of copper alloy, smaller and more plainly decorated with incised lines and stamps. (These quoit brooches, confusingly, are not decorated in Quoit Brooch Style.) They are used as costume fastenings in much the same way as annular brooches (ibid.).

All of the above round brooch forms are found over most of eastern Britain, although most show some marked distributions, with, for example, many saucer brooches found in

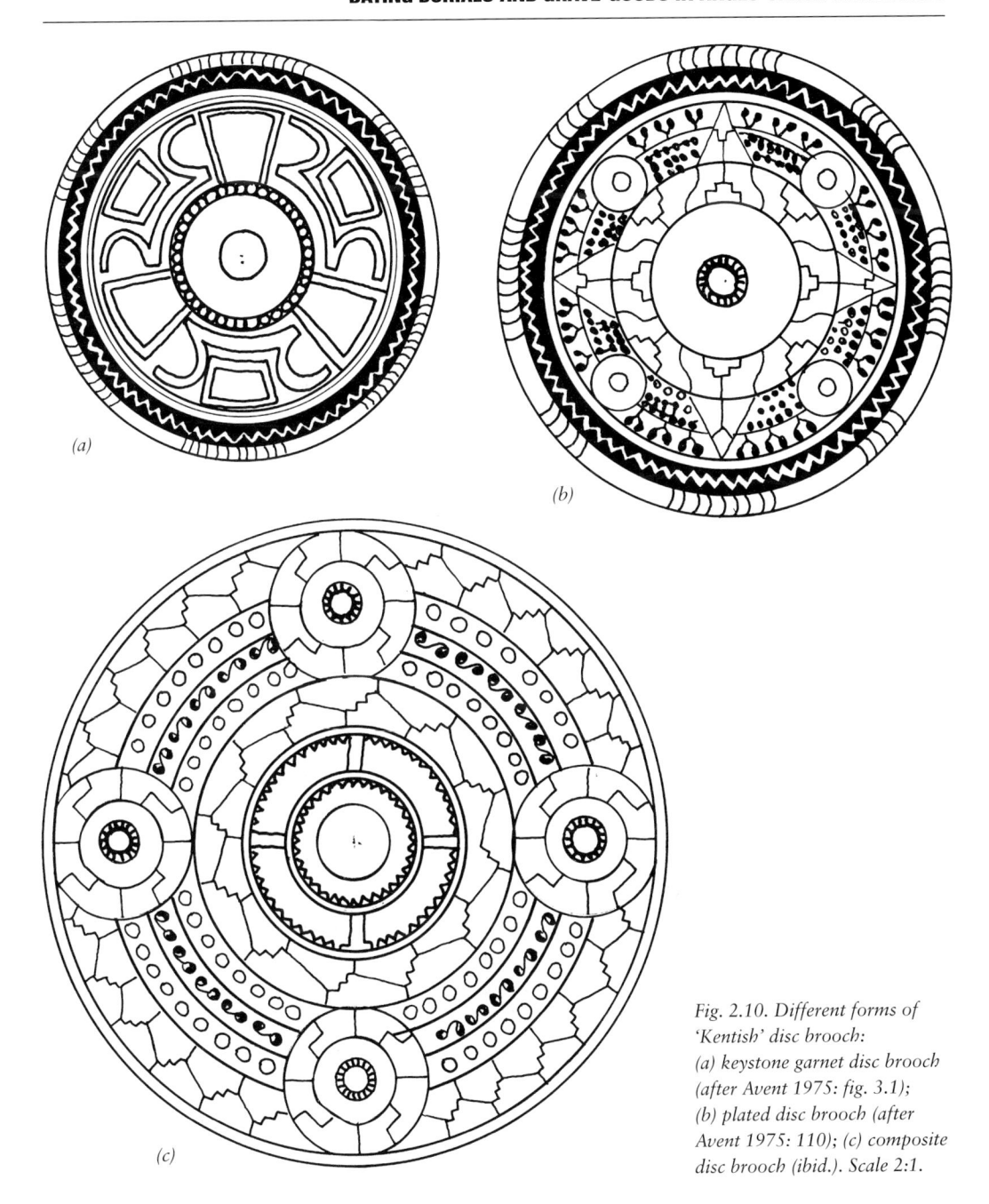

Fig. 2.10. Different forms of 'Kentish' disc brooch: (a) keystone garnet disc brooch (after Avent 1975: fig. 3.1); (b) plated disc brooch (after Avent 1975: 110); (c) composite disc brooch (ibid.). Scale 2:1.

the 'Saxon' Upper Thames area, while cruciforms and square-headed brooches are found mainly in the east and north. It is these distributions which archaeologists have attempted to use in inferring tribal distributions in the fifth and sixth centuries. There are some classes of brooch, though, with distributions which are quite localised in Kent. These are keystone garnet disc brooches, and plated and composite disc brooches (**Fig. 2.10**), which appear to form a developmental sequence, taking the single brooch-wearing custom into the seventh and early eighth centuries.

Keystone garnet disc brooches are made by casting, and have a predominantly Kentish distribution. Usually in silver, the brooch front is mounted with settings interspersed with cast panels of animal ornament. All brooches of this type have a circular central setting with either a plain stone or a white setting (flat or raised) with a central garnet. Radiating out from this centre are three or four triangular, wedge- or T-shaped settings, usually filled with garnet (Avent 1975: 1). Avent (ibid.: 23–41) divided keystone brooches into seven classes, mainly based on the style of animal ornament, but also on other features, and argued that these represent an approximate sequence of development (by comparison with associated grave-goods), beginning with Class 1 in the mid-sixth century and ending with the final examples of Class 7 around AD 630 (ibid.: 62). He argued for the development of this brooch type through a combination of influences: Jutish animal styles, combined with Frankish methods of inlay within the round brooch (ibid.: 66).

Plated disc brooches have a silver backplate and a gold frontplate with a central hole into which the main setting fits. This setting is surrounded by a ring of cloisonné inlay. Radiating out from this are three or four main triangular cloisonné settings, with minor settings and bands of filigree in between (Avent 1975: 1). Avent (ibid.: 62) argued that this brooch type forms a bridge between the keystone and composite brooch, and the associated grave-goods support a dating between the late sixth century and *c.* AD 720. The vast majority of these brooches are found in Kent (ibid.: 64).

Thicker than the keystone or plated disc brooches, **composite disc brooches** comprise three circular plates: a gold or bronze cloisonné wall frontplate (into which the settings are placed), a bronze or copper inner plate to which the frontplate is fixed, and a silver, gold or bronze backplate (Avent 1975: 2). These brooches seem to date from the early to mid-seventh century, on the basis of the goods that they are found with (ibid.: 62). Like the keystone and plated disc brooches, most of these are found in Kent (ibid.: 64).

Thus, while some round brooch forms are seen as being modelled on imported types, such as the applied and the cast saucer brooches, many others have been seen as having insular antecedents, and have been widely employed in arguments about the survival of the 'native British' (see Chapters Six and Seven for a detailed consideration of this debate).

Other dress fastenings and ornaments

Other dress ornaments comprise sleeve-clasps (**Fig. 2.11**), pins, beads and objects which were hung from a belt or garter. Hines (1993) proposed a typology (and relative chronology based on contexts) for **sleeve-clasps** (also called wrist-clasps). His Type A clasps are made of a length of wire with the ends rolled to form spirals; Type B employ one or more of a combination of buttons, plate and bar, while Type C are the ornate cast versions (which generally use zoomorphic ornament). He sees the initial nuclei of clasp use in Humberside and Norfolk, but by the end of the fifth century they had expanded into Suffolk, Cambridgeshire and Lincolnshire. These changes are seen by Hines as an element of Anglian English material culture in the sixth century: 'it reflected a common sense of – and desire for – group identity' (ibid.: 92). Occasionally, male graves are accompanied by

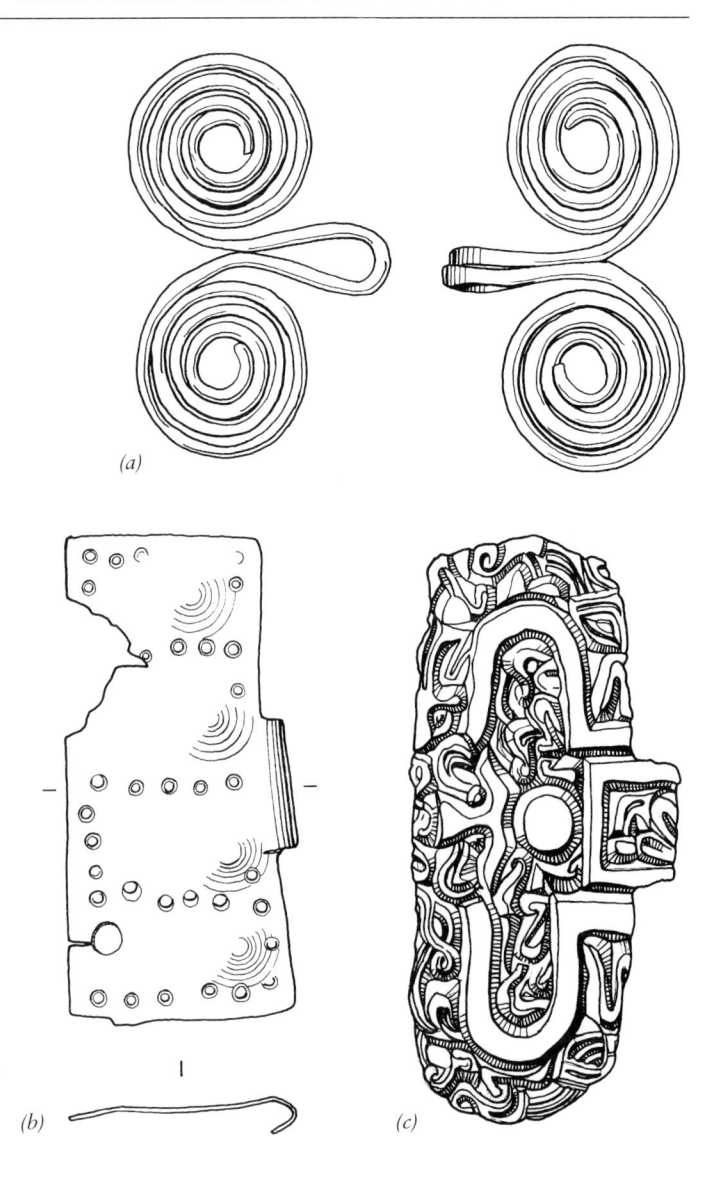

Fig. 2.11. Different forms of sleeve-clasp (under Hines' 1993 classification): (a) Type A from Empingham G91 (after Timby 1995: fig. 141); (b) Type B from Easington G1 (after Hamerow & Pickin 1995: fig. 3); (c) Type C from Morningthorpe G153 (after Green et al. 1987: fig. 348). Scale 1.5:1.

these clasps, but they are placed at the knees or ankles, and are thus serving a different function (ibid.: 78). One example of such usage has been seen recently at Tallington, Lincolnshire, although the sex of the burial was not given (Field & George 1998: 41). The type goes out of use by the end of the sixth century.

A vast range of **glass beads** are found in Anglo-Saxon burials, both in inhumations and as melted fragments in cremations. These take a number of different forms, such as truncated discs and spheres, cylinders, cubes, lobed and segmented beads (**Fig. 2.12**). They are found in clear and opaque glass, and can be multi-coloured, with the addition of polychrome trails, dots, zigzags, vertical and horizontal lines and spots. Other types found

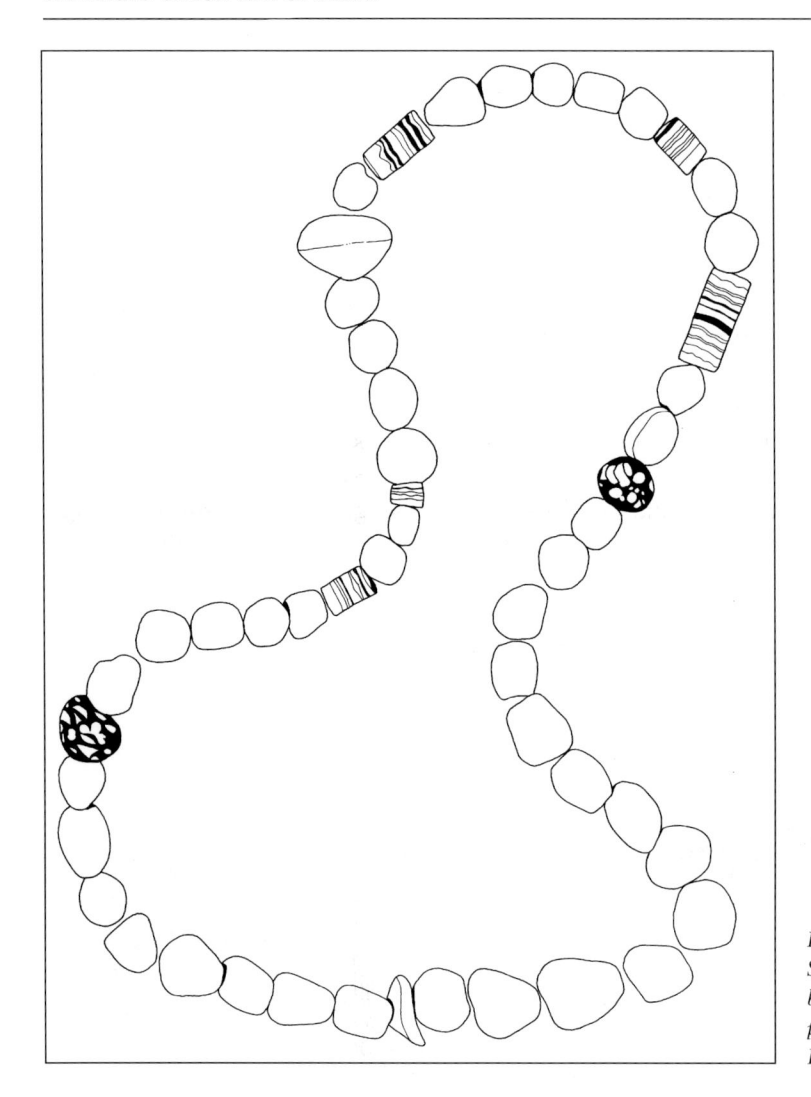

Fig. 2.12. Bead string from Sewerby G35, comprising both monochrome and polychrome beads (after Hirst 1985: fig. 25. Scale 1:2.

are faience 'melon' beads, millefiori, reticella (herringbone-overlaid) and metal-in-glass beads (Dickinson 1976: 208–10; Guido 1999; Hirst 1985: 62–85). Beads were worn in a variety of ways: as necklaces reaching all the way around the neck (as seen in G19 at Portway, Andover, Cook & Dacre 1985: 81); as festoons strung across the neck between two brooches; and sometimes sewn on to clothes, presumably as decoration. Sometimes all three uses have been noted within one site (Brush 1993: 102).

Amber beads are a relatively common find in Anglo-Saxon graves, especially in mid- to late sixth-century assemblages, although smaller numbers are still found into the seventh century, with a high proportion of these later examples being found with children (Geake 1997: 47). Although amber does occur in small quantities on the east coast of Britain, it is generally assumed that the amber found in graves was imported from the Baltic (Huggett 1988: 64). **Amethyst beads** are generally thought to have an east Mediterranean source (ibid.: 66), and are found in contexts dating from the very end of the sixth century to the third quarter of the seventh, mainly in Kent (ibid.). Outside Kent, only single amethyst beads are usually found in graves, though four were found in grave E2 at Marina Drive, Bedfordshire (Geake 1997: 41). Beads of **rock crystal**, usually found singly as part of a necklace, tend to be in sixth-century contexts (Dickinson 1976: 206).

A range of different pendant types may also be found (**Fig. 2.13**). Bucket pendants, small bronze semi-circular objects usually found in ones or twos, but sometimes in groups of up to twelve, arranged around the neck (and possibly sown on to a leather and/or metal object), have been recognised in a range of cemeteries from Kent to Cleveland (Dickinson 1993b: 50–2). Brush (1993: 100) has commented on the predominantly northern distribution of this type, found mainly in earlier cemeteries, and suggested that they may symbolise the social and ritual role of alcohol (see also Dickinson 1993b: 51). Pierced Roman coins were also often worn as pendants, and knotted silver wire rings became popular in the seventh century (Dickinson 1976: 213). Although these wire slip-knot rings (sometimes mounted with beads) are often interpreted as ear-rings, Geake (1997: 48–50) argues persuasively for them being the ends or components of necklaces. At Castledyke, Humberside, however, one pair was found *in situ* by the ears, held in place by the grave fill, in a grave probably dating to the seventh century (Drinkall & Foreman 1998: 274), suggesting a variety of functions for these rings.

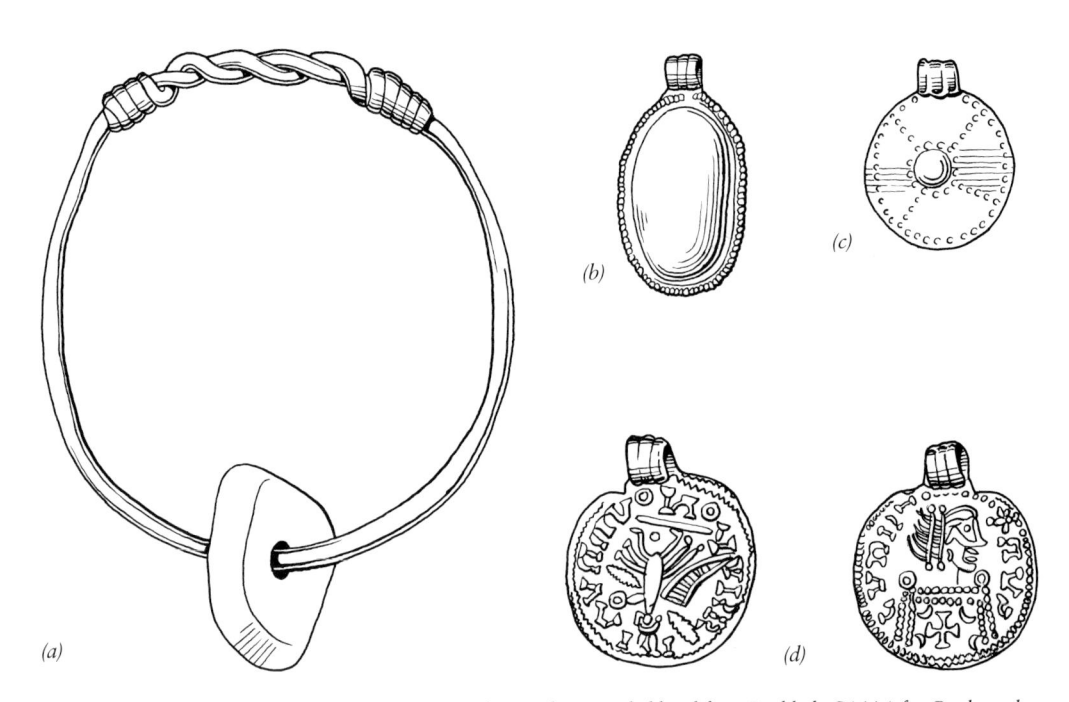

Fig. 2.13. Different types of pendant: (a) slip-knot pendant with suspended bead from Lechlade G144 (after Boyle et al. 1998: fig. 5.88); (b) cabochon garnet pendant from Lechlade G173 (ibid.: fig. 5.100); (c) scutiform pendant from Dover Buckland G67 (after Evison 1987: fig. 37); (d) bracteate from Dover Buckland (ibid.: fig. 64). Scale 1.5:1.

Bracteates are pendants whose form developed out of imitations of late Roman coins and medallions. Struck from gold, they usually consist of a central circular flan, surrounded by a stamped collar, and enclosed by a loop and frame (Gaimster 1992: 2). While they are divided on a typological basis into A, B, C, D and F types, their production appears to have lasted only two to three generations, with much overlap between the styles (ibid.). Mackeprang (1952) classified them as follows: (A) direct imitations of Roman gold medallions, i.e. with a portrait of a Roman emperor; (B) with a more debased form of head or figure; (C) with a stylised emperor head imitation and running animals; (D) with stylised Germanic animal ornament; and (F) with an animal in comparatively 'natural' proportions. They seem to have been produced mainly in Scandinavia, but around forty-five have been found, mainly in grave contexts, in Britain, the majority in Kent. Some of these may be imitations rather than imports. Silver and copper alloy examples are widespread in Britain, especially among the bracteates found outside Kent (Gaimster 1992: 8–9). Where their associations are known, virtually all are found in female graves as pendants on necklaces (ibid.: 9) – an interesting contrast with Denmark, where they are generally found in hoards.

Bullae are little metal pendants, spherical or hemispherical in shape, which were made from silver, bronze or gold, and probably dated to the later seventh and perhaps early eighth centuries (Geake 1997: 36–7). A variety of other pendants have been discussed by Geake (ibid.: 37–41), including silver and bronze **'scutiform' pendants** (with a central boss and punched decoration), **gold disc pendants** (often a coin mounted in a setting) and **'cabochon' pendants** (where the glass or garnet setting has a convex polished surface). While scutiform pendants are found in earlier cemeteries, with Hines (1984: 221–3) seeing them as having fifth-century Scandinavian origins but being a distinctively sixth-century type in England, these other pendant types are more characteristic of later cemetery assemblages.

A variety of pins are found, with various elaborations of the head, such as the addition of loops or solid knobs, and of the shaft, for example by facetting or the use of grooves (Dickinson 1976: 194–5). Pins were obviously used for a variety of purposes, as they are found in positions ranging from the head (where they perhaps served as hair-pins, or as a veil-fastener), right down the body to the legs. They could act as replacements for brooches, and they may have been used to fasten a shroud (Brush 1993: 93). Analysis of the pins from the Castledyke cemetery (Drinkall & Foreman 1998: 270) suggests that as most were found on the upper chest or neck, they were used to fasten a cloak, or perhaps a veil in some cases. The **linked pin suites** (two gold, silver or bronze pins, linked by a short delicate chain, which sometimes also have garnet settings), which may have fastened a veil to the cloak or shawl, seem to be another seventh-century artefact (Owen-Crocker 1986: 92–3; Geake 1997: 35–6). **Finger-rings**, made of gold, silver or bronze, and **bracelets** (found in a range of materials such as glass, metal and shale) are found across the whole date range of furnished cemeteries. Interestingly, these often show the persistence of Roman types into the fifth and early sixth centuries (Dickinson 1976: 198).

A range of apparently non-functional items has been classified by Meaney (1981) as having an amuletic function, i.e. protecting the owner from harm or misfortune, and these are often found associated with jewellery assemblages. They include objects hung from festoons around the neck, from chatelaines (an often long, linked chain) at the waist, or

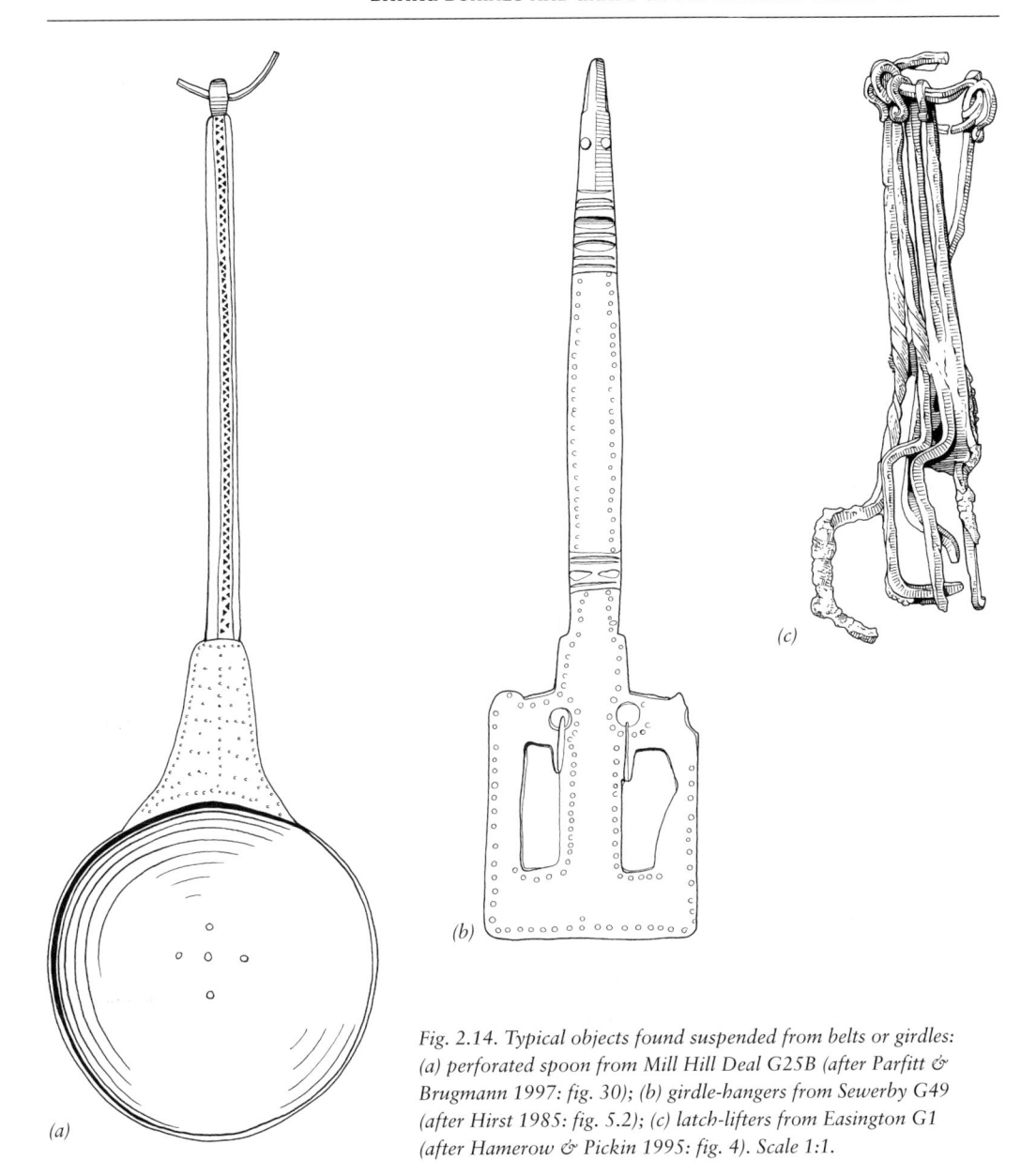

Fig. 2.14. Typical objects found suspended from belts or girdles: (a) perforated spoon from Mill Hill Deal G25B (after Parfitt & Brugmann 1997: fig. 30); (b) girdle-hangers from Sewerby G49 (after Hirst 1985: fig. 5.2); (c) latch-lifters from Easington G1 (after Hamerow & Pickin 1995: fig. 4). Scale 1:1.

kept in bags or boxes and deposited in the grave. Examples are crystal balls mounted in metal slings, perforated spoons (perhaps strainers or skimmers, which are often associated with the crystal balls in Kentish graves), quartz pebbles, fossils, mounted animal teeth and claws, cowry and other shells, miniature model weapons and tools, and girdle-hangers (**Fig. 2.14**), which are often found in matching pairs and seem to be symbolic household keys (Meaney 1981; Hines 1997: 263). Spindle-whorls (made from a variety of materials, such as bone, stone, shale, pottery, crystal, amber and glass) may also fall into this category, as

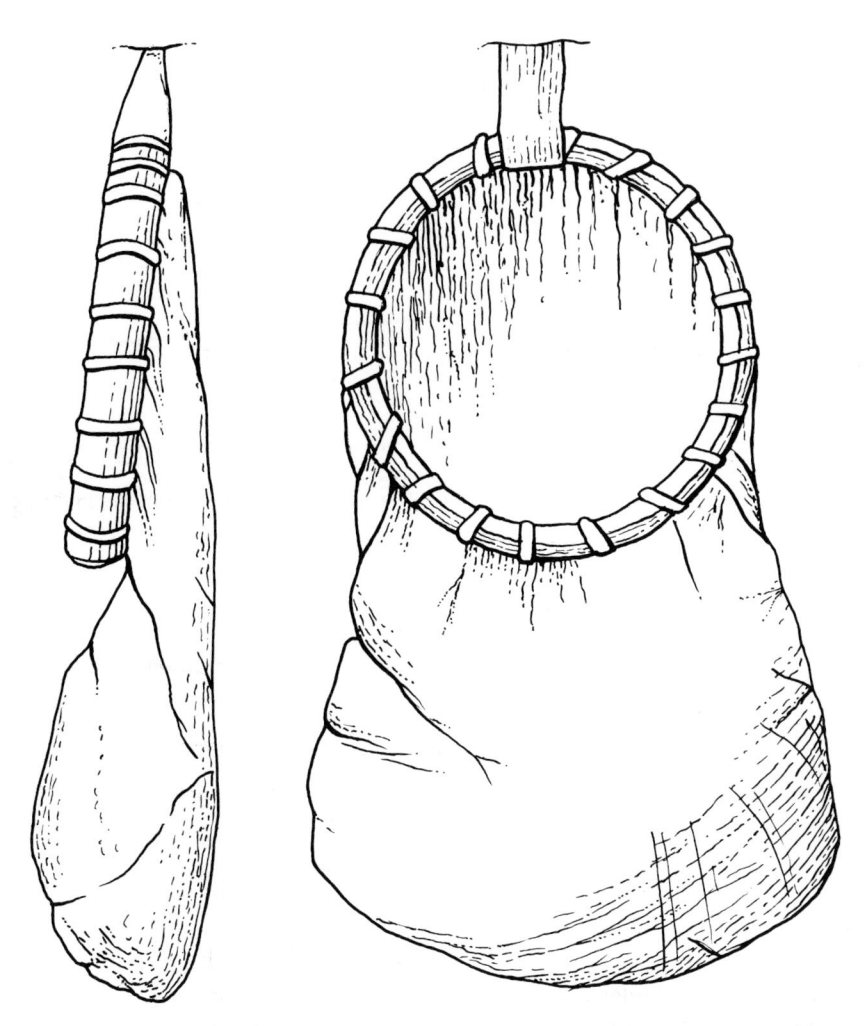

Fig. 2.15. Reconstruction of a bag suspended from an ivory ring (after Meaney 1981: fig. VII.l).

those with narrow bore-holes through the centre, or the faceted crystal beads, for example, could not have been functional (Dickinson 1976: 233). While some of these objects, such as the crystal balls and spoons, are found mainly in earlier cemeteries, with a strong concentration in Kent, many are predominantly found in graves of the late sixth and seventh centuries, for example the cowry shells (Huggett 1988: 70–2). Roman objects may also fall into this non-functional category, as old or unusual items which had been kept or collected for some reason, although they were sometimes employed in functional ways, for example the first-century AD brooches which were still used as dress fasteners in two graves at Portway, Andover (Cook & Dacre 1985: 96; see also White 1990).

Bags are found in graves throughout the period. They were made of organic material, and usually the only part to survive (excluding the non-organic contents) were the rings that formed the top – these are found in ivory, bronze and iron (**Fig. 2.15**). Although bags

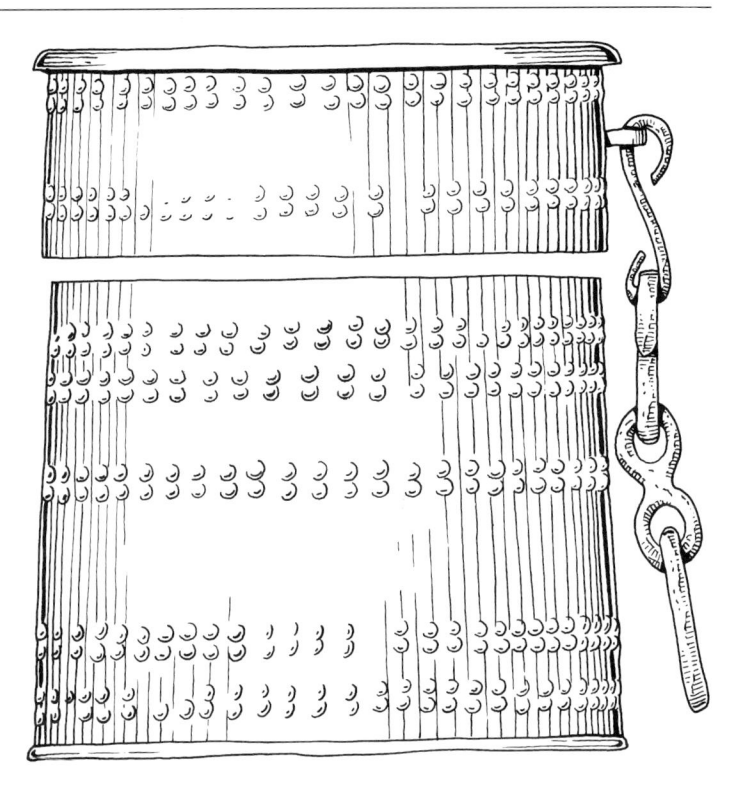

Fig. 2.16. Thread-box from Didcot G12 (after Boyle et al. 1995: fig. 97). Scale 1.5:1.

in seventh- and eighth-century graves are usually found with women, this may be because of their use by this time as containers of small objects (and it is these collections of objects near a large ring which often leads to the inference of a bag being present in the grave) (Geake 1997: 80–1). Amuletic items were often contained in bags too, as detailed in some depth by Meaney (1981: 249–52), who cites examples from Cassington (Oxon), Wheatley (Oxon) and Abingdon (Berks). An interesting range of objects, for example, was found in a grave at Orsett (Essex), contained in a bag. They comprised an iron ring, a seax-fitting, a shale bead and the mounts (escutcheons) from a hanging-bowl (Hedges & Buckley 1985).

Meaney argues (1981: 184–5) that the **bronze cylindrical boxes** (**Fig. 2.16**) sometimes found in late seventh-century graves are relic boxes, rather than thread- or work-boxes associated with embroidery or other needle-work, as they are usually interpreted. Sometimes they are decorated, usually with simple designs of punched dots, though the box from G42 at Burwell, Cambridgeshire, had Style II repoussé animal ornament (Geake 1997: 34).

While most of these amuletic items seem to be associated with the burials of women and children, the beads or rings that are sometimes found associated with the hilts of swords are also seen as having a symbolic function (Evison 1975; Meaney 1981: 196). Some of these objects, such as worked flints and Roman items, appear to have been curated, collected from older sites and reused. Many of these amuletic objects are found in graves of the late sixth century and after, with many from Kent, suggesting that external influences played a strong role in the use of these items (Meaney 1981: 264–5).

Weaponry

Burials with weaponry of the fifth and sixth centuries are usually provided with a combination of spear, shield and sword. Other types of weapon, such as axes and arrowheads, are also found but in much smaller numbers. As well as the dress ornaments, weapons also underwent a change in the seventh century, with the increasing use of the seax and of the sugar-loaf shield-boss (Geake 1997: 14–15), and it is only in these later graves that 'elite' pieces of armour such as helmets and chain-mail are found buried, albeit in exceptionally small numbers (**Fig. 2.17**). Weaponry does not exhibit distinct regional variations in type in the same way that dress ornaments do, and so they have not been interpreted in archaeology in quite the same way. Nevertheless, attempts have still been made to classify them, and arrange them in order of date.

Swanton's (1973; 1974) classification of over two thousand Anglo-Saxon **spearheads**, based on the common visible characteristics of profile, section, length and ratio of blade length to socket length, identified the following groups (**Fig. 2.18**): A, with barbs (this type is also known as the angon, and seems to have been designed as a throwing weapon); B, with a dominant midrib; C and D, with leaf-shaped blades; E and F, with more angular blades; G, with sword-shaped blades; H, with angular blades and a more concave curve to the angle; and I, J, K and L, with corrugated cross-sections. However, as Hills (1979: 321) has pointed out, 'the majority remain part of a somewhat amorphous mass, although he has managed to distinguish a few interesting small groups'. Types B (especially B1) and C appear to be relatively common in the seventh century, and angular Types E and F less so, although along with Type G they are occasionally found in seventh-century contexts (Geake 1997: 69). Types H, I, J and K are found in greatest numbers in the sixth century (at least in the Upper Thames region), and are almost entirely absent from Geake's sample of later graves, which corroborates this dating, while Type D spearheads seem to cover the entire date range (ibid.: 68–9, citing Dickinson 1976: 293–329). Type L seems to be predominantly early, dating to the later fifth and earlier sixth centuries (Swanton 1973: 137). Spears were usually placed to the left or the right of the body, with the spearhead itself typically at the head end of the grave.

The Anglo-Saxon **shield** consisted of a wooden board with a central iron boss and metal grip, sometimes with further board fittings or a leather cover. The boss (or *umbo*) is made up of the flange (or rim), the wall (or collar), the cone (or dome) and the apex (or spike) (Dickinson & Härke 1992: 1). Evison (1963) outlined the basis for classification of shield-bosses: the later it was, the taller it would be, until the extremes of the 'sugar-loaf' form were reached. Evison (ibid.: 38) distinguished the true sugar-loaf, with its high curved cone, from the straight-sided conical forms. While fifth- and sixth-century bosses in England are usually carinated, Evison saw bosses and flanges getting narrower, with less emphasis on the carination during the sixth century (ibid.: 39). She saw the emergence of the conical form in the decades just after AD 650, and the development of the true sugar-loaf in the last decades of the seventh century (possibly earlier than these forms appear on the continent) (ibid.: 65–6). These findings were largely confirmed by the multivariate analyses conducted by Dickinson & Härke (1992), who put forward a chronology for this artefact type, while noting that some strong regional preferences could be seen in

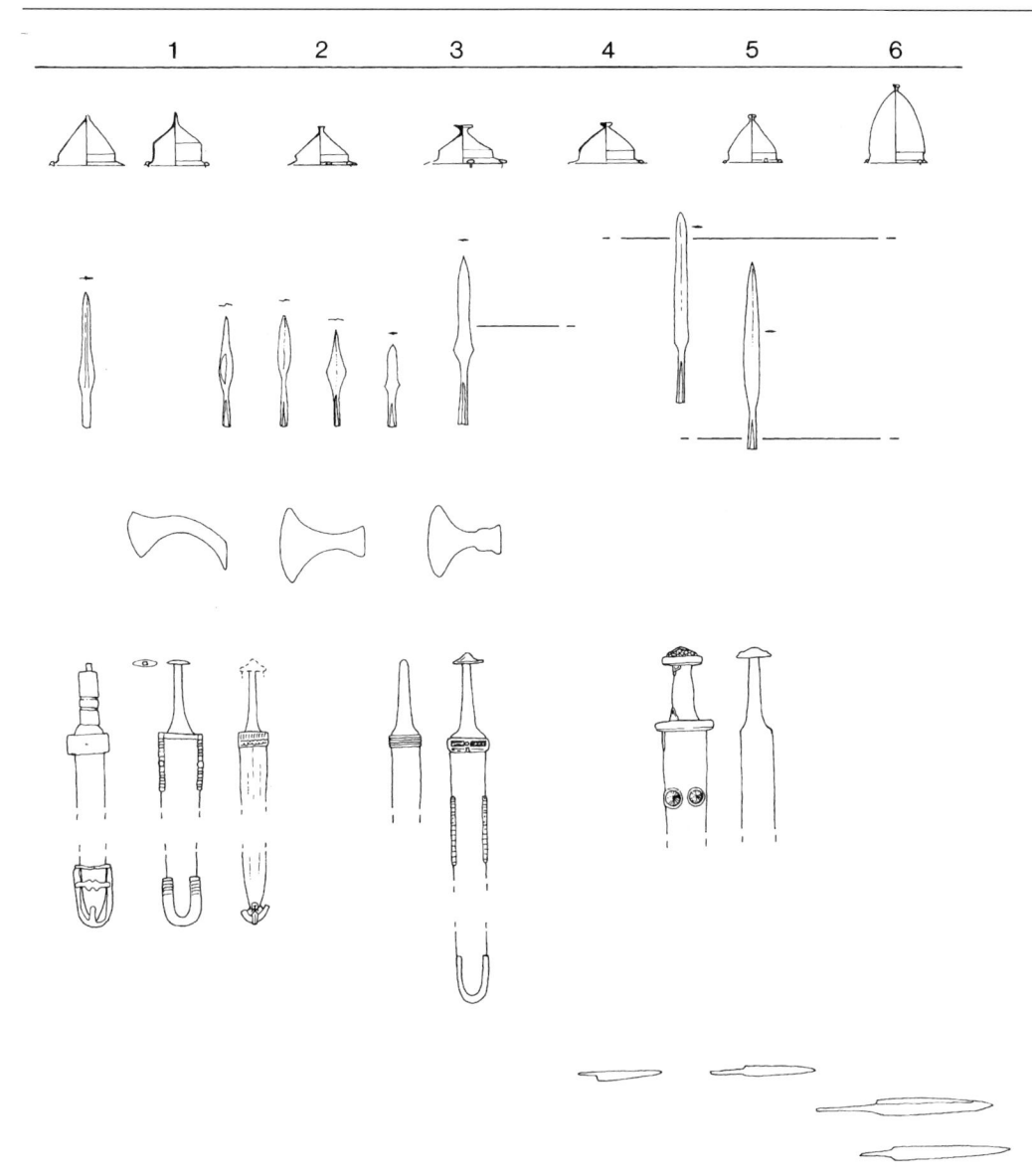

DATING BURIALS AND GRAVE-GOODS IN ANGLO-SAXON CEMETERIES

Fig. 2.17. Chronology of weapon development (after Härke 1992b: fig. 6).

operation (ibid.: 24). The early, pointed bosses were thought to have been used aggressively, while the lower examples of the later fifth and early sixth centuries seem designed more for defensive use in the parrying of blows (ibid.: 54). Their inclusion as grave-goods seems to owe much to symbolic expression, however. Shields in early Anglo-Saxon graves are only sometimes deposited as part of a functioning fighting kit, and are occasionally even the only piece of weaponry in the grave (ibid.: 67). They were rare in graves of children or juveniles (ibid.: 68–9) and were most often laid over the body itself (ibid.: 65).

49

THE ANGLO-SAXON WAY OF DEATH

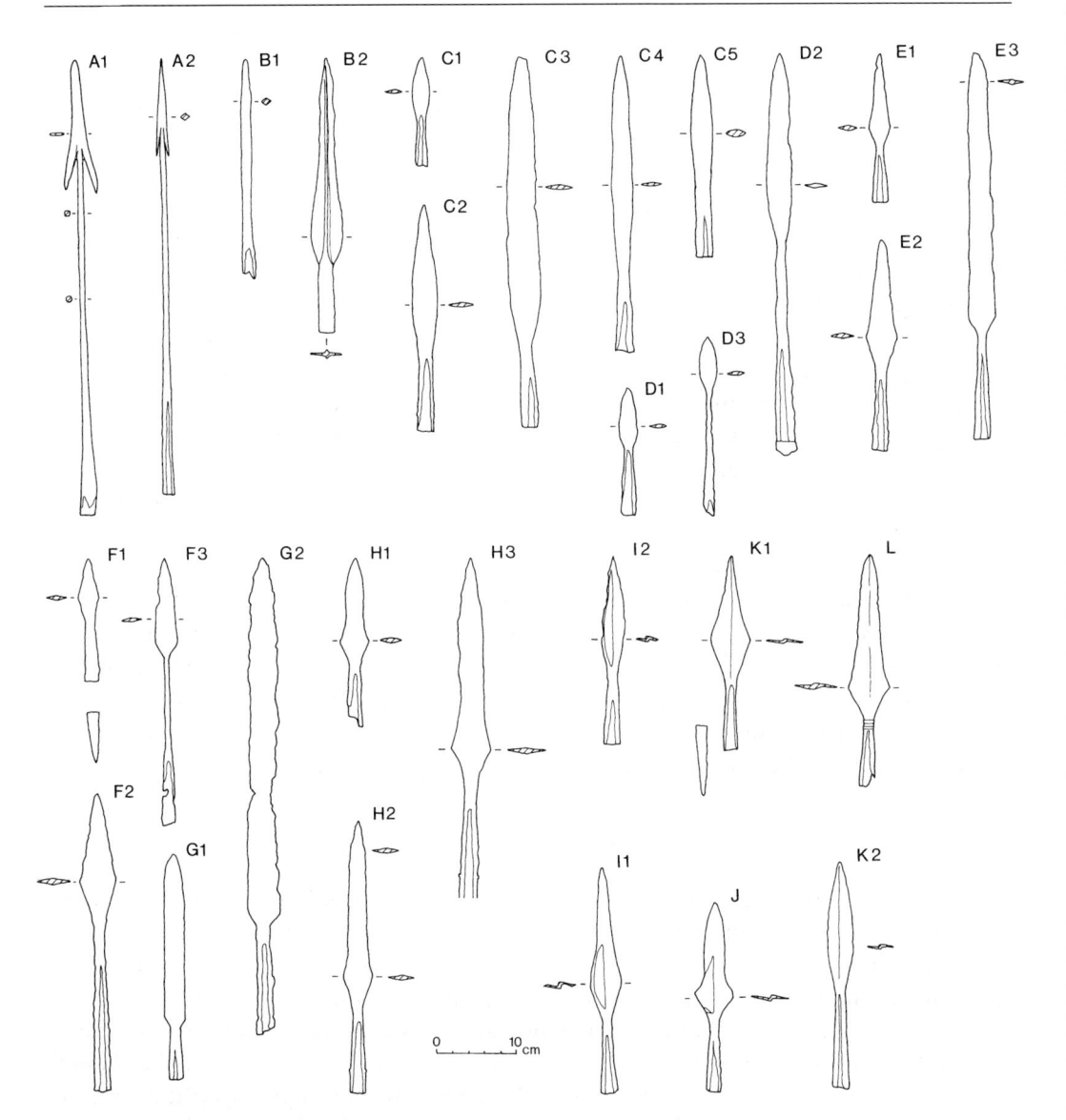

Fig. 2.18. The range of spearhead types, as classified by Swanton (1974: figs 1–8).

Swords are sometimes found as grave-goods. They were double-edged, and designed to be used one-handed (Bone 1989: 63–4). These swords consist of an iron blade which was sometimes pattern-welded (by welding together twisted iron rods, thus strengthening the blade, and adding to its aesthetic appeal), a metal hilt, sometimes wood, bone or horn upper and lower guards, often a richly decorated pommel and scabbard fittings, and sometimes a ring or bead attached to the pommel (Bone 1989: 65; Evison 1975). Judging by their comparative scarcity in graves (although they are more common in Kent than elsewhere), they were prestige goods and symbols of an aristocratic warrior class (Bone

1989: 69); although in decline as grave-goods, they carried on in use into the seventh century (Geake 1997: 1). They were also used in real fighting, to judge from the occasional evidence of sword cuts, found mainly on skulls.

The **seax** (sometimes mistakenly termed the *scramasax*) is a form of single-edged sword-knife which became popular as a grave-good in England during the seventh century. Evison (1961: 227–30, following Böhner 1958) distinguished three types: the narrow seax, which is the main form found in England during the seventh century and seems to have developed from a weapon type in use in the Trier region between AD 450 and 600; the broad seax (mainly found on the continent in the seventh century, although a few British examples are known); and the long seax (again, with mainly a continental distribution, but dating to the eighth century). These can be decorated, making use of a variety of incised lines, grooves and metal inlay (Gale 1989: 74). They may also have played a role in hunting, as well as fighting (ibid.: 80), but once again their inclusion as grave-goods was intended to signal status rather than actual fighting ability.

Other rarer types of weaponry found in Anglo-Saxon graves are arrowheads and axes (in contrast with contemporary continental graves which made much use of them). Härke (1992b: 112) notes the presence of **arrowheads** in graves at Dover Buckland, Mucking II, Pewsey, Berinsfield, Bidford-on-Avon, Stretton-on-Fosse and Empingham II (comprising only 1 per cent of his corpus). Burials with **axes** do not fare much better, with these graves comprising 2 per cent (ibid.: 104). **Helmets** have been found at Sutton Hoo, Suffolk (Bruce-Mitford 1968); Benty Grange, Derbyshire (Bateman 1861: 28–34); and Wollaston, Nottinghamshire (the latter two having a boar figurine as a crest on the top of the helmet). These all date from the seventh century.

Vessels and Other Grave-Goods

As well as weapons and jewellery, other items are found, both as grave-goods and as dress accessories, in Anglo-Saxon graves. These include vessels made from a variety of material, knives and buckles, and a range of other types which do not appear to be associated with either the jewellery or the weaponry assemblages, but can be found with both.

Pottery vessels are found both in inhumation graves as accessory vessels (probably once containing food or drink offerings) and in cremations as the container for the skeletal remains and grave-goods (**Fig. 2.19**). Some vessels may have been made specifically for the funerary context, but normal domestic cooking vessels are also found used in this way. Haith (1997) has described how Anglo-Saxon cremation urns were made. Clay was tempered (to enable it to better withstand the firing process) with either minerals, such as limestone or flint, processed temper, such as crushed fine clay, or organic material, such as chopped plant material or dung. Pots were handmade (pinched or coiled), dried, decorated and then fired under bonfires. They could also be burnished before firing by rubbing with a hard smooth object. Decoration could be linear (made by incising lines with a pointed implement), plastic (adding raised bosses or pushing them out from the inside) or stamped. Some pots have pedestal bases, and separate lids have also been found, but these are rare. Vessel forms range from shallow bowls to large carinated urns with wide mouths, and tall urns with narrow mouths. A unique find is that of the 'mammiform' vessel from

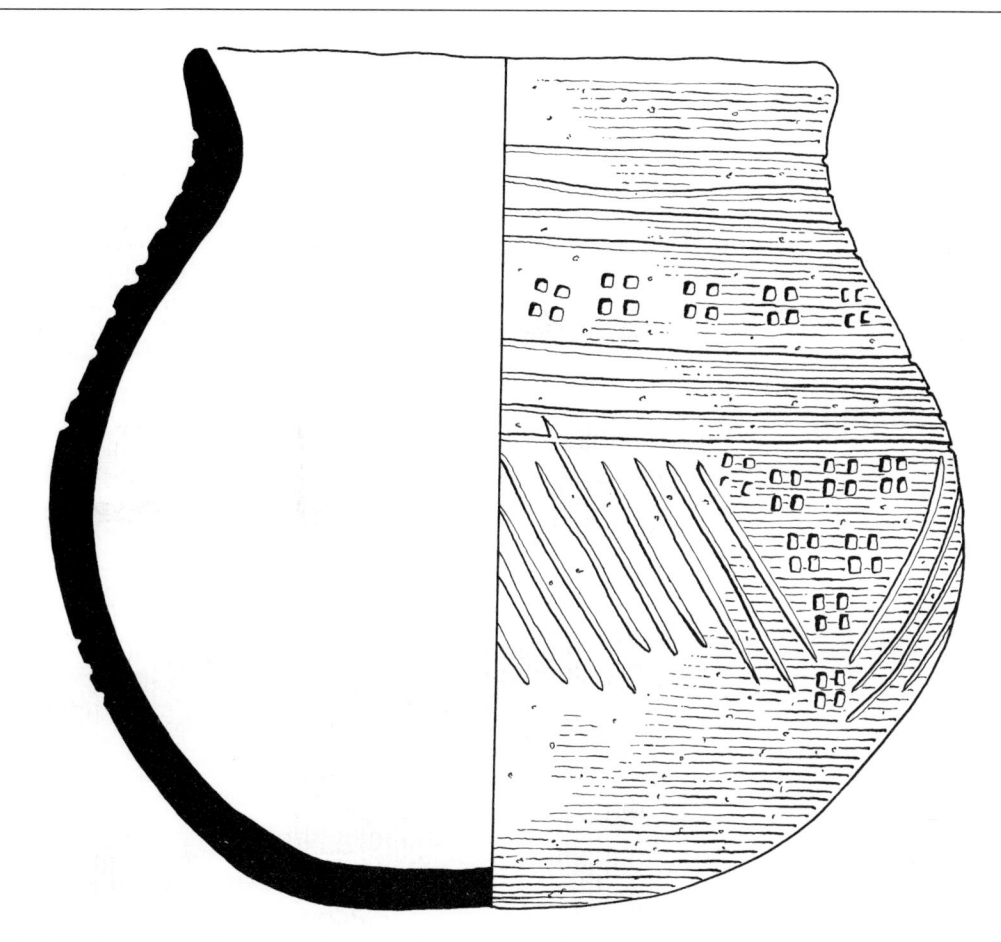

Fig. 2.19. Pottery vessel from Sewerby G38 (after Hirst 1985: fig. 47). Height of vessel 15cm.

Castledyke (South Humberside), which is interpreted either as a baby's feeding bottle or as a bottle for hand-rearing animals; it was deposited in a small grave, thought to have been that of an infant, although no skeletal remains were preserved (Drinkall & Foreman 1998: 309–11. They also cite a larger vessel with a nippled spout from recent excavations at Dover Buckland in Kent, which may be a partial parallel).

Pottery vessels are extremely difficult to date (although thermoluminesence dating may offer some future possibilities, and analysis of shape, fabric and technology changes, rather than decoration, may produce some interesting results). Presently, the only secure method is to use associated grave-goods, although in the case of cremation burials these are often damaged and distorted by fire. One interesting approach has been the attempt to identify pots which have been decorated using the same stamps (cf. Myres 1977: xxi). Hills (1983a: 95), for example, has shown that Spong Hill nos 1020 and 1021, which were buried in the same pit, had almost identical decoration. Four other pots from the same site were decorated using the same swastika stamp. Presumably, this would put them extremely close

Fig. 2.20. Wheel-made pottery found in Kentish cemeteries (reproduced from Faussett 1856: pl. xx).

together in terms of manufacture. Another odd 'stamping' feature had been identified by Briscoe (1986) who recognised that the feet and knobs of cruciform brooches and brooch springs were also sometimes used to create stamps, and that these seem to have been quite limited regional features (see Hills et al. 1994: 1–18 for an overall survey).

Myres (1977: 114–27) saw the following as potentially early features of pottery form and ornament: the carinated bowl form, simple linear, chevron or standing arch (also known as *stehende Bogen*) decoration, and finger-tipped rosettes. The *Buckelurnen* (elaborately bossed pottery) are also seen as early, while sixth-century pottery is characterised as having elaborate stamped decoration and using vertical lines and bosses as a dominant feature. Such schemes do, however, partly rely on historical frameworks, which Kennett (1978: 11) expresses succinctly: 'The earliest Anglo-Saxon pots are those of types found also in the continental homelands of the ancestral English. Types found only in the Netherlands, Germany and Scandinavia are presumed to be of fourth-century date or earlier; types found there and in England are assigned to the fifth century, when contemporary chroniclers and later historians such as Bede record a large-scale movement of people from the north European littoral to England. Pottery types found only in England are assigned to the sixth century or later.' Very recently, Ravn (1998: 214, following Høilund Nielsen) has analysed the decoration on the pottery vessels from Spong Hill using correspondence analysis, and has concluded that there is a chronological dimension to the schemes used, with simple hanging arches being replaced by plastic decoration and then by elaborate stamped decoration (supported by the association of elaborate cruciform brooches with the latter). Similar approaches on other bodies of material may thus have potential in this extremely difficult issue.

The pottery sequence in Kent is rather different (**Fig. 2.20**). Early pottery there is characterised by hard leathery black open bowls, and later on by probable continental imports of wheel-made pottery (Evison 1979). Wheel-thrown pottery is mainly found in Kentish contexts of the mid-sixth to seventh century, but some may have been earlier. These vessels have their strongest parallels in the Pas-de-Calais region of France (Huggett 1988: 74).

Hanging bowls (vessels of spun bronze with escutcheons, circular attachment plates which are often enamelled, **Fig. 2.21a**), **coptic bowls** (cast bronze vessels such as those

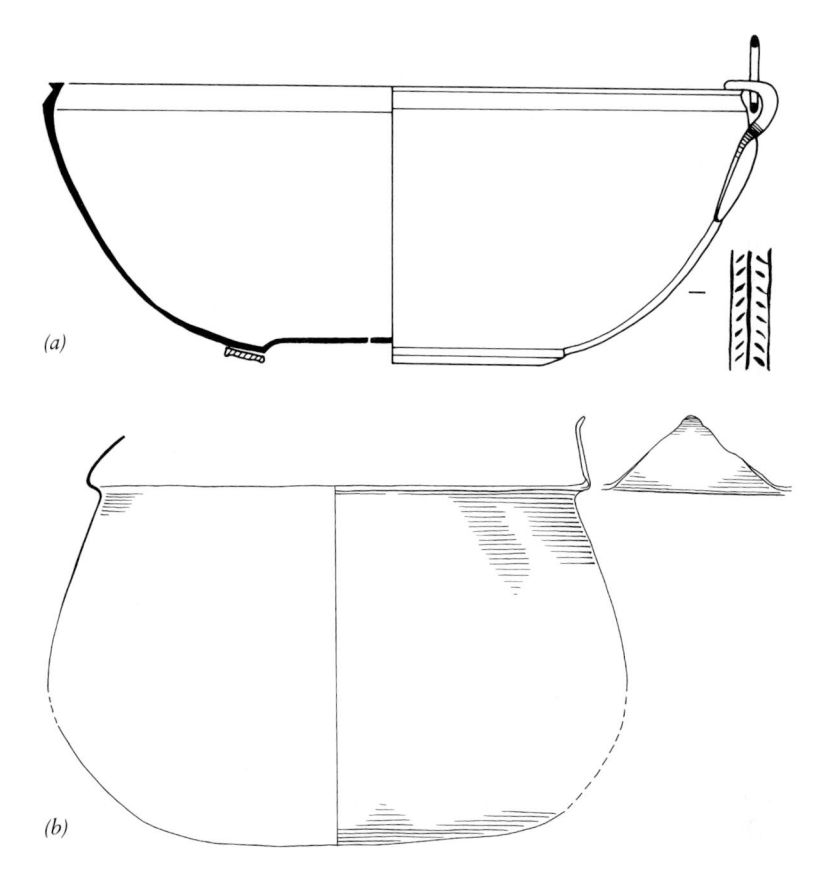

Fig. 2.21. Examples of metal vessels found in Anglo-Saxon graves: (a) hanging-bowl from Faversham (after Brenan 1991: 211); (b) cauldron from Lechlade G58/1 (after Boyle et al. 1998: fig. 5.60). Scale 1:2.

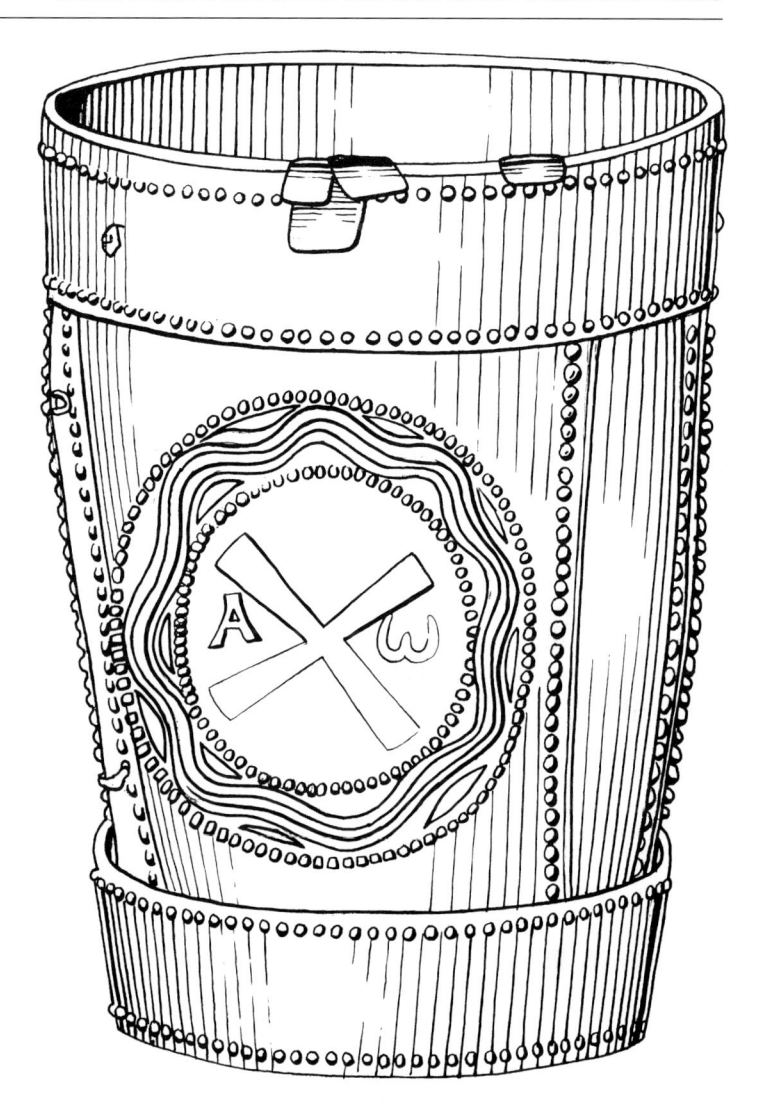

Fig. 2.22. The metal stoup found at Long Wittenham (after Smith 1923: fig. 78). Scale 1:1.

found at Taplow, Buckinghamshire and Asthall, Oxon) and **skillets** mostly appear in seventh-century contexts in England (Geake 1997: 15, 85–7). While the hanging bowls in particular have generated much debate of an art-historical nature as to their origin and date of manufacture (with Leeds (1936), for example, suggesting that they were of sub-Roman native British manufacture), a recent detailed study of their dates of deposition (Brenan 1991) concluded that they were probably of late sixth- and seventh-century manufacture, although there is some evidence for their having been made in Scotland (Geake 1997: 87). Other metal vessels found include the so-called Vestland and Gotland sheet bronze cauldrons with upright triangular lugs (**Fig. 2.21b**). Other obviously imported vessels include the probably Gallo-Roman stoup (**Fig. 2.22**) found at Long Wittenham I (Berkshire) with a child who had probably been buried in the

THE ANGLO-SAXON WAY OF DEATH

Stemmed beakers

Claw beakers

Cone beakers

Drinking horn

Bell beakers

Bag beakers

Pouch bottles

Squat jars

Bottle

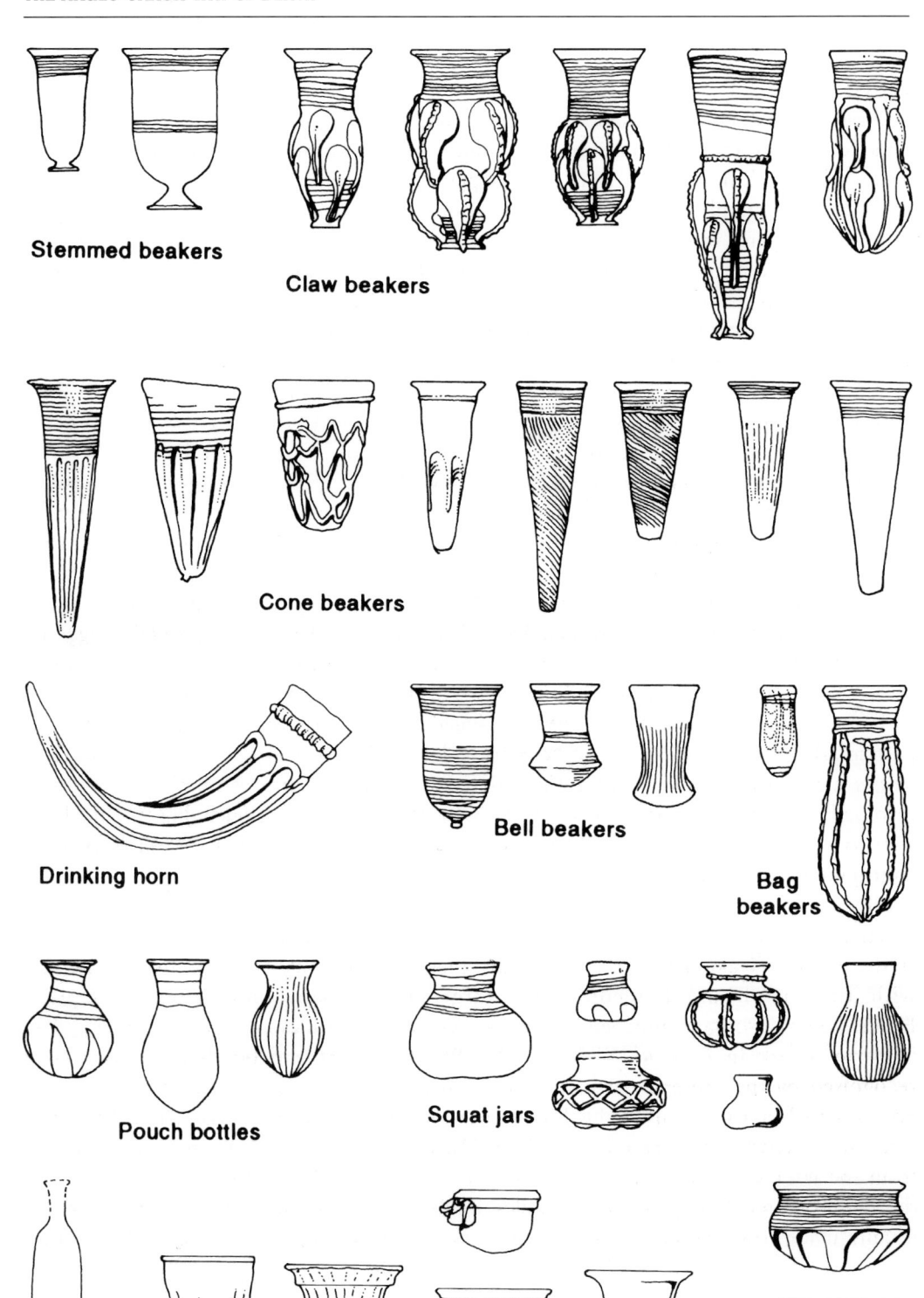

Palm cups

Bowls

sixth century, to judge by the associated spearhead, knife and cauldron (Akerman 1861).

Glass vessels (**Fig. 2.23**) found in Anglo-Saxon graves in Britain were made using the same techniques as late Roman examples, but standards of production seem generally to have declined (clear glass, for example, disappears, and only greens, yellows, browns and deep blues are found), and there is less variation in the decoration applied (Harden 1972: 78–80). This glass was soda glass, not potash, which is why it does not weather in the grave and become black or brown (Harden 1977: 1). While northern Gaul and the Rhineland seem to have been the main production centres in the post-Roman period, vessels were exported to Britain, Scandinavia, north Germany and Holland. There also seems to have been some production in Britain, at least from the seventh century, of window glass in the monastic centres in Northumbria, and in Kent (Harden 1972: 87). Forms which span the fifth and sixth centuries are stemmed beakers, claw beakers, cone beakers, pointed bell beakers and shallow bowls. Forms which are found through the sixth century are claw beakers, cone beakers and bell beakers, with the addition of ribbed palm cups, while late sixth- and seventh-century forms comprise the tall claw beaker, bag beakers, pouch bottles, squat jars and plain palm cups (ibid.: 89–91). Some of these later types – squat jars, bag beakers, pouch bottles and some types of claw beaker – may have been made in England, as they are rare on the continent. They have a high concentration in Kent, especially in the cemetery at Faversham. (Evison (1982; 1983; 1994b) suggests that 'Kempston-type' claw beakers may have been produced in Britain from the fifth century; a proviso to the apparent Faversham concentration was added by Harden (1956: 133 n3), who noted that 'I have heard it suggested that "Faversham" proveniences are particularly suspect, as it was the "correct" place to which a dealer should attribute a Saxon glass'; this site was heavily plundered in the nineteenth century, and was not recorded well.) Some unusual forms have been added to this list, including the bucket-shaped vessel in G62 at Westgarth Gardens, which has its closest parallels in late metropolitan Roman glass (Harden 1977: 5).

Fifth- and early sixth-century **buckets** (**Fig. 2.24**) have their wooden staves held together by bronze hoops, which are replaced by iron bindings from the middle of the sixth century (Geake 1997: 90–1). Usually there are three metal hoops plus a handle, with iron-bound buckets tending to be larger in size than bronze-bound examples. Buckets often also have attached mounts – these are sometimes bifurcating or triangular in form (Cook in Evison 1994a: 22–4). **Wooden cups and bowls** are sometimes recognised by the presence of pieces of metal that were used to repair them, or had bronze or silver rim-mounts added as decoration; these latter types date from the later sixth and seventh centuries (Geake 1997: 92). **Boxes**, too, are found in graves, mainly from the later sixth century and predominantly in Kent. Again, they are identified by their non-organic fittings, such as handles, angle irons, hasps and hinges, and they were usually made from wood, although antler and leather examples are known. The larger

(Opposite) Fig. 2.23. The different types of glass vessel found in Anglo-Saxon graves (after Harden 1956: fig. 25). Scale 1:6.

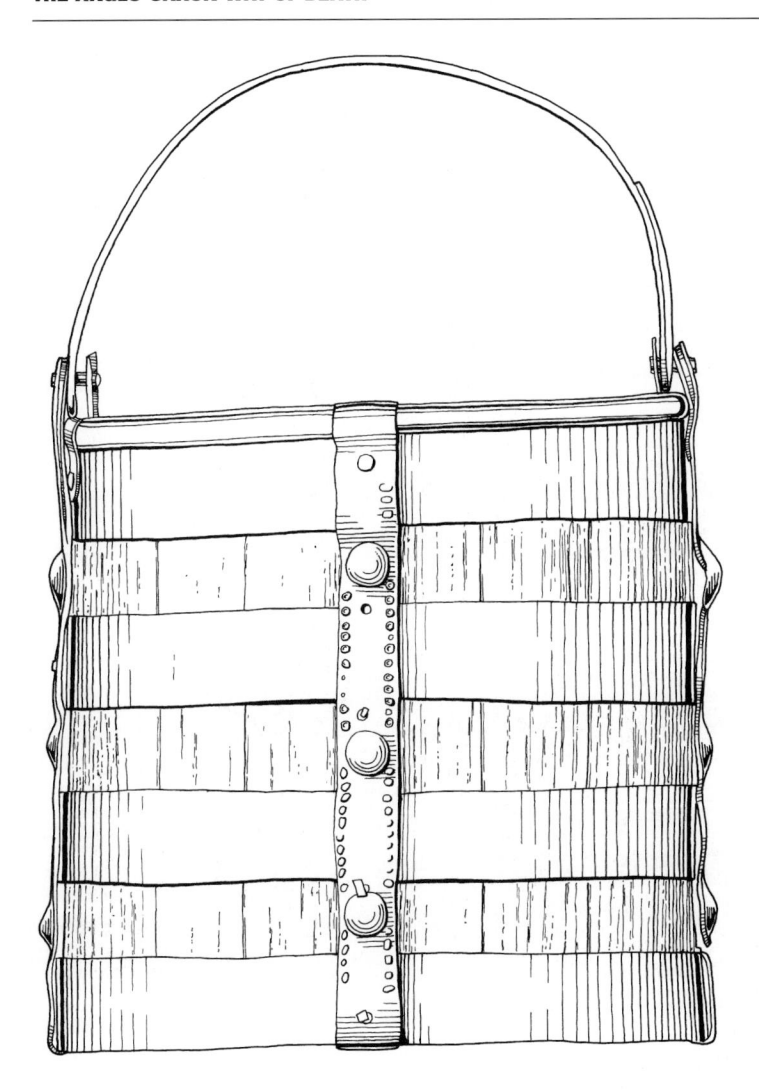

Fig. 2.24. The wood and bronze bucket from Alton G2 (after Evison 1988: fig. 23). Diameter of bucket 13.8cm.

caskets seem to be associated with females, while smaller boxes are sometimes associated with males (Geake 1997: 81–2).

Buckles and **knives** are near-ubiquitous items in Anglo-Saxon furnished graves of all periods (**Fig. 2.25**). Buckles with animal ornament seem to date largely to the fifth century; those with round-, heart- and kidney-shaped plates to the later fifth and earlier sixth century; those with D-shaped loops, round or oval bronze loops and the 'shield-on-tongue' buckles seem to be largely sixth century; while those with smaller loops and buckles with triangular plates are found in the sixth and seventh centuries, mainly in Kent but in smaller numbers across the rest of the country as well (Dickinson 1976: 252–3; Stoodley 1997: 58; Geake 1997: 76–7). Openwork buckles and those with a double tongue also seem to be late (Geake 1994; 1997: 78). Buckles were usually used to fasten a belt or girdle at the waist, but could also be used as part of a bag or baldric (Brush 1993: 96).

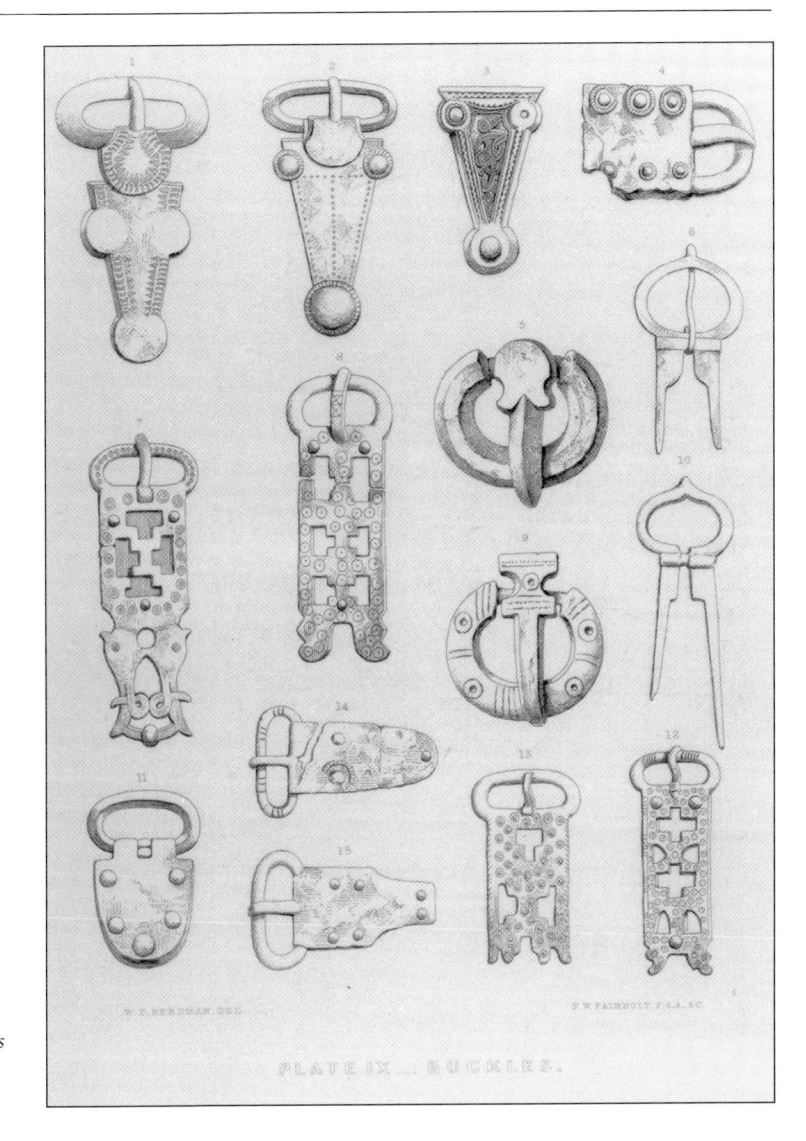

Fig. 2.25. Examples of buckles and buckle-plates found in Kentish cemeteries (reproduced from Faussett 1856: pl. ix).

No wide-ranging study of the knives used as grave-goods in England in this period has ever been carried out, so use is often made of Böhner's simple classification developed for the knives of the Trier region (1958), which divides them into those with straight backs, those where the back and the edge curve to a point, and those with humped backs. In her study of the cemeteries of the Upper Thames region, Dickinson (1976: 331) concluded that straight and curved-back knives seem to be the standard types in the fifth and sixth centuries, with humped-back and also seax-shaped knives more characteristic of the seventh century. More recently, however, Evison (1987: 113–17) has put forward a new classification, dividing knives into six groups, based on whether the back is curved, straight or angled, and whether the cutting edge is curved or straight. Knives seem to have been worn mainly suspended from, or tucked into, a belt or girdle, as they are usually found point down near the waist or on the upper thigh in graves, but occasional examples have been found associated with the arms or lower leg, suggesting different uses (Brush 1993: 105). Judging from organic traces found preserved, most if not all were contained within a sheath, usually of leather (Drinkall & Foreman 1998: 283). There may be some correlation between knife length, and the age and sex of the person buried with it (Härke 1989).

Iron tools, such as awls, spatulate tools and chisels, seem to be used as grave-goods only in the seventh and eighth centuries, although they are found on settlement sites in the fifth and sixth centuries (Geake 1997: 93–5). Another type of tool that is sometimes found is the 'sword-beater' or weaving baton or batten (Chadwick 1958: 30–5). This was a specialised type of tool used in north and west Europe on an upright warp-weighted loom. They are found in wood, whalebone and iron, and were used two-handed for beating up the weft at regular intervals. They have an odd tongue-shaped formation of the tip, and are sometimes adapted from real swords or spearheads (and perhaps thus mis-identified as weapons, with corroded blunt tips and edges not being recognised, cf. Drinkall & Foreman 1998: 293–4). Most of the examples in Anglo-Saxon cemeteries come from late sixth- and seventh-century contexts, and the concentration in Kentish graves may suggest connections between Kent and the Merovingian world (Millard et al. 1969: 17–22). Hones, or sharpening steels, are also found occasionally.

An item whose function has been disputed is the iron or bronze **'purse-mount'**, a shaped piece of metal with usually curled ends (**Fig. 2.26**). Brown (1977) examined fifth- and sixth-century finds from British and continental cemeteries and argued that many 'purse-mounts', even those with buckles, are in fact fire-steels, which were often attached to the outside of a pouch containing tinder, and could be used to strike a spark. Geake (1997: 79–80) discussed examples from seventh- and eighth-century cemeteries in England, finding that they tended to be of iron, undecorated, and only one or two had attached buckles. Examination of the associated finds and the positions of these artefacts in the graves led Geake to conclude that while two may have formed part of a tinder pouch (one of these was the only example to be associated with a flint), the others appear to have been attached to chatelaines or contained within bags (although this does not preclude their use as fire-steels).

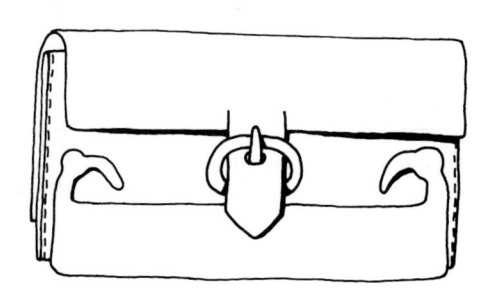

Fig. 2.26. Reconstruction of a 'purse-mount' or 'fire-steel' (after Brown 1977: fig. 4).

Various different types of **comb** are found in Anglo-Saxon burials (**Fig. 2.27**). In the Upper Thames cemeteries of the fifth and sixth centuries, inhumations tended to have three-piece double-sided combs (although combs are relatively rare in such graves), while cremations tended to have composite triangular or single-piece non-functional miniature versions made of bone or antler. In the seventh century, inhumations were more often associated with complete three-piece single-sided combs (Dickinson 1976: 216–18). Parts

Fig. 2.27. The bone comb from Lechlade G145/2 (after Boyle et al. 1998: fig. 5.89). Scale 1:1.

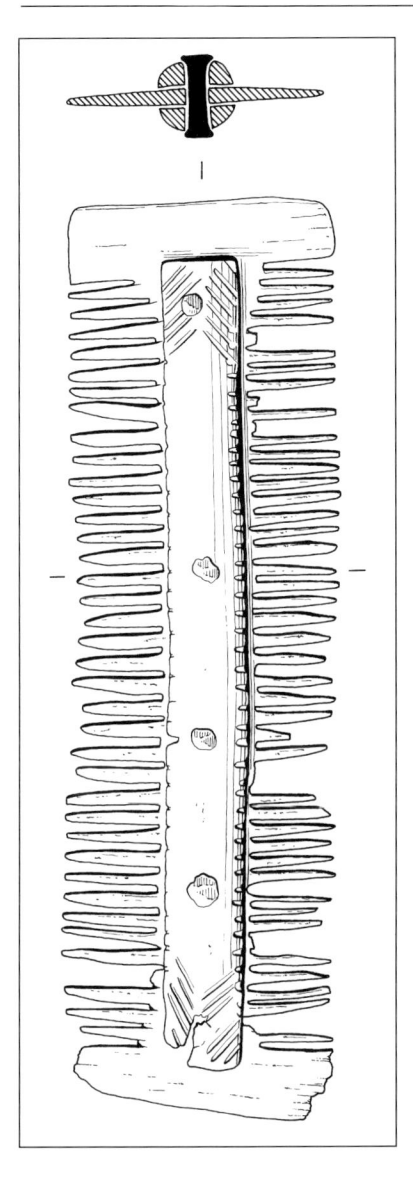

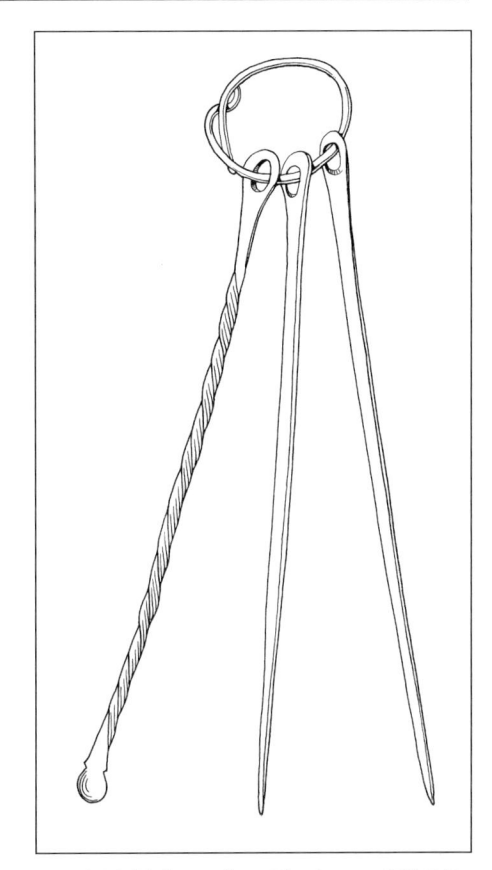

Fig. 2.28. Toilet-set from Blewburton Hill G12 (after Collins & Collins 1959: fig. 4). Scale 1:1.

of a double-sided comb case were found in G110 at Dover Buckland (Evison 1987: 119), and others are known from cremated remains at Spong Hill. Other items associated with appearance include so-called **toilet-sets** (**Fig. 2.28**). In her study Dickinson (1976: 220) found that inhumations were buried with functional tweezers, picks, 'ear-scoops', bronze-sheathed brushes (cf. Brown 1974) and 'scrapers', while cremations were given non-functional miniature knives, shears and tweezers (razors are found in some areas). Shears are found in inhumation graves, but these are full-size versions which are predominantly found in seventh- and eighth-century inhumations, and are strongly associated with the burial of females (Geake 1997: 96). A miniature set of shears, tweezers, two files, a knife-

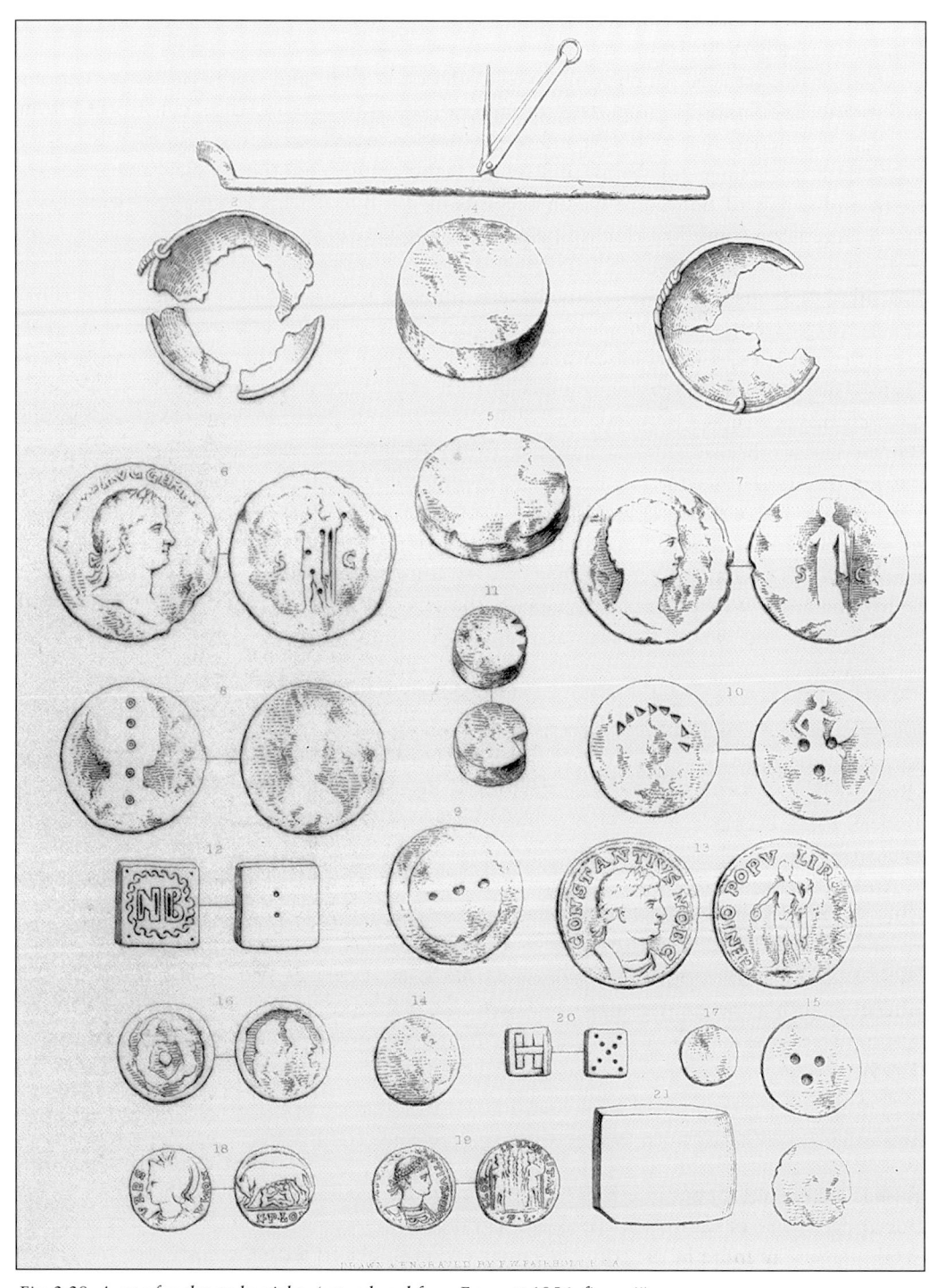

Fig. 2.29. *A set of scales and weights (reproduced from Faussett 1856: fig. xvii).*

like blade and a point was, however, found with inhumation 86 from Apple Down, Sussex (Down & Welch 1990: 103).

Another artefact type which is relatively common in fifth- and sixth-century cremations and in later inhumations are **playing counters** or draughtsmen and dice, constructed from a range of different materials. Typical of the later inhumed examples would be the forty-six bone draughtsmen (probably of Roman manufacture), another made from a horse's tooth and a pair of bone dice which accompanied a burial with a bronze hanging bowl and a large bone comb found in a flower garden at Keythorpe Hall, Tugby, Leicestershire, in 1860 (Smith 1907: 239).

Scull (1993) discusses the relatively rare finds of **balances and weights** in furnished graves (**Fig. 2.29**). These objects are known from nine cemeteries of the sixth and seventh centuries, six of which are in Kent, one in South Humberside and two in Oxfordshire. Detached balance pans are known from a further three sites. Scull's analysis of six weight groups with available and reliable data indicate that all except the Barton-on-Humber set (by far the most northerly example) were very close to the ideal weight standards of contemporary continental gold coinages. These would thus have been used to judge the weight and fineness of coins, and probably also uncoined bullion, in areas where no coins were minted at the time, but where foreign coinages were circulating. The Barton-on-Humber set, in contrast, is judged to be a jeweller's or smith's balance. Where data are available, the sets of balances and weights accompanied male graves (and weapon graves at that), while the two graves with balances but no weights were of females.

Other rare grave-goods include stringed instruments, some of which have been identified as lyres, which have been found in G22 at Bergh Apton and possibly in G97 at Morningthorpe, both Norfolk (Lawson 1978; Green et al. 1987: 63), Sutton Hoo, Suffolk (Bruce-Mitford 1968) and Dover Buckland, Kent (Evison 1987: 121). Grave 185 at Butler's Field, Lechlade, had two hundred uncut garnets deposited in the burial – a unique occurrence.

Another form of grave-good which should not be forgotten are **animals and food offerings** (see Chapters Three and Four for more detail). Crabtree's survey of the inclusion of animal remains in funerary contexts has shown these can encompass whole animals, such as horses and dogs, portions of animals, probably as food offerings, amuletic offerings, such as perforated bones and teeth, as well as artefacts made from bone such as gaming counters, and these seem to span the whole period of furnished burial (Crabtree 1995).

THE MEANINGS OF THINGS

As has been shown above, a wide range of artefacts are made use of in the Anglo-Saxon burial rite. Some of these artefacts are integral to the costume, holding parts of it together, while others are more in the form of grave offerings, placed with the body into the grave. Individual artefacts can be used to help assign an approximate date to a burial, but in practical terms this is often hard to pin down to a span of less than one or two generations. While many of these artefacts, such as tools, weapons or vessels, would have had practical functions in life, in their inclusion in the burial rite they are also taking on symbolic meanings. In this chapter a few instances have been mentioned where specific artefacts are restricted either in geographical extent, or in the identity of the people they were interred with – some artefacts are only found buried with adults, for example, or with males or females.

It can be argued that artefacts do not have inherent meanings. Archaeologists have long since learned that in assuming that they know what artefacts represented, they may just be projecting their own assumptions on to the past. Rather, we need to look at *how* artefacts are used in the burial rite, and which grave-goods the mourners assigned to which people, before we can infer things about their significance. The next two chapters will look firstly at the inhumation burial rite and then at cremation, in terms of what can be inferred from these burial rites, and what patterns they include.

THREE

INHUMATION BURIAL PRACTICE

INTRODUCTION

The previous chapter reviewed the nature of the main categories of grave-goods which are found in Anglo-Saxon cemeteries, and the evidence for their dating. There is more to a burial, however, than just the objects that were placed with the deceased in the grave. How those artefacts were used would have conferred on them some meaning and significance, with the deposition of a rare and valuable artefact, for example, having very different meanings for the mourners when compared with a common knife or buckle. Treatment of the dead was important to the living in this period: if it was not, we would not have the rich variation in burial rites that we reveal through excavation. This chapter will deal with unburnt burial – inhumation – a type of burial from which a great deal of information can be inferred. Often we can tell the sex and age of the person buried, and something about their health and lifestyle, the position in which they were buried, as well as how the grave-goods were arranged on or around them. The grave itself may yield interesting features – the remains of barrows which have been ploughed flat and are otherwise invisible, for example, or a child buried in a grave that was far too large for them. All this evidence can be used in interpreting the meaning of the variation that we observe.

INTERPRETING SKELETAL REMAINS

Inferring information from skeletal remains is, of course, reliant on those remains surviving in the grave. The degree of skeletal preservation is dependent on a number of factors, including depth of burial, ground temperature and the amount of water present, and the soil type in which the burial was made. Some soil types have a notoriously destructive effect on unburnt human bone. Sand, for example, tends to be very acidic, and this environment can completely destroy a skeleton, so that the remains may be visible only as a soil stain. At the recent excavations at Sutton Hoo, directed by Martin Carver, some innovative techniques were developed for the recording of burials where the bone had almost completely disappeared in the sandy soil, which resulted in three-dimensional 'sand-bodies' (**Fig. 3.1**). Chalk, on the other hand, tends to be alkaline, and can result in excellent bone preservation. Even in alkaline conditions, though, if there are free-draining soils (as was the case at Mucking, Essex), the passage of water may completely leach out the bone mineral, resulting in only fragments of bone remaining (Mays 1998: 21). The nature of the bone itself may affect preservation – poorly mineralised infant and juvenile remains seem more susceptible than adult bones to decay in hostile soil conditions, for example (ibid.: 21–2). In eastern

THE ANGLO-SAXON WAY OF DEATH

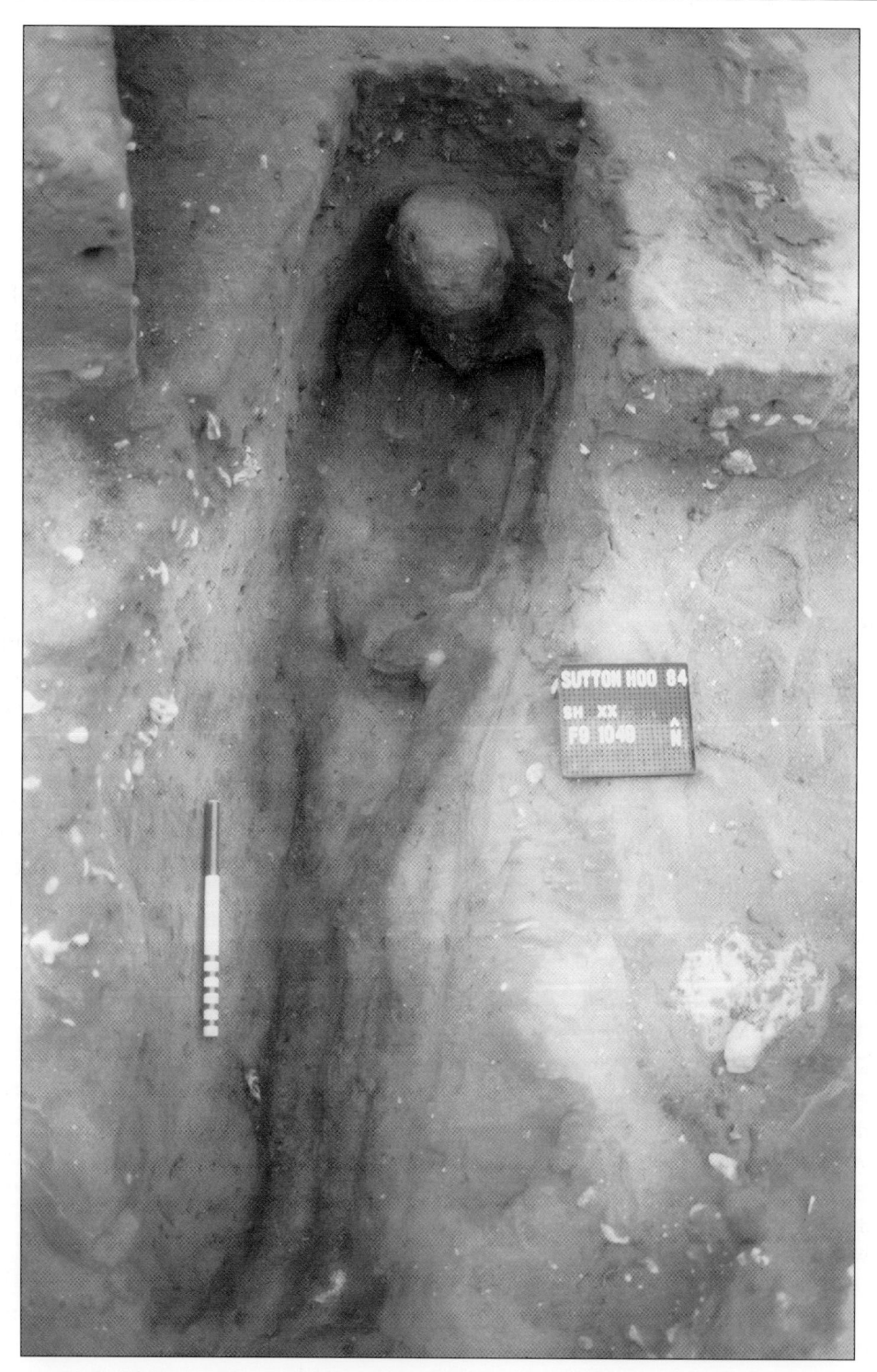

Fig. 3.1. Burial 17, one of the 'sand-bodies' excavated at Sutton Hoo. (Copyright Martin Carver and the Sutton Hoo Research Trust. Reproduced by kind permission of Martin Carver and British Museum Press.)

Britain we have no extreme environmental conditions, such as permafrost or peat bogs, which can result in the remarkable preservation of human organic remains, so archaeologists excavating Anglo-Saxon cemeteries are usually dealing with 'dry' bones (although recently, at West Heslerton in Yorkshire, contact with a brooch caused an ear to be preserved, and occasional reports are made of hair being preserved, such as at Greenwich Park (Smith 1908: 378) and Broome, Norfolk (Smith 1901: 336)). If bone preservation is reasonable, osteoarchaeologists ('bone' archaeologists) can use various techniques to gauge the approximate age, sex, and sometimes other information about the dead person.

People under the age of around twenty-three undergo more or less rapid skeletal development, so it is much easier to age younger remains. Up to the age of about eighteen, tooth eruption is a very good guide, as both deciduous (milk) teeth and permanent teeth emerge at predictable times, and diet and environment seem to make little difference to tooth formation. Teeth also have the advantage that they survive quite well in burial environments, as the enamel serves to protect them to a certain extent from destruction – indeed, tooth crowns may still be present even when the rest of the skeleton has entirely disappeared. As well as teeth, the osteoarchaeologist can also look at the extent to which certain parts of the skeleton, for example the ends of the long-bones (known as epiphyses, which ossify and develop separately) and the top rim of the pelvis have fused on to their associated long-bone shafts (a process known as epiphyseal fusion). In addition, the ends of different long-bones fuse on to the shafts at slightly different ages, and comparison of which epiphyses have fused and which have not can produce quite a narrow age range (Mays 1998: 48–9). As young bodies grow very rapidly, the length of long-bones can also be used as an approximate guide to age, although this method (and others based on similar statistical techniques) is turning out to have some inbuilt inaccuracies that must be remedied (Gowland 1998).

In people over the age of around twenty-three, however, the skeleton has stopped growing and any judgement of age has to be made from looking at degenerative changes. These may be seen most easily in the teeth, although dental wear is greatly affected by cultural practices and the incidence of tooth decay (Brothwell 1981; Miles 1963), and in certain parts of the skeleton, such as the front joint of the pelvis where the two bones meet (the pubic symphysis) (Katz & Suchey 1986; Meindl et al. 1985), the rib-ends (Işcan et al. 1984; 1985) and the auricular surface, where the base of the back articulates with the pelvis (Lovejoy et al. 1985). Cranial suture closure (the joining of the gaps between the various bones of the skull) is still used, despite doubts about its accuracy (Mays 1998: 50). None of these techniques can, however, be used reliably to age anyone over about forty-five, and there is a possibility that a significant proportion of burials are being given drastically younger ages than should be the case (see, for example, the results from the Spitalfields crypt excavations, where historical records were available for testing against many of the bodies recovered, enabling actual age and age derived from skeletal methods to be checked (Cox 1996: 93)).

While it is easier, therefore, to age younger individuals with a degree of accuracy than adults, the opposite picture is seen when it comes to determining sex. Adult skeletons exhibit varying degrees of sexual dimorphism, but many of these features, such as the widening of the pelvis in females, do not appear until puberty, meaning that skeletons younger than this are very difficult to sex. In adults, the main features used for sexing are the wider, shallower pelvis in females, and the narrower, taller pelvis in males. The size of the angle at the front of the pelvis where its two halves meet (the sub-pubic angle) is often a good guide, although in a supine skeleton (i.e. one that has been buried on its back) this is often the first bone to be damaged if, for example, the site is disturbed by ploughing. The sciatic notch, another angle towards the rear of the pelvis, is also a good guide (Mays 1998: 33). Features of the skull can also help: adult males tend to have heavier brow-ridges than females, and more prominent ridges where the neck muscles attach (Chamberlain 1994: 10–11). Overall size of the skeleton can also be used, but there is a great deal of overlap, meaning that generally only large males and small females can be distinguished in this way (ibid.: 11). Very recently, DNA testing has started to offer the possibility of sexing skeletons of all ages by detecting the presence of a Y-chromosome in the DNA; even infant males can be identified in this way. Unfortunately, DNA testing necessitates the destruction of a single tooth, and some of the early studies have found archaeologists and curators of skeletal material reluctant to allow this, in spite of the important information it can offer.

Certain illnesses and indications of trauma can be identified from examination of skeletons, although these will obviously only be those conditions (often of a long-term nature) which have had an effect on the bones themselves (see Roberts & Manchester 1995 for an overview). As bones remodel themselves after they have been damaged (as long as the victim survives), there are often quite obvious indications of such events (**Fig. 3.2**). Broken arms and legs, for example, will fuse back together, even if they have not been set properly (this can often cause shortening of the limb, as the two parts will heal when still overlapping). An example of this was seen at Burn Ground, Hampnett, Gloucestershire, where a male skeleton was found to have one leg which had been broken and had fused together improperly, leading to shortening of the limb (Grimes 1960: 113–25).

Conversely, where bone has been injured and has not remodelled, inferences about cause of death can sometimes be made. Grave 1 at Puddlehill, Bedfordshire, for example, was assumed to have been killed by a sword blow, as there were severe unhealed cranial injuries (Matthews & Hawkes 1985). The youth with a sugar-loaf shield-boss, spearhead and knife from Ewell, Surrey, had lost his left foot shortly before death (*Antiquaries Journal* 43, 1963: 294–6). Grave 2 at Puddlehill had had the left leg amputated at the knee, and placed in the grave (Matthews & Hawkes 1985). At Buckland Denham in Somerset, a female burial was found to have a broken neck – presumably the cause of death (Meaney 1964: 218), and this may also have been true of the female with a hole through her skull at Hadleigh Road, Ipswich, Suffolk (Layard 1907).

Sometimes unusual circumstances of death have been identified. There are a number of burials with foetal or neonatal bones apparently inside the pelvis, indicating death of mother and child during labour or in late pregnancy, including cases from Dover Buckland G110 (Evison 1987: 18), Castledyke G146 (Drinkall & Foreman 1998: 231), and two cases from Great Chesterford, Essex (Evison 1994a: 59). Probable battle mortalities have been suggested, such as the large man from Cross Barrows, Compton, Berkshire, with a javelin head fixed into his pelvis (Peake 1906: 279), the male from Letchworth with a spearhead embedded in his chest (Kennett 1973: 103), and the male skeleton G7 at Harwell with a spear deeply embedded into the left side (this, incidentally, was an Anglo-Saxon spear type, and the man was buried in an Anglo-Saxon furnished cemetery, which has interesting implications) (Brown 1967: 73–4). A note of caution should, however, be sounded here as a knife laid on the chest can slip between the ribs on decomposition. Of a more convincing nature was the treatment of a man from the cemetery at Eccles in Kent, who had been shot with a bow and arrow, before suffering a sword blow to the skull (Manchester & Elmhirst 1982). Two probable victims of murder have even been identified: the male with a knife protruding from his ribs who was found during the excavation of a Roman bridge at Aldwincle, Northamptonshire (Jackson 1970: 38) and the female from Poulton Down, Wiltshire, who was found 23ft down a Roman well. She had fallen on top of a rock, and had another thrown on top of her, shattering many bones. Accompanied by an iron knife, a bronze pin, two iron buckles, one amber and two other beads, this woman appears to have been thrown fully dressed into the well in the later sixth century; to judge by the blood stains remaining on some skull fragments, she met a violent death (Meyrick 1950).

Some interesting medical conditions have been inferred from Anglo-Saxon skeletal evidence. Down & Welch (1990: 186), for example, mention evidence for periostitis on the lower legs (tibiae, fibiae or both in some cases) of six male skeletons of different ages from the Apple Down cemetery, suggesting that the condition might be associated 'with ulceration of the lower legs, possibly connected with the wearing of leggings which were not removed very often'. A female example of this was suggested for Sk119 at the Barrington Edix Hill cemetery in Cambridgeshire, where a young woman with evidence of severe infection of the lower legs – inferred to have been caused in the same way by chronic leg ulcers – was found buried (in a grossly contorted position) in the top of an Iron Age ditch (Malim & Hines 1998: 179). Again, care is needed, however, as periostial new bone formation can occur as the result of a vast number of causes including trauma as well as infection, and it is very difficult to tie it to one specific condition (R. Gowland pers. comm.). Other work on skeletal material has suggested the diagnosis of leprosy, secondary bone cancer possibly associated with primary breast cancer, and a possible brain tumour causing hydrocephalus ('water on the brain') (Manchester 1981a; 1981b; 1983). A weapon burial, Sk146, from Barrington Edix Hill was judged to have advanced cancer, from the characteristic destructive lesions in this mature male's entire axial skeleton and parts of the long bones. This tall and robust but incapacitated man was nevertheless buried with a buckle, knife, spear and shield-boss (Malim & Hines 1998: 194).

Most intriguing is a female burial, Sk42B, from Edix Hill, who was interred on a bed-like structure (of which only a few examples are known) and was discovered to have been a leper. Although the disease was affecting the skull and the lower legs, but not yet the hands or feet, she would have had (at least) lepromatous nodules over her face and a profuse discharge from the nose. Despite this obvious facial disfigurement, she was distinguished by her bed burial and by the range of grave-goods which accompanied her, including silver rings, a key, two knives, a bucket, a weaving baton, a comb, a spindle-whorl, and possible amulets including a fossil sea urchin and an astralagus from a sheep (Malim & Hines 1998: 52–3, 176–7). Other burials with leprosy are now known from grave A8 at Beckford in Worcestershire and suspected in a further two burials at that site (Evison & Hill 1996: 23). Probable tuberculosis has also been identified in graves 72, 98 and 151 at Castledyke,

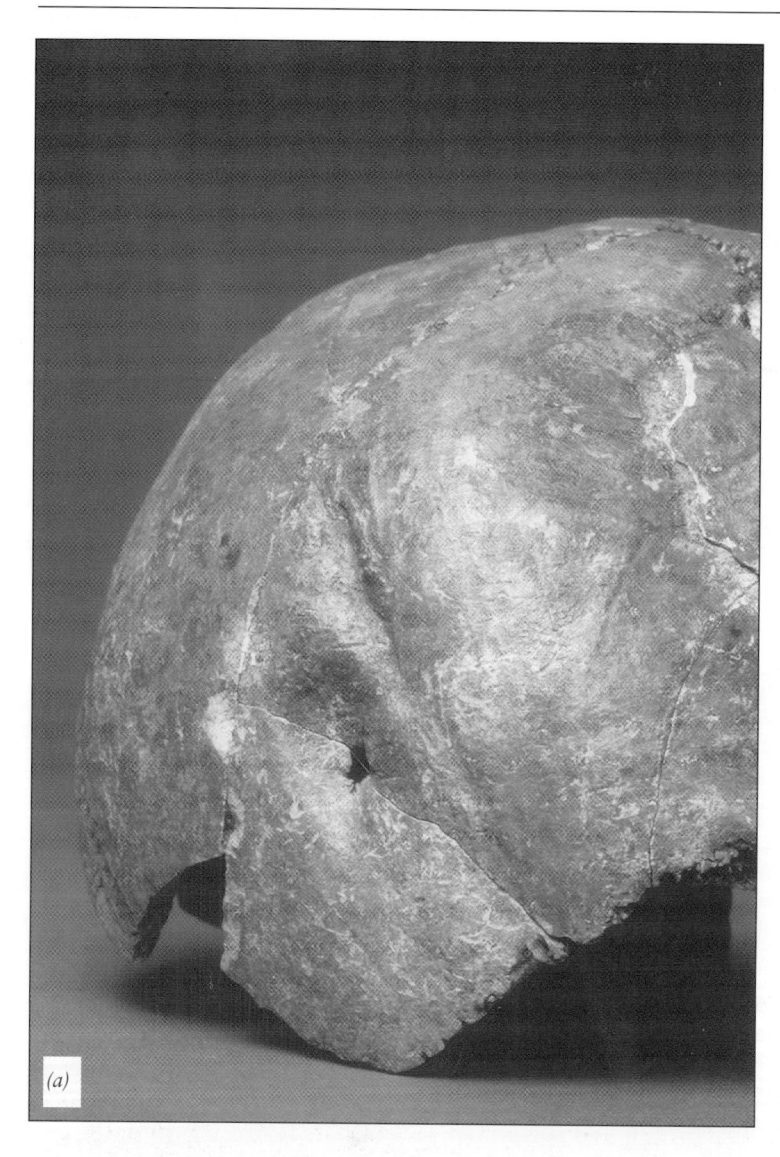

Fig. 3.2. (a) The skull from the mixed burial context 62/63/64 at Broughton Lodge, Willoughby-on-the-Wolds, showing a healed injury and a trepanation (copyright Charlotte Roberts); (b) (Possible) healed depressed fracture on posterior portion of parietal. Blacknall Field, Pewsey Cemetery, Skeleton 62. (© Wiltshire Archaeological and Natural History Society); (c) G100 at Camerton, a seventh-century female burial with foetal remains visible in the pelvis (copyright Cambridge University Museum of Archaeology and Anthropology, Acc. No. LS44869).

South Humberside (Drinkall & Foreman 1998: 231). Grave 60 from Apple Down (Sussex), a fifteen- to seventeen-year-old, showed a number of interesting skeletal changes. Almost all the bones were abnormal, with the limb-bones being extremely slender, and the pelvis and ankle bones of unusual shape, leading to the suggestion that this was the skeleton of someone who had been paralysed in life (Down & Welch 1990: 187). Such cases throw interesting light on the caring nature of the communities in which these people lived, for care of the disabled and sick seems to have been prevalent.

Sometimes quite lurid (and unjustifiable) interpretations have been made on the basis of skeletal evidence. For example, grave 78 from Worthy Park, Hampshire, was found to have a lesion on the back of the femur. This burial, of a female aged around sixteen years,

(b)

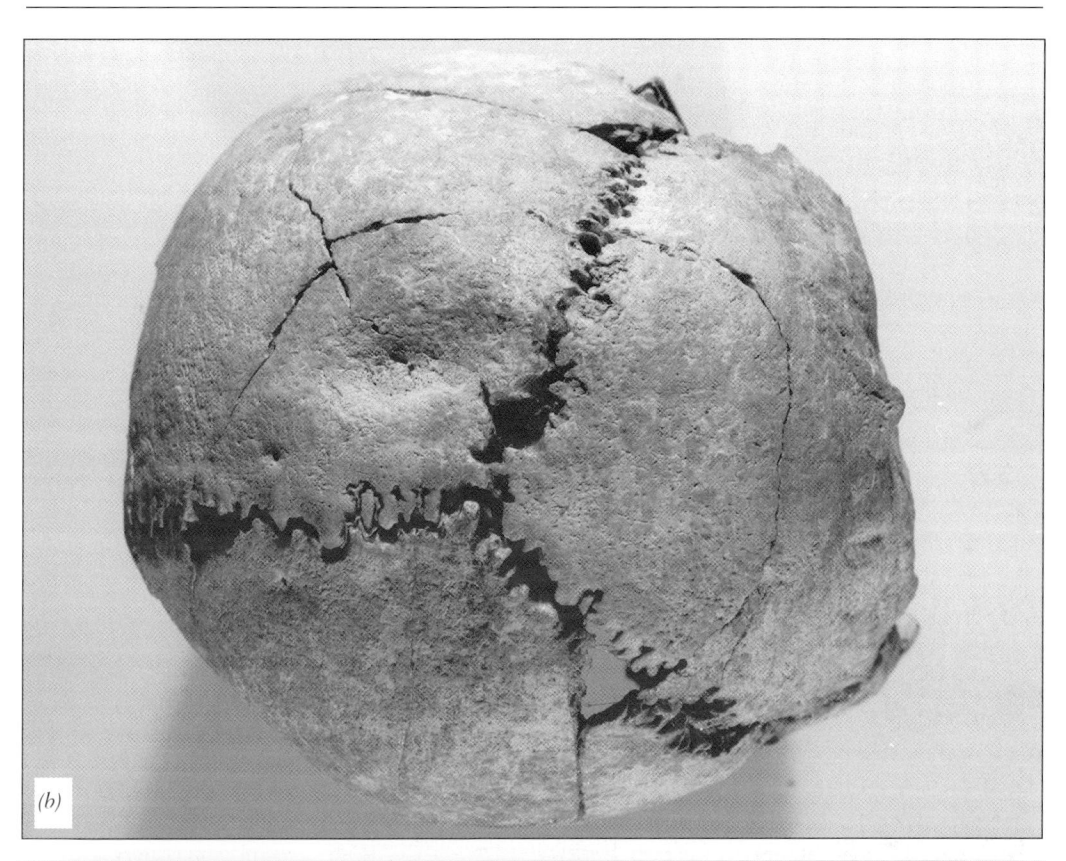

(c)

was found in a prone position. Hawkes & Wells (1975: 119) stated that such a lesion 'is typically the result of a brutal rape which was strongly resisted by the victim', and inferred that, as the lesion showed signs of healing for around four to six months, she had concealed the crime in shame, but 'Perhaps some five or six months later, no longer able to conceal her swelling pregnancy, she was done to death by her dishonoured kindred and outraged neighbours' (ibid.: 121). Reynolds (1988: 716) prefers a more prosaic explanation, arguing that such lesions are far more likely to occur from rough riding on a horse. He also notes that a prone female five or six months pregnant would not have a straight backbone as this skeleton did. Knüsel (1993: 206) criticises both the rape and the horseback riding interpretations, however, arguing that a whole range of activities can produce such generalised trauma to this part of the leg, and it is impossible to narrow it down to just one interpretation.

Occasional evidence for surgical interventions has been found. Calvin Wells (1974), for instance, describes four sixth-century adult male skulls from Norfolk and one from Suffolk which all have a well-healed perforation of a similar nature. Another, female, example is now known from Oxborough, Norfolk (*Medieval Archaeology* 35, 1991: 177). Wells suggests that these are healed trepanations, and, moreover, that they were all performed by the same surgeon, who, he (only half-jokingly) suggests, might be known as the 'Master of the Gliding Gouge' (see also Parker et al. 1986). Further examples have been identified at Sleaford, Lincolnshire (Thomas 1887) and G55 at Castledyke (Drinkall & Foreman 1998: 236), and other possible cases have been noted in G55 at Portway, Hampshire (Cook & Dacre 1985: 65), and G25b at Mill Hill, Deal, Kent (Parfitt & Brugmann 1997: 230). The remarkable thing about all these cases is that the individuals seem to have survived, for a certain time at least, as the bone around each perforation shows regrowth. We can only presume that such operations were attempts to cure some kind of mental or physical disorder.

Skeletal evidence can also give indications of a range of degenerative conditions. Degenerative joint disease, such as osteoarthritis (where joint surfaces are damaged, and sometimes even polished smooth when the cartilage has completely deteriorated), is, as might be expected, more common in older members of a community, so higher rates would be expected in a cemetery which had a generally long-lived population (and also in populations involved in a lot of strenuous activity). Where it occurs in certain joints only, it may be a result of specific activity, such as the adult male, Sk101, from Mill Hill, Deal, who had degeneration of the left wrist only (Parfitt & Brugmann 1997: 225). However, some conditions, such as spondylolysis, where the neural arch of the vertebrae separates from the body, can indicate stresses imposed on the lower back. The high rates of this condition, especially among the males at Castledyke, suggested heavy, probably agricultural, activity undertaken in adolescence at this site (Drinkall & Foreman 1998: 235–6). Dietary deficiencies have also been suggested. The pitting of the upper roof of the eye sockets known as *Cribra orbitalia* is usually regarded as being evidence of iron deficiency (although it can have other causes), and examples have been detected, particularly in sub-adult skeletons, at Caistor-on-Sea, Norfolk, and West Heslerton, Yorkshire (Parfitt & Brugmann 1997: 229–30), and is present to a greater or lesser degree in most Anglo-Saxon cemetery populations.

Teeth can also offer evidence about health and lifestyle. As well as being able to reveal evidence of caries (the relative incidence of which can suggest attitudes to oral hygiene, as well as the amount of sugary food in the diet (Mays 1998: 148–55)), some Anglo-Saxon skeletons exhibit 'dental enamel hypoplasia' – depressed lines or bands of enamel which run across the tooth crown (ibid.: 156). Disease (perhaps high fever in childhood) and poor nutrition seem to be the main causes. Interestingly, while the incidence of dental enamel hypoplasia is rather high in Anglo-Saxon skeletal populations, caries, especially in sub-adults, is low, indicating that the standard of oral health was higher than is found in more recent populations. Sub-adults at Caistor-on-Sea and West Heslerton are not reported to have any tooth decay whatsoever, compared to approximately one-third of the milk teeth of modern-day children (Parfitt & Brugmann 1997: 238). Loss of teeth before death is also easily detectable, as the empty sockets close over again, as are abscesses, which leave visible sinuses in the jaw bone.

Chemical analysis of bone is a recent development, and may also offer potentially interesting information. Techniques can include looking at the proportions of carbon and nitrogen isotopes, which can indicate the reliance on marine as opposed to agricultural dietary components, and identifying trace elements such as strontium and lead which are present in minute quantities and can also reveal patterns of diet as well as possibly food preparation methods (the use of leaden drinking and storage vessels, for example) (Mays 1998: 182–96).

Finally, studying DNA extracted from skeletons, as well as being able to determine sex, may also indicate genetic relationships between members of populations (Mays 1998: 197–206); combined with other archaeological evidence, such as burial practice, or the position of the grave within the cemetery, this may start to give us a clearer idea of the role of the family in the burial rite. While such studies are still in their infancy, attempts have been made to use some non-metric traits in the same way. These traits are, often slight, skeletal abnormalities, such as unfused metopic sutures in the skull, or extra bone growth or loss of bone in an area. Some have been suggested to be hereditary, and have been used to argue for family groupings in the spatial distributions of individuals in cemeteries (for example at Alton, Hampshire – Evison 1988: 37), while others appear to be indicators of certain patterns of physical activity. An example of the former are the six individuals from Apple Down in Sussex who have both six vertebrae (rather than five) in the lumbo-sacral region and wormian bones in the sagittal suture (i.e. extra bones in the skull) (Down & Welch 1990: 184), while an example of the latter are the so-called 'squatting facets', which usually appear on the lower legs, presumably as a reaction to long periods of time spent in a squatting position. Different rates of occurrence between the sexes at one cemetery might indicate sex-related activity patterns (Drinkall & Foreman 1998: 227).

Care does need to be taken with some diagnoses. Heinrich Härke (1990: 36), for example, cited the case of a weapon burial, G110, from Berinsfield with 'spina bifida', from which he inferred that that man would probably have been severely disabled and possibly unable to use the weapons with which he was associated. While weapons have certainly been found with people patently unable to use them, the medical condition in this case was *spina bifida occulta*, where one or more vertebrae has failed to fuse at the neural arch. This is not detectable in life, and would have had no impact on the physical abilities of that person (Boyle et al. 1995: 54).

Traditional racial or ethnic interpretations of skeletal data can also be questioned. In their discussion of the human remains from East Shefford (Berkshire), for example, Peake & Horton (1915: 104) stated: 'I believe we have examples of the original Saxon invaders of the district, represented by our Male type, the Romano-British women whom they married represented by our Female type, and their offspring, our Intermediate type, comprising the first generation of their progeny.' While such interpretations are understandable, given the period in which they were put forward, more recently other authors have suggested similar interpretations of 'ethnic' difference based on skeletal data (thus ignoring much recent sociological and anthropological research which demonstrates that there is no necessary connection between them). Härke, for instance, in a series of papers (1990; 1992a; 1992b), has argued on the basis of a slight average difference in height between fifth- and sixth-century burials with weapons and those buried without weapons, that the weapon burials are those of immigrant Germans, who are taller and more slender than the 'native' Britons. As there seems to be no difference in the incidence of enamel dental hypoplasia between these two groups, and some individuals within each group have similar non-metric traits, he argues that these stature differences are a result of familial descent groups, rather than a result of differential nutrition or health status. There are a number of problems with this interpretation. Firstly, estimation of stature from long-bone length is an extremely imprecise technique, which has a wide error range associated with it. The average stature difference of between 0.2cm and 4.7cm which he identifies on the basis of small sample sizes from just five sites (1992b: 197) should be taken with caution, as correlations of long-bone length with height carry with them an error range of around 4cm (Trotter & Gleser 1952). Moreover, his arguments about nutrition and health status are also not as well founded as they might seem. His association of dental hypoplasia with malnutrition is not the only explanation for this condition, as incidence of high fever in childhood can also be a contributing factor (something which is presumably not related to nutrition in any direct sense). If his stature differences are real, which is debatable, they may have been caused by differential access to food, something which need not be reflected in teeth. Finally, his reliance on epigenetic traits to indicate family links is also rather tenuous. As his tables show (1992b: 200–8), the traits which he discusses are not found exclusively with either weapon or non-weapon burials at any of his cemeteries, and it is not enough to use just one indicator as evidence of genetic links – non-metric variation is much more complex than this (A. Tyrrell pers. comm.). Perhaps what is most worrying about such interpretations is how quickly they become accepted as fact.

Work in recent years has thus shown the wealth of information which can be derived from studying the skeletal remains of inhumation burials, giving evidence as to age, sex, health, lifestyle, diet, oral hygiene and disease. In combination with other aspects of the burial rite, such as the way the body is laid out, and the goods with which they are furnished, a rich and detailed picture can be drawn of the community which buried its dead in a particular location. Some caution must be exercised, however, when interpreting this specialist skeletal information, as human bones rarely offer clear-cut indicators of any medical condition or activity, and interpretation should be left to experts, with detailed knowledge of how trauma, illness or activity can present themselves on human bone. The rest of this chapter will move on to look at the other sorts of information which can be gained from the study of inhumation burial.

Pre- and Post-mortem Burial Rites

Evidence from skeletal remains can suggest special treatment of the body, either before or after death (**Fig. 3.3**). Mutilation of the body, including decapitation, is a practice which, although not common, is found in small numbers at a surprising number of cemeteries (Harman et al. 1981). Sometimes all burials in a cemetery are found to be decapitated, and the cemetery should be seen as an 'execution cemetery', a subject on which Andrew Reynolds has produced some interesting new work (Reynolds 1999). While the majority of these seem to be late, often dating to the tenth or eleventh centuries, such as (probably) Five Knolls, Dunstable (Dunning & Wheeler 1931) and Bran Ditch, Fowlmere, where the burials were found in 'Hangman Field' near 'Gallow Gate' (Fox & Palmer 1926: 31; Lethbridge 1929: 87), others may be earlier. The small cemetery at Littleton, where the burials were decapitated and the heads placed at the foot of the graves, is dated by the presence of a few buckles to the seventh or eighth century, although as there was also an infant skeleton here this is not necessarily an execution cemetery as such (*Medieval Archaeology* 35, 1991: 157).

One site with a number of decapitated and otherwise mutilated burials which does seem to be early is the famous barrow cemetery at Sutton Hoo in Suffolk (**Fig. 3.4**). In the recent excavation campaign, a number of burials which had been hanged, beheaded or mutilated were found around mound 5 and on the eastern edge of the barrow area (Carver 1998: 137). Around mound 5, several were found in quarry pits associated with the construction of the mound, the earliest being contemporary with it. Others in this group have produced radiocarbon dates possibly as early as the seventh century, and continuing into the tenth or eleventh century (ibid.: 137–9). In a group to the east, associated with a probable gallows structure, remains of bodies were found which probably had the wrists or ankles bound, while others had the head removed, or were buried in unnatural positions. Again, these show evidence for a similar date span as those around mound 5. While this may be a 'normal' execution cemetery of the ninth or tenth century, suggestions of early dates from the scientific evidence may possibly indicate that the existing barrow cemetery was deliberately chosen for these burials in the seventh century, with the mutilation associated with the exercise of Christian kingship (ibid.: 139–40).

In 'normal' Anglo-Saxon cemeteries these practices are also found, in both earlier and later cemeteries. One particularly strange example was seen at Loveden Hill, where one burial had the head placed on the stomach, and a pottery urn just beyond where the head should have been (Meaney 1964: 158). At Great Addington, Northamptonshire, three headless skeletons were found in 1847, with stones in place of the heads (Smith 1902: 241–2), and two more at Chadlington, Oxon, had the heads placed by the legs (Leeds 1939: 357–8). At Mitcham (Surrey) extra skulls were found in a number of graves, and some graves were without heads, or with heads at the feet. Many, if not all, of these anomalies may simply be the result of disturbance of this site in the nineteenth century (Wilson 1992a: 93). A more peculiar practice is seen at Kemble II, Gloucestershire, and Loveden Hill, Lincolnshire, where individual burials had their feet detached and placed by the knees at burial (King et al. 1996: 28; Wilkinson 1980: 230); even more unusually,

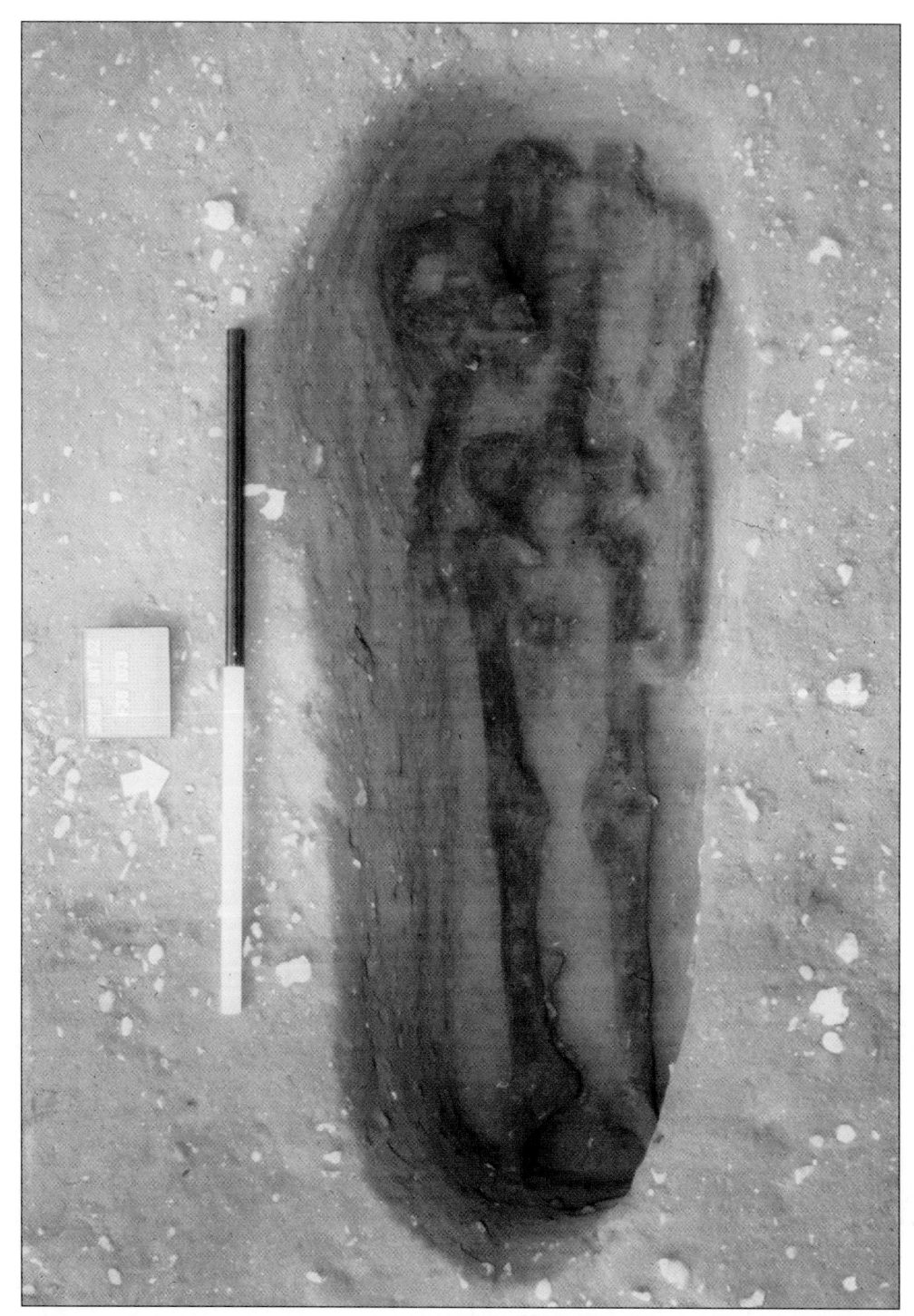

Fig. 3.3. A decapitated burial from Sutton Hoo (Burial 35) with the detached head lying on the shoulder. (Copyright Martin Carver and the Sutton Hoo Research Trust. Reproduced by kind permission of Martin Carver and British Museum Press.)

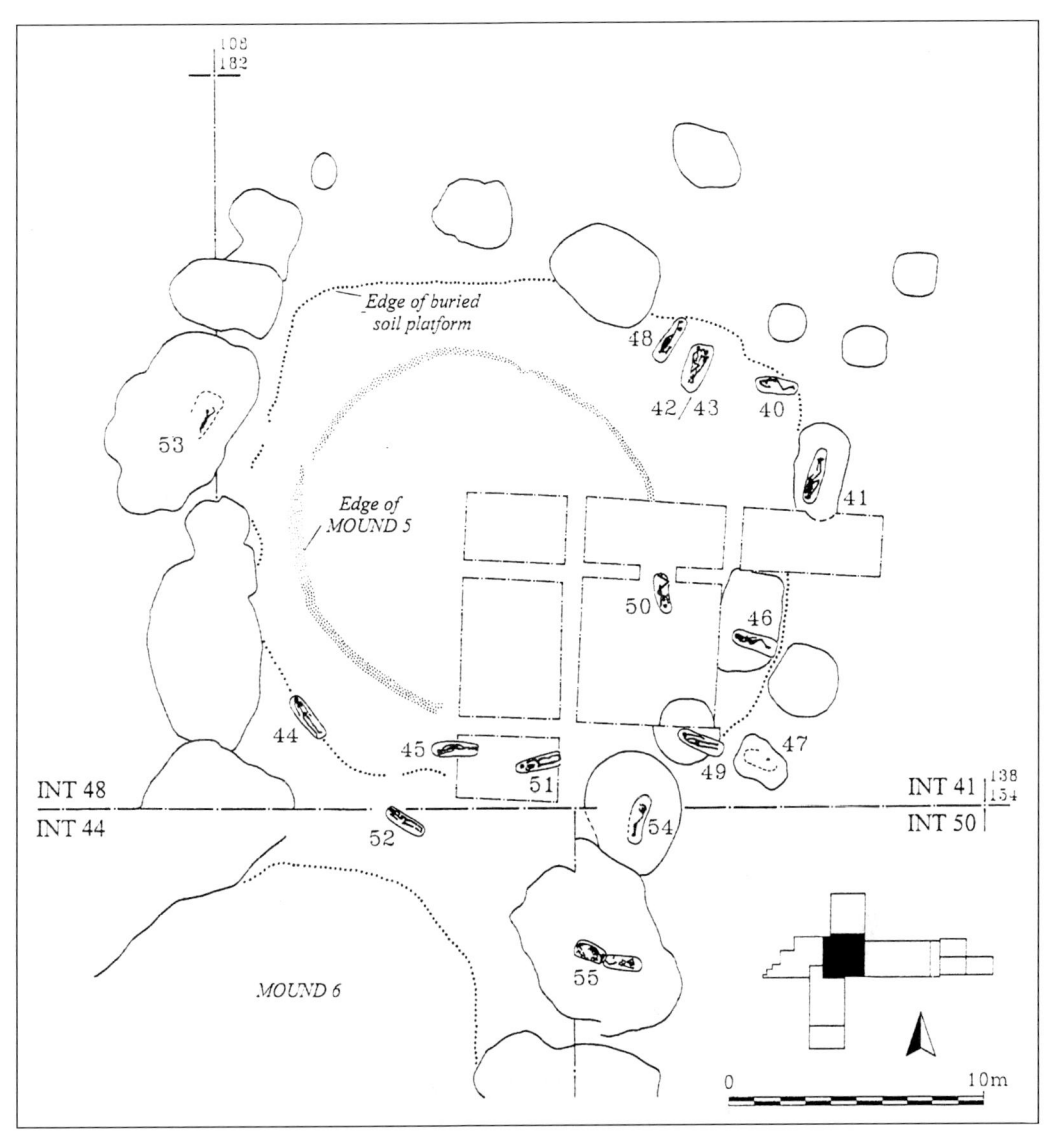

Fig. 3.4. *The unusual burials around Mound 5 at Sutton Hoo. (Reproduced by kind permission of Martin Carver and British Museum Press.)*

skulls seem to have been buried on their own at Bidford-on-Avon, Warwickshire, and Portway, Hampshire (Wilson 1992a: 95). One burial at West Heslerton in Yorkshire had the legs bent right back, as if they had been bound in position (Powlesland in press).

Other forms of evidence can offer some information about the treatment of the body before burial took place. In a few cases, such as in G39 at Mill Hill, Deal, Kent (Parfitt & Brugmann 1997: 26), graves 10 and 14 at Apple Down, Sussex (Down & Welch 1990: 18) and at Wakerley, Northamptonshire (Adams & Jackson 1989: 78), insect pupa cases found preserved on the back of metalwork suggest that the body was left unburied for long enough, probably days or even weeks, for eggs to be laid and start to hatch. In most cases the excavated skeletons reveal how the body was placed in the grave at the time of the funeral. This is important information, as it may convey messages about belief and status, and the way that person was viewed in life.

Variations in Skeletal Position

Bodies in Anglo-Saxon cemeteries are found arranged in a variety of positions. The body can be placed on the back (supine), front (prone), or on one side. The legs can be arranged straight out, be crossed at the lower leg or ankle, be slightly bent (flexed), or even pulled right up to the chest in a foetal position (crouched or contracted). References to skeletons in a 'sitting' position are very occasionally found, such as at Caenby, Lincolnshire (Jarvis 1850), Kempston, Bedfordshire (Smith 1904: 176–84), Beakesbourne and Breach Downs (both Kent) (Smith 1908: 343–4, 348–9) but these tend to be from older excavations where the recording is not necessarily reliable. One, however, was recorded from a more recent excavation at Butler's Field, Lechlade, Gloucestershire (Boyle et al. 1998: 37) which suggests that this is an occasional position which was employed. In addition, in one grave (G27) from Alton, Hampshire, a ten-year-old had been propped up in the grave in a half-sitting position (Evison 1988: 18).

Burial face down (prone) has always excited comment among excavators (**Fig. 3.5**). Occasionally such burials are also interpreted as 'live', when burial position is particularly unusual. Grave 43 at Worthy Park, for example, was 'lying askew with her faced crushed against the grave floor, her forearms and hands doubled up under her chest, her knees bent to her left and her feet together. There was an air of suspended animation about this skeleton, as if the woman had been committed to the grave when still alive and had been attempting to raise herself to her knees as the earth was thrown in upon her' (Hawkes & Wells 1975: 118). Grave 41 at Sewerby, East Yorkshire, was found in a similar position – face down, with her arms doubled back at the elbows and her feet splayed, as if she was trying to push herself up. She also had a large stone placed on her back. This too was interpreted as a live burial, perhaps one made as punishment for witchcraft, especially as it formed part of an unusual double burial, where G41 lay over a younger well-furnished female grave (G49), and both were covered by a stone cairn (Hirst 1985: 38–43). However, as Reynolds (1988: 717) notes, if G41 had been held down in the position she was found in, 'someone must have had a hard job shovelling earth underneath her lower limbs'. A more likely explanation was that the disintegration and collapse of the coffin of the burial underneath would have caused the peculiarities in position in G41. Knüsel et al. (1996) suggest an alternative explanation for her odd position, noting that it seems to be due to contraction of the flexor muscles in the hands, arms and thighs – a response which is sometimes seen in fire victims. In a thought-provoking article, Hirst has restated her arguments for this being a live burial, arguing against such rational and 'sanitising' explanations, and remarking that 'in the later 20th century we may be seeking a relief from the uncertainties, vulgarity and brutality of our society in a vision of the past as a more civilised place, where death always came quietly and rationally' (1993: 43). She

INHUMATION BURIAL PRACTICE

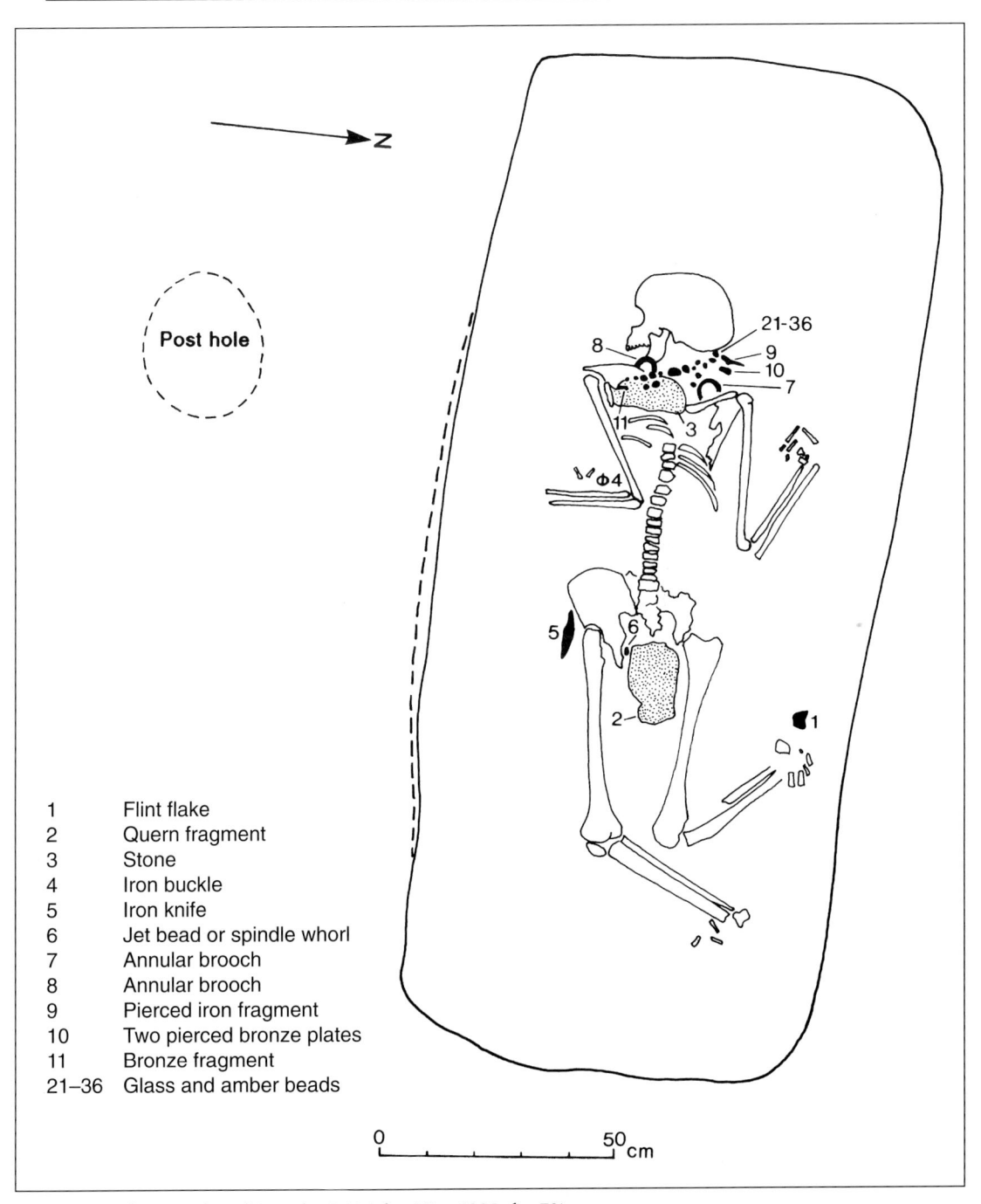

1	Flint flake
2	Quern fragment
3	Stone
4	Iron buckle
5	Iron knife
6	Jet bead or spindle whorl
7	Annular brooch
8	Annular brooch
9	Pierced iron fragment
10	Two pierced bronze plates
11	Bronze fragment
21–36	Glass and amber beads

Fig. 3.5. The prone burial Sewerby G41 (after Hirst 1985: fig. 73).

certainly has a point here, in that we may project our own expectations on to the interpretations we make of burials in the past.

There is probably no single explanation for the use of prone burial. In some cases it may be accidental, especially if the burial was in a coffin which had been clumsily handled. In other cases it might have specific significance attached to it, as in the double burial at Sewerby (assuming the two burials were contemporary). Likewise the female found face down between a male weapon burial and the burial of a twelve-year-old child at Farthingdown in Surrey, who was 'lying prone in a sprawled position, apparently thrown in the grave' (Meaney 1964: 241). Grave 32, the only prone burial at Westgarth Gardens, Suffolk, was marked out as different in a number of ways: he was one of only two or three adults in a flexed position, his left hand was missing, his grave was an odd shape and he had been trepanned (West 1988: 28). G103 at Great Chesterford was a prone female who had brooches and beads deposited with her, not as fastenings for a costume, but between the back of the skull and the corner of the grave (Evison 1994a: 30). The only well-furnished grave at Westbury-by-Shenley was, however, the only prone burial at this small late cemetery (Ivers et al. 1995: 71), suggesting that there was nothing 'odd' about this burial, and the eight prone burials from Empingham II were treated in otherwise 'normal' ways (Timby 1995: 21). Some prone burials have even been treated in ways which can be interpreted as sentimental. G86 at Great Chesterford, Essex, for example, was an eight-year-old child, buried prone with a spearhead and a mended shield, and with an elderly male dog, presumably a pet, buried above his feet (Evison 1994a: 30). Very often, though, prone burials are not marked out as special in any way, and we must assume that this was just one of a range of positions, albeit an unusual one, which could be employed during the burial rite.

Various studies have found burial laid out straight (or reasonably straight) on the back to be the dominant burial position in both early and late cemeteries across much of the country. In her study of 2,216 burials of the fifth and sixth centuries from forty-five cemeteries across the country, Brush (1993: 221) found that between 50 and 75 per cent of burials at most sites were in the extended, supine position, while between 10 and 25 per cent were usually semi-flexed, with the legs slightly bent at the knees. Some burials are found in crouched positions. Sometimes this is the dominant rite used within a cemetery, for example at Uncleby, Yorkshire (**Fig. 3.6**), and Sleaford, Lincolnshire, or a major position, with between 20 and 30 per cent of burials deposited in this way, as at Norton, Cleveland (Sherlock & Welch 1992), Castledyke, Humberside (Drinkall & Foreman 1998), and at Driffield and Cheesecake Hill in Yorkshire (Brush 1993: 221). More often, though, it is a minority rite used by a small percentage of burials. It is not true, as Brush stated from the basis of her sample, that crouched burial is absent or rare south of the Wash – they are found in just over one in ten of cemeteries of all dates, both early and late, and are as common south of the Wash as north. There may be a chronological dimension here. One study of the Anglo-Saxon cemeteries in East Yorkshire found crouched burial to be far more common in this area in later cemeteries than in earlier ones (Lucy 2000). While some people have argued that this position may be an indicator of 'British' individuals being buried in Anglo-Saxon cemeteries (e.g. Eagles 1979: 46; Faull 1979: 85; Higham 1992: 184), again it seems to be just one of the alternative rites which could be employed.

INHUMATION BURIAL PRACTICE

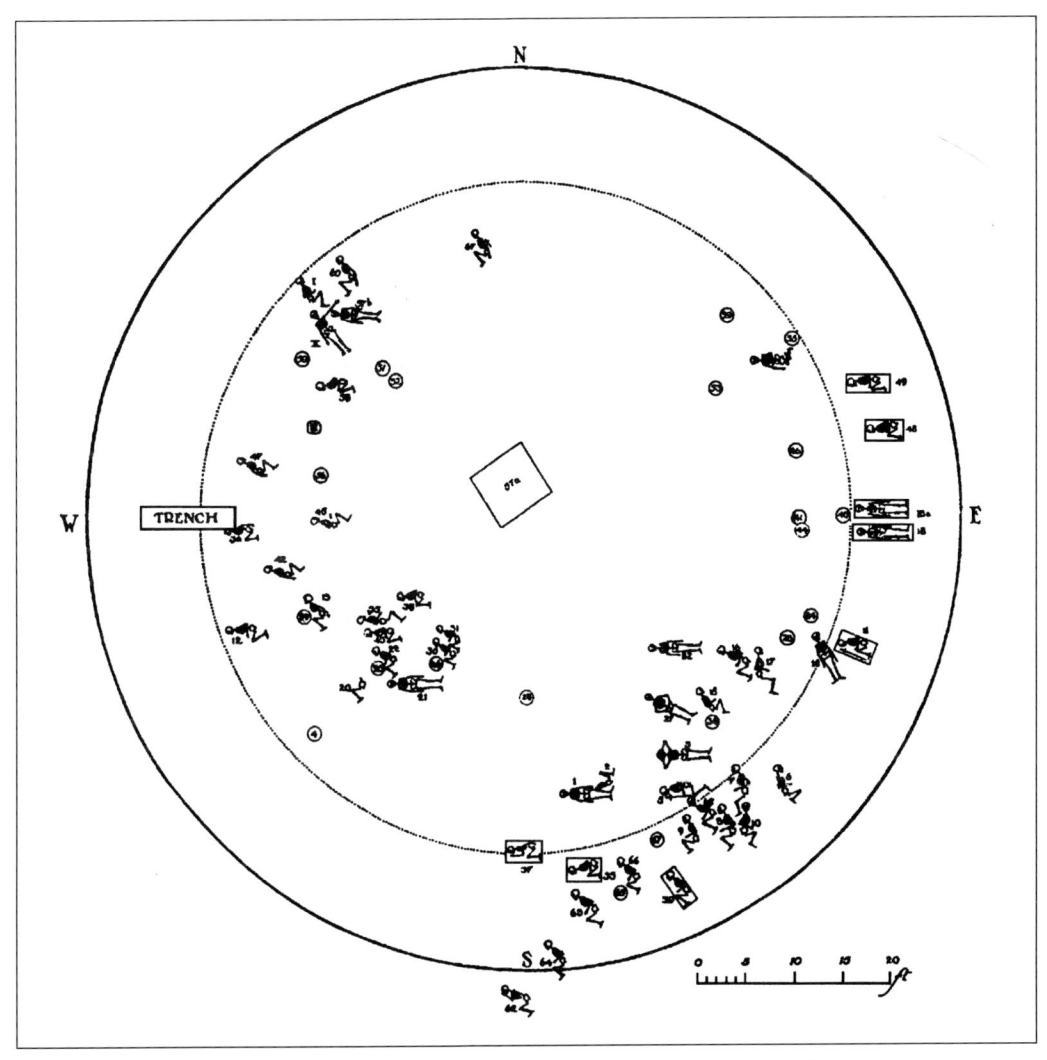

Fig. 3.6. Plan of the cemetery at Uncleby (after Smith 1912a: fig. 1). Numbers in rings show burials whose direction could not be determined, and the dotted circle indicates the extent of the original Bronze Age barrow.

Similarly, burials which were placed on their side are also found in a number of cemeteries. These can be extended, flexed or crouched, and examples from both early and late cemeteries are known from all areas of the country. Sometimes different positions can be seen to be determined by the shape of the grave itself. The burials at Horton Kirby, Kent, for example, a site on hard chalk, were often bent at the heads and feet to get them into small graves (Spurrell 1889: 314–15), and this explanation was also suggested for the crouched burial on the left side of the tall man in a short grave in G37 at Portway (Cook & Dacre 1985: 56). This is not the universal reason for bent, crouched or flexed graves, however, as many such burials are in graves which are of ample size and sometimes of quite large dimensions.

Multiple Burials

The burial of more than one person in a grave is a reasonably common feature of Anglo-Saxon cemeteries. Usually just one extra person is represented, but there are instances where there are more. For example, at Argyll Avenue, Luton (Bedfordshire), G6 contained six adult skeletons, both males and females, with a mixture of orientations, but only a knife and spear as grave-goods (Austin 1928). At Stowting, Kent, one very odd circular grave 9ft in diameter contained six female skeletons oriented north–south, accompanied by an openwork disc, a small square-headed brooch and a silver and garnet brooch (Smith 1908: 365–6). Grave 81 at Lechlade (Boyle et al. 1998: 37–8) was a large stone-lined grave which contained five individuals, and was thought perhaps to have been a family 'vault', especially as it seemed to have had at least two phases of use.

Burials containing two individuals tend either to have them side by side, usually representing contemporaneous burial as in the double weapon burial G96 from Dover Buckland, Kent (Evison 1987: 239), or to have one interred on top of the other, either buried at the same time, or with the first grave reopened to take the second burial (see Stoodley forthcoming for a detailed review). Unusual instances of the latter include the case from Cotgrave, Nottinghamshire, where the grave of a prone female was reopened in order to insert a male burial, who was also prone and who had to be crammed into the grave (Bishop 1984). Sometimes these double burials are marked out on the surface as well. Another double grave from Cotgrave contained a female on top of an adolescent, both covered by large amounts of stone, and this is paralleled by the above-mentioned double grave from Sewerby where G49, a supine female in a coffin, had a prone uncoffined female interred on top, and both were then covered by a stone cairn (Hirst 1985: 38–43). These burials are interpreted as taking place close in time, as in G166 at Castledyke, where a prone elderly female was found sprawled over an extended youth (Drinkall & Foreman 1998: 334). An unusual example was G99, an early seventh-century weapon burial from Apple Down, Sussex, which had the female burial G93 placed at ninety degrees to his feet (Down & Welch 1990: 15). Also odd was Burial 2 at Portway, Andover, a crouched male on his back with wrists possibly bound, found immediately above an older female, Burial 2A, who was in a supine, extended position (Cook & Dacre 1985: 56).

Perhaps the most common combination within multiple burials is of an adult and child or infant. This practice is seen right through the period from the burial of an adult female and a child of around four years in G13 at Portway (Cook & Dacre 1985: 27) to the 'Kingston Brooch' grave which was of a woman in an iron-bound coffin within a grave 10ft long and 8ft wide, accompanied by the late elaborate composite Kingston Brooch, a gold bracteate, a casket, two bronze bowls, a green glass cup, and other grave-goods, plus a child buried at her feet outside the coffin (Smith 1908: 345–8). While such burials are often assumed to be mother and child, as is suggested for five of the ten double burials at Empingham II in Rutland (Timby 1995: 17), cases are known where this cannot be the case. At Uncleby, Yorkshire, a child was found to lie across a man's knees (Smith 1912a: 150), and a child was placed by the lower legs or feet of the man in G68 at Castledyke, Humberside (Drinkall & Foreman 1998: 334). Grave 67 at Apple Down, Sussex, had a seven- to eight-year-old child laid at right angles over his lower legs (Down & Welch 1990: 43).

Variations in Costume and Related Grave Furnishings

As Anglo-Saxon inhumations were often buried clothed, the various fastenings which held the clothing together can give indications as to the type of garments worn at the time of death. While this costume could have been one reserved specifically for burial, finds of similar brooch and buckle types on settlement sites suggest that they largely consisted of items in everyday use. It is now being recognised more and more that where textiles and other organic materials are buried in contact with metal artefacts, impressions of those materials can be preserved through a process of mineral replacement, and left on the back of the artefact is often a 'rusty' version of the original textile. Analysis of such organic materials has led to studies of textile production and use throughout northern and western Europe (Bender Jørgensen 1992). Attempts have also been made at costume reconstruction by looking at such information, aided by examining where brooches and other fastenings were placed on the body (Owen-Crocker 1986), as well as by noting patterns of wear on brooches (Leigh 1985). Pictorial sources have also been used, from which Brush (1993: 128) concluded that males in this period may have worn coats, tailored tunics and trousers, whereas females probably wore tailored gowns, loose overgowns and possibly veils. Both men and women may have worn cloaks. Interestingly, she also concludes that none of these costumes required the use of fasteners, so the female costume, for example, could have been worn despite there being no brooches or buckles found in a grave.

Spatial and chronological variations in the female costume

Chapter Two mentioned that the types of grave-goods found in burials of the fifth and sixth centuries are different from those of the late sixth, seventh and eighth centuries, highlighting the fact that throughout much of this period the furnishings found in eastern Kent often stand out as distinct from the rest of eastern Britain. The earlier costume often featured pairs of brooches worn usually on the shoulders (but occasionally in the south of England on the breast) of female costumes, holding together a type of tubular gown (Brush 1993: 87), whereas different female dress is inferred from the switch to single brooches towards the end of the sixth century. Brush (ibid.: map 2A) highlights some interesting distinctions between the later fifth- and sixth-century costumes employed in (a) Kent (although only two cemeteries from East Kent were included in her sample), (b) the south of England and the Upper Thames region and (c) the east coast and East Anglia. In broad terms she found that north of the Thames the main brooches used were wide, flat annular, cruciform and great square-headed brooches, usually combined in sets of three to five brooches worn on the upper torso. Other types of jewellery accessories used mainly in these areas were sleeve-clasps, bucket pendants and girdle-hangers (ibid.: 110). South of the Thames, disc, saucer, applied, and button brooches were characteristic, as were brooch pairs worn low on the chest, Roman coins worn as pendants and 'pelvic festoons' – strings of beads worn low on the body (ibid.). These distinctive types are those which have, on the basis of brooch types, been classified as 'Anglian' and Saxon' costumes respectively (Fig. 3.7). In more detail, the 'Anglian' costume is seen to consist of two cruciform, annular or small-long brooches worn on the shoulders and a brooch on the chest, fastening a cloak, while the 'Saxon' variant consists of two disc or saucer brooches worn at the shoulders (Parfitt & Brugmann 1997: 113). A variation on this is the use of multiple brooches – usually four – in rows down the torso, a practice that appears to reflect fifth- and sixth-century Merovingian fashion (Parfitt & Brugmann 1997: 113). Brush (1993: 89, 252) found examples at Alfriston and Highdown in Sussex; at Dover Buckland and Finglesham in Kent; at Sewerby in Yorkshire; and at Bergh Apton, Morningthorpe and Swaffham, all Norfolk; and three examples at Holywell Row, Suffolk, in her sample. Mill Hill, Deal, provides other examples.

It should be noted, however, that Brush's study was based on just forty-five sites (albeit with numerous burials and good recording), which naturally creates a more clear-cut picture than if she had included the hundreds which are known in total. Even within this smaller sample, however, the distinctions were not as clear as one might expect. Although sleeve-clasps, annular and cruciform brooches were mainly found to the north and saucer, button and disc brooches to the south of the Thames, there were several sites in her sample where both costumes were in use, for example, at Barrington Edix Hill and Hooper's Field, Little Wilbraham, in Cambridgeshire, and at Wasperton in Warwickshire (Brush 1993: 85). Within these sites individuals were also found to have 'mixed' costumes. At Barrington Edix Hill, for example, graves 68 and 106 wore sleeve-clasps together with saucer brooches (Malim & Hines 1998: 71, 85). Thus our ideas about 'Anglian' and 'Saxon' costume are akin to stereotypes – the 'proper' costume is found occasionally, with all its attributes, but the reality is that there was a great deal more variation in the way that these artefacts were used in the burial rite.

Fig. 3.7. Reconstruction of Anglo-Saxon female costume (after Owen-Crocker 1986: fig. 30).

Geake (1997; 1999) has demonstrated how the same types of grave-goods are found across all the Anglo-Saxon kingdoms in the seventh and early eighth centuries, arguing that many of them derive their inspiration either from earlier Romano-British material or from contemporary Byzantine practice. These new types, as described in Chapter Two, were several varieties of pendants, bullae, silver wire rings and mounted animal teeth. The long strings of amber, crystal and polychrome glass beads disappear, as do most of the sixth-century brooch types (although round-section annular, penannular and garnet-set disc brooches remain in use, but worn singly rather than in pairs). Different types of object are worn from the belt – small iron spoons, toilet-sets, amulets, bags and bronze workboxes, rather than the earlier crystal balls and sieve spoons (these mainly in Kent) and girdle-hangers. Geake describes how this development, intriguingly, makes the now historically documented kingdoms appear archaeologically invisible, for the former regional distinctions have disappeared.

As noted above, east Kent always appears slightly distinct in its costume types. In a study of the Kentish jewellery chronologies, Brugmann (1999) has identified two main fashions: a primary phase in which Kentish brooch types (bow brooches, and disc brooches of Avent's classes 1 and 2) are worn in combination with continental brooch types, D-bracteates, shield-on-tongue buckles and/or shoe-shaped rivets and reticella beads (with the brooches being worn down the torso); and a subsequent fashion in which a single Kentish disc brooch (of Avent class 3 and later, or a composite brooch) was worn at the neck, in combination with other types of pendants and amethyst beads. She dates the transition between these two fashions to around 580/590. Owen-Crocker (1986) thinks that this earlier fashion may indicate the use of a different type of gown: open-fronted and secured by brooches at the waist and neck. Even in Kent, however, 'mixed' costumes are found, for example grave 39 at Lyminge which wore a pair of saucer brooches and a pair of Kentish small square-headed brooches (Parfitt & Brugmann 1997: 113), while graves 61, 71 and 73 at Mill Hill followed the odd practice of wearing their brooches in a single line from the neck to the waist (ibid.: 48), as suggested above, perhaps imitating contemporary Merovingian costume. In addition, 'Anglo-Saxon' costume is also found in Kentish cemeteries, with 'Anglian' or 'Saxon' brooch types worn in the usual way on the shoulders (and more typical Kentish artefacts used in ways that do not conform to continental practices) (ibid.: 116).

Recent examination of the textile evidence from the Castledyke cemetery in Humberside has provided some important new information relating to costume changes over time. It is argued that there was a chronological shift in the types of fabric being used for burial towards the end of the sixth century, with a greater use of linen tabby weaves (Drinkall & Foreman 1998: 274–5), which appears to occur from Kent up to the north of England. From the earlier evidence at Castledyke, women appear to have worn the usual tubular *peplos* gowns, either fastened at both shoulders with a brooch, or stitched at one side and fastened with a brooch at the other. The front of the gown could be attached to the undergown with a pin, to prevent it sagging open. The overgown was sometimes fastened by a belt with a buckle, although non-detectable braid girdles may have been used (ibid.: 275–6). Several burials with this costume were found to have cloaks fastened by central cruciform brooches, and there was also evidence for the use of short veils (ibid.: 278). There was also some indication of the use of a front-opening gown at this site, in three graves with a single central brooch on the chest (ibid.: 278).

As mentioned above, many of the artefacts found in graves are also known from settlement sites, although not in such numbers. In addition those found in the graves frequently show signs of wear, and sometimes repair, likewise suggesting their everyday use. However, some brooches appear to have been sewn on to clothing, which presumably meant that a 'burial costume' was in use, rather than garments which could have been easily put on and taken off in life (cf. the notion of *tracht* used by continental authors such as Vierck 1978). In grave 346 at Morningthorpe, Norfolk, the cruciform brooch had been stitched on to a garment (Green et al. 1987: 133–4), as had button brooches from the cemetery at Brighton, Sussex (Smith 1988: 31). At Marston St Lawrence, no brooches had pins (Dryden 1882), suggesting that something similar was going on here, as it may have been in graves 1, 6 and 96 at Norton-on-Tees, Cleveland, where the brooches also lacked pins (Brush 1993: 86). Likewise, at Winnall II, Hampshire, a burial was found with a pinless composite brooch, which had been lain on where it would have been worn (Meaney & Hawkes 1970).

Other brooches are found used in odd ways. Grave 9 at Soham Waterworks (Cambridgeshire) was found with annular brooches at the leg, rather than the shoulder, suggesting that they were performing a different function from usual (Lethbridge 1933), while the annular brooches found above the head and at the waist in G15 at Wallingford (Berkshire) suggests a different usage again (Leeds 1938). A grave at Wigston Magna was accompanied by the backplate of an applied brooch, but this may have been in use as a pendant rather than a brooch (Liddle & Middleton 1994). Sleeve-clasps, too, are used in different ways. A grave at Little Wilbraham had these at the knees as well as at the wrists (Lethbridge & Carter 1928), and a grave at Tallington had them on the lower legs (Field & George 1998: 41). Sometimes grave-goods are placed with, rather than on, the body. Grave 90 at Lechlade had beads, pendants, a pair of matched saucer brooches, and a hooked pin laid in the lap of this adult female, possibly in a bag – her possessions had been buried with her, rather than as part of her burial costume (Brush 1993: 78; Boyle et al. 1998: 94–5).

Occasionally, burials are found to contain obviously old jewellery, which presumably can be interpreted as heirlooms. Brooches, especially, are often noted in this way, perhaps because they are the objects which seem to be most closely datable. At Marina Drive (Bedfordshire), grave E2, an eight-year-old child, was buried with a collection of late sixth- and seventh-century objects, but also with an early sixth-century small-long brooch which had lost its pin (Matthews 1962). G86, an elderly female, at Mill Hill, Deal, had a set of three abraded annular brooches and three fresh Frankish brooches, perhaps suggesting acquisition of a new set of brooches late in life (Parfitt & Brugmann 1997: 50). Grave 106 at Abingdon, Berkshire, was of an adult female with an applied brooch and a fragment of a repaired late fourth-century tutulus brooch (Leeds & Harden 1936). Brooches can also be used in other ways, for example at Dinton Folly (Buckinghamshire) where G11 contained an old bow brooch attached to a ring at the waist (Hunn et al. 1994); likewise a grave at Burwell in which an annular brooch was reused in a chatelaine (Lethbridge 1931) and another at Osengal where a similar brooch was used as a key-ring (Baldwin Brown 1915: 700–1). Whole assemblages very exceptionally stand out as being old. G104 in the Anglo-Saxon cemetery at Alton (Hampshire) was a sixty- to eighty-year-old female, who was buried with a necklace of eleven Romano-British glass beads, two perforated Roman coins, a Romano-British brooch and two D-shaped buckles at either shoulder (*Medieval Archaeology* 37, 1993: 263).

Spatial and chronological variations in male costume

There is little evidence for male costume (as opposed to provision of weapons as grave-goods) in the fifth and sixth centuries, although there are occasional finds of pins and brooches, and knives, tweezers and shears could be carried at the waist, presumably from a belt which may have secured trousers or a tunic (Owen-Crocker 1986: 65–84). Evidence from Castledyke, Humberside, suggests a male costume of trousers and a tunic (one burial, G55, had two belts, fastening different items of clothing) (Drinkall & Foreman 1998: 28). In the seventh to ninth centuries there seem to be a few innovations, as buckles and the remains of strap equipment are sometimes found at the breast or shoulder, perhaps indicating a type of baldric (a diagonal strap across the chest plus belt). In some high-status burials waist-clasps (as at Taplow) and shoulder-clasps (such as the exceptional pieces from Sutton Hoo) are found. Occasional finds have been made in seventh-century graves of garments of fur (or at least of a shaggy appearance), perhaps cloaks. In addition, the Frankish fashion for fancy gartering on males seems to reach Kent in the seventh century, to judge by the lace tags found at Finglesham and Polhill (Owen-Crocker 1986: 107–29). Again, Castledyke provides some support for this change in male costume as well as in female costume at the end of the sixth century. Grave 126 contained a male who was interpreted as wearing a jacket or coat of linen twill with a patterned braid as a border, which he wore wrapped around his body, fastened by a belt. Artefactual evidence suggests a seventh-century date for this costume (Drinkall & Foreman 1998: 278–9). Likewise, the late seventh-century primary barrow burial at Banstead Common in Surrey was a tall man in his late twenties or early thirties, who was wearing soft leather boots, his legs covered with plain fabric, above which was a twill coat (Barfoot & Price Williams 1976).

Correlations of costume and grave-goods with age and sex

As well as different burial costumes, there are broad differences in the range and types of grave-goods with which at least some male and female inhumations were provided. It should be remembered that in all areas, a greater or lesser percentage of all burials were unfurnished, perhaps buried in just a sheet or shroud, or perhaps in a costume which used no metal fittings and so is archaeologically undetectable. Those burials which are provided with grave-goods generally fall into one of three main categories: (a) those buried with items of weaponry (usually adult males or older children, but not exclusively); (b) those buried with items of jewellery (usually females, but not always); and (c) those buried with other types of goods (i.e. neither weaponry nor jewellery), such as pottery vessels, knives, buckles etc. (although, of course, burials with weapons or jewellery are often provided with such goods too).

Based on his extensive analysis of the weapon burial rite in England, Härke (1990: 25) noted that 18 per cent of his corpus of 3,814 inhumations from 47 cemeteries contained weapons (comprising 47 per cent of all identifiable male adult inhumations). A spear was found in four out of five of these weapon burials, half contained a shield, while one in ten or fewer contained another type of weapon such as a sword, seax (single-edged battle knife), axe or arrows. Helmets and mail corselets have been found in a very few graves (ibid.: 25–6). These associations change over time, with axes and arrows generally found in fifth- and sixth-century contexts, while seaxes appear in the sixth century, becoming more popular in the seventh (ibid.: 26). Härke (ibid.: 30) estimates that the weapon burial rite itself, however, is relatively rare in the fifth century, reaches a peak in the mid-sixth, and sharply declines after that, virtually going out of use by AD 700. While the people buried with these weapons were thought to be virtually all male, they ranged in age from twelve months to sixty years, and some exhibited disabling conditions such as severe osteoarthritis and broken long-bones which had not healed together well (ibid.: 36). Nor was there a strong positive correlation between burial with weapons and evidence of fighting (mostly in the form of sword cuts to the skull) – of seventeen such injuries, only five were buried with weapons (ibid.; see p. 74 for doubts about the rest of Härke's argument based on skeletal data).

Occasionally, tools are found as male grave-goods. Grave 1 at Soham Waterworks (Cambridgeshire) contained a man buried with a hammer and a whetstone, and G40 at the same site was buried with a spear and an adze (Lethbridge 1933). A grave at Sarre was similarly accompanied by both tools and weapons. At Gilton, Kent, G98 was buried with two putative surgeon's instruments. As mentioned in Chapter Two, other items with interesting associations occasionally accompany a burial with weapons, such as functional sets of scales and weights (Scull 1993), and draughtsmen. It is now largely accepted that such provisioning of goods does not necessarily reflect the real-life activities of the people so buried, but that provisioning of weapons was an act of a more symbolic nature, perhaps reflecting that person's position in their community, or their membership of a certain lineage (Lucy 1997).

As well as work on the weapon burial rite, the past two decades have also seen in-depth studies of burials with other grave-goods. Improvements in cemetery reporting and detailed skeletal reports mean that grave assemblages can now be compared against the age and sex (and often other details) of the people they were buried with, rather than simplistic assumptions being made about the meanings of such artefacts. The first of these studies was a detailed analysis by Pader (1980; 1982) of two cemeteries in East Anglia, Holywell Row (Lethbridge 1931) and Westgarth Gardens (West 1988), which examined assemblage against age, sex and location of the grave within the cemetery. Although these sites were broadly contemporary and located only 19km apart, Pader found subtle but significant differences in the way the dead were treated at the two sites, on top of distinctions already made within individual sites on the basis of age and sex differences. At Holywell Row she found that women and children were symbolically linked in terms of their grave-goods and skeletal positioning, while adult males were distinguished, whereas at Westgarth Gardens, it seemed to be adults in general who were demarcated from infants and children.

Building on this approach, Brush carried out a study of burial costumes across a range of Anglo-Saxon cemeteries of fifth- and sixth-century date, finding that burial assemblages became more diverse with the age of the person buried (Brush 1993: 164–5). She argued that children's costume was a simpler version of adult dress (ibid.: 172), and that there were various artefacts which were restricted to older children and adults, such as keys, girdle-hangers, sleeve-clasps and shields (ibid.: 169). These findings are echoed by Stoodley (1999b; 190–1), who suggests that bracelets and arrowheads may have been associated primarily with infants and young children. Lucy (1998) came to similar conclusions in a study of cemeteries in East Yorkshire, which compared grave-good provisioning to a range of other aspects of the burial rite. Again, provisioning was highly structured by sex and age, with square-headed brooches, shields, swords, tweezers and tools being confined to adult burials over the age of twenty-five, while a range of other goods were only found with those over twelve years of age. Moreover, the burial rite itself was structured by sex and age, but differences between sexes and people of different age groups were marked in different ways at each cemetery (something which was also found for East Anglia by Fisher 1995: 162).

Stoodley (1999a) reported on a study of 351 undisturbed adult burials from seventeen cemeteries in Wessex, which he investigated in terms of their gender construction. He, like Brush, Pader and Lucy, also found two dichotomous assemblages: weapons on the one hand and dress fasteners, jewellery and personal equipment on the other. Through analysis of the associated skeletal material, he found that these assemblages were strongly (though not completely) constrained by sex – there were no females with weapons in his sample, and only two possible and one probable male with jewellery. The probable male with jewellery, G9 from Portway, Andover, was an interesting case: the skeleton was accompanied by a pair of annular brooches and a bead necklace, but there was carbonised bread-wheat under the pelvis and a large flint placed on the chest (Cook & Dacre 1985: 25–6). Stoodley suggests that this burial was being marked out as special by these unusual practices. There are a few other skeletal males who were buried with supposedly female jewellery. A male with disc brooches was found at Burn Ground, Hampnett, Gloucestershire (Grimes 1960: 113–25); male graves were said to contain bronze brooches at Kenninghall, Norfolk (Smith 1901: 339–40); at Broughton Lodge (Nottinghamshire) a male grave was buried with a Roman and an annular brooch and sleeve-clasps (Kinsley 1993); one at Filkins, Oxon, had two annular brooches (Akerman 1857: 140–3); and an elderly male was found with a knife, a bronze pin, two annular brooches and a pair of tweezers on a ring at Lakenheath Aerodrome, Suffolk (*Medieval Archaeology* 2, 1958: 189). Roach Smith (1868: 169) mentions a tall man buried at Kempston, Bedfordshire, with a pair of long brooches, a large circular brooch, a spearhead and a shield-boss, while two weapon burials at Basset Down, Wiltshire, were reported as each having brooches and a pair of clasps (Goddard 1896). Such burials, with both weapons and jewellery, are extremely rare, and perhaps the circumstances of discovery of these last two cemeteries should cast doubt on the accuracy of these reports.

Females, too, are sometimes buried with the 'wrong' goods. In a recent study Stoodley (1997) re-examined several cases where this appeared to be the case. While the majority of these had, in fact, been wrongly assigned as males on the skeletal evidence, a group from Dover Buckland in Kent (Evison 1987: 125) were confirmed as female weapon burials. There are also several weapon burials from West Heslerton, Yorkshire (Powlesland in press), which have been skeletally sexed as female and one of these sexings has now been confirmed by DNA testing (Flaherty 1999). There may thus have been some localised communities where burial of weapons with females was an acceptable practice. Moreover, Flaherty's findings from West Heslerton suggest that burial of males with annular brooches was a common occurrence at this site (ibid.)

In the past some archaeologists have been extremely reluctant to accept such 'anomalous' sexings, where weapons are found with a skeletal female, or jewellery with a skeletal male. Both Hirst (1985: 53) and Evison (1987: 123), for example, chose to accept the grave-goods at Sewerby and Buckland respectively as the 'true' indicators of sex, despite osteological reports to the contrary. While such associations might seem obvious, the evidence above shows that we can question whether there is anything inherently male or female about these goods – perhaps in certain instances the grave-goods were being used to symbolise something other than the deceased's gender. Recently a more enlightened approach has come from the Netherlands, where one of the thirty-five inhumations from the cemetery at Oosterbeintum was identified as male on osteological grounds, but was accompanied by two brooches, forty beads and a bracelet. The excavators chose to publish this grave as a man/woman, recognising the ambiguous nature of the evidence (Knol et al. 1996: 301–2).

Animal, food and other offerings

Animals, or bits of animals, are sometimes found interred with inhumations. Examples of dog burials include Foulden (Norfolk) where a dog had its head on the knees of a male burial (Meaney 1964: 175) and Minster Lovell (Oxon), where a female had been buried with a small lapdog (Meaney 1964: 211; Prummel 1992: 175–6). Grave 1 at Loveden Hill was a multiple burial of a very elderly man with a five-year-old child in his arms and an elderly lame dog at his feet (Wilkinson 1980: 229–30). A more unusual case was the goose which was found with a burial in G180 at Castledyke, Humberside (Drinkall & Foreman 1998: 239). Rather more inhumations have been found accompanied by horses (Hills 1999a: 149; **Fig. 3.8**). Often these are 'warrior' burials, with weapon assemblages, such as that in G44 at Little Wilbraham, Cambridgeshire (Lethbridge 1938: 317), G142 at Great

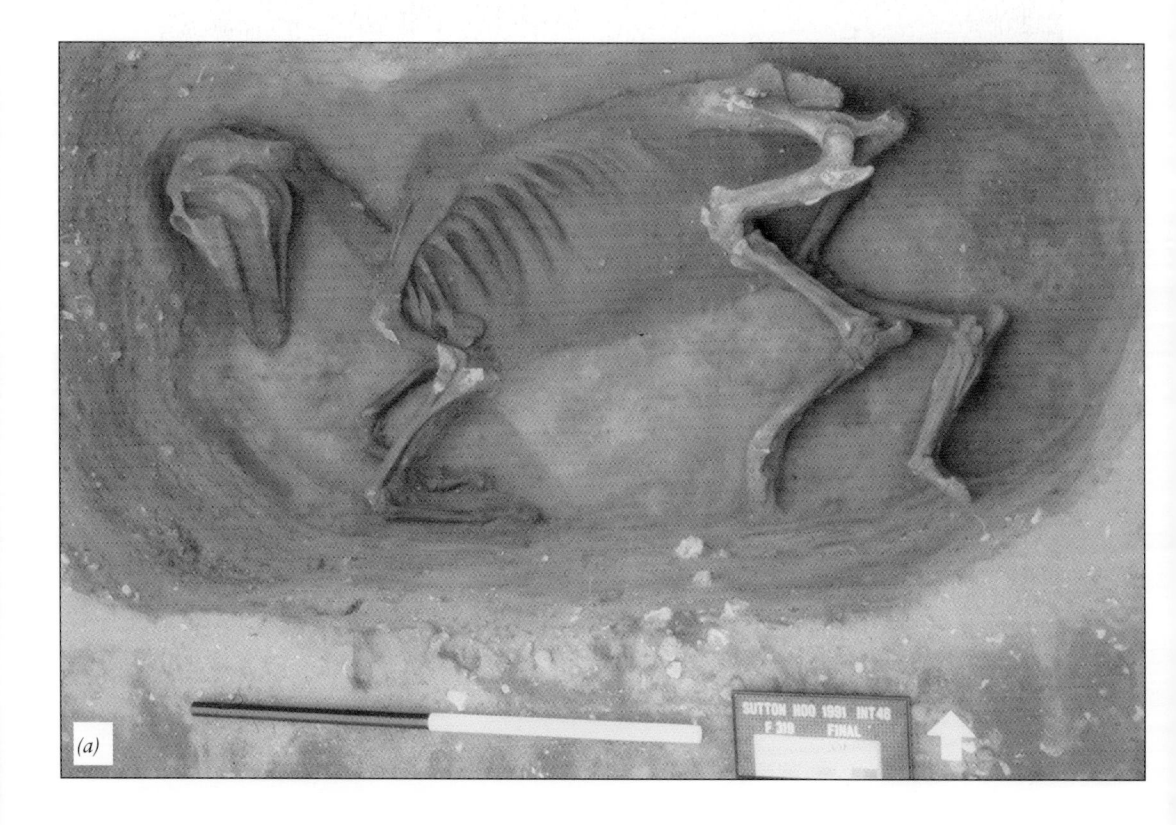

(a)

INHUMATION BURIAL PRACTICE

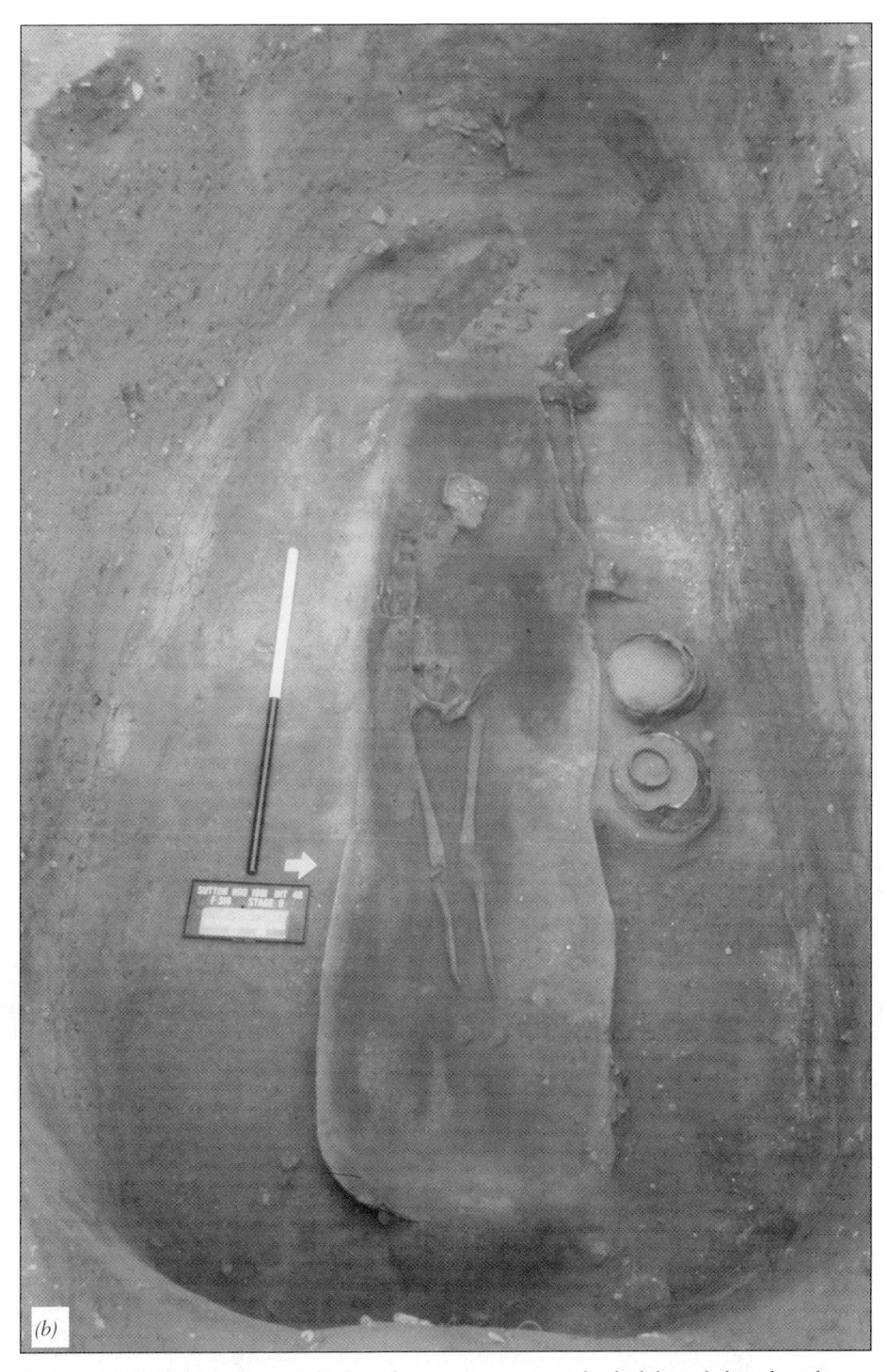

Fig. 3.8. (a) The horse-burial and (b) the rich grave it accompanied, which lay side-by-side under Mound 17 at Sutton Hoo. (Copyright Martin Carver and the Sutton Hoo Research Trust. Photo: Nigel Macbeth. Both reproduced by kind permission of Martin Carver and British Museum Press.)

Chesterford, Essex (Evison 1994a: 29), and the recent find at USAF Lakenheath (Suffolk Archaeological Service *Annual Report* for 1997–8: 13–14). Other horse-burials are given their own grave, for example at Marston St Lawrence, Northamptonshire, where the animal was buried with its headgear (Dryden 1882: 328); at West Heslerton (Yorkshire), where the horse, a five-year-old mare, had been decapitated and the head placed between its legs (Powlesland et al. 1986: 163); and probably at Great Chesterford, where a horse had been placed in a grave and its tack placed at the foot and burnt *in situ* (Evison 1994a: 29). In a more unusual case a horse's head was found in a pit in the cemetery at Springfield (Essex), complete with bridle fittings (Tyler 1996: 110–13).

O'Connor (1994) comments on the burial of a five- to six-year-old male horse found in 1991 at Sutton Hoo, buried in a parallel grave to a probably contemporary human burial. This horse would have stood about fourteen hands high, and was of a fairly heavy, muscular build (about the size of a very large pony). O'Connor also briefly surveys the evidence for horse burials (as opposed to finds of horse bones from settlement contexts), and finds that most northern and western continental examples of the fifth to tenth centuries are also of male horses, but of variable ages, though some are not complete or were disarticulated at burial. He also notes that horse bones are far more common in cremation burials (see Chapter Four).

Food remains are also found. The hanging bowl accompanying the barrow burial at Ford, Laverstock, Wiltshire, contained onions and crab-apples, as well as string (Musty

(a)

1969: 109), and is closely paralleled by the hanging bowl from Banstead Common (Surrey), also under a barrow, which contained textiles as well as what were thought to be crab-apples (Barfoot & Price Williams 1976). Bronze bowls containing nuts were found at Faversham (Roach Smith 1868: 144), and fruit as well at St Peter's Broadstairs (both Kent) (*Medieval Archaeology* 19, 1975: 223), where it accompanied a weapon burial. More unusual offerings include the unopened oysters in a grave at Sarre, Kent (Smith 1908: 357–61). Grave 26 at Portway, Hampshire, appeared to have a domestic fowl at the top of the left femur (Cook & Dacre 1985: 57), and a male was accompanied by a goose wing at Farthingdown, Surrey (Meaney 1964: 241). Eggs, too, could be food deposits; these were found in a grave at the Sibertswold-Barfreston cemetery in Kent (Faussett 1856: 135–43), and were placed in accessory vessels in a grave at Holywell Row, Suffolk (Lethbridge 1931: 33–4), and in the grave of a young man at Great Chesterford, Essex (Evison 1994a: 35). G7 at Roche Court Down, Wiltshire, was buried with the complete leg of an ox (Stone 1932: 567), and a female burial at Wigber Low, Derbyshire (**Fig. 3.9a**), with a side

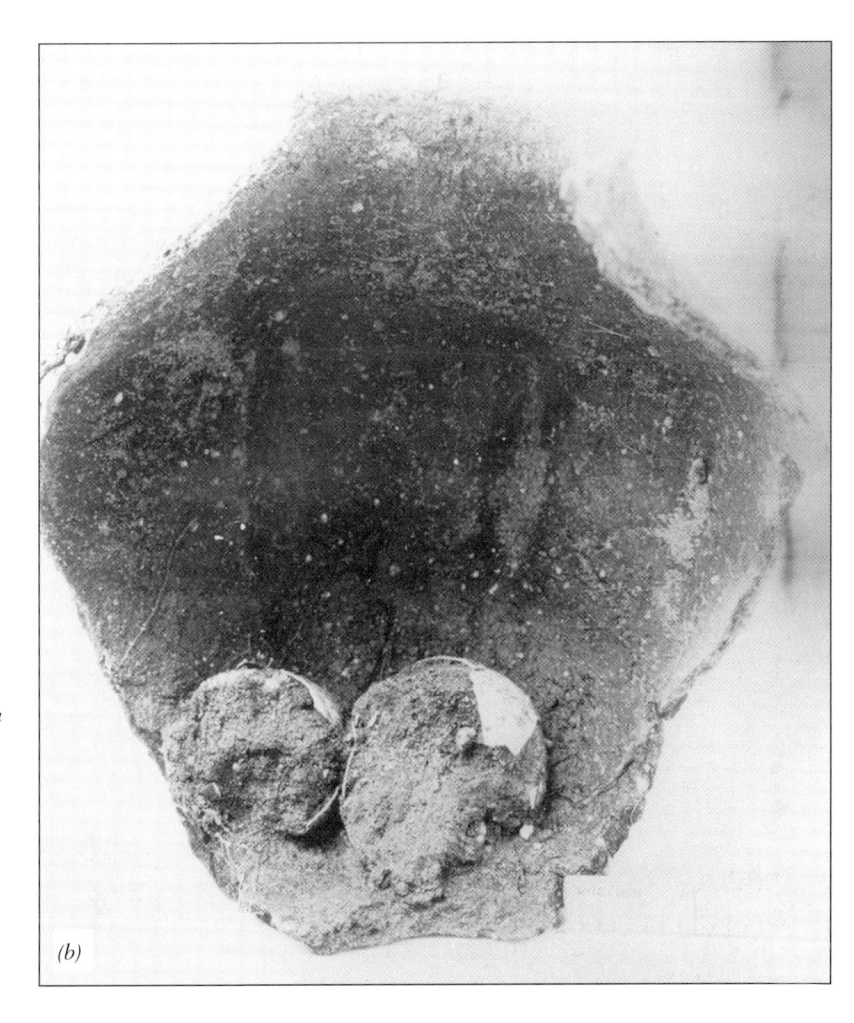

Fig. 3.9. (a) Grave 4 at Wigber Low, showing the side of beef placed on the left thigh (reproduced by kind permission of John Collis, University of Sheffield); (b) section through the 'food offering' of duck eggs in a pottery urn from G69 Holywell Row (Cambridge University Museum of Archaeology and Anthropology, Acc. No. LS44871).

of beef (Collis 1983). Joints of meat seem to be a relatively common offering, and are found particularly in later cemeteries, at least in East Yorkshire (Lucy 1998: 74). A different sort of offering may be represented by the finds of animal bone fragments inside accessory vessels with G10 and G13 at Great Chesterford – these may represent a stew given to the dead person (Evison 1994a: 35). Other food or drink remains in pottery accessory vessels are suggested by the pots from Spong Hill which had organic residues on their inner surfaces (e.g. Hills et al. 1984: 7).

Other animal remains may have had more amuletic purposes. For example, the boars' tusks found at Stowting, Kent (Smith 1908: 365–6), Offchurch, Warwickshire (Burgess 1876: 466–7), Downton, Wiltshire (Davies 1985), Great Chesterford, Essex (Evison 1994a: 35) and Kingthorpe, Yorkshire (Bateman 1861: 235), the eagle talon from Alfriston, Sussex (Griffith 1915), and suspended dog teeth from Milton-next-Sittingbourne in Kent (Smith 1908: 373–4) do not seem to fulfil any practical function. An intriguing parallel to this is the occasional discovery of human teeth, which seem to have been contained in bags round the necks of skeletons, for example in the male graves B5 and C9 at Marina Drive, Bedfordshire (Matthews 1962), with the female burial G1 at Portway, Andover, (Cook & Dacre 1985: 23–4) and in G25, G42 and possibly also G26 at Castledyke, Humberside (Drinkall & Foreman 1998: 289).

Unusual treatment of grave-goods

Some objects were treated in unusual ways. Some, for instance, have been found with runic letters and other symbols added to them. A seventh-century spearhead from Snodland, Kent, had a runic symbol on the blade in metal inlay (Evison 1956: 97–9). Grave 93 at Buckland had a spearhead with an inlaid swastika (not a runic symbol, but one which was used on various artefacts in this period) on one side of the blade (Evison 1987: 238, 314), a sword pommel from Bifrons, Kent, had an incised swastika on one side (Smith 1908: 343), and a cruciform brooch from G143 at Sleaford, Lincolnshire (**Fig. 3.10**) and a small-long brooch from an isolated burial at King's Walden, Hertfordshire, both had roughly incised swastikas on the headplate (Wilson 1992a: 119). Other artefacts have runic inscriptions. In Kent, sword pommels from Sarre and Gilton have produced enigmatic

Fig. 3.10. Cruciform brooch engraved with swastika symbol from Sleaford (after Smith 1923: fig. 18). Scale 1:1.

inscriptions, as has a sixth-century scabbard mouth-piece from Chessell Down, Isle of Wight (ibid.: 120–2). Brooches with runic inscriptions include a Kentish disc brooch from Dover Buckland (G126) with two short illegible inscriptions on the back (Evison 1987: 46–7), a square-headed brooch from Wakerley, Northamptonshire (ibid.), and a more recent example from West Heslerton, Yorkshire (Powlesland forthcoming).

Some grave-goods, especially weapons, appear to have been deliberately damaged before burial. Spears at Field Farm, Burghfield, Berkshire (Butterworth & Lobb 1992), and Woodingdean, Sussex (Welch 1983: 424–6), appear to have been treated in this way, as were shield-bosses at Barrington Edix Hill, Cambridgeshire (Malim & Hines 1998), at Snodland, Kent (Evison 1956), and at Sporle, Norfolk (Roach Smith 1852a: 234), where one shield-boss had been pierced by a spear. Weapons were broken prior to burial in three graves at Alfriston, Sussex (Griffith 1915), and 'goods' at Alvediston, Warwickshire, had similarly been broken before burial (Clay 1927: 432–7). While some of these instances may be the result of actual warfare, others appear to be 'ritual' damage, perhaps as a way of 'killing' the weapon (and preventing it being used beyond or from the grave?). G1 from Puddlehill (Bedfordshire) had a broken spear, a shield-boss and a smashed skull (Morris 1962: 66), which adds interesting overtones to this practice.

OTHER VARIATIONS IN BURIAL PRACTICE

One very unusual practice is interment of the corpse within a boat or ship (cf. Carver 1995). Definite examples of this in England are only known from Sutton Hoo and Snape, both in Suffolk (**Fig. 3.11**). This seems to date to the later sixth and seventh centuries. While burials from Caistor-on-Sea were thought to parallel this (Parker Pearson et al. 1993: 41), this site is now recognised as being a later cemetery, in which boat strakes were used as coffin lids (Rodwell 1993: 252–4) or in one case as a bier (Carver 1995: 117). Clench nails in burials at Rochester, Sarre and Osengal may represent a similar practice (see map in Carver 1990; Carver 1995: 123). Bolts found in G23 at Half Mile Ride, Margate, were likewise suggested to be the remains of a small boat which had been used as a grave cover (Perkins 1987). The boat burial at Snape was in a 3m-long log boat, accompanied by an iron knife, an iron buckle and stud, and a pair of drinking horns, and seems to date to the late sixth or early seventh century (Filmer-Sankey 1990). From the same site comes an earlier report of an 1862 excavation of the reuse of a Bronze Age mound by a larger ship burial, 46–48ft long, which contained fragments of glass from a claw beaker, two disturbed iron spearheads and a fine gold finger-ring set with a late Roman intaglio (Smith 1911: 326–9; Filmer-Sankey 1992: 41; cf. Carver 1995).

The now famous ship burials at Sutton Hoo were found under mounds 1 and 2. In mound 2 lay a wooden chamber-grave containing an elaborate weapon burial (later robbed and heavily disturbed), with a ship about 65ft long placed on top, sealing the chamber (Carver 1998: 116–21). At some point afterwards, a massive mound was constructed from soil and turves, standing 13ft high. This was not, however, as spectacular a burial, or a mound, as mound 1, the miraculously undisturbed grave which was excavated on the eve of the Second World War, in May, June and July 1939. In this case the whole ship, all 90ft of it, was buried below ground, and a wooden burial chamber constructed amidships (ibid.:

Fig. 3.11. The original excavation of the boat under mound 1 at Sutton Hoo. (Reproduced by kind permission of Martin Carver.)

121); when excavated, this was found to contain an extraordinary grave-good assemblage, consisting of garments, vessels, drinking bottles and horns, weapons, a baldric and shoulder-clasps, and helmet, as well as an iron standard and a lyre (Bruce-Mitford 1975; 1978; 1983). The whole was eventually covered by a mound several metres high. Carver (1995: 121) has argued that this rare use of ship burial represents a 'symbolic vocabulary' shared by the seventh-century peoples around the North Sea, with this short-lived rite enacted as a protest against the encroaching tide of Christianity.

Other structures found in burials include the use of a bed on which the corpse was placed. This seems to be a late seventh-century feature, as examples have been found from the Cambridgeshire cemeteries at Barrington Edix Hill, in graves 18 and 60 (Malim & Hines 1998: 261–8), at Cherry Hinton (G4) (Kennett 1973: 102) and at Shudy Camps (G29) (Lethbridge 1936), while further examples are known from Ixworth, Suffolk, and a small group in Wiltshire including the isolated burial at Swallowcliffe Down (Speake 1989: 98–102). At the latter site, a primary Bronze Age burial in a barrow had been destroyed to make way for the probable adult female in a large grave filled with Gault clay and the remains of the bed furniture, along with two buckets, an iron pan, a barrel, a wooden casket containing a bronze sprinkler, a silver spoon, four silver brooches, a pair of knives, two beads and a comb, a satchel, and two glass palm cups, suggesting a high status for this grave, and perhaps thus for the use of a bed (ibid.: 110). Seven of the eleven known examples are of females, with only one, that from Lapwing Hill, being a definite male (Malim & Hines 1998: 268).

Burials could also be covered over with organic materials, which though not often detectable are sometimes preserved in contact with metalwork. At Wallud's Bank, Luton (Austin 1928: 177–8), and Roxby, Lincolnshire (*Medieval Archaeology* 42, 1998: 144), skeletons were noted as being covered with tree branches, while at Field Farm, Burghfield, G145 contained carbonised plant remains which were thought to represent burnt turves in the grave (Butterworth & Lobb 1992). The young man in the primary barrow burial at Roche Court Down in Wiltshire was also covered over with a thin layer of turf, before his grave was capped by white chalk rubble and sealed with a large quantity of flint nodules (Stone 1932: 578). G5 at Woodingdean, Sussex, which contained a heavily built elderly man with buckle, knife and spearhead, was lined with cut grass or hay (*Medieval Archaeology* 3, 1959: 300), and this was paralleled by G19 from Monkton, Kent, which was either covered or lined with grass (Hawkes & Hogarth 1974), and G19 from Sewerby, Yorkshire, which was covered with grass or plant stems (Hirst 1985: 31, who also cites graves from Mucking, Essex, as covered or lined with bracken and moss). Two graves at Berinsfield, Oxon, were associated with similar organic coverings: G104 was found to have the grave lined with charred oak logs, while G102 was partly covered by the remains of decayed rushes – perhaps a woven mat (Boyle et al. 1995: 121). At Chelmorton, Derbyshire, the remains of an animal skin were found along the right side of a barrow burial with a knife (Bateman 1861: 51), while graves 29 and 32 at Leighton Buzzard were covered with coarse cloth, and graves 160 and 163 at Sleaford, Lincolnshire, and G24 at Spong Hill may have been covered with leather (Brush 1993: 66).

The grave itself is sometimes elaborated. G27 at Wheatley (Oxon) had a bed of crushed sea-shells on the base of the grave (Kenward 1885), G3 at Haddenham (Cambridgeshire) similarly contained a bed of pebbles (Robinson & Duhig 1993: 15), while at Biscot Mill, Luton (Bedfordshire), G11, a powerfully built adult male with a pot and an iron arrowhead, had red clay forming the grave fill which had been transported from two hundred yards away (Hagen 1971: 23).

VARIATIONS IN GRAVE STRUCTURE

Graves can differ in a number of ways. They can vary widely in size, from a shallow scoop in the ground to a large pit with regular sides over 2m long and over 1m deep. They can

THE ANGLO-SAXON WAY OF DEATH

GRAVE STRUCTURAL FEATURES: Integral

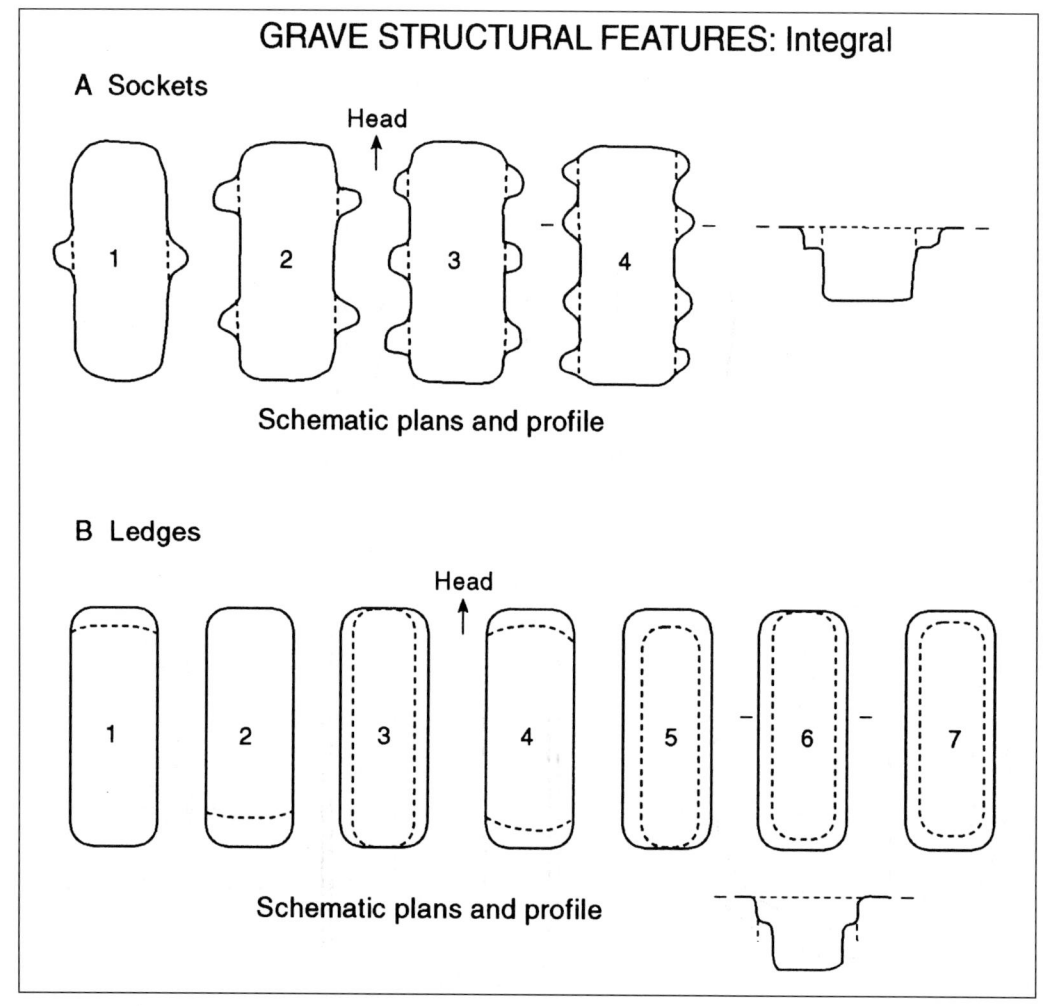

A Sockets

Schematic plans and profile

B Ledges

Schematic plans and profile

Fig. 3.12. (Above and right) The various types of grave structure (after Hogarth 1974: figs 7 and 8).

have barrows raised over them, or other types of surface feature or marker. They can also be elaborated with the use of external and internal structures, which are a particular feature of later cemeteries (**Fig. 3.12**). Hogarth (1974) put forward a classification of possible grave structures, with types I a–d comprising graves with sockets, ledges and slots internal to the grave, types II a–d being graves with external post-holes, penannular or fully circular ditches, or 'kerb-slots' around the grave, and types III a–b having a stone-lining or flints placed in the grave. Looking at the incidence and dating of these features in the cemeteries of Finglesham, St Peter's Broadstairs and Bradstow School in Kent, he argued that penannular ditches and other external features (i.e. type II structures, excepting post-holes) should be seen as later seventh century, rather than earlier (ibid.: 118–19), which would seem to be supported by the fact that at Broadstairs and

INHUMATION BURIAL PRACTICE

GRAVE STRUCTURAL FEATURES   External

a Post-holes   b Penannular ditches   a/b

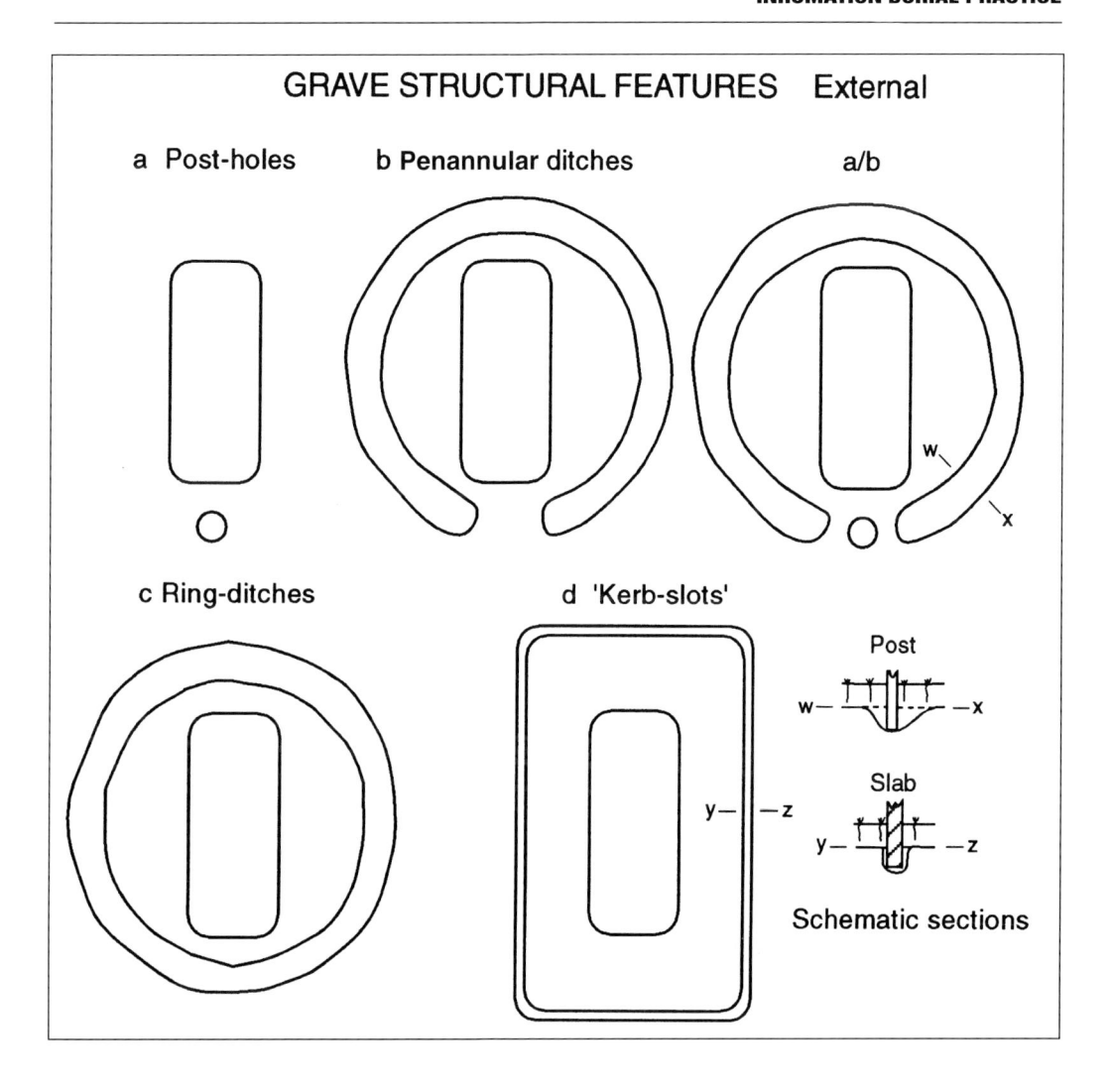

c Ring-ditches   d 'Kerb-slots'

Post

Slab

Schematic sections

Finglesham these ditched features were seen to be clustered, and were at or near the perimeters of these cemeteries (**Fig. 3.13**), suggesting their use late in the life of the site (Wilson 1992a: 60). At St Peter's Broadstairs the penannular ditches around some of the graves may have contained palisades (*Medieval Archaeology* 15, 1971: 128). Hills (1977a) demonstrates that while these external structures in east Kent are indeed probably later seventh century, earlier examples are known from East Anglia. Inhumations 31 and 32 from Spong Hill, for example, were placed inside a ring-ditch with an external diameter of 10m, with an oval pit or post-hole between them, beyond the west end of the graves (Hills et al. 1984: 80–2). They are now also known from Orsett, Springfield and Stifford Clays (all in Essex) where they may have surrounded cremations (Tyler 1996: 108–13), from Morningthorpe, Norfolk, where they surrounded at least two inhumations (*Medieval*

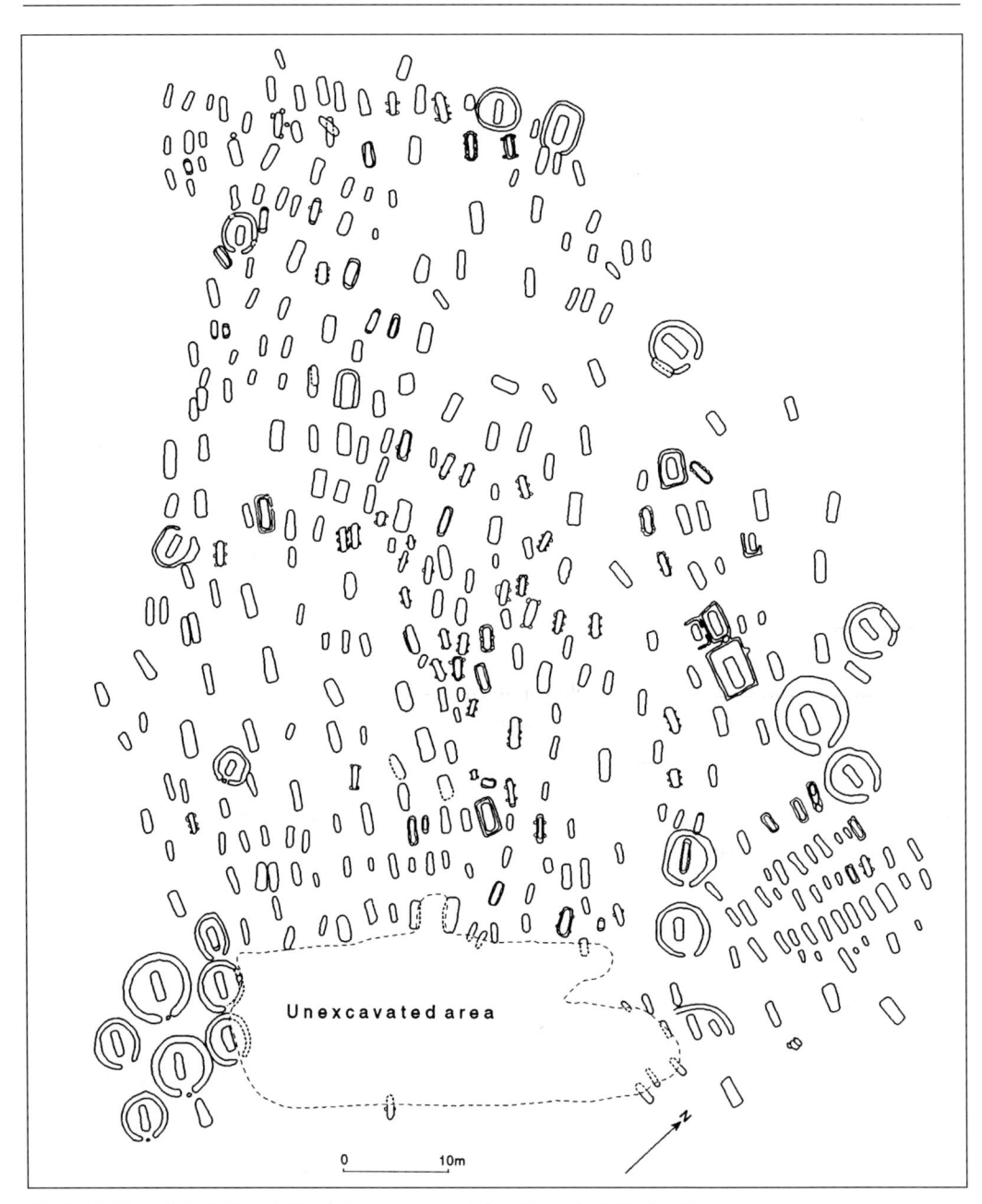

Fig. 3.13. Plan of the St Peter's Broadstairs cemetery (after Hogarth 1974: fig. 4).

Archaeology 20, 1976: 167), and from Butler's Field, Lechlade, where one surrounded an adult female inhumation (Boyle et al. 1998: 38). In addition, a rectangular enclosure around three of the inhumation burials at Westhampnett in Sussex was also probably of the later seventh century (Fitzpatrick 1997: 294).

Shepherd (1979: 49) identified a pattern of ring-ditches associated with flat graves in the mid- to later sixth century being replaced in the early seventh partly by barrow cemeteries (where small mounds are found erected over the majority of burials within a cemetery) and partly by larger barrows erected over a single individual. On the geographical locations of these larger barrows, he noted how there were hardly any in the south-east of England, but that those with a diameter of between 7.5 and 30m were concentrated in Derbyshire and Wiltshire. He suggested that this represented a social difference, with the flat and barrow cemeteries being structured by age and sex, whereas the isolated burial represented a person of superordinate rank (ibid.: 67–70).

Some large barrow burials, like those from Sutton Hoo discussed above, have indeed been found to contain extremely elaborate goods, which have led to them often being described as 'princely' burials. The grave at Taplow (Buckinghamshire), for instance, was found on its excavation in October 1883 to have a central grave 20ft down from the summit (6ft below the original ground level). Fragmentary human bones indicated a skeleton with the head to the east, with an elaborate gold and garnet buckle which seemed to have fastened a gold braid and wool garment. Around the body lay a selection of vessels and weapons, including two spearheads, a shield-boss, vessels such as a bucket, a bronze bowl and a small drinking horn with silver-gilt bands and terminals, and a large tub containing, among other items, two glass tumblers, two large and one smaller drinking horns (Burgess 1886: 331–5; Webster 1992). The grave at Broomfield in Essex (Smith 1903: 320–6) contained a male skeleton with a sword in a wooden sheath, gold and garnet items that probably formed the pommel, a spear, a knife, a bronze pan which contained part of a cow's horn, two dark blue glass vessels and two wooden cups; resting on top of a mass of folded woollen fabric were two wooden buckets, an iron lamp, an iron cauldron and the coffin. The significance of this development in burial furnishing and construction will be discussed in Chapter Seven.

Sometimes burials are found to have stones, either as grave covers or forming a lining to the grave. At Loveden Hill, Lincolnshire, a double inhumation burial had been covered by the upper part of a Roman column (*Medieval Archaeology* 3, 1959: 297). One very rare instance is of a young person who was interred in a coffin of barnack stone at West Stow, Suffolk (Smith 1911: 338–40). Some of the inhumations at Kempston (Bedfordshire) were reported as having limestone slabs placed over them (Smith 1904: 176–84; Roach Smith 1868: 170–1), while many other sites produce reports of stone slabs forming a grave-lining. At Portway, Andover, several of the burials had large flints placed around the inside of the grave (Cook & Dacre 1985: 54), and this practice was also seen at the nearby site of Winterbourne Gunner, Wiltshire (Musty & Stratton 1964). While this may have had ritual significance, Evison (1987: 18) prefers a more pragmatic explanation for its occurrence at Dover Buckland; she sees the flints as adding to the volume of the grave fill, and thus producing a higher mound as a more distinctive marker on back-filling. At Great Chesterford, Essex, however, she sees it filling a different function, firming up the edges of grave pits where they had been dug into softer soil (Evison 1994a: 28).

Other 'external' features such as four-post structures have now been identified in recent excavations at Osengal and St Peter's Broadstairs, Kent (Down & Welch 1990: 15;

Medieval Archaeology 15, 1971: 128). The cemetery at Apple Down, Sussex, produced many of these four-post (and also single examples of five-post and six-post) structures, mainly over cremations, where they were interpreted as 'the remains of miniature houses to commemorate the dead' (Down & Welch 1990: 29). Examples found associated with inhumations may indicate places where inhumations have either been dug through a cremation structure or had a canopy erected over them (ibid.: 15). A similar canopy structure could be argued for at Morningthorpe, where G148, a possible double burial, had a post-hole at each corner of the grave (Green et al. 1987: 76–7; Wilson 1992a: 53).

A wooden chamber-grave has been identified at Selmeston, Sussex (Welch 1983: 389–90), and large chamber-graves at both the Boss Hall and Buttermarket cemeteries at Ipswich, Suffolk (*Medieval Archaeology* 34, 1990: 211; *Medieval Archaeology* 33, 1989: 209). Evidence from Spong Hill inhumation 40 shows that the body was housed inside a rectangular wooden chamber (with the wood showing in the grave pit as dense black staining), roofed with turf and situated inside a ring-ditch 10m in diameter, which probably once surrounded a mound (Hills 1999b: 20). Similar structures may have been seen (though not recognised) in the seventh-century burials at Taplow, Broomfield and Asthall (Hills 1977a: 172). These dense layers of decayed wood may be what Meaney (1964: 16–17) was misinterpreting as 'half-cremations'. Reynolds (1976) argued, on the basis of some post-burial movement identified in some of the graves at Empingham, that some of the graves had been covered with a form of timber planking, on top of which earth had been piled. The decay of this timber had caused the overlying earth to collapse on to the also decaying skeleton, causing the observed dislocations. More common is the use of wooden coffins or chambers for the interment of the dead. While the practice increased through the seventh century, it is found in earlier sites too. Also seen in earlier cemeteries is the use of biers or open 'coffins' for the burial of the dead, although in practice it is often difficult to distinguish between different types of enclosing wooden structure and other wooden features, such as the timber lining along the sides of the grave (Cook & Dacre 1985: 55). Other graves may have been marked by single posts. This is suggested for G33 at Portway, Andover, where a post-hole was found near the head of the grave (ibid.: 53), and may, if it was a widespread practice, partly account for the relative rarity of overlapping or intercutting graves in these cemeteries.

Another feature of the later Kentish cemeteries is that some graves seem to have been robbed in antiquity, a practice which is seen at Osengal (*Medieval Archaeology* 26, 1982: 189–90) and Sarre (Perkins 1991; 1992), as well as at Broadstairs (*Medieval Archaeology* 15, 1971: 128), where it seems to have taken place on a large scale, and at Margate, where the robbing was thought to have taken place within living memory of the burials being made (Perkins 1987: 231). Other, earlier, graves may have been deliberately left empty. G8 at Portway, Andover, was entirely empty, while G34 at the same site had a buckle and knife but no body. While this would not be unusual on a sandy site, where the soil conditions do not favour skeletal preservation, Portway is on chalk, and has otherwise good bone preservation. That G23 contained a skull, a knife, beads but no body suggests a practice perhaps peculiar to a single community (Cook & Dacre 1985: 25, 32). Grave 6 at East Shefford contained only animal remains (Peake & Horton 1915), perhaps suggesting a similar symbolic deposit.

INTERPRETING VARIATIONS IN BURIAL RITES

This chapter has, I hope, given an idea of the vast range of variation which is found in inhumations in eastern Britain from the fifth to the seventh centuries AD. Information can be derived from skeletal material as well as from artefactual and environmental evidence, and together these sources can be used to give a contextual and detailed picture of the ways in which individuals were buried during this period, and perhaps some ideas as to why various practices were employed. Detailed analyses, often using computing technology and statistical testing to shed light on the patterning within the data, are helping to offer new interpretations of the role of the burial rite within its contemporary society. By showing a complex, highly structured burial rite, it is gradually being accepted that people in this period did not blindly follow rules in their burials; there were different practices and grave-goods available, and the mourners made a deliberate selection of those that were felt most appropriate for the person being buried by that community. The next chapter will deal with cremation burials in a similar way, looking at the types of information which can be justifiably derived from the cremation burial rite, which brings with it its own particular problems and possibilities of interpretation.

Four

Cremation Burial Practice

Introduction

Cremation is a very different form of burial ritual from inhumation. In burning the body (and often associated goods) the physical appearance of the deceased is destroyed, and the goods often become virtually unrecognisable. This chapter will look at the information which can be gained from the study of cremation burials, and the patterning and variation within this burial rite as it is currently understood. Until quite recently, archaeologists did not believe that any useful evidence could be gained from the study of cremated human bone, an attitude which very often led to the picking out of any obvious grave-goods from the urn, and then the disposal of the bones (Hills 1980: 197). In this process minor grave-goods and those made from bone or antler were often discarded as well. Recent work, especially by McKinley in her studies of the cremated material from Spong Hill in Norfolk, where around 2,300 cremations and 57 inhumations were excavated between 1968 and 1981, has, however, shown that these skeletal remains (human and animal) *can* be interpreted, and much useful data gleaned from them (McKinley 1994a; 1994b).

The Cremation Process

In technical terms, cremation is the process of dehydration and oxidation of the organic components of the body (i.e. ridding the body of water and the non-mineral components such as body tissue, fat and internal organs). As organic components make up an average of 34.2 per cent of bodyweight, and water a further 57.1 per cent, the remaining mineral component after cremation (the 'ashes') represents only 5.7 per cent of initial bodyweight – about 2.5–3kg (McKinley 1994b). Cremated bone is still recognisable as human – in modern crematoria the skeleton is still largely visible after cremation, although quite fragmented (McKinley 1994a: 75); the remains which are today handed back to the relatives have been deliberately crushed into powder, to avoid offending sensibilities. The colour of the cremated bone depends on the degree of oxidisation, ranging from grey to black/blue to white (where oxidisation is complete, and the organic remains have been totally destroyed). Successful cremations require temperature and fuel, as well as oxygen (ibid.: 77). The range of temperature in Anglo-Saxon cremations seems to have been from 400 degrees Celsius up to a possible maximum of 1,200 degrees, although this can be influenced by the physical makeup of the person being cremated: individuals with more body fat cremate more easily as the body fat itself is used as fuel (ibid.: 72, 84).

CREMATION BURIAL PRACTICE

While Calvin Wells (1960) thought that cremations at Illington had taken place with the body laid out on the ground surface, covered by the pyre (owing to the tips of shoulder-blades often not being fully cremated, and some distortion of the long-bones, which he saw as the result of the pyre collapsing on top of the bones), McKinley (1994a: 83) disagrees, arguing that this technique would have led to incomplete cremation, as there would not have been enough oxygen to burn the body, being smothered by the pyre. Rather, she thinks that Anglo-Saxon funeral pyres probably consisted of a criss-cross framework of large timbers infilled with brushwood, possibly with a shallow pit underneath to provide an under-pyre draught, on top of which the body was laid out, probably extended on the back (ibid.: 80; **Fig. 4.1**). She points out that extremities, such as feet and hands, are often found not to be fully cremated, as these would have been away from the centre of the heat (especially if the pyre was slightly too small for the person being cremated), and they are also harder to cremate, as they have less fat on them. Judging by the occasional finds of glass and metal deriving from dress ornaments which are fused on to the bones, the body seems to have remained on top of the pyre for some length of time before its eventual collapse (ibid.: 83–4).

The weight of bone recovered from the cremation urns at Spong Hill ranged from 117.2g to 3,105.1g (where the remains represented a single adult with no animal bone present). While the top end of this range is close to the 2,500–3,000g which one would expect from an adult cremation of either sex, most cremations must represent only partial collection of the remains from the pyre (McKinley 1994a: 11, 72). As the Spong Hill cremated bone appeared to be very clean, with very little pyre debris (charcoal, from the burnt wood, was only found in 131 urns, for example), this collection of bone seemed quite deliberate and careful, and may even have involved cleaning the bones (ibid.: 82, 85).

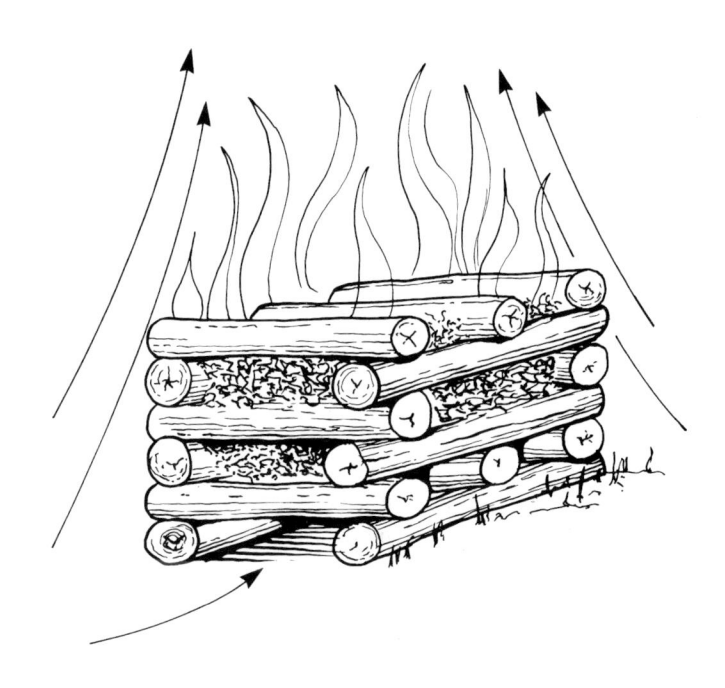

Fig. 4.1. Tentative reconstruction of a cremation pyre (after McKinley 1994a: fig. 19).

105

Cremation Pyres

Surprisingly few pyre sites have been excavated in early Anglo-Saxon cemeteries. Even the complete excavation of the site at Spong Hill revealed no evidence for where the cremations had actually taken place, leading to suggestions that cremation had taken place off-site and the filled urns then brought to the cemetery, perhaps from quite a long distance (McKinley 1994a: 82). The remains of possible pyres have been noted under mounds at Chavenage (Gloucestershire) and Asthall (Oxon), and another was recently identified at Snape, Suffolk (Carnegie & Filmer-Sankey 1993). Little Wilbraham, Cambridgeshire, is also reported to have had a pyre area (Lethbridge & Carter 1928), and Sancton in Yorkshire had an area of scorched clay, burnt bone and charcoal (Myres & Southern 1973: 10). A letter dated 13 January 1848 recording the levelling of a mound in a field at Chavenage by a labourer reported that a yard and a half below the surface many large flag-stones, placed horizontally over several square yards, were met with, which exhibited evident marks of cremation (Wright 1849: 50–4). The abundance of wood-ash, half-burned human bones and black earth formed a layer up to 4–5in deep. No cremation urns were noted here, however, only inhumation graves in stone cists, and this site could conceivably represent the reuse of a prehistoric barrow by an Anglo-Saxon inhumation cemetery. A more convincing case was given by excavations between 1923 and 1924 of the barrow at Asthall which involved sinking a shaft through the centre, whereupon a clay floor was found beneath a burnt layer with the probable remains of a pyre, including visible posts, comprising human and animal bones, and fragments of bronze, silver, bone and pottery, which seemed to represent a set of gaming pieces and die, three pottery vessels (one wheel-made and Merovingian), fragments of a silver vessel, two copper alloy vessels (one being a cast Byzantine bowl), the ivory inlay of a possible casket, and a Style II pendant object, which would date this find to the first half of the seventh century (Leeds 1924; Dickinson & Speake 1992). A recently excavated feature at the mixed inhumation and cremation cemetery at Snape, Suffolk, consisted of a spread of burnt bone, fragmentary pottery vessels and burnt grave-goods, which might also represent the remains of a cremation pyre (Filmer-Sankey 1992: 48–9).

The cemetery at Liebenau in Germany has produced some very well-preserved examples of cremation pyres, which give an idea of what might be found in future. Areas with a diameter of 2–3m were blackened by charcoal and found to be strewn with cremated bones and a remarkable quantity of grave-goods (Genrich 1981: 59). Analysis of these pyres showed that whole series of pots were broken during the cremation rite, with some of the sherds falling into the pyre and being reburnt (as was suggested for some of the Spong Hill sherds, described below). Afterwards, some of the grave-goods, the broken pottery sherds and burnt bones were selected and buried in cremation pits, cremation heaps or urns within the funeral pyre or nearby (ibid.: 59–60).

Interpreting Cremated Skeletal Remains (Fig. 4.2)

The process of cremation shrinks and deforms bone, and makes it more liable to fragmentation, especially if the remains are then moved or if, for example, the pyre collapses (McKinley 1994b). Cremated remains can, however, sometimes be aged and

Fig. 4.2. An urn from Spong Hill with cremated remains visible inside (including a comb). (Norfolk Aerial Photography Library. Copyright Norfolk Museums Service, BNX7. Photographer Dave Wicks.)

sexed, as this shrinkage and breakage happens in predictable ways (McKinley 1994a: 11). For immature remains, tooth development can be used in the same way as with inhumed material, as can evidence for the fusion of the iliac crest (the top rim of the pelvis). Similarly, cremated remains sometimes show the degenerative changes which can be used to help age adult remains (ibid.: 16). Sexing cremated remains can be difficult, owing to fragmentation of the bones, but if, for example, the remains of the angle of the sciatic notch are preserved, or of the significant skull features, and several features agree with each other, then an identification can be made (ibid.: 19–20). Evidence for palaeopathological changes can also occasionally be detected on cremated bone. Conditions seen in the Spong Hill evidence, for example, include tooth loss, joint diseases such as osteoarthritis, and bone lesions as a reaction to infection (ibid.: 106–18).

Sometimes multiple cremations are identified, with the remains of more than one person represented in one urn. Most dual cremations at Spong Hill seemed to be of an adult with an immature individual. In addition, all the sexed adult remains which were accompanied by a very young child, or a even foetus, were female, suggesting complications in childbirth leading to the death of mother and child (McKinley 1994a: 100–1). Similarly, at Newark, the seven certain double cremations all contained burials of an infant or child with an older person (Kinsley 1989: 23). The difficulties of distinguishing two adults within one cremation should, however, be pointed out, as it is much easier to distinguish a mature from an immature skeleton than it would be to distinguish, for example, two adult females (unless the remains of, for example, two left brow-ridges were seen to be present, which would necessarily indicate two separate individuals). Problems of bone collection from the pyre and recovery by archaeologists may also serve to under-represent this practice, as young bones, especially of infants, are small and delicate – they may not have been spotted on the pyre by the mourners (especially if only partial collection of any adult remains was taking place), and they may also be missed by archaeologists, in particular if the cremation urn has been disturbed, scattering the contents, or if the burial was unurned to begin with.

Cremation Grave-goods

A reasonably high proportion of cremations are found to be associated with pyre- or grave-goods (items either placed on the pyre with the body, or added later to the cremation urn unburnt – **Fig. 4.3**). About 70 per cent of the cremations from Spong Hill, for example, contained such goods (Hills 1999b: 17). In an extensive study of the cremation burial rite, Richards (1987: 109) identified two different classes of artefacts associated with cremation burials: those that were rare, occurring in low proportions on a limited number of sites, and those that appeared to be more common equipment. Grave-goods commonly associated with cremations include brooches, glass beads and vessels, spindle-whorls, tweezers, shears and combs.

Brooches found at Spong Hill comprised mainly cruciform types, as well as small numbers of small-long, applied, supporting-arm, saucer, equal-armed, penannular and annular examples (Hills 1977b: 24; Hills et al. 1987: 41; Hills et al. 1994: 18). A more restricted range was seen at Newark, with just one applied brooch, two or perhaps three small-longs and four cruciform brooches (Kinsley 1989). In general, long brooches seem more common than round brooch forms in cremations.

Glass beads were found in many cremations at Spong Hill, although they were often melted to a point where shape and colour was difficult to distinguish. Although most beads from this site were monochrome, polychrome beads and a possible millefiori bead were also found (Hills 1977b: 28). Glass vessels could also be included as cremation grave-goods, for example the cone beaker in pot E19 from Caistor-by-Norwich (Myres & Green 1973), the bowl found in a plain pot from Lackford (Harden 1956: 134) and a glass cone beaker found with an urn at Loveden Hill (Meaney 1964: 159). At Spong Hill, fragments of around a hundred glass vessels were found, with the blue claw-beaker in C2921 probably used to contain the burial itself (Evison 1994b: 30; Hills et al. 1994: 18).

Tweezers and shears can be made of bronze or iron, and were often combined into 'toilet-sets' with combs and sometimes single blades, razors and 'ear-scoops' (often a twisted rod with a small rounded scoop at the end). These are sometimes suspended from rings, presumably designed to be hung from a belt. Some of these may have been made specifically for the burial context, as the tweezers and shears are often miniatures, and some did not appear to have had cutting edges (Hills 1977b: 23). Around 350 cremations

Fig. 4.3. (a) Heat-damaged small-long brooch from burial 3095 at Spong Hill (Norfolk Aerial Photography Library. Copyright Norfolk Museums Service, EYU8. Photographer Dave Wicks); (b) heat-damaged wrist-clasp from burial 2765 at Spong Hill (Norfolk Aerial Photography Library. Copyright Norfolk Museums Service, CNM13. Photographer Dave Wicks.) Scale (a) 1:1; (b) 2:1.

at Spong Hill contained bone combs, of which seven were miniature versions made from a single piece of bone into which rudimentary teeth were cut (C. Hills pers. comm.). The others were all made from three layers of bone, with the tooth-plate riveted between upper and lower plates. Usually these combs were single-sided, but occasional examples were seen of combs with two rows of teeth. Types found included triangular and barred examples, which are sometimes found housed in the remains of cases. Combs are sometimes decorated, often with simple ring and dot designs, or groupings of incised lines (Hills 1977b: 28–9). An interesting feature was seen at Newark, where the combs, although largely unburnt, were in a rather fragmentary state, with ends especially being represented, suggesting that they had been deliberately selected for burial (Kinsley 1989: 19).

Playing pieces are also a reasonably common find from cremations – fifty-nine cremations at Spong Hill contained these small bone plano-convex counters (C. Hills pers. comm.). At Caistor-by-Norwich one burial contained thirty-three gaming pieces and over thirty-six astralagi (ankle-bones) of sheep and roe deer, of which one had a runic inscription (Myres & Green 1973: 98–100), while in a pair of adult cremations at Loveden Hill one urn contained sixteen fragments of sheep astralagi, and the other fourteen (Wilkinson 1980: 28). At Cold Eaton, Derbyshire, an unurned deposit of cremated human bone was found to be the primary burial under an earthen barrow, and was accompanied by twenty-eight bone playing pieces, as well as by parts of two bone combs and some fragments of iron (Bateman 1861: 179–81). While most of these associated goods were cremated along with the body, combs and toilet-sets were often found unburnt. Although combs may have been used in the hair, and so may have fallen off the pyre at an early stage in the cremation, toilet-sets seem to have been added to the urn as grave-goods (McKinley 1994a: 91).

Other, rarer, finds at Spong Hill include occasional occurrences of sleeve-clasps and sword–fittings, a bell with clapper in C1281, bone casket fittings in C1645, a silver pendant in C1743, girdle-hangers in C2346 and C2758, and a small iron needle in a bone case in C1664 (Hills 1977b: 26; Hills & Penn 1981: 22; Hills et al. 1987: 12; Hills et al. 1994: 18). One outstanding burial from the site, C2376, contained a silver finger-ring, silver-bound iron rings from a necklace, a chip-carved equal-arm brooch and a pair of saucer brooches, as well as more common goods such as a comb and beads (Hills et al. 1987: 12). Rare finds are seen at other sites, too. In 1831 a small bronze ewer, on three legs with two handles, was found inside a cremation urn from Markshall, Norfolk (Clarke 1940: 225).

Although razors are a relatively common find at Spong Hill, they are rare elsewhere. Other differences among rarer goods were also detected between sites by Richards (1987: 109): the use of coral and cowry shells at Elsham, for example, and iron nails at Caistor and Newark. Among the more common goods, relative proportions also differed between sites. At Caistor, for instance, the high proportion of cremations with miniature toilet implements and the relative scarcity of glass objects and fragments contrasted with the picture seen from sites such as Elsham and Newark, which both had poor representation of miniatures but high numbers of combs, ivory fragments and spindle-whorls (ibid.: 110–11). Other cremation cemeteries, such as Mucking and South Elkington, had relative scarcity of all types of grave-goods (ibid.). Oddly, these similarities do not seem to bear much relation to geographical proximity, as might be expected.

One interesting feature is the occasional discovery of reburnt pottery sherds, seen in a few cremations at Portway (Cook & Dacre 1985: 57), as well as at major cremation cemeteries such as Spong Hill, suggesting the addition of accessory vessels to the pyre, in the same way that inhumations are sometimes provided with them. This interpretation is supported by the discovery of cereal grains in nine urns, and nutshell fragments in another, suggesting food offerings within such urns, although these may have been accidental inclusions (McKinley 1994a: 91–2). Some of the urns from Markshall in Norfolk were also found to contain wheat grains (Clarke 1940: 225). Incidentally, while Richards (1987: 83) cites Spong Hill C2022 as an example of a complete accessory vessel placed inside a cremation urn, Hills & Penn (1981: 49) see it as a piece of a plain pot, which may have been used as a lid (and, indeed, was reconstructed as having been upside down in the top of the urn).

Interesting differences are seen in the nature and range of goods which are found included with cremations as opposed to those with inhumations. In an initial study of the grave-goods from Spong Hill, Brush (1988) found that while two-thirds of the inhumations contained clearly gender-linked items such as jewellery and weapons, cremations presented a very different picture. Jewellery and weapons were found with cremations but they were very rare. While beads were highly correlated with female graves (identified from their skeletons), they were also found with males, and the only sword found with sexable remains was with a female. Most artefacts, such as combs, spindle-whorls and knives, were found with both sexes, leading Brush to suggest that sex/gender had played only a minor role in structuring the provision of grave-goods: 'The act of cremation itself may be seen as gender and sex destroying while inhumation may be seen as gender preserving' (ibid.: 83). Later studies of the whole assemblage from Spong Hill, which included all the sexing and ageing data, largely concurred with these results, but added some new information (McKinley 1994a: 86–91, citing C. Hills pers. comm.). Most brooches and groups of more than ten beads were associated with females, while all five ear-scoops from sexed graves were with males. Most goods, however, were not exclusively associated with one sex rather than another, though some showed strong tendencies. Items found with more females than males included spindle-whorls, fragments of bronze, ivory and crystal, and bone and antler rings. Those found with more males than females comprised tweezers, shears and razors (often miniature versions), knives, blades, antler or bone beads and worked antler and bone objects. No difference in terms of sex could, however, be seen in the provisioning of a whole range of other items such as bowls, buckets, glass vessels, playing pieces, combs and iron rings.

As part of his wider study of cremation urns Richards (1987: 126–29) also looked to see which grave-goods were associated with sexed remains. To his surprise, he found very few, with just ivory (possibly representing bag handles) being significantly associated with females, and the small numbers of miniature iron shears and tweezers being associated with males. No items were exclusively found with males or females, something which contrasts strongly with the picture from inhumation burials, where the grave-goods such as jewellery and weaponry appear to be strongly sex-linked. Spong Hill may thus be unusual in its (still fairly low) degree of sex association of artefacts with cremations. The detail of the Spong Hill associations has been recently elaborated on by Ravn (1998: 226–8), who used correspondence analysis to study these assemblages. He was able to distinguish a single female assemblage, characterised by coins, glass beads, ivory, spindlewhorls, silver pendants, crystal and amber, from three distinct male assemblages. The first of these consisted solely of miniature artefacts, the second of shears, playing pieces, glass vessels, horse and sheep bones (this assemblage was linked with adult males), and the third of honestones, bronze tweezers, bone beads and weapons. Ravn (1998: 228) thus argues for internal divisions being marked among the males at this site, and disagrees with Brush (1988) about cremation being gender-destroying. He sees it as destroying the body, but this is compensated for by the provision of symbolically loaded grave gifts (Ravn 1998: 251–2).

Age may also have played a part in the provisioning of goods. In total, 53 per cent of the infant cremations at Spong Hill had goods. These largely resembled the types associated with females, with the exception of sets of miniatures, including the only three miniature spearheads or arrowheads, which were all found with infants (McKinley 1994a: 90). Richards (1987: 130–4) also looked at age in relation to grave-goods and found a few interesting associations. Iron tweezers and playing pieces were linked with old adults, iron shears with child burials, glass with adults and bone rings with adolescents. In addition, Ravn (1998: 231) found that, while arrowheads were associated with children at Spong Hill, weapons were linked to adult males (contra Brush 1988). The provisioning of grave-goods with cremations thus seems to be partly age-linked, occasionally sex-linked, and subject to a great deal of variation between sites. Similar patterning can also be seen in the provisioning of animal remains in cremations.

Animal Remains as Grave Offerings

Animal remains have been recovered from many cremation cemeteries, although, as mentioned above, this may be an under-represented practice owing to problems of detection and recovery. The best study is now that by Bond on the Spong Hill material, where 43.7 per cent of the cremations were accompanied by some form of non-human bone (and it is indicative that further animal remains were found by McKinley during her analyses of the supposedly human bone from this site). The range of animal bone found at Spong Hill included sheep/goat (which are hard to distinguish from each other), horse, pig, dog, fox, deer, bear, beaver, fowl, hare, goose, birds and fish, although of course the cremation process may have led to some of these being under-represented (fish bones in particular are hard to detect). Of the cremations with animal bone, 20 per cent contained more than one species, and five cremations contained at least four different species (McKinley 1994a: 92–3). Horses appear to have been placed on the pyre whole. There is some evidence for dismemberment of cattle and pigs, but again all skeletal elements are represented, suggesting that the entire remains of the animal were used. Sheep/goat could be either treated in this way or placed on the pyre as joints of meat. 'Suckling' pigs, however, were placed on whole, as were dogs. Thus, while horses and dogs seem to have been personal possessions, sheep/goat, cattle and pig were probably intended as food offerings, though the lack of fine knife-marks suggests that these bones do not represent feasting remains (ibid.: 94–6).

Bond (1996) compared the animal bone from Spong Hill with that from excavated cremation urns at Sancton in Yorkshire. She found that 43 per cent of cremations at Spong Hill and 40 per cent at Sancton contained animal bone, including domestic and wild animals, fowl and fish. At Sancton, like Spong Hill, she found that the most common animal represented was horse (whereas previous studies of cemeteries at Newark and Illington had found that sheep/goat remains were more common). In addition, all skeletal elements of horse have been found at both sites, suggesting that the whole animal was placed on the pyre (although one horse from Sancton showed signs of decapitation). Sheep and pig bones tended to have butchery marks, indicating that they were included as joints of meat. Dogs were found in twenty-six cremations at Spong Hill and three at Sancton, although this seems to be rare in other cremation cemeteries, with only Illington recording their presence elsewhere. Spong Hill also seems unusual for the range of 'wild' species present, and overall has a wider range of animals than other English sites (McKinley 1994a: 92)

Intriguingly, bear phalanges were found in six urns at Spong Hill and two at Sancton, which may represent the inclusion of bear-skins on the pyre in these cases. Other finds of unusual animal remains have been made at various sites, such as the mammoth tooth in an urn at Markshall (Myres & Green 1973), and the major parts of an antler (or antlers) with an ageing adult, possibly male, at Newark (Kinsley 1989: 24), and with a large male at Lackford, Suffolk, where this was tentatively linked to magical or shamanistic activity (Lethbridge 1951: 17–18).

An interesting feature found at Spong Hill was the discovery of a few urns which contained almost nothing except animal bone – these 'animal accessory vessels', as they have been termed, are often found in pits paired with urns which contain virtually all human bone, and there is strong evidence that the human and animals in question were cremated on the same pyre, with fragments of the human remains found mixed in with the animal bone and vice versa. Occasionally animal bone was found in the cremation-pit itself, around or under the urn, rather than in a separate vessel (McKinley 1994a: 93). Many of these 'animal accessories' contained horse bones, but most were of multiple species. This practice seemed to be linked to the cremation of adults rather than other age groups (ibid.). Vessels containing only animal bone have also been found at Baston, Sancton and Newark (ibid.: 94), and in a possibly parallel find, the excavation of a dark patch in the small cemetery at Wanlip, Leicestershire, in 1960 produced charcoal and ash, bones and horse teeth, two crushed shield-bosses and a bridle-bit, perhaps suggesting the *in situ* cremation of a human and horse double burial (Liddle 1981).

An early study by Calvin Wells of cremations at Illington in Norfolk concluded that the occurrence of animal bones in the cremations appeared to be linked to sex and age, with the only horse being found with a male, sheep and oxen with both males and females, but pig remains being associated only with adolescents (Wells 1960: 37). The more recent study of the remains at Spong Hill in Norfolk, based on a much larger database, suggests that adults, especially male adults, are more likely to have animal bones in general, albeit with a wider range of species being found with adult females (McKinley 1994a: 99–100; see also Richards 1987: 128–9). Bond (1996) discounts any sex-linking of horse remains (as argued by Wells), however, as horse bones were found with both males and females at Sancton and Spong Hill. Another study of a wider range of cemeteries found that horse and cow bones were more strongly linked with adults, and sheep bones with children (Richards 1987: 132), a finding which is largely agreed with in the study of animal bones from Newark, although at this site both sheep and pig bones were found with individuals of all ages (Kinsley 1989: 24). These rather inconclusive and sometimes contradictory findings support the idea that cremation burial practice is subject to a great deal of variability between burial grounds.

Interpreting Cremation Urns and Containers

Another aspect of the cremation burial rite that displays much variation is the form and decoration of the (largely hand-made) pottery urns themselves (**Fig. 4.4**). Decoration on urns takes a number of forms. As well as bosses, stamps and linear incised marks (see Chapter Two), freehand designs have been noted, such as the sequence of animals on C2594 at Spong Hill, which may represent a hunting scene (Hills et al. 1987: 153). Pot 67 from Newark has a unique form of raised relief in the form of two four-legged animals, one of which resembles a spread-out bear-skin (Kinsley 1989: 11–12). Stamps in the form of animals are also known from Newark, Spong Hill, Caistor-by-Norwich and Loveden Hill. A variant on this is the 'wyrm' figure, supposed to represent a dragon or serpent (but in practice looking more like a modern-day worm). Other motifs, such as swastikas and runic symbols, have been interpreted as magical or protective devices (Wilson 1992a: 142–50). The form of the urns is also varied, ranging from shallow bowls to tall, narrow-necked vases. Decoration is usually found on the upper parts of urns, although it is sometimes found to extend below the shoulder, and very occasionally, on to the base (Cook & Dacre 1985: 105).

Sometimes cremation urns are found to have lids of one form or another, which also raises interesting questions about how the contents were regarded, as there seems to have

Fig. 4.4. Urns from Spong Hill showing plough-damage. (Norfolk Aerial Photography Library. Copyright Norfolk Museums Service, BQG4. Photographer Dave Wicks.)

been a need to thoroughly contain them, thus removing them from view. Matching lids are seen in examples from Baston, Lincolnshire (Mayes & Dean 1976), and Drayton, Norfolk (Smith 1901: 333–4), while that from Newark's Millgate cemetery was decorated with figures of birds (now lost, and known only from an antiquarian drawing (Bateman 1853: 189)). It was reported of the cemetery at Kingston-on-Soar that a piece of sandstone had been laid over the mouth of each urn (Henslow 1847: 60–3), and the large number of urns at King's Newton (Derbyshire) also usually had their mouths covered with thin stones (Briggs 1869: 1–3), while some of the urns at Castle Acre (Norfolk) had a large flint placed over the mouth (Housman 1895). It is thought that some of the urns at Spong Hill may have had perishable covers, as the upper parts of the urns had sometimes collapsed in upon empty space on top of the bones in the pot – empty space that would have been filled with earth had the urns been open when buried (Hills 1977b: 11). The most impressive lid, however, is Spong Hill C3324, which depicts a seated human figure, with its head in its hands (Hills et al. 1987: 162). Unfortunately, this lid was found unstratified in a rabbit-hole, and so its associations are unknown (Hills 1980: 52).

Other occasional finds are the so-called 'window urns' which have a piece of glass inserted into the fabric. Examples are known from Castle Acre, Norfolk (Meaney 1964: 172); Helpston, Derbyshire (ibid.: 189–90); Broughton Lodge, Nottinghamshire (*Medieval Archaeology* 9, 1965: 173); Girton, Cambridgeshire (Lethbridge 1938: 313); Kempston, Bedfordshire (which was of an unusual fluted design – Roach Smith 1857: 159–61); Haslingfield, Cambridgeshire (Lethbridge 1938: 313–14); Westbere, Kent (Jessup 1946: 21); and Loveden Hill, Lincolnshire (Meaney 1964: 159). An exceptional example from Elsham, Lincolnshire, had five of these 'windows' arranged around the shoulder of the pot, almost as bosses (*Medieval Archaeology* 21, 1977: 209–10). An urn from Little Wilbraham, Cambridgeshire, was found to have a fragment of lead inserted into the base (Lethbridge & Carter 1928), as did others from Wolterton, Norfolk (Clarke 1940: 232–3) and pots 2 and 342 from Newark, Nottinghamshire (Kinsley 1989). Very occasionally, late Roman vessels are found to have been used for cremations. One burial at the large, predominantly cremation cemetery at Cleatham, Lincolnshire, was contained in a large and elaborately decorated fourth-century Romano-British jar (Field 1989: 53).

Richards (1987) set out to study Anglo-Saxon cremation urns as symbolic artefacts, with the aim of answering social questions such as the nature of the underlying symbolic system, rather than the historical questions that had traditionally been posed. Using a contextual approach, he compared the form and decoration of the pottery urns with indications of the age, sex and number of associated individuals (gained from the analysis of cremated bones within the pots), and information derived from associated objects. By identifying various correlations between 'pottery attributes', such as the form or decoration of the urn, and 'identity attributes', such as the age or sex of the person inside, he was able to show, to a certain extent, that pots had been selected as appropriate for the individual interred. There were close correlations between the age and sex of the cremated individual and the size of the vessel: from infants in the shortest vessels (see also McKinley 1994a: 102, on Spong Hill) to old adults in the tallest (Richards 1987: 136). Females tended to have vessels with wider rims (ibid.: 139), and Richards (ibid.: 205) concluded that pottery attributes were being made use of to mark different aspects of social role, with the level of visibility of the attribute reflecting the size of the audience being broadcast to. It is interesting in this respect that some urns may have been the product of workshops rather than made on a domestic basis, for example the group of pots found in Cambridgeshire and East Anglia which have been attributed to the Illington/Lackford workshop (Green et al. 1981), for it implies that there was a range of available pottery from which an appropriate urn could be chosen, as opposed to one being made specifically for the burial.

It is not only pottery urns that were used as containers for cremations, however. The use of bronze bowls has been noted at Illington, Norfolk (Clarke 1957: 406), Snape, Suffolk (West and Owles 1973) and Coombe, Kent (Ellis Davidson & Webster 1967), a bronze cauldron at Field Dalling (*Medieval Archaeology* 20, 1976: 167), and at least five cremations were in bronze bowls at Sutton Hoo in Suffolk. One (or possibly both) of the hanging bowls found at Loveden Hill (Lincolnshire) contained a cremation (another was found between two inhumations), and both these vessels had been 'killed' by stabbing them through the bottom (*Medieval Archaeology* 1, 1957: 148). Some pottery urns, at this site and at Sancton and Elsham, also appear to have been intentionally damaged or broken prior to burial. One form of intentional damage is the deliberate holing of vessels identified by Richards (1987: 97) at several sites; he found it to be most common at Spong Hill (where over 10 per cent of the complete urns were treated in this way), followed by Elsham (with 7.3 per cent) and then Caistor (with 4.0 per cent).

In recent years more unurned cremations are being reported, owing to the improvements in excavation techniques and recording. These are now known from Portway, Hampshire (Cook & Dacre 1985), where there are twenty-two examples, some of which were placed in their own cremation pit, Thurmaston, Lincolnshire (Williams 1983), Brettenham, Norfolk (*Medieval Archaeology* 10, 1966: 172), RAF Lakenheath in Suffolk (SMR Records), Apple Down, Sussex (Down & Welch 1990) and Loveden Hill, Lincolnshire (Meaney 1964: 158). At Spong Hill, however, McKinley (1994a: 103) concludes that there were no deliberately unurned cremations, although in a number of cases some bone from the urned cremation was placed in the pit beneath or around the urn.

INTERPRETING VARIATIONS IN GRAVE STRUCTURE

Usually, cremated skeletal remains were collected from the pyre and placed in pottery urns, or other vessels, and then deposited in pits in the ground. In the vast majority of cases the urns were put in upright, but inverted examples are known, such as one or two

(a)

from King's Newton (Derbyshire), where the cremated remains had been placed on a small flat stone and the urn placed mouth down over them (Briggs 1869: 1–3). Sometimes the urns have stones placed around them in a sort of packing, as at Baston, Lincolnshire (Trollope 1863). They can be found in individual grave pits, or in groups of urns placed in the same pit (**Fig. 4.5**). That these groupings represent contemporary burial is inferred from various clusters at Spong Hill, such as urns 1133 and 1134, which were buried together under a large piece of sandstone (Hills 1977b: 11, fig. 140).

There are cases of cremation barrow burial though, for example the fourteen cremations which were found to be the primary interments under a barrow at Pitsford, Northamptonshire (Smith 1902: 224) and at Brightwell, Suffolk, where the remains of four individuals, plus animals, were deposited in a bronze bowl and placed under a barrow (Meaney 1964: 225). The probable double cremation from Coombe (Kent), found in a handled bronze bowl associated with unburnt grave-goods including two swords wrapped in cloth, a spearhead, beads and a brooch, was also under a barrow (Ellis Davidson & Webster 1967). At West Stoke in Sussex two small barrows were

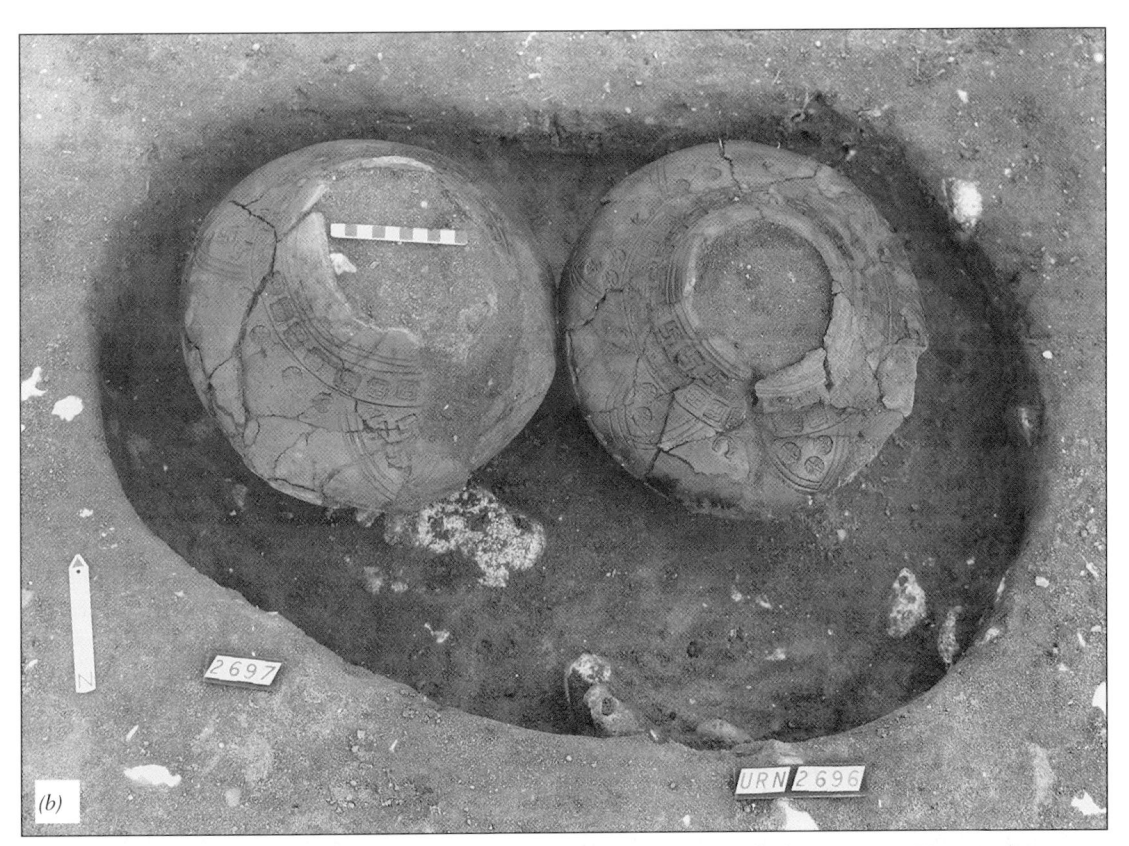

Fig. 4.5. (a) An early excavation of the cremation cemetery at Lackford (Cambridge University Museum of Archaeology and Anthropology, Acc. No. LS44870); (b) urns 2696/2697 from Spong Hill, showing modern excavation standards (Norfolk Aerial Photography Library. Copyright Norfolk Museums Service, BNX7. Photographer Dave Wicks.)

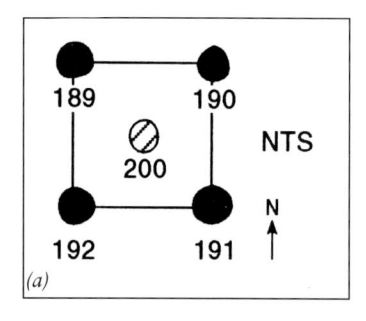

Fig. 4.6. (a) Plan and (b) reconstruction of one of the 'cremation-houses' at Apple Down (after Down & Welch 1990: fig. 2.16, pl. 53).

excavated, and found to have urns containing human bones placed mouth downwards (Smith 1870: 59–62).

Some cremation graves appear to have wooden structures associated with them (**Fig. 4.6**). At Apple Down in Sussex the four-post structures were mostly found over cremations (Down & Welch 1990: 25–33), as was a single example at Croydon, Surrey (Nielsen 1992: 6–7), and a similar structure was found with one of the few cremations from Berinsfield, Oxon (*Medieval Archaeology* 19, 1975: 227). Down & Welch (1990: 29) reconstruct the structure over cremation 146 at Apple Down as having corner uprights supporting a pitched roof, perhaps with a thatched or wooden shingle roof, and they think there may well have been side walls of planking or wattle and daub to protect the inside, and brace the structure. These structures at this site range from a metre square to 2.7m by 2.5m, and the excavators viewed them as being built specifically to house the cremation deposits of a single family. Secondary burials could have been inserted during repairs or post-replacements to the structure (ibid.). Comparable structures are known from earlier and contemporary sites on the continent, but some of these represent cremation pyre supports, rather than cremation houses (ibid.: 32). A similar structure was found surrounding cremation 7 at Alton, Hampshire, which consisted of four post-holes linked by narrow round-bottomed gulleys (Evison 1988: 34). Single examples of a four-post structure and a rectangular ditched enclosure, both with central cremations, were found in the predominantly inhumation cemetery at Butler's Field, Lechlade (Boyle et al. 1998: 38).

Ring-ditches surrounding cremation burials are known from Springfield, Essex (Tyler 1996: 110–13) and suspected from Stifford Clays, also Essex (ibid.: 108). Nineteen examples survived from Apple Down, Sussex (although only four were still associated with burials), and these seem to have been intended to delimit the area around the central cremation on this chalky site, rather than to provide the material for a barrow over the cremation pit, as the ditches were rather shallow (Down & Welch 1990: 25). Three other ring-ditches at Portway are interpreted as being cremation structures (Cook & Dacre 1985: 59), although these have also been found surrounding inhumations (see Chapter Three). More unusually, a cremation in a stone cist at Loveden Hill, Lincolnshire, was accompanied by two decorated combs, a knife and the remains of a drinking horn with a fine bronze terminal (Meaney 1964: 158–9).

Interpreting Variations in Cremation Burial Rites

Cremation is often cited as being a minority rite south of the Thames (cf. the map in Meaney 1964: 8). However, recent excavations at Apple Down, Sussex (Down & Welch 1990), Alton (Evison 1988) and Portway, Andover (Cook & Dacre 1985), both in Hampshire, have produced large numbers of both urned and unurned cremations. Inadequate excavation methods, plough damage and little expectation that cremations would be found have probably contributed to the under-representation of this rite in southern England (Down & Welch 1990: 25). Meaney (1964: 15) is, however, still correct when she notes that 'pure cremation' cemeteries – those with large numbers of cremations, and no (or only a few late) inhumations – are found in 'Anglian' areas, i.e. those north of the Thames. The only 'cremation-only' cemeteries found south of the Thames are those with either single, or between two and five, documented cremations. In addition, with the exception of Apple Down, Portway and Croydon, all sites with more than fifty cremations are found to the north of the Thames (**Fig. 4.7**).

Although cremation as a popular burial rite seems to have been reintroduced to eastern Britain in the later half of the fifth century, it is occasionally found in the later Roman period in Britain (and was a common Iron Age and early Roman period rite). Weller et al. (1974), for example, reported on a number of cremation burials from Billericay in Essex of the second and third centuries. The latest burial in the series was a cremation in a decorated jar, which had a red colour-coated bowl placed upside down on it as a lid. The burial urn was wheel-made and of fine grey fabric, and it had twenty-one bosses on the shoulder, all but one of which were decorated with an incised diagonal cross. Other decoration on the urn included punched rosettes. Myres, commenting on this vessel, suggested that this decorative scheme had strong parallels with Germanic pottery of the time. In general, cremation belongs to the fifth and sixth centuries AD, although examples of late cremations are also known. As mentioned above, the burial from Coombe (Kent)

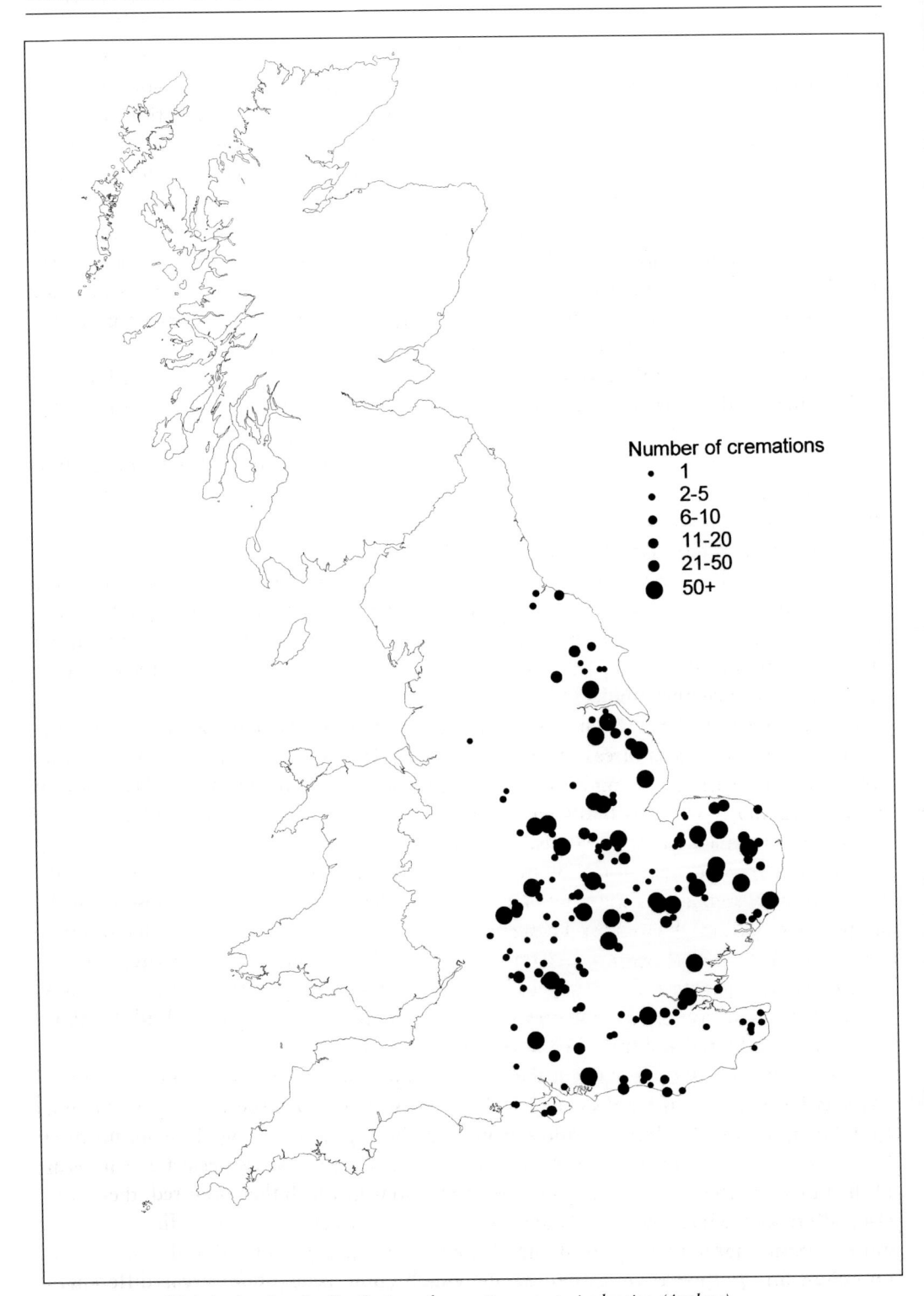

Fig. 4.7. Map of Britain showing the distribution of cremation cemeteries by size. (Author.)

appears to date to the late sixth century (Ellis Davidson & Webster 1967), the cremation under a barrow at Asthall to the first half of the seventh century (Dickinson & Speake 1992), and the wheel-turned vessel that apparently contained a cremation, and was associated with a spear and sword, at Churchover (Warwickshire) would also seem to be later (Thurnham 1867: 481). Down & Welch (1990: 108), moreover, argue for cremation continuing at Apple Down, Sussex, into the second half of the seventh century.

Much effort has gone into trying to identify the cultural antecedents of the cremation burial rite in eastern Britain, both through examination of the pottery forms and the associated grave-goods. Fourth-century pottery from the area between the rivers Elbe and Weser (the 'Elbe–Weser triangle') includes large narrow-necked pots of globular, shouldered and biconical forms. By the end of the fourth century a variety of elaborate decoration was being applied to these, including applied cordons, bosses, indented dimples and stamps, and linear patterns (Hills 1979: 315). Pottery of a similar date from the 'Anglian' areas of Schleswig, Holstein, Mecklenberg and Fyn tended to be decorated with alternately horizontal and vertical lines, grooves or cordons, with both tall and shallow forms being found (ibid.: 316). Various archaeologists have attempted to identify similar differences in the pottery types found within Britain, and thus to delimit the 'tribal' areas, but such attempts have largely failed. While 'Saxon' pots are found in the Thames Valley and 'Anglian' pots in East Anglia, there are also many 'Saxon' pots in Anglian areas, and by the sixth century the pottery styles were thoroughly mixed (ibid.: 316–17). This may have been both a result of the chronological development of pottery styles in Britain, but also a reflection of the mixing of these styles that was already occurring on the continent in the late fourth century (ibid.: 317).

Similar attempts have been made with the grave-goods. Late Roman Iron Age cremations in the 'Saxon' areas of the continent tended to be accompanied by miniature tweezers and shears, bone combs, pieces of late Roman belt equipment and brooches, of both round and bow forms (Hills 1979: 315). Cremations from the 'Anglian' areas were found with a similar range of goods, but the only brooches were of the bow form – no round brooches were found in Schleswig or the areas to the east (ibid.: 316). As we have seen, although cremations were popular in the 'Anglian' areas of Britain, those from the supposedly 'Saxon' areas may be seriously under-represented in the archaeological evidence. Moreover, as we know from looking at the inhumation burial rite, it is not enough merely to note the presence of distinctive artefact types within a given cemetery, and thereby claim continental ancestry for the people using it to bury their dead, for those goods can be adopted and then used in rather distinctive ways.

While very few studies looking at the contextual information available from cremations have yet been carried out, Hills (1993: 308–9) conducted a comparison of the cremations from Spong Hill in Norfolk and those from Süderbrarup in Schleswig-Holstein, northern Germany. She found that while there was similarity between these two cemeteries in terms of the range of artefact types used and the proportions in which they occurred, there were also differences. More glass beads and ivory were in evidence at Spong Hill, as well as more 'Saxon' material, such as stamped pottery and saucer, applied and equal-armed brooches. She proposed various scenarios which could account for these differences: 'a mixed group of Germanic settlers from various parts of northern Europe at Spong Hill.

Or a group of predominantly Anglian origin could have acquired pots and brooches from other peoples, or they might have included a small number of wealthy or productive Saxons. The accident of a single skilled Saxon potter might have started a fashion for stamped pottery amongst people who had hitherto never used this kind of decoration' (ibid.). These comments illustrate the difficulties associated with attributing artefact styles to origins, even in the presence of detailed contextual information.

The next chapter will take a wider view of the cemetery evidence from eastern Britain during this period, looking at the overall incidence of these types of furnished burial, at where they were located in the landscape, at what information can be derived from the spatial distributions of graves within individual cemeteries, and at what we can say about the distributions of various items of material culture.

Five

Studying Cemeteries

Introduction

In the past, when grave-goods were the main focus of enquiry, perhaps not as much effort as was desirable was put into recording all the other details of cemeteries, such as the precise position of each grave within it, the exact location of the cemetery in the landscape, and the relationship of those graves with other features, such as prehistoric remains or other structures. However, if this information is recorded, it can help to add another dimension to our interpretations of cemeteries, for they can start to be seen as places with long histories. There must have been, for example, an initial decision to make the original interment in a particular spot in the landscape. What prompted this decision? Was it proximity to the settlement site where the community lived, or were there other factors involved? We know in the Bronze Age, for example, that barrows under which the dead were interred were often located in particular landscape locations, such as on ridges and false crests. Were similar considerations an issue in the Anglo-Saxon period? Or were particular places regarded as special, and thus appropriate for burial, for some reason. Did the existence of earthworks, such as a Neolithic barrow or an Iron Age hill-fort, mean that burial was more likely in such a spot?

For a cemetery to be created in a particular location, there must be more than the first burial. What prompted people to carry on burying their dead in one place; did they carry out other activities there, in the same way that people lay flowers on graves today? Detailed analysis of the archaeology and layout of cemeteries can start to tell us more about the history of use of such sites. Looking at the location of datable graves may indicate whether there was gradual expansion of the burial area over time from a single core, or whether various different areas of a cemetery were in use at once. Sometimes, pre-existing features seem to have been made use of as boundaries, which helps to shed some light on the ways in which these places were separated off, physically as well as ideologically, from the arenas of the living.

As well as an initial burial, there must similarly be a final interment. Why would a group of people, who had buried their dead in a particular location for perhaps one or even two hundred years, decide to stop? Again, looking at the layout of graves and their nature may give us indications as to why burial ceased in a particular location, perhaps shifting to a nearby site. The data drawn on in this chapter represents a wide-ranging survey of Anglo-Saxon cemeteries in Britain conducted by the author. An attempt was made to collate data on every cemetery (both published and unpublished) with a recorded location. A total of 937 sites were recorded in a database, which was used to generate the accompanying distribution maps.

The Landscape Context of Cemeteries

From an early point in the history of the excavation of Anglo-Saxon cemeteries, there have been frequent mentions of remains of different periods being present. Sometimes these can be inferred from the excavation report, even where the excavators themselves failed to recognise them, for example at Crundale, Kent, where Faussett (1856: 177–98) did not realise that he was excavating both Roman and Anglo-Saxon burials. Often such coincidence of site is the result of the later cemetery reusing an earlier earthwork. At times, this remains obvious, for example the burials inserted into highly visible Iron Age hill-forts at Maiden Castle in Dorset (Wheeler 1943: 78–9) and Blewburton Hill in Berkshire (Collins & Collins 1959: 52–73). However, if the site has been ploughed for any length of time, earlier, less prominent remains such as Bronze Age round barrows or Neolithic hengiform enclosures may no longer be visible. In such cases it will only be with modern excavation techniques, especially the use of open area excavation which reveals the whole of the site surface, that the relationship between the Anglo-Saxon burials and the remains of the barrow ditch or other feature will become clear. The excavations between 1986 and 1988 at Mill Hill, Deal, for example, revealed the sixth-century Anglo-Saxon cemetery, with over eighty inhumation burials, clustered around a prehistoric barrow cemetery (Parfitt & Brugmann 1997).

Williams (1998: 92) argues that around a quarter of all known Anglo-Saxon burial sites have relationships with ancient monuments, most of which were Bronze Age round barrows, but Neolithic, Iron Age and Roman structures were also made use of. This practice was found throughout the areas in which furnished burial was employed, and is seen in the fifth and sixth centuries, though it seems to gain in popularity during the seventh century (ibid.: 95). Indeed, he argues that it may have provided the impetus for the phase of barrow construction which characterises many late sixth- and seventh-century cemeteries (ibid.). My own analyses generally support these conclusions, although there does seem to be some chronological variation in terms of which types of monuments or features are reused at particular times (differences with the figures which Williams (1997) cites are caused by different methods of classification). Reuse of Roman sites, such as towns and forts, and burials made through the surface of Roman roads is predominantly a feature of early Anglo-Saxon cemeteries (**Fig. 5.1a**). Of a total of fifty-three examples of Roman reuse, thirty-eight date to the fifth or sixth century and a further three are of fifth- to seventh-century date. There seems to be no localised patterning of where this type of reuse takes place; it is known from Northumberland right down to Sussex. Examples include the small cemetery of twenty-two cremations and two inhumations found at Longthorpe, Cambridgeshire, in 1968 which had been placed in the north-west corner of a first-century Roman fort (Frere & St Joseph 1974: 112–22), and the sixth-century cemetery at Little Chester (Derbyshire) which had been established in the ruins of a Roman fort and vicus (*Medieval Archaeology* 17, 1973: 138). Similarly, at Fordcroft, Orpington, Kent, a late fifth- and early sixth-century cemetery of nineteen cremations and fifty-two inhumations had been situated in the remains of a Romano-British occupation and bath-house site of the first to fourth centuries AD (Tyler 1992: 73–5). The extensive cemetery at Cestersover (also known as Churchover and Bensford Bridge) stretched for

STUDYING CEMETERIES

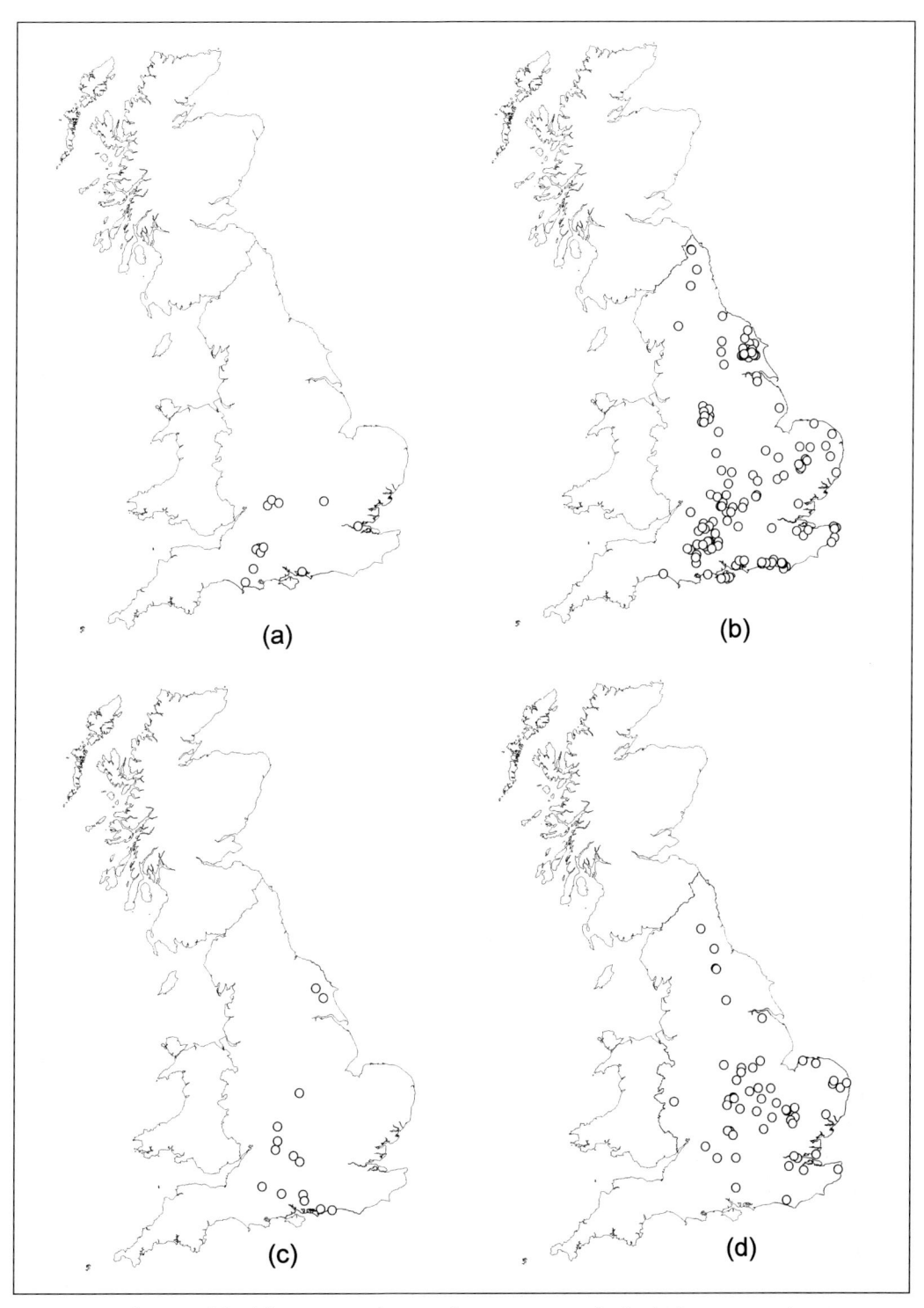

Fig. 5.1. Distributions of the different types of re-use of past monuments by Anglo-Saxon cemeteries: (a) Neolithic sites; (b) Bronze Age sites; (c) Iron Age sites; (d) Roman sites. (Author.)

half a mile along the Roman Watling Street on the border between Warwickshire and Leicestershire, with the inhumation graves in the centre and along both sides of the road (Thurnham 1867: 481). One of the graves around Barton Farm, Cirencester, found in 1909 was cut through the Orpheus pavement of the villa at Barton Mill (Brown 1976: 31). At Eccles a large number of burials had been made in the ruins of a Romano-British villa, the earliest of which dated to the seventh century, to judge by the limited number and type of grave-goods. As the later burials were unfurnished, and aligned east–west, it is difficult to be sure for how long this cemetery was in use, but as there were three layers of burial to the north-east of the villa it seems to have been a number of generations (Detsicas 1973: 78, 212; 1974: 129–30). It was not just settlements and roadways which were made use of, though. The primary burial in the barrow reused by the Anglo-Saxon cemetery on Linton Heath, Cambridgeshire, was thought to have been a Romano-British one (Lethbridge 1938: 315), and the Anglo-Saxon cemetery at Great Chesterford in Essex was found to have been situated outside the Roman town in an area already used by Romano-British burials (Evison 1994a: 30). The excavator thought that these later burials had possibly been attracted by existing grave-markers, which may have included visible traces of at least four Roman tumuli (ibid.: 30, 41).

In contrast, reuse of Neolithic monuments was more of a minority rite, with only thirteen examples known, of which the majority are late cemeteries, dating to the later sixth century and after (**Fig. 5.1b**). These have a predominantly southern distribution, with small clusters in Dorset, Gloucestershire and Wiltshire. The only example of this sort of reuse from the fifth and sixth centuries is seen at Burn Ground, Hampnett (Gloucestershire), where a Neolithic long barrow was used as the focus of a Bronze Age round barrow cemetery, and this in turn was reused by a small mixed cemetery of the late fifth and sixth centuries (St J. O'Neil 1948: 32). More typical is the late solitary burial with a seax and small knife which was found near the end of a Neolithic long-mound which was itself enclosed by the Iron Age hill-fort at Maiden Castle in Dorset (Wheeler 1943: 78–9). A similar example of 'multiple' reuse is seen at West Heslerton in Yorkshire, where the fifth- to seventh-century cemetery was situated in an area already occupied by a late Neolithic and early Bronze Age ritual complex consisting of a hengiform enclosure, an associated post-circle and a series of round barrows, as well as a major boundary feature dating to the Iron Age (Powlesland et al. 1986).

Reuse of Iron Age sites is also fairly rare, with just fourteen examples known (**Fig. 5.1c**). Again, these are predominantly late, but unlike the Neolithic sites have a widely scattered distribution. At Garton Station (**Fig. 5.2**) a late cemetery reused an Iron Age square barrow cemetery in the Yorkshire Wolds (Stead 1991), while an Iron Age religious site was reused by a small late inhumation cemetery at Westhampnett in Sussex (Powell & Fitzpatrick 1997). At Noah's Ark Inn, Frilford (Bedfordshire), an isolated seventh-century skeleton had been buried on an Iron Age site, disturbing a hoard of Roman coins which had been deposited in the same place. Some of the disturbed coins appeared to have been deliberately placed back on to the corpse (Bradford & Goodchild 1939: 37–9).

The most popular monuments for the interment of the dead were, however, Bronze Age barrows (**Fig. 5.1d**). Perhaps it was their landscape location, often visible on the skyline – for example, the three distinct sites around Soham, Cambridgeshire, all with late fifth- and

STUDYING CEMETERIES

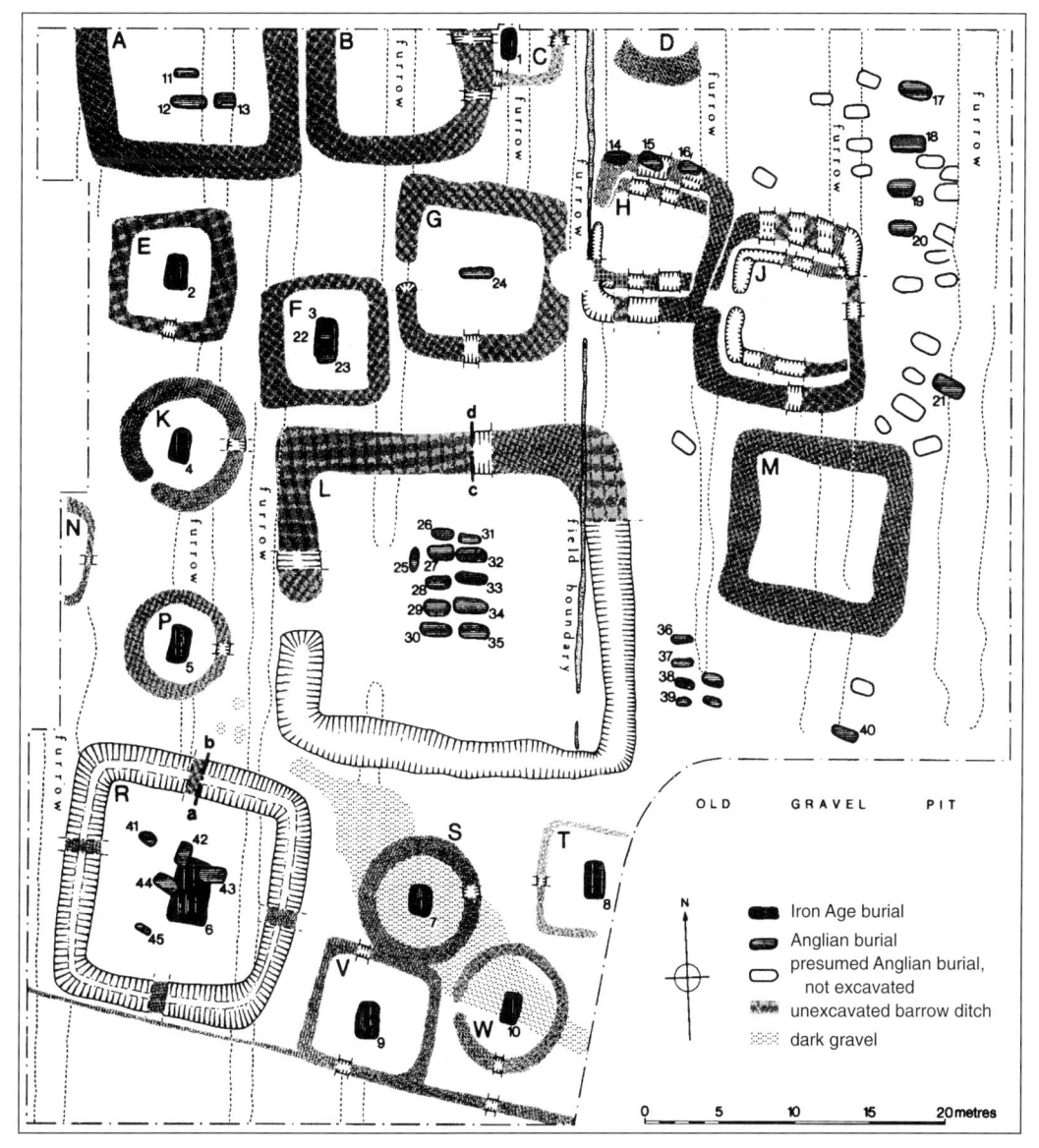

Fig. 5.2. Plan of Garton Station (after Stead 1991: fig. 20).

sixth-century goods, distinguished by Lethbridge (1938: 316), who thought it possible that the dead had been buried in a series of barrows along a ridge – which encouraged this, or perhaps it is an accident of excavation histories: these barrows were often the targets for the diggings of early antiquarians in their search for antiquities, and Anglo-Saxon burials made as secondary deposits in these mounds were often excavated along with the primary interments. A total of 140 examples of this form of reuse are known, with no particular bias shown either to late or early cemeteries. Particular geographical clusters are seen,

127

however, when these places are reused by later sixth-, seventh- and eighth-century cemeteries, especially in Derbyshire, Sussex, Wiltshire and Yorkshire. This does seem to be a genuine pattern, rather than one caused solely by intensive antiquarian activity in these areas. While this would have caused these sites to be excavated in the first place, the bias towards later cemeteries in these areas seems to be real.

While it might be thought that reuse of Neolithic and Bronze Age remains, in particular, was a response to existing places for the burial of the dead in the landscape, the use of settlement sites from other periods may suggest that it was the presence of earthworks (rather than necessarily burial mounds) that served to attract Anglo-Saxon burials. The site at Sutton Hoo, for example, lay over a prehistoric settlement, and it has been suggested (Carver 1989: 150) that this would have been visible as earthworks when the decision was made to erect the barrow mounds there. Other cemeteries, such as Sewerby in East Yorkshire, were made on natural ridges or mounds in the landscape, and this may be part of the same phenomenon (Hirst 1985; see also Williams 1998: 94).

Very occasionally burials are found within near-contemporary settlement sites. The burial in Room I at Sutton Courtenay, Berkshire (a sunken-featured building), was of an adult male, with head to WNW, outstretched but with the left leg bent under the right. He was accompanied by a knife and an ivory comb, and had been deposited on the floor of the house and covered in a 'blanket' of clay (Leeds 1923: 169).

As well as attracting Anglo-Saxon cemeteries in the first instance, earlier remains can also sometimes be seen to structure the ways in which the graves were laid out within those cemeteries. Some prehistoric earthworks were used as boundaries within cemeteries. At Springfield, Essex, a Bronze Age circular enclosure ditch appeared to have been used as the northern boundary of a cemetery containing over 250 inhumations and cremations of the late fifth and sixth centuries (Tyler 1996: 110–13). The cemetery at Lechlade, Gloucestershire, made use of a Roman ditch as the south-eastern boundary of the site, and this also formed a topographical feature upon which the graves were aligned (Boyle et al. 1998: 38), while at Finglesham one side of the site was bounded by a prehistoric trackway (Hawkes 1976: 33). At Thornham, Norfolk, the fortified enclosure of a Roman signal station was used for the site of a small seventh-century inhumation cemetery (*Medieval Archaeology* 1, 1957: 148). At Portway, Hampshire, a linear ditch, which was probably partially silted-up at the time, was used as the eastern boundary of the cemetery, also influencing the orientation of the inhumations which followed its curved alignment (Cook & Dacre 1985: 52, 54). Intriguing examples of this practice are seen at Spong Hill in Norfolk, where the majority of the cremations were found within an earlier enclosure ditch, while the fifty-seven inhumations lay in a cluster outside to the north-east (Hills et al. 1987), while the single cremation at Castledyke, Humberside, actually lay in the probable enclosure ditch, spatially separated from all but one of the large number of inhumations – literally beyond the pale (Drinkall & Foreman 1998: 354–5).

Burials are sometimes found associated with linear earthworks, which served to structure their layout, such as those with late fifth- and sixth-century metalwork and jewellery buried in the filled-in ditch of Fleam Dyke, Cambridgeshire (Lethbridge 1958), and the later cemeteries, similarly in linear ditches, at Garton II (Mortimer 1905: 247–57; **Fig. 5.3**) and Garton Slack I (Mortimer 1905: 264–70). At Empingham II in Rutland an

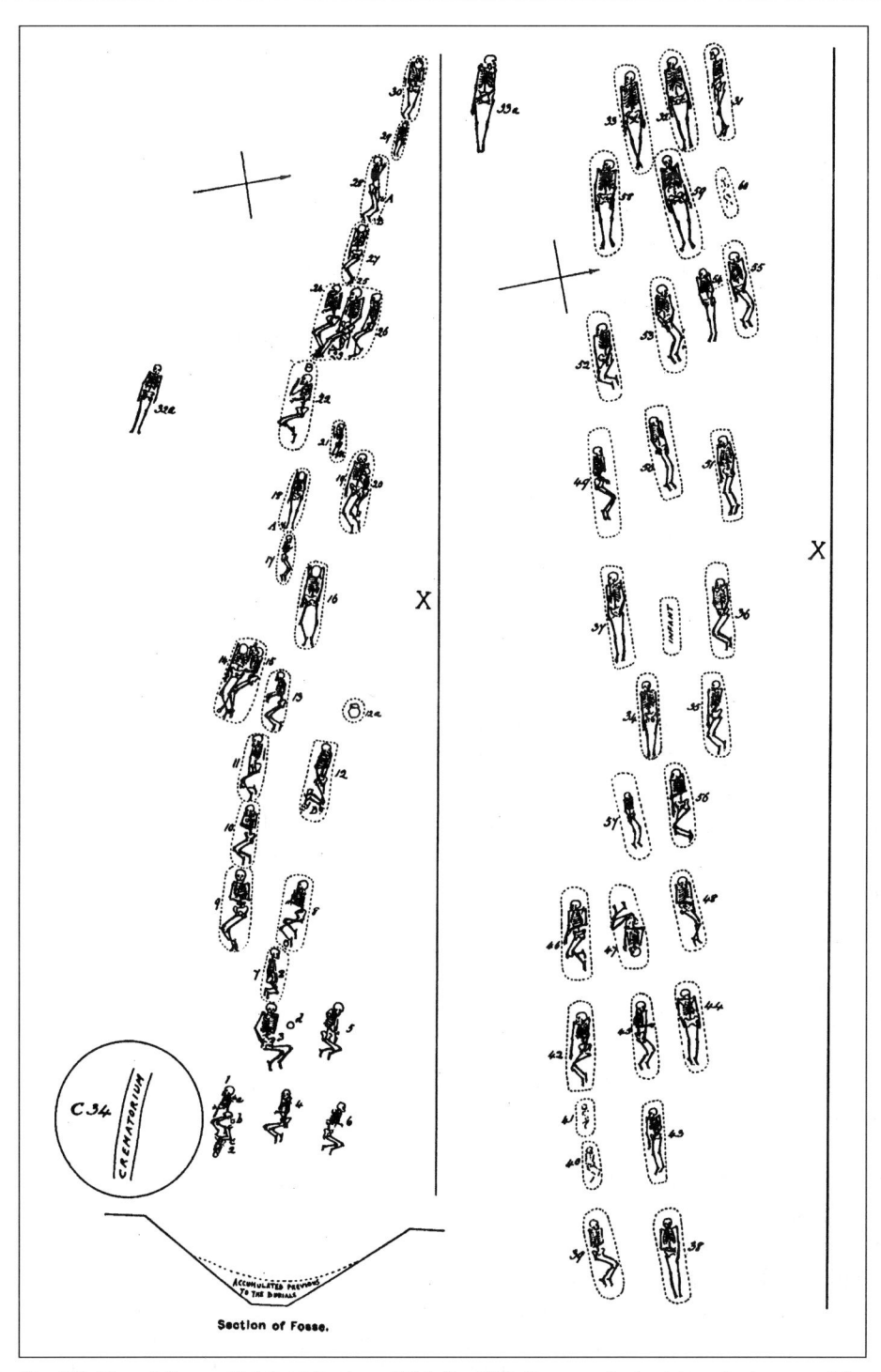

Fig. 5.3. Plan of Garton II (after Mortimer 1905: fig. 621). Between the burials at the bottom of the left-hand column and those at the top of the right-hand column is a space of 46ft, which contained no burials.

early Roman or Iron Age trackway was used as the southern boundary of the cemetery, and the burials were strung out alongside it (Timby 1995: 15).

In addition to being used as a boundary within which burials were placed, earthworks could also be used as a focus for the orientation of later burials. At Mill Hill, Deal, for example, the heads of some of the earlier burials at the site were aligned to the centre of the Bronze Age barrow (Parfitt & Brugmann 1997: 13; **Fig. 5.4**), as were some at Dover Buckland (Evison 1987: 152), and the majority of burials were aligned in this way at Oxborough, Norfolk (Penn 1998) and Kelleythorpe, Yorkshire (Mortimer 1905: 271–83). Burials were arranged around the periphery of a Bronze Age barrow at one of the Dorchester cemeteries (Meaney 1964: 208), while in one part of the cemetery at Newport Pagnell (Buckinghamshire), graves were found in two concentric circles, with their feet to the centre (Smith 1905: 204), from which we might infer the presence of a former barrow or other central feature. At Cuddesdon, Oxon, a cemetery was found in 1847 in which the skeletons were arranged in a circle, prone, with their heads outwards and legs crossed. While a number of seventh-century goods were found 'near' these burials, the assemblage has been argued to represent a single grave, possibly under a barrow around which the other burials were placed – perhaps this represents an execution or sacrificial cemetery (Dickinson 1974).

Clearly the foundation of cemeteries in areas with existing features is an aspect of early Anglo-Saxon cemeteries which has been underestimated in the past (see Williams 1998), and appears to be a dominant feature in some, if not all, areas. Why was this so? Williams (1998: 96) thinks this practice may have served to embody an idealised community of ancestors linked to the distant past and the supernatural (in the same way that certain anthropologists have suggested for contemporary societies in other countries). In addition, it could have helped to support claims and rights to land, wealth and other resources (ibid.: 103; Lucy 1992). Thus by associating their dead with these places, the mourners may have been either manipulating or drawing on associations with the distant past (Lucy 1998: 99).

Cemetery Layout

As well as looking at how burials are arranged with regard to existing features, some interesting patterning emerges when examining how they are arranged in relation to each other; whether uniformity of orientation is the norm, for example, or whether certain groups of people are found in specific locations within a cemetery. Around one-third of cemeteries of the fifth to sixth centuries where data is available have the bodies laid out with heads predominantly to the west, but this figure increases to just over one-half of the later period cemeteries, although there is still variability in the large proportion of these sites which do not have such uniform west–east orientation.

Sometimes different age groups are found to be distinguished by orientation. At Long Wittenham I (Berkshire), most of the adult burials were W–E or SW–NE, while the children were usually buried N–S (Akerman 1860: 328). At Alton, Hampshire, only five burials were buried north–south, four of which were of children (Evison 1988: 40–1). Similar distinctions were seen to be made at the Yorkshire site of West Heslerton, where

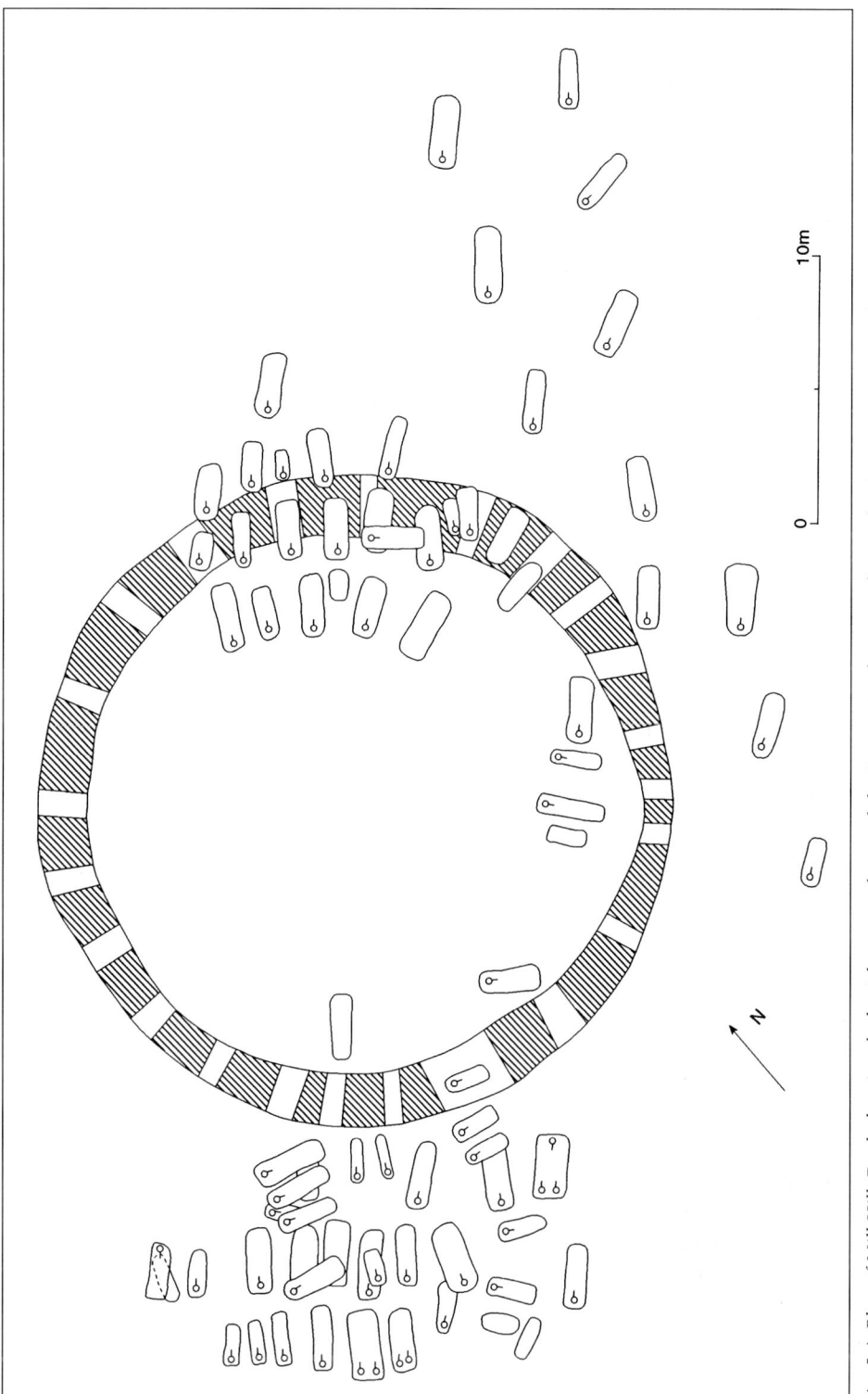

Fig. 5.4. Plan of Mill Hill, Deal, showing the burials arranged around the Bronze Age barrow (after Parfitt & Brugmann 1997: fig. 4).

orientation seemed to be quite heavily structured by age, as well as assemblage, for jewellery burials and those of adults were more likely to be buried to the west, while burials with other assemblages, as well as sub-adults, were more likely to be given a non-western orientation (Lucy 1998: 54-5). Sex, too, could be significant, with jewellery burials at Sewerby (also Yorkshire) more likely to be oriented to south or south-west, while weapon burials seemed to actively avoid this direction (ibid.: 57). Predominant orientation could also change through the period of use of a cemetery. At Butler's Field, Lechlade, the seventh-century burials tended to be NW–SE, often cutting across the earlier burials which were mainly oriented NE–SW (Boyle et al. 1998: 35). Again, selection of an orientation for individual burials seems to have been determined by local traditions, and by a sense of what was appropriate for the person being buried.

Much ink has been spilt over questions of the significance of burial orientation within Anglo-Saxon cemeteries, especially where minor variations are seen within a generally uniform direction. Based on a study of the cemetery at Finglesham in Kent, Hawkes (1976) argued that the variations within the generally westerly head directions of the burials were not random, but rather related to the direction of sunrise on the morning of burial. She argued that as the sunrise could be seen over the sea from the site on clear mornings, and that as the majority of the seventh- and eighth-century burials fell within the range of such sunrise orientation, this was a deliberate practice, putting forward the idea that the burial party must have spent part of the night in the cemetery, in order to observe the sunrise on the day of burial. Variations in orientation were thus thought to relate to time of year of burial. Brown (1983), however, disagreed with this 'sunrise dating' hypothesis. Looking at modern and historical data recording the incidence of death throughout the year, it was argued that the solar arc model used by Hawkes vastly underrepresented the number of deaths likely to have occurred between November and February. Instead the idea was put forward that the burying party were attempting to bury bodies with their feet to the east, and that the discrepancies resulted either from their inability to accurately judge east, or because they were making use of a local referent. Moreover, Rahtz (1978) demonstrated the range of possible factors which could give rise to such variation. Again, we come to the conclusion that there is no single explanation which can be uniformly applied to a particular aspect of Anglo-Saxon cemeteries. Indeed, when such aspects are examined more closely, taking other information into account, detailed and intriguing patterning often comes to light.

At Howletts, Kent, there appeared to be spatial distinction of burials according to sex: male graves were found mainly in the northern part of the cemetery and female graves to the south (Meaney 1964: 125). Likewise, at Lechlade, Gloucestershire, females were consistently buried in the north-west corner of the site (Stoodley 1997: 209). In the earlier phase at Polhill, Kent, there appeared to be three rough plots for burial, separately containing males, females and children (Stoodley 1997: 215). Graves 29–32 at Empingham II in Rutland formed a spatially distinct cluster of adult males buried with weapons, and there was also clustering of male weapon burials to the east end of the site (Timby 1995: 15). While these examples do not approach the clear-cut distinctions seen at the continental sites of Hornbek and Hamfelde (cited by Stoodley 1997: 209), which were restricted to male and female burials respectively, they do hint at strong gender segregation on occasion.

Presence of a particular artefact type also seems to be a determining factor within some cemeteries. At Empingham, Rutland, for instance, Stoodley (1997: 221) distinguished a group of separate weapon burials, and he also saw a similar pattern at Broadstairs in Kent, where the cemetery was focused on three Bronze Age barrows, and the weapon burials at this site tended to be to the east side of these (ibid.: 214–15). Similarly, at Orpington, also in Kent, at a distance around the grave of a man aged around fifty years, who was possibly buried under a barrow, were most of the weapon burials from the site, as well as a proportion of the sub-adult burials (ibid.: 215–16).

At Stretton-on-Fosse, Warwickshire, there appeared to be spatial distinction on the basis of brooch type, with those accompanied by small-long brooches being found apart from those with saucer brooches (Ford 1996: 60). A parallel pattern was seen at Dinton Folly, Oxon, where two groups with differing orientations were also distinguished by the brooches buried with them; the NW–SE group had saucer brooches, while the SW–NE group had disc brooches (Hunn et al. 1994).

This observation brings us on to the question of whether brooch types do indeed represent different cultural groupings, as has often been assumed. As stated in Chapter Three, the stereotype of the Anglian costume is one that employs cruciform and wide, flat annular brooches, along with sleeve-clasps and girdle-hangers, while the Saxon costume makes use of saucer, applied, button and simple disc brooches. Indeed, this assumption is so strongly held that histories of the settlement of an area by these different cultural groupings are often written on the basis of it, with Anglian areas to the north of the Thames and Saxon areas to the south, with 'Jutish' Kent and the Isle of Wight different again. However, when we look at the actual distributions of these artefacts, the picture is not nearly so clear-cut.

Although cruciform brooches are absent from many of the southern counties, including Hampshire, Surrey and Wiltshire, their distribution stretches into Kent and the Upper Thames valley, but it is more concentrated in East Anglia, the Midlands, Lincolnshire and Yorkshire (**Fig. 5.5a**). This overall distribution is largely mirrored by that of the square-headed brooches (**Fig. 5.5b**) (and also small-long brooches (**Fig. 5.5c**), perhaps supporting Leeds' suggestion that the latter was used as a substitute for the two larger brooch types), and by the use of girdle-hangers, though these are predominant in East Anglia and Kent. The one item which does appear to have the 'right' distribution for the supposed Anglian area is the sleeve-clasp (**Fig. 5.5d**), which is tightly limited to the northern parts of East Anglia, the east Midlands, Lincolnshire and Yorkshire (the single example in the south is only half a clasp, and therefore not used as a sleeve-clasp, from the site at Saxonbury, Lewes). John Hines (1994: 52–3) may well be right when he argues that the use of this artefact is indicative of a regional costume in this area (especially in light of the fact that his Phase 3 great square-headed brooches appear to have the same tightly delimited distribution – see map at Hines 1997: 203), although it should be noted that only in Rutland and Cambridgeshire do over 50 per cent of sites datable to the fifth and sixth centuries employ these clasps – in all the other areas there are many more sites which do not use them, compared with those that do. It is interesting, though, that this sleeve-clasp distribution is much more limited than those of the supposedly characteristic brooch types, which find their way into Kent, southern Essex and the Upper Thames valley in

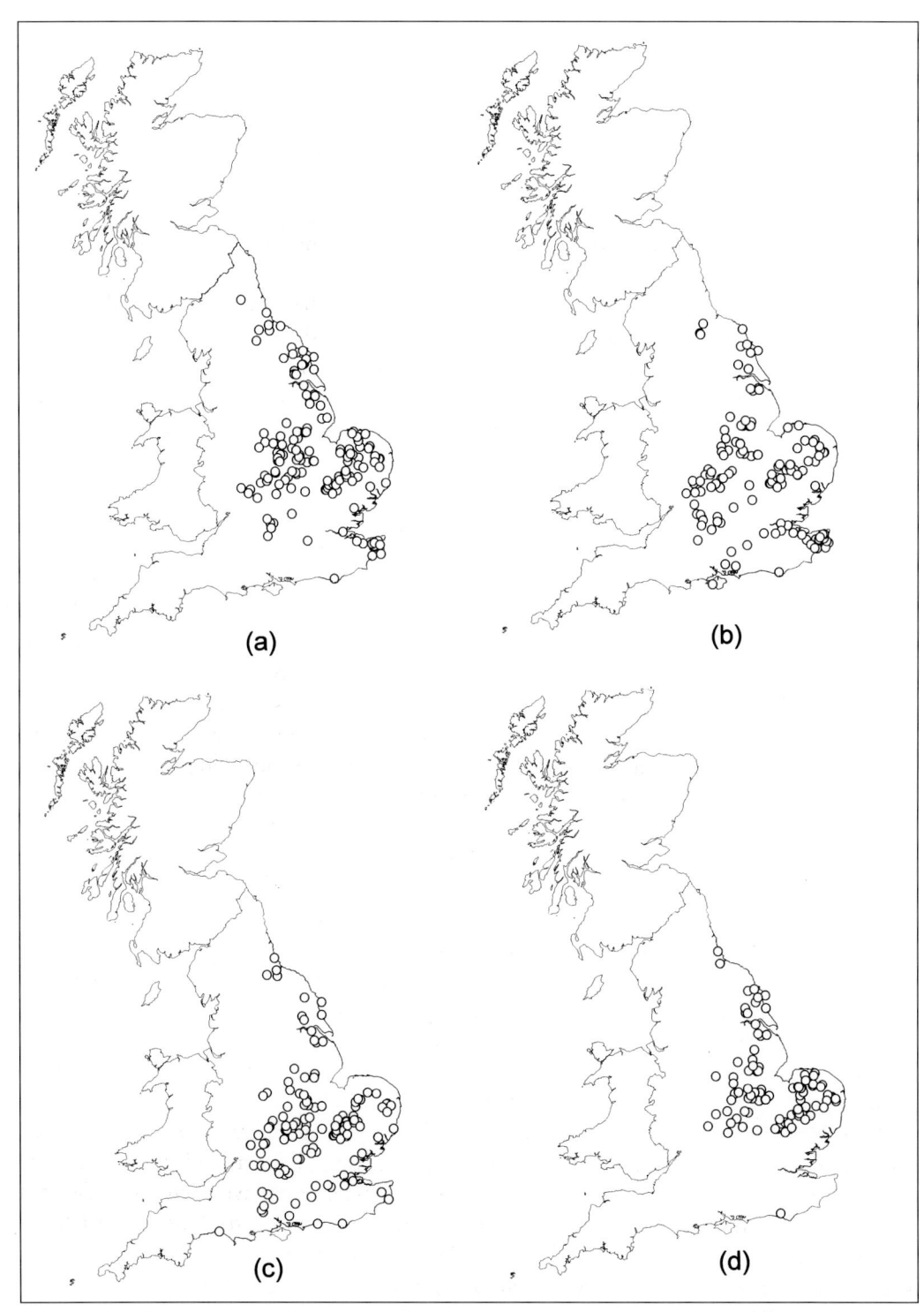

Fig. 5.5. Distributions of typical 'Anglian' artefacts: (a) cruciform brooches; (b) square-headed brooches; (c) small-long brooches; (d) sleeve-clasps. (Author.)

substantial numbers. One other artefact within the northern region which does have a reasonably tightly delimited distribution is the openwork 'swastika' brooch, a variant of the annular and/or disc brooch. This is clustered in the Midlands area, particularly Northamptonshire and Rutland, and may conceivably represent the produce of a local workshop (**Fig. 5.6d**). Negative evidence may also be of interest – there appear to be no annular brooches, of any type, recorded from Bedfordshire, Hertfordshire or Middlesex, and they are recorded only from one site in Buckinghamshire; penannular brooches are absent from the same areas. Perhaps not wearing certain brooches could be as significant as wearing them?

Turning to the 'Saxon' brooch types, saucer brooches are heavily clustered in the Upper Thames valley, but concentrations are also seen in Warwickshire and Worcestershire, well to the north, and in a general spread across much of the Midlands and into Cambridgeshire (**Fig. 5.6a**). They are also seen at a number of sites in Kent, though the majority of these are in west rather than east Kent. Applied brooches have a slightly tighter distribution, with fewer examples in the south-eastern counties, and particular clusters in Berkshire and Cambridgeshire (**Fig. 5.6b**). Button brooches, however, look rather different. These are found at fewer sites, and are almost exclusively used in the Thames valley and to the south, and also in East Kent (**Fig. 5.6c**). The prominent exceptions are the sites at Sleaford, where the button brooch was only a tentative identification, but which anyway stands out as distinctive in a number of ways, and that at Alveston Manor in Warwickshire where the button brooches were riveted to the centre of saucer brooches (Meaney 1964: 262–3). Finally, simple disc brooches, while clustered in the Upper Thames region, are found in a wide spread across the Midlands, into East Anglia and into east Kent. Thus, these distributions, with the sole exception of button brooches, overlap substantially with those of 'Anglian' artefacts, including sleeve-clasps.

The material culture of early cemeteries in east Kent seems thus to be an intriguing mixture, with cruciforms and girdle-hangers being used along with button and disc brooches, as well as some more regionally distinct types, such as the garnet keystone disc brooches which are heavily clustered there (**Fig. 5.7a**), bracteates (**Fig. 5.7b**) (although numbers of both of these are also seen outside of Kent), and sixth-century mounted crystal balls and perforated spoons. Kent is otherwise distinguished in terms of distribution maps only by the finds of swords (**Fig. 5.7c**) and glass vessels (**Fig. 5.7d**) in a high number of cemeteries, and the incidence of weaving swords or battens. The high incidence of other characteristic seventh- and eighth-century objects in Kent, such as amethysts, wooden boxes, seaxes, full-size shears, work-boxes and cowry shells may merely reflect the higher numbers of late cemeteries in that area (**Fig. 5.8a–d**).

What these very brief summaries of the evidence do not portray are clearly defined cultural areas on the basis of distinctive brooch types. Even the items which do have clear-cut distributions – the button brooches and the sleeve-clasps – have been much debated over in terms of their significance; both of these are also seemingly sixth-century artefacts, and can tell little of fifth-century cultural origins. More mileage may come out of in-depth studies of how these artefacts were used, along the lines of Brush (1993) and Parfitt & Brugmann (1997), but distributions alone tell us little – merely that those artefacts were transmitted to an area by some means, or were manufactured there, and, possibly decades

THE ANGLO-SAXON WAY OF DEATH

Fig. 5.6. Distributions of typical 'Saxon' artefacts, compared with swastika brooches: (a) saucer brooches; (b) applied brooches; (c) button brooches; (d) swastika brooches. (Author.)

STUDYING CEMETERIES

Fig. 5.7. Distributions of artefacts showing a strong Kentish clustering: (a) keystone garnet disc brooches; (b) bracteates; (c) glass vessels; (d) swords. (Author.)

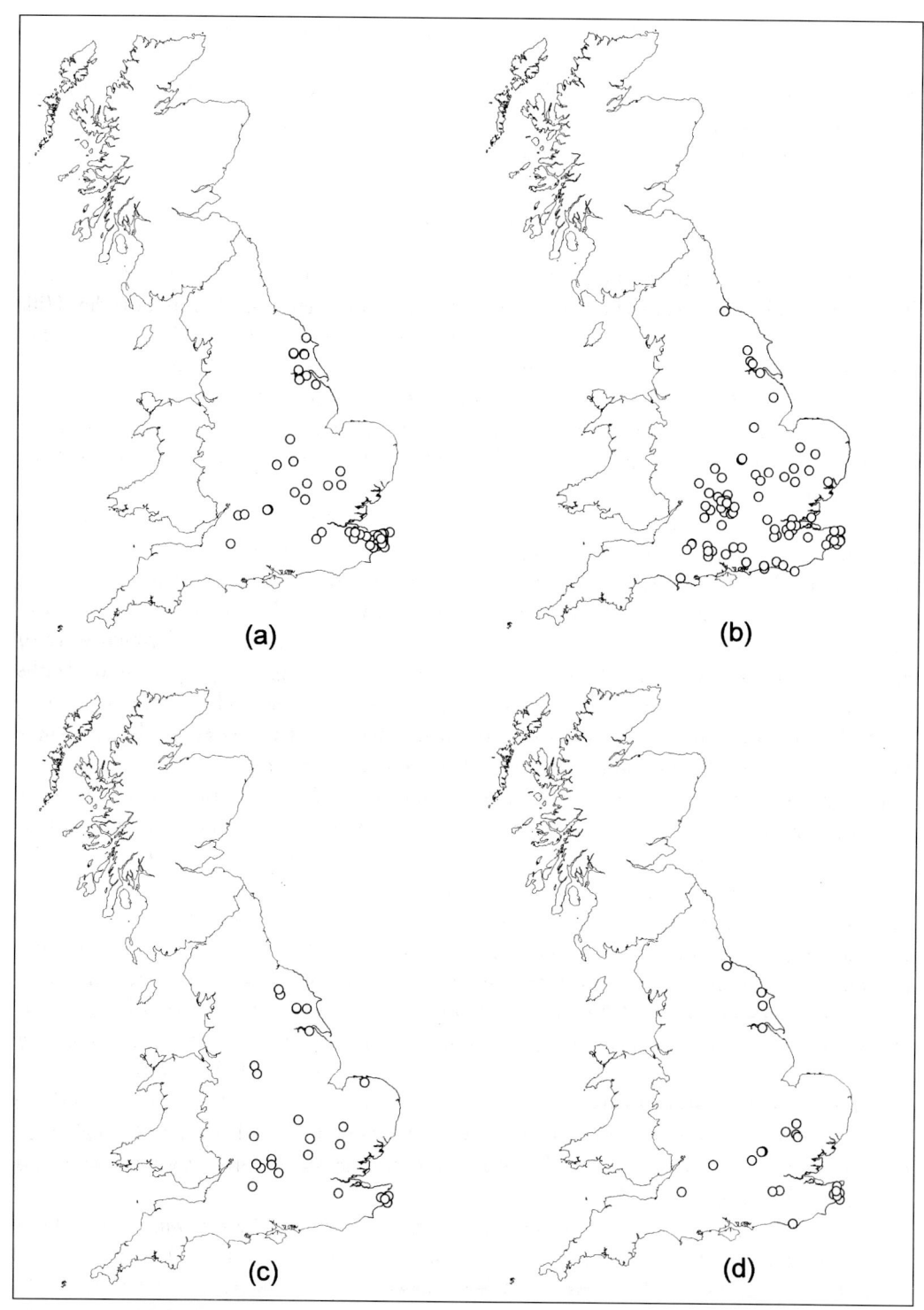

Fig. 5.8. Distributions of typically 'later' grave-goods: (a) amethyst beads and pendants; (b) seaxes; (c) workboxes; (d) cowry shells. (Author.)

later, were deposited in a grave. They may, however, give some important information about the manufacture, exchange and trade of objects, as clusters may represent the products of local or regional workshops, as suggested by Dickinson (1976: 49) for the majority of all the brooches in the Upper Thames region, rather than anything necessarily 'ethnic'. These issues will be further explored in Chapter Seven.

CEMETERY COMPOSITION

Cemeteries range greatly in size, from the solitary grave (often a characteristic of later burial practice), to the very extensive, often cremation, cemeteries, such as Loveden Hill, Lincolnshire, with almost two thousand burials (Fennell 1974: 285–6). These very large cemeteries may be serving more than one community. Spong Hill, for example, is argued by Hills (1980: 202) to have served perhaps a whole region, rather than just a single settlement (see below for more on settlements and cemeteries). Often, though, the latter is assumed to be the case, and the age and sex structure of the cemetery is examined for what light it can shed on the burying population. However, in order to estimate population structure accurately, there needs to be a reasonable degree of confidence that *all* members of a community are being buried, and are subsequently recovered through excavation. This is patently not the case for the vast majority of Anglo-Saxon cemeteries. The cemetery at Great Chesterford, Essex, is unusual for the high proportion of infant and foetal burials found there. At this site, there were 171 inhumations, 65 of which were of infants and foetuses (Evison 1994a: 28), and it was suggested that the percentage of deaths in these younger age groups was similar to that in some underdeveloped countries now (ibid.: 59). In other words, the figures from Great Chesterford are what we should expect from a cemetery in the pre-industrial past, rather than an exception.

That we do not generally have a similar picture at other sites is something that needs explanation. It may be that under-representation of younger remains is a result of preservation conditions, with small infant bones being dissolved more thoroughly by acidic soils, or small skeletons in shallow graves being more easily disturbed; sometimes it may be due to inadequate excavation – poorly preserved infant bones can easily be missed, especially if grave-cuts are hard to see (see Crawford 1991; 1993). It may also be the case, though, that younger individuals were deliberately not buried in these cemeteries, except in unusual cases like Great Chesterford. While we do not have cemeteries which consist exclusively of infants in this period (unlike the preceding Roman period, where a number of these are known), infant remains are occasionally found in other contexts, including (shocking as it may seem to us now) in rubbish deposits at West Heslerton (Powlesland 1997b). Regardless of where these younger remains were deposited, their general absence from these cemeteries means that calculation of demographics is extremely difficult, if not impossible (Boddington 1987).

Other types of interesting data can, however, be generated by examination of how cemeteries are constituted with regard to age and sex. At Portway, Hampshire, for example, the majority of the unfurnished inhumation graves were those of children (Cook & Dacre 1985: 73), suggesting that the furnished burial rite was not thought appropriate for many of the younger individuals at this site. At Dover Buckland in Kent the arrangement of the cemetery was interpreted as the spatially clustered evidence of family groupings (Evison 1987: 145–6), yet these families (if that is what they were) comprised only older burials, as in the whole cemetery there was only a single child under the age of five years (and this was distinguished by having its head placed at the east end of the grave) (ibid.: 146). Here, burials of the young seem to have been distinguished by not being buried within the cemetery at all.

Occasionally, cemeteries stand out as peculiar within their regional context. The mixed inhumation and cremation site at Sleaford, Lincolnshire, for example, with over six hundred graves, produced evidence for a range of unusual practices, such as many crouched burials, the use of cists, and the peculiar placing of brooches, with only children not being found regularly interred crouched on the left-hand side (Phillips 1934: 139–41). Yet other cemeteries in the region showed a more 'normal' rite.

Burning and Burying the Dead: Cremation and Inhumation

Of all the recorded sites of Anglo-Saxon furnished burials in eastern Britain, there is a large imbalance between inhumation and cremation as burial rites: 692 sites have inhumations but no cremations, while just 70 sites have cremations but no inhumations (175 sites have both rites, **Fig. 5.9**)). As stated in the previous chapter, the majority of cremations belong to the earlier phase of burial, with just a few late examples known, while inhumations are found throughout the period of furnished burial, making up the vast majority of later sites (**Fig. 5.10**). The distribution of furnished burials changes with time, however. In the earlier phase they are concentrated in East Anglia (Cambridgeshire, Suffolk and Norfolk), Kent, Lincolnshire, Northamptonshire, Oxfordshire and Yorkshire, with each of these counties having at least twenty cemeteries of fifth- and sixth-century date. Most of these counties, with the exception of Kent, Oxfordshire and Yorkshire, have fewer late cemeteries than many other areas, suggesting a waning of the furnished burial rite in East Anglia and the east Midlands in the seventh and eighth centuries. Other counties though, such as Dorset and Wiltshire, have many more late than early cemeteries, suggesting widespread adoption of the furnished burial rite at a later stage in these areas. The overall distribution of all sites produces some interesting patterns which seem to result from geographical features. Cemeteries are entirely absent from the Weald of Kent and the Sussex Downs, although there are numerous sites in other downland areas. Other 'blank' spots on the map are around the Wash, much of north London, Hertfordshire and Essex, the north-east Lincolnshire coast, north Nottinghamshire and South and West Yorkshire. While some of these areas would have been unattractive for settlement, and so presumably also for burial, at this time, others would have been prime agricultural areas, and so cultural reasons should be sought for the lack of the 'Anglo-Saxon' burial rite in these areas.

Cremation is rare in some areas of the country (**Fig. 5.11**). East Kent, for example, has only small collections of cremations, although they are known; an iron spearhead (or sword) was found with an urn filled with calcined bones near Folkestone (Smith 1908: 364), which was noted as extremely unusual at the time. As pointed out in the previous chapter, cremation is now being increasingly recognised south of the Thames, as a result both of improved excavation techniques and of changing expectations. The discoveries of

Fig. 5.9. Map of Britain showing the distribution of (a) inhumation cemeteries; (b) cremation cemeteries; (c) cemeteries of mixed rite. (Author.)

THE ANGLO-SAXON WAY OF DEATH

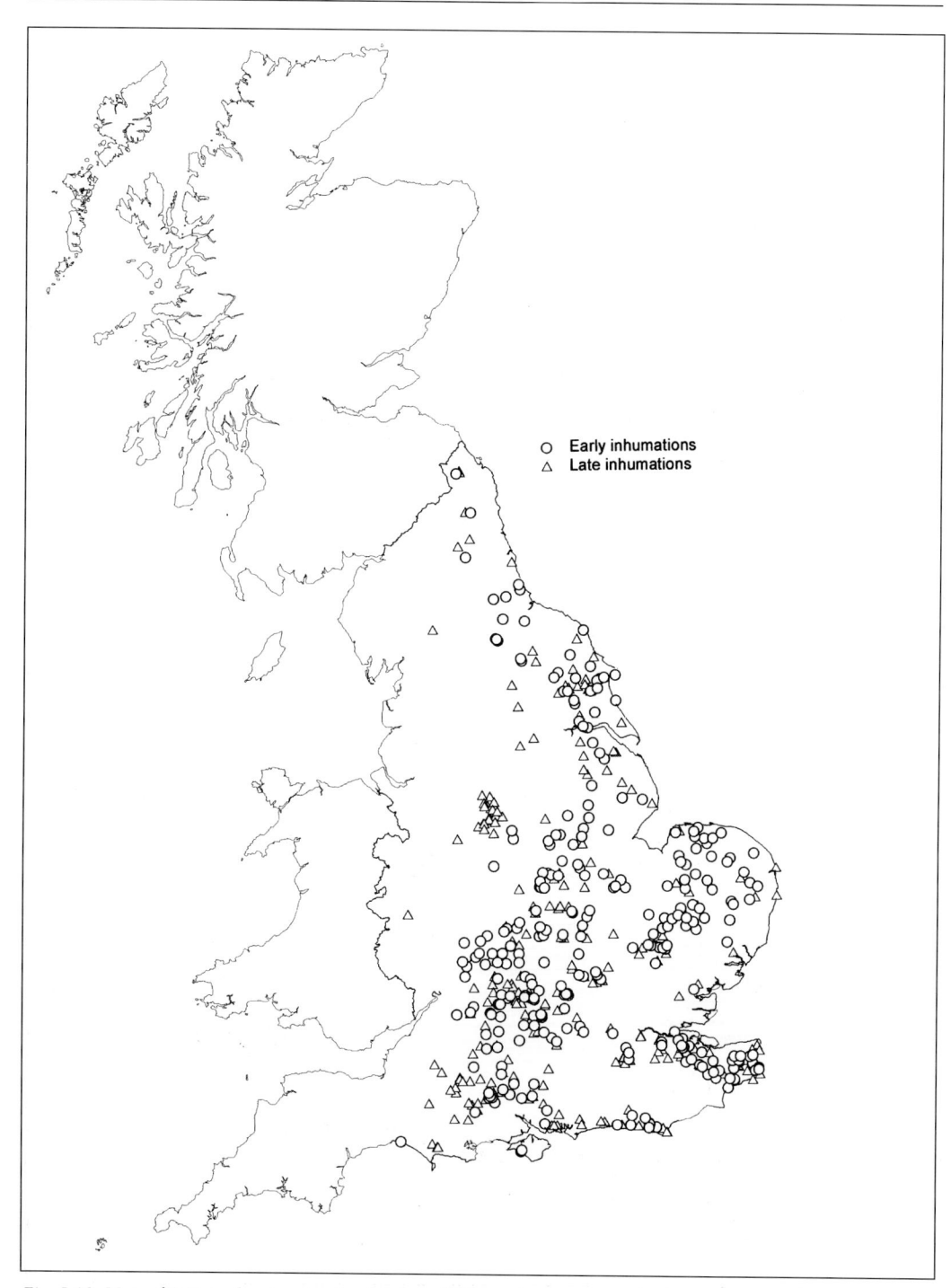

Fig. 5.10. Map of Britain showing the distribution of inhumation cemeteries by date. (Author.)

STUDYING CEMETERIES

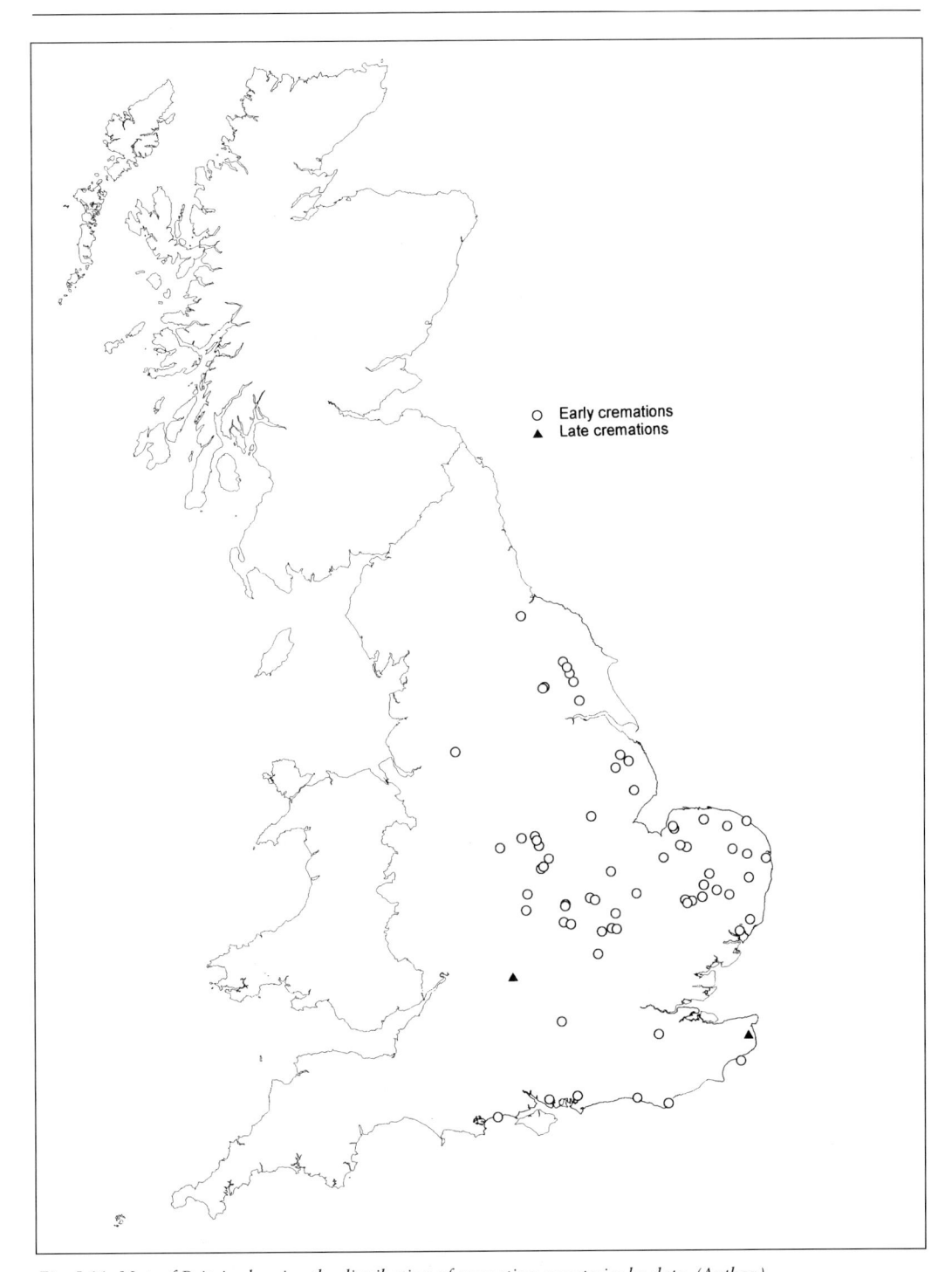

Fig. 5.11. Map of Britain showing the distribution of cremation cemeteries by date. (Author.)

substantial numbers of cremations at sites such as Apple Down in Sussex and Portway in Hampshire has highlighted that this may be a more common rite in this area than was once suspected. It is still true, however, with these rare exceptions, that the large cremation cemeteries, with many hundreds of burials, are confined to East Anglia (including Essex), Yorkshire and the Midlands.

Sometimes cremations were found to accompany inhumations, for example the young woman from Kempston (Bedfordshire) who was provided with a bronze finger-ring, brooch fragments and a fine urn (identical to pottery found in the Midlands and East Anglia) containing cremated bone (Roach Smith 1868: 167–8). The rites were certainly in use at the same time at a number of sites, for example at Spong Hill, where inhumations both disturb and are disturbed by cremations in some instances, with some of these juxtapositions looking deliberate (Hills 1999b: 20). In broad terms though, at Spong Hill inhumations and cremations appear to be spatially distinct (**Fig. 5.12**), although at the nearby site of Snape, Suffolk, cremations and inhumations were thoroughly intermixed, and likewise were in use at the same time (Filmer-Sankey 1992: 46). At the latter site it is suggested that the ship burial, which dated to around AD 550, was the 'founder grave' of an inhumation cemetery in a pre-existing cremation cemetery (ibid.: 47). Of especial interest here is the fact that the barrow covering this ship burial appeared to swamp the existing Bronze Age barrow which may well have been the original focus of the cremation cemetery (ibid.). Other sites where both rites were in use at the same time include Portway, Hampshire, where the two rites were largely spatially distinct. Inhumation was predominant in the eastern part of the site and cremation in the west (Cook & Dacre 1985: 52), although here they seem to be contemporary throughout the whole period of use of the cemetery (ibid.: 106). Intriguingly, unurned cremations at this site seem to form an intermittent line along the south and west sides of the cemetery (ibid.: 57). This particular cremation rite is suggested to be later than the bulk of urned cremations, especially as one, cremation 49, was associated with one of the three annular features discovered here (ibid.: 59) – features which elsewhere are seen as late.

There does not seem to be any uniform explanation for why some people were inhumed and some cremated at such sites. At Caistor-by-Norwich inhumations were buried with annular brooches only, whereas cremations were found with a variety of brooch types (Myres & Green 1973), but as Brush (1988) showed, cremations and inhumations tend to be buried with very different assemblages, so such a finding should occasion little surprise. It may be that, as has been argued for Spong Hill, the adoption of inhumation was a deliberate tactic employed by an up-and-coming family group, perhaps in an attempt to assert their superiority, but this does not seem to be a satisfactory explanation for those sites where the rites co-existed for the life of the cemetery. Cremation is usually seen as being an intrusive continental rite in fifth-century contexts, though it should be noted that there are small numbers of unurned cremations dating from the second half of the fourth century at late Roman cemeteries such as Lankhills (Clarke 1979: 128–30). This is an area which clearly needs more detailed and contextual research, especially into similarities and differences with continental rites, along the lines proposed by Hills (1999a).

Fig. 5.12. Plan of Spong Hill excavations 1972–84. (Illustrator Robert Rickett. Copyright Archaeology and Environment Division, Norfolk Museums Service.)

Cemeteries Through Space

In the previous two chapters, various instances have been noted where burials have been marked out on the surface, for example by the construction of a barrow over the grave, or the use of a ring-ditch or a mortuary house. While most barrow mounds of Anglo-Saxon construction are thought to date from the later sixth or seventh centuries, there may be a few earlier examples. Farley (1992: 11–13) argues that the Cop round barrow at Bledlow (Buckinghamshire) was constructed in the early Saxon period and used for both inhumation and cremation burials; it was previously thought to have been a Bronze Age barrow that had been reused (cf. Head 1938). The fifth- and sixth-century cemetery at Marston St Lawrence in Northamptonshire was in a field formerly called Barrow Furlong, and Smith (1902: 228–30) thought the graves may have been marked by small hillocks. Two 'slight eminences' which produced similarly dated inhumation and cremation burials at Beddington, Surrey, were thought by one commentator to be 'evidently Saxon tumuli' (*Journal of the British Archaeological Association* 30, 1874: 212–13). Barrows which are now ploughed out are sometimes suggested by field names recording their former existence. The discovery of the cemetery at Feering (Essex) in Barrow Field (Smith 1903: 326–7) may be a case in point. As mentioned previously, some cemeteries are thought to have perhaps had the graves marked in some way, for instance at Portway (Cook & Dacre 1985: 53), where small mounds over graves were suggested as the reason why the shallow graves had not been ploughed away, and formed an orderly arrangement. In general, though, on the available evidence, the erection of primary mounds over graves would seem to be a later feature.

Four areas appear to have a strong tradition of barrow building (rather than just reuse) in the seventh century (**Fig. 5.13**). While Kent and, to a lesser extent, Sussex are characterised by entire cemeteries in which the individual graves are covered by small mounds (for example, many of the sites excavated by Faussett and Douglas in the eighteenth century), Wiltshire and the Peak District have more large individual barrows (although in both these areas reuse is still a strong tradition at this time). Primary barrow burials in Derbyshire include the weapon burials at Lapwing Hill (Bateman 1861: 68–70), where the body was laid in a shallow grave cut into the rock on hide-covered wood, accompanied by a sword in a sheath, a knife, two small spearheads and coffin-fittings, and Benty Grange (ibid.: 28–34), where the offerings included a helmet decorated with a silver cross and a boar figurine on the crest, a decorated cup and three hanging-bowl escutcheons. Secondary burials in Derbyshire include that in the prehistoric barrow at Cow Lowe, which had linked gold pins and a padlocked bronze-bound wooden box containing a necklace, a glass palm cup, a bone comb and a fox or dog tooth, among other items (Ozanne 1963: 28–9).

Very occasionally, Anglo-Saxon burials are thought to be both primary and secondary on the same site. At Arreton Down on the Isle of Wight, for instance, the seven burials in Barrow 1 were thought to be secondary in a Bronze Age barrow, while in the centre of Barrow 2 a skeleton was found with part of an iron axe, a pair of tweezers and a spearhead, and was thought to have been primary (Arnold 1982b: 75–6). Nearby, at Bowcombe Down, two large Bronze Age barrows produced secondary cremations and

STUDYING CEMETERIES

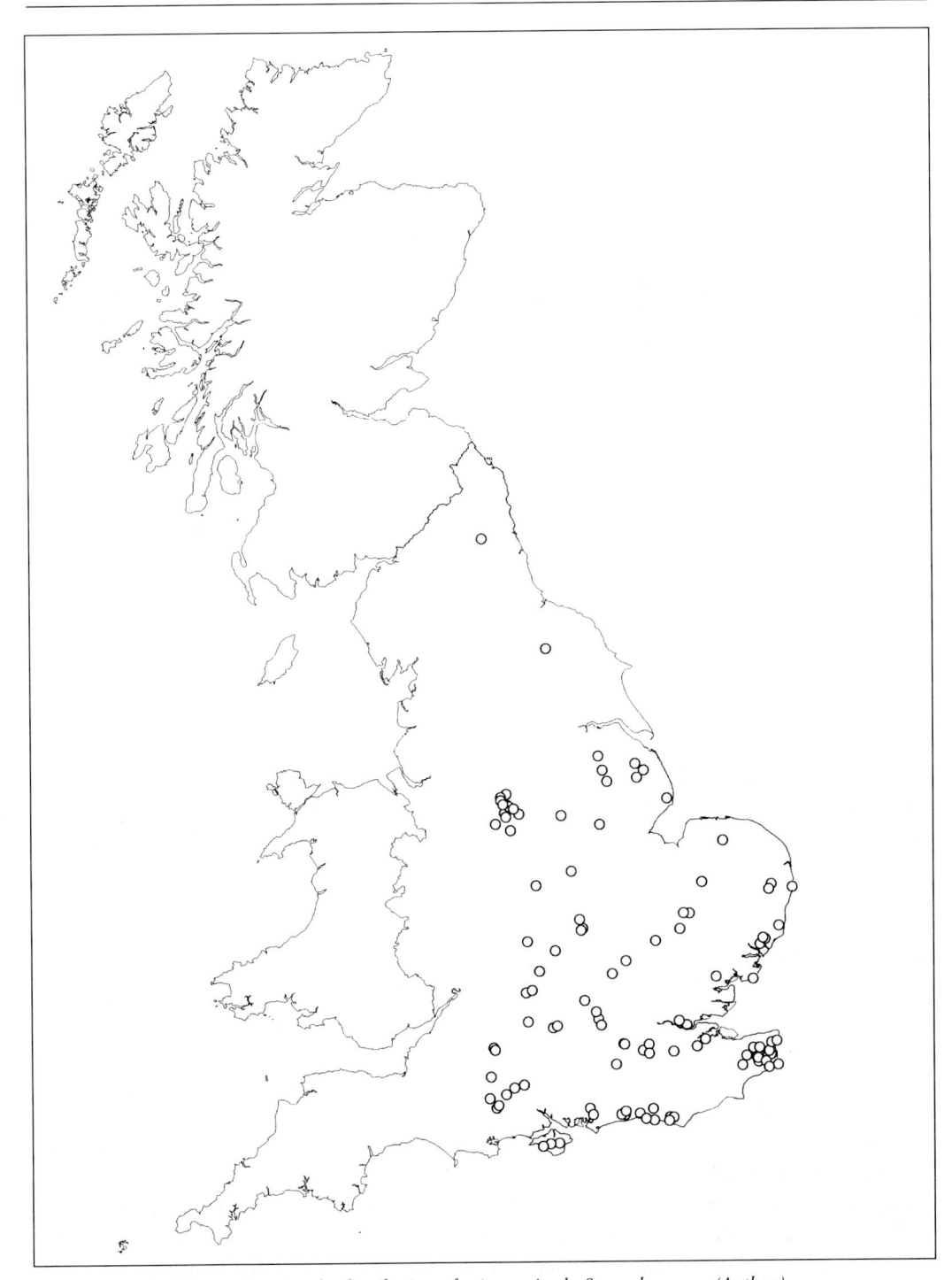

Fig. 5.13. Map of Britain showing the distribution of primary Anglo-Saxon barrows. (Author.)

inhumations, while on the same ridge eleven smaller barrows produced Anglo-Saxon primary inhumations and cremations, which appeared to be spatially distinct (ibid.: 89–96). At Laverstock, Wiltshire, two barrows were excavated in 1964. One produced the tip of an iron sword and a bronze strip, suggesting a destroyed secondary burial in a Bronze Age barrow, while the other produced the seventh-century primary burial of a powerful male, forty to fifty years old, with two spears, a sugar-loaf shield-boss, a seax with silver and garnet pommel, a garnet-decorated double-tongued buckle, a bone comb and a bronze hanging bowl containing onions, crab apples and lengths of string. It has been suggested that this barrow was a Saxon version of a disc barrow, and intriguingly pottery had been dropped in the interior just subsequent to burial, suggesting perhaps either post-burial rituals or return visits to the graves (Musty 1969).

The practice of reusing prehistoric mounds and constructing new burial mounds has been argued to be a response to church-graves (which also offered an opportunity for elaborate and long-standing monuments to the deceased), while expressing the opposition of non-Christians to the Christian elite (Carver 1986: 99; Carver 1992b: 365; van der Noort 1993). However, the reuse of prehistoric monuments, as detailed above, was a long-lasting aspect of early Anglo-Saxon funerary practices, which in its earliest instances dates back well before any influence from Christianity can be discerned. The construction of massive primary mounds, such as at Sutton Hoo, may represent a distinctive development as such, and the idea may have come from the practice of secondary barrow burial (especially as secondary barrow use is also found concentrated in Derbyshire and Wiltshire), but the latter should not be seen only as a contemporary phenomenon of this (see also Williams 1998: 95).

One interesting aspect which has been commented on extensively is the apparent coincidence in a number of areas of cemeteries and barrow burials with territorial divisions such as county, hundred and parish boundaries. In a series of papers Bonney (1966; 1972; 1979) appeared to demonstrate that earlier burials (identified both by the excavations of cemeteries and barrows, and by the use of 'heathen burials' mentioned in charters) lay on the boundaries of ancient ecclesiastical parishes. There are a couple of problems with Bonney's argument, however, which have been recently discussed by Reynolds (1999). Firstly, the work on Wiltshire parishes identified proximity as being within 500m of a boundary. However, the downland nature of many of these parishes means that they are long and thin, and thus a substantial proportion of their area lies within 500m of such a boundary. Secondly, while there is no argument over the location of the excavated Anglo-Saxon cemeteries, Reynolds disputes Bonney's reading of 'heathen burials' as indicating fifth- to seventh-century burials. Rather, he demonstrates convincingly that this is a reference to tenth- and eleventh-century burials of social and legal outcasts, excluded from the Christian burial rite within defined churchyards and instead relegated to burial on the boundary, often the hundred boundary. Excluding the mentions of heathen burial from Bonney's maps (e.g. that at 1979: 43) produces a much less coherent distribution, weakening his argument for the pre-existence of such land-units in the earlier Anglo-Saxon period in many instances, though of course his cases based on excavated evidence still stand.

In a more rigorous study, Goodier (1984) also looked at this issue, with a simple comparison of recorded Anglo-Saxon furnished burial sites against civil parish boundaries.

She found that 17.9 per cent of all sites were on or within 50m of the parish boundary, a figure which was statistically significant (i.e. unlikely to have been generated by chance). She also found that more of these boundary burials were either primary or secondary in barrows, and that more were of sixth- or seventh-century date rather than earlier, but there were considerable regional variations in this. Examples include the solitary burial from Farndish (Bedfordshire) found in 1828 and accompanied by a pair of tweezers, a knife, a buckle, a comb, three mostly amber necklaces and a horned small-long brooch which was interred in a bank which formed the county boundary here (Smith 1904: 189; Morris 1962: 66). The linear ditch which acted as a boundary to the Portway cemetery may also have formed part of a territorial division, in which case it is interesting that the female burial in G50 on the east side of that boundary was distinguished in other ways, which the excavators suggest might indicate that she was an 'outsider' from that neighbouring territory, marked out as such in the burial rite (Cook & Dacre 1985: 53)

Finally, there has been some discussion of features which seem to be contemporary with burials, and serve to structure their layout. At Lyminge, Kent, two gulley features on the edge of the excavated area, possibly the remains of rectangular structures, appeared to be respected by the burials (Warhurst 1955; Wilson 1992a: 48), as seemed to be the case for sub-circular slot features at Portway, Hampshire and Sewerby, Yorkshire (Wilson 1992a: 52). Clearer evidence is available for the square enclosure 581 at Spong Hill, which was 6-7m long, and both cut through and was cut by inhumation burials in the north-east corner of the site, indicating that it was contemporary with a brief phase of the cemetery (Hills et al. 1984: 12). Wilson (1992a: 48–53) suggests that some of these features may have served to demarcate 'sacred areas', or they may be the foundations for more solid structures such as shrines or mortuary houses. In a recent wide-ranging review John Blair (1995) argues for a late sixth- to seventh-century tradition of square enclosures and structures, derived from a continuing Iron Age/Romano-British tradition, and often focusing on existing monuments (for example, at Garton Station, where he argues that the rectangular enclosures are largely Anglo-Saxon additions to the Iron Age barrow cemetery). With modern excavation techniques now standard (i.e. the use of open-area excavation), more evidence for such structures can be expected to emerge.

Cemeteries Through Time

Of all cemeteries of known date, 469 date from the earlier phase of burial (i.e. fifth to sixth century), while 261 belong to the later phase (i.e. later sixth century and later). Just 61 have evidence for both early and late rites. In addition, many undated cemeteries may be later, but these are often difficult to date owing to their characteristic scarcity of grave-goods.

There are a small number of instances of seemingly very early 'Germanic' graves found in late fourth- or early fifth-century contexts. For example, a grave found outside Richborough Castle in Kent has been argued to be that of a late Roman soldier of Germanic ancestry, for it was interred with a long sword, spear, shield and pewter bowl – an assemblage typical of late Roman military burials on the continent (Bushe-Fox 1949: 80; Hawkes & Dunning 1961: 17–18). Of perhaps similar date is the male burial found in Dyke Hills, Dorchester, Oxon, with a late fourth- or early fifth-century Gallo-Roman belt set (Leeds 1939: 350). However, the arguments about the 'Germanic' nature of weapon burial in the fourth and fifth centuries are not as sound as they could be. These graves may well represent an unusual variant of late Roman burial practice.

Searches for continuity between late Roman and early Anglo-Saxon burial rites have been largely unproductive, although there are some suggestive exceptions. At Sandy, Bedfordshire, an early Saxon cremation cemetery was very closely associated with a large Roman cemetery, which included a group of thirteen early fifth-century cremations, outside a Roman town (Morris 1962: 70; Bilikowska 1980: 29). Likewise at Hassocks, Sussex, Anglo-Saxon cremation urns were found in a Roman cremation cemetery, primarily of the third century AD (Lyne 1994).

At Frilford I (Berkshire) fourth-century Romano-British burials were found in 1864–8 in the same place as early Anglo-Saxon cremations and inhumations (Smith 1906: 235–7). The earlier burials included those oriented to WNW, with fourth-century coins placed in their mouths, plus many unfurnished skeletons with their heads to the west, while the Anglo-Saxon burials comprised cremations in plain or decorated urns, inhumations laid at full length with the 'usual grave furniture', and also a group with their heads to the west and stone slabs in the grave, including a number with pillow-stones. These findings suggest a long period of use for this cemetery. Later excavations in the Roman part of the cemetery in 1937–8 found a further six graves, one of which contained a coin hoard dating to not earlier than AD 440, suggesting that Roman burial at this site had continued well into the mid-fifth century. It is unfortunate that the area where the Roman and Anglo-Saxon type burials appeared to overlap had been destroyed by quarrying (Bradford & Goodchild 1939), meaning that the questions arising from these excavations will never be resolved.

Coincidence of Roman and Anglo-Saxon burial was also seen at the cemetery underneath Girton College on the outskirts of Cambridge. Excavations in the 1880s revealed extensive Roman buildings, plus at least six undoubted Romano-British burials (both inhumations and cremations), as well as many Anglo-Saxon burials, some of which had Roman brooches while others were accompanied by Roman vessels (Lethbridge 1938: 313). At West Lane, Kemble in Gloucestershire, the eleven burials in a small late Roman rural cemetery were oriented N–S and provided with hobnailed boots, equipment and food offerings; in the same area were six poorly furnished Anglo-Saxon burials, which all had their heads either to north or south (King et al. 1996). Although poorly furnished cemeteries tend to be late, there is nothing categorically seventh century about these burials, which may thus be reasonably close in time. At Itchen Abbas a fifth-century weapon burial and a young man in a coffin with hobnail boots and a late Romano-British coin in a purse were found, suggesting something similar (*Medieval Archaeology* 29, 1985: 180–1; *Medieval Archaeology* 39, 1995: 211–12).

A convincing case of Roman–Saxon burial continuity is seen at Great Casterton, Rutland, where two groups of Roman burials were followed by a small group of Saxon inhumations, then cremations and finally further Saxon inhumations, with all these burials post-dating the counterscarp bank of the Roman town (Whitwell 1967: 41; Fennell 1974: 287). More recently, excavations at Wasperton in Warwickshire produced an intriguing series of both cremation and inhumation burials, which appear to show Roman burial practices mutating into Anglo-Saxon rites (Crawford 1983: 25–7). Further consideration must, however, await full publication. If any similar sites are excavated in future, they would be ripe for the application of DNA analysis, in order to determine whether there is, in fact, any continuity of population represented by such sites, despite the changing burial practices.

Within the Anglo-Saxon period, one cemetery is sometimes thought to be superseded by another close by. This may be the case at the recently excavated sites of Roxby, Lincolnshire, where cemetery 1, a sixth-century site with around forty-three inhumation and two cremations, seemed to be set within a pre-existing field, while cemetery, 2, consisting of eighty-two burials with characteristic seventh-century goods, was set within an adjoining field (*Medieval Archaeology* 2, 1998: 144). Similarly at Portway a small group of seventh-century burials was found 800m to the west of the larger fifth- and sixth-century cemetery (Cook & Dacre 1985: 22), while a similar shift in location at the end of the sixth century was suggested for the two sites near Sancton in Yorkshire (Faull 1976; Myres & Southern 1973; Timby 1993). The later site here was also smaller, replacing in this instance a large cremation cemetery. What we may be seeing here is the establishment of new cemeteries serving more local populations at this time (Faull 1976).

Two nearby cemeteries at Beckford (A and B) were found to be contemporary. Evison & Hill (1996: 38) suggest that the smaller site, cemetery A, with twenty-four inhumations, represented the establishment of a separate cemetery for a group inflicted by leprosy (this site contained one probable and two possible cases of this condition) and possibly a family group, as there were also five cases of *spina bifida* (presumably *occulta*, though this is not stated in the report). They also see the comparatively high number of non-adult burials from cemetery A as representing the premature deaths of a closely in-bred group (ibid.). Some caution needs to be exercised here, however, as the bones from cemetery B were very poorly preserved, and any existing medical conditions or non-metric traits would be very difficult to distinguish. It remains interesting, though, that two cemeteries should co-exist within a small area.

Looking at the seventh- and eighth-century cemeteries, some interesting regional distinctions are seen. One peculiarity of east Kent is the number of extensive late cemeteries which have been discovered. One example is the Updown, Eastry, site, where a large number of burials surrounded by penannular ditches are visible on aerial photographs; thirty-six were excavated in 1976 and a further fifty-four (thirteen of which turned out to have been excavated in 1976) in 1989. The site had been scheduled, and these excavations were carried out in advance of pipeline construction and the building of the Eastry by-pass. These excavated burials were largely oriented west–east, in large and deep graves, and were accompanied by a range of goods, such as sugar-loaf shield-bosses, Style II ornamented jewellery, thread boxes and seaxes, which suggested use of the cemetery between approximately AD 650 and AD 750 (Willson 1990: 229–30). Occasionally, such cemeteries can be seen to have earlier origins, rather than being new foundations at the start of the seventh century. The large (unfortunately still unpublished) cemetery from Finglesham contained four exceptionally rich burials which were interpreted by the excavator as founders' graves from the first half of the sixth century, as well as a number of other sixth-century burials and over two hundred burials probably dating to the seventh and early eighth centuries (Hawkes 1976: 33–7). Other possible founders' graves have been interpreted by Stoodley (1997: 218) at Petersfinger. Grave 2 was a male with a sword, axe, shield and spear, while G29 was a female with brooches, a necklace, pin, bracelet and ring. Both were early in the history of the cemetery and on the southern fringe of the site.

Sometimes furnished cemeteries themselves are reused. At the Goblin Works cemetery in Leatherhead, Surrey, a small sixth- and seventh-century cemetery was reused as the site of an execution cemetery dating from the seventh to the twelfth century. The earlier graves were oriented west–east and were deposited either supine or crouched into well-cut graves in the chalk, while the execution burials were oriented north–south and were carelessly interred in shallow graves, some having their hands tied behind their backs, and others prone or decapitated (Poulton 1987: 311–17). Likewise at Banstead Common, Surrey, the primary Anglo-Saxon barrow was later used as the site of a gallows, and the burial of five victims of hanging had disturbed the primary grave. These execution cemeteries may have deliberately used a known site with pagan or pre-Christian connotations for the burial of those deemed to be excluded from Christian burial within a churchyard.

Tracing the development of cemeteries through time is a difficult and time-consuming exercise, which is heavily reliant on the use of grave-good chronologies. Perseverance, however, can produce worthwhile results, as we start to get a picture of these sites as places which were maintained as areas of the dead, sometimes possibly even over the traditional period boundary of Roman–Saxon. Looking at cemeteries as sites which have chronological depth forces us to think about the people who used them over such a long time span, and about the various decisions they made regarding how to bury their dead. When these cemeteries go out of use, we can start to discern major social changes, affecting all aspects of society, which meant that whole communities were impelled to break with tradition, and start burying their dead in different costumes, and very often in different landscape locations. Possible reasons for this dramatic change will be explored in Chapter Seven.

THE LIVING AND THE DEAD: CEMETERIES AND SETTLEMENTS

Another way to focus on the living people creating and using the cemeteries is to examine the settlements in which they lived. Even now, however, very few cemeteries have been found to have accompanying settlements. The general lack of excavated settlements means that we cannot know whether the general settlement pattern was one of nucleated villages or more dispersed farmsteads (Hills 1979: 310). Large cemeteries, especially the very large cremation cemeteries like Spong Hill, may have served several communities, or even formed a focal point for the whole neighbourhood (ibid.), while smaller cemeteries presumably served a more localised community. We may get some indication of relations between the living and their dead by looking at the general distributions of settlements and cemeteries. Cemeteries are often located on high ground, whereas we would expect settlements to be founded in more sheltered valley sites (ibid.). This is precisely the situation found in East Yorkshire, where the bulk of the known settlement sites were located in and around the valleys of the eastern Yorkshire Wolds, with the cemeteries located higher up in the Wolds (intriguingly, they seem to move higher up through the

STUDYING CEMETERIES

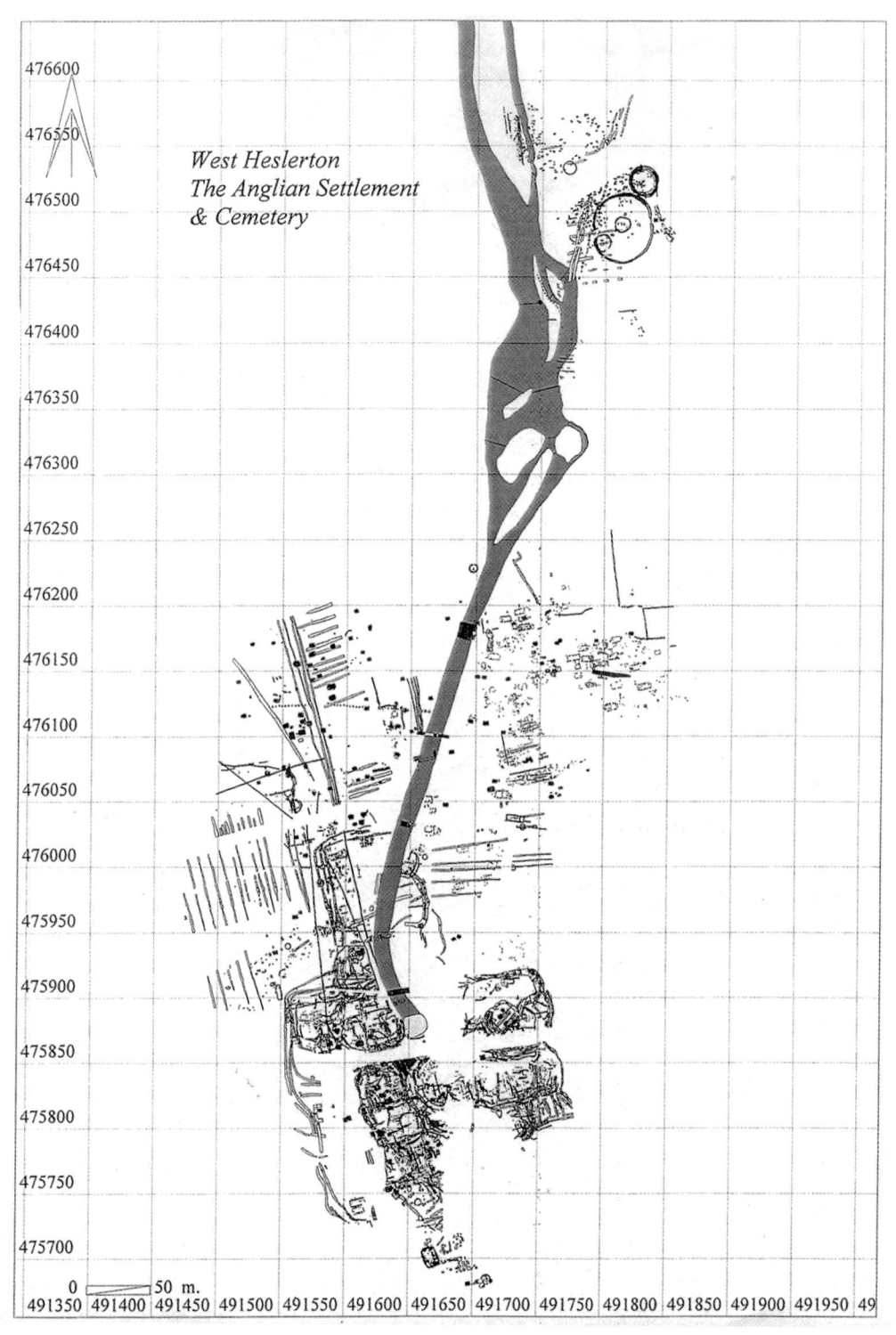

Fig. 5.14. Plan of West Heslerton, showing the cemetery in relation to the settlement site (reproduced by kind permission of Dominic Powlesland).

period (Lucy 1998: 98). These findings have interesting implications for studies which try to map 'settlement' through looking at distributions of cemeteries.

Of more potential would seem to be the study of a paired settlement and cemetery, to see if any social structures discernible within one can also be seen in the other. Again, however, we suffer from lack of evidence. The settlement and cemetery complex at Mucking in Essex unfortunately remains half-published, with only brief accounts of the cemetery finds being currently available. Two separate early Anglo-Saxon cemeteries were excavated close to the extensive settlement site (as well as three Romano-British cemeteries), producing a total of seventy inhumations in the disturbed cemetery 1 and nearly 800 inhumations and cremations in cemetery 2, which was completely excavated (Jones & Jones 1974: 29). The finds indicate dates from the early fifth to the early seventh century, making this a long-lived settlement and burial area. Three graves have late Roman military belt-equipment and early Anglo-Saxon metalwork in association, and it is unsatisfactory that a site which is so important for the understanding of this transitional period should remain unpublished. At West Stow the settlement evidence is well published, but the cemetery was excavated in the nineteenth century and only partial records survive (West 1985).

The site at West Heslerton offers more possibility for interpretation, as it is on schedule to be published within the next few years (**Fig. 5.14**). Here a cemetery of around two hundred burials (ten of which were cremations) was located a few hundred metres away from an extensive settlement area, with sunken-featured buildings and halls, which appeared to be divided into activity zones (Powlesland 1997a). The precise and detailed recording used in the excavation of this site means that very detailed reconstructions will be available for analysis and comparison with the cemetery data.

This chapter has shown how there is a great deal of potential evidence which can be extracted by looking at cemeteries in their wider context. Rather than just seeing them as potential 'mines' for grave-goods, examination of the places in which they are founded, the ways in which they develop over time and the distinctions which are drawn spatially between different groups of people, can all help add to the detailed and interesting picture which this book has been attempting to show. What, though, do these cemeteries mean in even wider terms, such as long-term historical sequences? The following two chapters will examine the various historical debates in which cemeteries of this type have been used as evidence, and will argue what these sites can and cannot legitimately be used as evidence for.

SIX

FROM MIGRATION TO INVASION

The earlier chapters of this book have described the nature of the evidence for Anglo-Saxon burial rites in the fifth to eighth centuries, and have attempted to show the limits of that evidence and what it can be reasonably used to infer. I have tried to show how all the different types of evidence – skeletal, artefactual and burial practices – must be used with care, in order to prevent false and unjustifiable statements being made. In the past, however, the frameworks of interpretation were very different – for example, the assumptions about what artefacts could be seen to represent. A 'Germanic' artefact in a grave was interpreted in an extremely straightforward manner as evidence for a Germanic person being present in that grave, in the same way that jewellery was thought to denote a female. In this chapter and the next I shall trace the history of ideas about Anglo-Saxon cemeteries, and how they should be interpreted. This chapter will deal with what can be called the more 'traditional' interpretations – largely those that rely on some form of invasion or migration from the continent in the fifth and sixth centuries – to explain the various changes in material culture seen in Britain. The following chapter will look at some alternative views which are being developed to explain not only these transitions but also those which occur in the later sixth and seventh centuries.

THE IMPACT OF THE HISTORIANS, 1800–1900

Before looking at how the archaeological evidence was dealt with, it is important to understand the historical frameworks that were current in the nineenth and twentieth centuries. These versions of the past, based on the sparse documentary sources, have strongly influenced the stories that have been told from the archaeology and they cannot be ignored. It is useful first to look at the documentary sources themselves, and then at how historians of various periods have interpreted them.

Interpreting the documentary sources

The earliest, almost contemporary, source which we have for the period in which furnished cemeteries were in use is Gildas' *De excidio Britanniae et conquestu*, where in Book One he depicts events from the fourth century to his own day (probably sometime in the sixth century), as a punishment by God, in the form of barbarian onslaughts, for the failings of the British church and its leaders (Winterbottom 1978; Lapidge & Dumville 1984). In colourful Latin text, this British cleric paints a picture of his people under attack by the Picts and Scots, and appealing to a Roman commander for help; the Roman armies having been earlier withdrawn, their appeal went unheeded. A while later, under threat again, 'the proud tyrant' invited the 'ferocious Saxons' into the island 'like wolves into the fold, to beat back the peoples of the north' (Winterbottom 1978: Ch. 23). As the current translation puts it:

> Then a pack of cubs burst forth from the lair of the barbarian lioness, coming in three *keels*, as they call warships in their language . . . On the orders of the ill-fated tyrant, they first of all fixed their dreadful claws into the east side of the island, ostensibly to fight for our country, in fact to fight against it. The mother lioness learnt that her first contingent had prospered, and she sent a second and larger troop of satellite dogs. (Ibid.)

These 'barbarians' are then depicted as demanding more supplies, and breaking their agreement to protect their hosts; instead 'all the major towns were laid low by the repeated battering of enemy rams; laid low, too, all the inhabitants – church leaders, priests and people alike, as the swords glinted all around and the flames crackled' (ibid.: Ch. 24). Some of the survivors of this onslaught were caught in the mountains and butchered, others surrendered and were enslaved, while yet more 'made for lands beyond the sea' (ibid.: Ch. 25). Gildas then talks of a resurgence, when the 'cruel plunderers had gone home', under Ambrosius Aurelianus, and 'from then on victory went now to our countrymen, now to their enemies', culminating in the siege of Badon Hill 'pretty well the last defeat of the villains, and certainly not the least. That was the year of my birth; as I know, one month of the forty-fourth year since then has already passed' (ibid.: Ch. 26).

This text has been tremendously influential, for it seems to give a dating for 'the Coming of the Saxons', on which so many historical interpretations have been based. It was used heavily in *The Ecclesiastical History of the English People*, written by the monk known as the Venerable Bede, writing in Jarrow in the eighth century AD (see Goffart 1988: 235–328 for details of the historical context and political purpose of Bede's work). Bede certainly thought that Gildas could be used to date the *Adventus Saxonum*, for it was his main source for this period, despite the obvious vagueness of the *De Excidio* in terms of chronology and geography. Bede also did not have much choice in his sources – continental writers of the fifth and sixth centuries had largely ignored Britain in their works, and two of the sources which do mention this country were unknown here in the eighth century (Sims-Williams 1983: 5). Much of the debate surrounding the events of the fifth century rests on a now well-known passage from Bede's work (I, 15), which appears to be an authorial interpolation into a narrative largely based around Gildas, which rests at least partly on the political nomenclature of Bede's own day:

> They came from three very powerful Germanic tribes, the Saxons, the Angles and the Jutes. The people of Kent and the inhabitants of the Isle of Wight are of Jutish origin, and also those opposite the Isle of Wight, that part of the Kingdom of Wessex which is still today called the nation of the Jutes. From the Saxon country, that is, the district now known as Old Saxony, came the East Saxons, the South Saxons, and the West Saxons. Besides this from the country of the Angles, that is the land between the

kingdoms of the Jutes and the Saxons, which is called *Angulus*, came the East Angles, the Middle Angles, the Mercians, and all the Northumbrian race . . . as well as the other Anglian tribes. *Angulus* is said to have remained deserted from that day to this. (Colgrave & Mynors 1969: 51)

Bede, like other historians after him, placed the arrival of the tribes in the middle of the fifth century, presumably on the basis of the one datable fact in Gildas – the letter sent by the Britons to a named Roman commander (Sims-Williams 1983: 6, 16–17). Unfortunately 'Agitus', Gildas' version of the name of this commander, is not recorded anywhere, so historians (of whom Bede was the first) assumed that it was a form of 'Aëtius', a military leader active in Gaul in the 440s, who died in 454 (Brooks 1994: 91). Although this seems to over-compress the long series of events (the defeat of the Picts and Irish, a period of luxury, and a plague) which Gildas describes between the appeal and the decision to invite the Saxons (ibid.; Sims-Williams 1983: 20), the date of around AD 449 for the 'Coming of the Saxons' has been largely accepted. This was certainly true of the later *Anglo-Saxon Chronicle*, compiled in its earliest current form in the late ninth century. Sims-Williams (1983: 26) accepts that some entries from the mid-seventh century onwards seem to be derived from contemporary annals, but states that it is uncertain when the narrative was extended back to cover the fifth and sixth centuries. He also argues that this earlier part of the *Chronicle* is peculiar in annalistic terms, with none of the eclipses and natural disasters one might expect from contemporary annals, but instead it comprises the origin legends of Kent, Sussex and Wessex (ibid.: 27), many of which seem to be based on folk etymology – taking current names for places, and inventing stories to explain them. For example, Portsmouth is interpreted as being founded by Port who landed with two ships in 501, although its actual origin lies in a derivation from the Latin *portus* (ibid.: 29).

Sims-Williams (1983: 40) is thus highly sceptical about the veracity of these early sources: 'It is one thing to admit that there "may be something in" the traditions reported by Bede and the *Chronicle*; it is quite another to imagine that we can divine what that something is.' Furthermore, 'the accounts of the settlement in Bede and the *Chronicle*, in so far as they do not derive from Gildas, are of value only for the light they shed on early Anglo-Saxon dynastic, heroic and topographical tradition and learned historiography' (ibid.: 41). In an analysis of the documentary sources for sub-Roman Britain, Dumville (1977) likewise argued that the only one that could be used with any confidence was Gildas. Dumville argues that Gildas is the prime text for the fourth to sixth centuries, as he alone had access to contemporary sources for the fifth century, and he was an eyewitness to events of the earlier sixth (ibid.: 191). Yet if Gildas is our only reliable source for this period, what is he actually referring to in his passage, and what is his intention in relating his narrative?

It is clearly not a straightforward historical account – it is allegorical and polemical. In a wider context, the first twenty-six chapters of Gildas' work are a prelude to a complaint to the rulers of his day, a sort of political sermon. Brooks (1984) sees it as outlining a programme of reform for the current corrupt leadership, which Gildas saw as lacking legal claims to power and ruling without social justice. Given, then, that Gildas did not set out to write a coherent history, but was putting forward arguments for change, with the

'Saxons' invoked as a form of divine punishment, how much weight can we put on the interpretation of his text, even if we can clearly discern what that text means (something which has defeated many historians)?

What we certainly cannot do is use the chronological framework inferred from it by Bede, and elaborated on in the *Anglo-Saxon Chronicle* as the historical basis on which to pin archaeological sequences. These works were written for specific purposes, in contexts of emerging and stabilising kingdoms and territories. Susan Reynolds (1983) argues that this desire to classify the peoples of Europe (seen in passages like Bede's) began in the sixth to seventh century AD, that such myths of common origin served to increase or express the sense of solidarity of such peoples, and that their origins lay 'in the desire of learned clerics both to find honourable origins for their own peoples and to make sense of the contemporary world in the light of classical and Christian learning' (ibid.: 375). She emphasises that all origin myths, including those that derive descent from the Trojans or from the north German peoples, are just that – myths – and that 'we have very little evidence at all, outside stories that were told and elaborated after the sixth century, that a larger proportion of the population of Europe moved around during the "Age of Migrations" than at any other time' (ibid.: 379). These myths came to have particular appeal when ideas about the common descent and customs of a group came to coincide with a territorial definition of a people – when all those living within an area claimed allegiance to the same leader (ibid.: 382–823). Thus, in the eighth century Bede ascribed slightly different origins to the Angles, Saxons and Jutes, and did not question the right to independence of the separate kingdoms, yet a sense of 'English' solidarity was only evident from the tenth century (ibid.: 383–4). In this theory Reynolds is supported by Wood (1990: 96): 'the *adventus Saxonum*, whatever it was, is scarcely noticed by 5th and 6th century writers; it is only Bede, interpreting Gildas, who transforms the 'Coming of the Saxons' into a major event in the emergence of England.'

Peopling England

However, when versions of the English past were penned in previous centuries, it was these historical sources which were first turned to, for they were accepted as more or less true records of the events of the fifth, sixth and seventh centuries, which were the beginnings of the inexorable process of the 'rise of the English nation'. The 'Coming of the Saxons' is now so much a part of our national mythology that it is not often realised that the origins of the people who lived in the eastern and southern part of Britain, now known as the English, have not always been traced back to Germanic invaders or migrants from the continent. Although this was the case from about AD 700 to AD 1100, and from around AD 1600 through to the present, for a large part of the medieval period a different 'origin myth' was in place, that of the *Brutus*, which traced the origins of the Britons back to the Trojans, with the advent of the Saxons seen as an unimportant episode (MacDougall 1982). The Brutus myth (seen in its most popular form in Geoffrey of Monmouth's *History of the Kings of Britain*, written around 1136) was widely accepted as historical truth in Britain from at least the twelfth to the sixteenth century, in many different versions. This is also the version of the history of Britain that introduced the mythical Arthur as a key historical figure. However, owing to political and religious conflicts, this origin story came to be replaced in the course of the sixteenth and seventeenth centuries by a different version of the past, which saw characters such as Hengist, Horsa and Alfred as the pivotal figures in the creation of the English people and nation (see Lucy 1998: 5–9 and MacDougall 1982 for a fuller account of this replacement). This 'Anglo-Saxonist' version of the past is still, to a large extent, historical dogma, although it is not as powerful as it once was, for many people in England, especially those schooled before the 1960s, still regard themselves as being descended from the Germanic peoples said to have settled in Britain in the fifth and sixth centuries.

The Anglo-Saxonist version did not remain static, however. At the beginning of the eighteenth century there was a widespread belief in the Germanic nature of English institutions such as parliament and trial by jury, but by the later nineteenth century this had mutated into depictions of the fifth and sixth centuries as a time when the native inhabitants of Britain were exterminated, or driven into Cornwall and Wales, by massed forces of Germanic tribes (although this view is seen as early as 1762, cf. Hume's *The History of England, 11–19*). This is clearly related to changing ideas about the nature of 'peoples' and nations, with the introduction of a strong racial element into interpretations of history during the nineteenth century.

The development of such attitudes can perhaps be linked to the increasing importance of issues of nationhood and nationalism (cf. Hobsbawm 1990). After the Act of Union with Scotland in 1707, Britain was a Protestant state. Successive wars with France, a Catholic country, throughout the eighteenth century provided an 'other' in opposition to which Britons defined themselves, and thus an idea of 'Britishness' was superimposed over an array of internal English, Welsh and Scottish differences (Colley 1992). French contamination was perceived as an evil, and many believed that Britons needed to become more moral and united. Evidence for this was sought in the past: in 1756 John Frere called for the English, Lowland Scots and the Hanoverian Kings, all of whom were descendants of the Saxons, to live in harmony with the Ancient Britons (the Welsh) (ibid.: 90).

Likewise, the French Revolution in 1789 prompted Burke (1790) to eulogise the British constitution and social system, stressing its antiquity and emphasising national differences in government and history (Peardon 1933: 163–4). The Napoleonic Wars and the loss of America in the War of Independence around the turn of the century also served to bring the ties between England and Scotland closer together (Colley 1992: 144). Such patriotic feeling in Britain at this time prompted an interest in periods of national origin and glory, and specifically renewed enthusiasm for the medieval period, both pre- and post-Conquest (Peardon 1933: 229–30; Smith 1987: 56). The uniting of a Protestant Britain also facilitated the creation of oppositions with Catholic Ireland, and antagonism to increasing Irish immigration into Britain after 1800 (Colley 1992: 330).

The first historian to make full use of the Anglo-Saxons in this patriotic sense was Sharon Turner. In *A History of the Anglo-Saxons* (1799–1805) he stated that 'the subject of Anglo-Saxon antiquities had been nearly forgotten by the British public; although a large part of what we most love and venerate in our customs, laws and institutions, originated among our Anglo-Saxon ancestors' (Turner ibid.: vii). In 1820 (in the preface to the 3rd edition: v–viii) it could be related of him that, looking back, 'his favourite desire has been fulfilled – a taste for the history and remains of our Great Ancestors has been revived, and is visibly increasing'. Turner was the first of the 'Germanist' historians, who believed that the Germanic element was responsible for the finest features of the English: 'This nation exhibits the conversion of ferocious pirates, into a highly civilized, informed and generous people – in a word, into ourselves' (1799–1805, vol. II: xi–xii) and that: 'Our language, our government, and our laws display our Gothic ancestors in every part. They live, not merely in our annals and traditions, but in our civil institutions and perpetual discourse' (ibid., vol. I: 188–9). Turner wished to demonstrate that the English language was principally Saxon, in reaction to Hume's view that it was predominantly of French origin (Peardon 1933: 221). Likewise, the Revd James Ingram, in his Inaugural Lecture as Professor of Anglo-Saxon at Oxford in 1807, made an appeal for Anglo-Saxon studies to be based on patriotic grounds (ibid.: 244–5). All aspects of the subject – archaeology, language and architecture among them – could be used to reinforce the current opinion of the English (and hence British) nation.

In a similar manner, from 1800 to 1850 historical scholarship in Germany had been undergoing dramatic changes, linked to ideas of national cultural independence and a rise in respect for the non-Classical past (Burrow 1981; Hale 1967; Rowlands 1988). Rather than a source of national shame, barbarian origins came to be seen as a dynamic impulse in a people, prompting continuous innovation and cultural change (Rowlands 1988: 59). This new attitude at first had little impact on English historians of the time, although after the 1830s there was some editing and translation work being done by Thorpe and Kemble (Burrow 1981: 119). Thorpe had translated Lappenberg's *A History of England under the Anglo-Saxon Kings* (1834) in 1846, but it was not until 1849 that an English historian again turned to the subject of the Anglo-Saxons.

In 1834 Kemble had studied philology under Grimm at Gottingen, having become interested in the Anglo-Saxon language while a student at Cambridge. In 1849 he published *The Saxons in England* in which he questioned the narratives of Bede and the *Anglo-Saxon Chronicle* reproduced in the works of Turner and Lappenberg (Sims-Williams 1983: 1): 'I confess that the more I examine this question, the more completely I am convinced that the received accounts of our migrations, our subsequent fortunes, and ultimate settlement are devoid of historical truth in every detail' (Kemble 1849 I: 16). He regarded the earliest historical sources as 'a confused mass of traditions borrowed from the most heterogeneous sources, compacted rudely and with little ingenuity, and in which the smallest possible amount of historical truth is involved in a great deal of fable' (ibid.: 3). Although he was the first historian to deal with the Anglo-Saxons in a critical and narrative manner, he nevertheless showed signs of deeply entrenched Germanism in his work. He did not doubt that the migrations took place, and that the current population of England were Germanic in their spirit and institutions, but he saw the transformation as a gradual process beginning in the third century AD, with AD 449 being an episode within this, rather than a decisive event in the history of England. In addition, he did not require the extermination of the native population: 'the mass of the people, accustomed to Roman rule or the oppression of native princes, probably suffered little by a change of masters, and did little to avoid it' (ibid.: 20). Such ideas, however, attacking the English national story with the weapons of foreign scholarship (Sims-Williams 1983: 1) were not found congenial by the increasingly nationalistic public.

Far more in favour were the works of Edwin Guest, and the historians of the so-called 'Oxford School' (in fact a group of close friends who were clerics and men of independent means, largely on the fringes of academe), such as E.A. Freeman, William Stubbs and J.R. Green, whose works were thoroughly reliant on the historical framework found in the pages of Bede and the *Anglo-Saxon Chronicle* (Freeman 1869; 1872; 1881; 1888; Green 1874; 1881; 1883; Guest 1850; 1883; Stubbs 1870; 1880; 1906). Broadly, these works promoted 'Anglo-Saxonism', a position which held that the Anglo-Saxons were an identifiable and historically attested race, with common ties of blood, language, geographical origin and culture; that Anglo-Saxon societies were the fullest expression of civil and religious liberties, a fact which was directly attributable to their peculiar genius in political affairs; that the Anglo-Saxons of Britain had virtues and talents which made them superior to all; that those attributes (which included reason, restraint, self-control, love of freedom, hatred of anarchy, respect for the law and distrust of enthusiasm) were transmissible from one generation to the next; and that serious threats came from physiological or biological forces inside the nation or race, including deterioration, limitation or contamination (Curtis 1968: 11–12). Such ideas were obviously derived from the racial theory which had emerged in the course of the nineteenth century, with its view of historical peoples as distinct 'races', the inheritable characteristics of which are threatened by mixing with the blood of another 'race'.

Kemble, although not so vehement in his views, was still susceptible to the general atmosphere of the period, which saw the characteristics of one's ancestors as passed down through generations. Such thinking is apparent in both his history and his archaeology (1849; 1856; 1863). Others took the tenets of Anglo-Saxonism to greater extremes, especially during the 1860s and 1870s, when the influence of the 'Oxford School' was at its peak. This historical tradition attributed Victorian success directly to their Teutonic forebears: 'our forefathers really became the people of the land in all that part of Britain which they conquered' and 'were thus able to grow up as a nation in England, and their laws, manners and language grew up with them, and were not copied from those of other nations' (Freeman 1869: 28), to the extent that Freeman was able to see 'fagging' in public schools as 'a trace of the Teutonic *comitatus*' (1872: 46). Green thought that 'the English conquest was a sheer dispossession and slaughter of the people whom the English conquered' and that 'the new England . . . was the one purely German nation that rose upon the wreck of Rome' (Green 1874: 9, 11). Such ideas plainly relied on extermination of the native population.

Stubbs, the first trained historian to hold the Chair of Modern History at Oxford (from 1866 to 1884), was convinced that England rested on Teutonic foundations: 'The political institutions that we find established in the conquered land . . . are the most purely German institutions that any branch of the German race has preserved' (1880, vol. I: 6). Such historical models were heavily dependent on the atmosphere of racial determinism which pervaded these years, an attitude well illustrated by Kingsley (the historical novelist who held the Chair of Medieval History at Cambridge from 1860), who asserted in a lecture that Teutonic purity 'had given him, as it may give you, gentlemen, a calm and steady brain, and a free and loyal heart; the energy which springs from health; the self-respect which comes from self-restraint; and the spirit which shrinks from neither God nor man, and feels it light to die for wife and child, for people, and for Queen' (1875: 46).

Ideas of 'national' characteristics were extremely prevalent at this time, with Anglo-Saxons often being compared favourably to Celts, who were assigned the traits which were deplored or despised by the upper and middle Victorian classes, such as femininity, violence, emotional incontinence and indolence (Curtis 1968: 64–5). Such nationalistic feeling was thus a way of justifying manifestos of hostility to 'foreigners', such as the Irish (Hobsbawm 1990: 109). One rather disturbing aspect of this emphasis on race as the primary determinant of behaviour were the attempts made by anthropologists to correlate cranial size, intelligence, national character and race (Curtis 1968: 67). The most notorious example of this was John Beddoe, who published his 'index of nigrescence', claiming that one could find in Ireland residual survivals of primitive people who had affinities with 'Africanoid' man ('proving' this by his survey of Cambridge undergraduates, which found a correlation between those with firsts and those who had light hair and blue eyes – obviously those of 'Anglo-Saxon' parentage) (ibid.: 72).

The influence of the 'Oxford School' was so great because of the popularity and accessibility of their writings. Green's *Short History* (1874), for instance, sold hundreds of thousands of copies, and became a manual for schools and a companion for advanced students (Gooch 1952: 331). As the first one-volume account of the civilisation of the English nation, it was only superseded by G.M. Trevelyan's *History of England* in 1926. Kingsley's lectures at Cambridge were far more popular than those of the academic historians. Their work influenced the ideas of a whole generation of children and young people. Although by the 1880s the more extreme forms of invective were no longer generally current, and strident Anglo-Saxonism was toned down by its former proponents in the face of a long tradition of criticism of such ideas by other writers (e.g. Allen 1880; Nicholas 1868; Palmer 1885; Pearson 1867; Pike 1866; Saint John 1862), its influence was still pervasive in popular thought. Allen (1880: 487) offers an amusing observation on this point: 'The idle, ignorant, superstitious Kelt has so often been contrasted with the clear-headed, energetic, pushing Anglo-Saxon, that everybody has hastened to enroll himself under the victorious Anglo-Saxon banner . . . [yet] . . . "Silly Suffolk" is the conventional phrase for the most purely Teutonic country in Britain.'

In the last two decades of the nineteenth century history became a more scholarly discipline, with growing emphasis on the use of primary sources, such as original documents, of which in-depth studies were made (Jann 1985: 218–19). Broad generalisations thus gradually fell out of favour within the academic profession (although even in the next century, they were still to be found in popular writings (Churchill 1956; Loyn 1962; Whitelock 1952)). Even Freeman and Stubbs discounted ideas of total extermination of the native Britons in their later works (Freeman 1888; Stubbs 1906). While Freeman could state in 1869 (Freeman 1869: 28) that by the end of the sixth century 'there seem to have been hardly any Welshmen left in the English part of the country except those who were slaves', in 1888 he asserted that 'I most strongly insist on the survival of a large British element in a large part of what we now call England' (Freeman 1888: 91), and that 'I think we may say that this fashionable doctrine of the extermination of the elder British population has never really been taught by anyone' (ibid.: 92). The agenda, however, had by this time been defined, and the actual fact of the migrations hardly ever questioned. There remained an implicit assumption that English success and superior qualities could be equated with Germanic origins. These assumptions were to have far-reaching effects on the interpretation of Anglo-Saxon cemeteries and the material found within them.

Tracing the Conquest Through Pots and Brooches, 1850–2000

In Chapter One we saw how, as early as 1850, Roach Smith was able to link the emerging regional distinctions of brooch types, such as Kentish, cruciform and saucer brooches, to the divisions between tribal areas outlined by Bede in the eighth century. Such direct linkages between the material culture found in the graves and reconstructions of political history are a common theme in interpretations made of this early archaeological evidence. The grave-goods and associated evidence were used to reconstruct the nature of the conquest, its date, the identity of the conquerors and the fate of the natives, as outlined below. The now-questioned historical sources have thus served to heavily influence the ways in which archaeological evidence has been interpreted.

The nature of the conquest

Lennard pointed out that in 1874 (the year of publication of the first volume of Stubbs' *Constitutional History*) few people would have questioned that the conquest 'was the result of a series of separate expeditions, long continued and perhaps, in point of time, continuous, but unconnected, and independent of one another' (Stubbs 1874: 59). Since 1907 and the publication of Chadwick's *The Origin of the English Nation*, however, he noted that the opinion of historians had undergone a radical change (Lennard 1934: 204). H.M. Chadwick (1907) had asserted that we must reject the notion 'that the invasion was carried out by small groups of adventurers acting independently of each other. It seems to me incredible that such a project as the invasion of Britain could have been carried out successfully except by large and organised forces' (1907: 12). He also did not doubt the truth of Gildas' statements about the extermination of many of the natives (ibid.: 184). This view can certainly be seen to have been adopted by Åberg, who in *The Anglo-Saxons in England* (1926) suggested that the actual invasion 'as far as can be judged, was undertaken with large and organised forces' and that a date for it between AD 400 and 450 tallied well with the archaeology (ibid.: 1). This debate can perhaps be related to the political events of this period which culminated in the First World War, and the resultant fear of conquest by the highly organised armies of other countries. Current situations were perhaps providing useful analogies for the past.

Not all agreed, however. Leeds (1913: 14) thought: 'They came in the first instance not as a proud military power seeking fresh fields to conquer, but in search of loot and plunder, mere bands of ravening pirates . . . once the legions were withdrawn, they descended in hordes on the shores of Britain . . . Force of circumstances, or natural bent, drove them to seek a new home; they came as true immigrants.' There were others, too. Baldwin Brown's *The Arts in Early England* (1903–15) was a survey of all the available evidence for the pagan period, from which he concluded that: 'In the case of the Teutonic migrations in general the moving mass was made up of families not individual men-at-arms, and the women accompanied their husbands and fathers along the march and to the verge of the battlefield.' In addition, early female finds 'seem to attest the presence of women even in the earlier stages of the westward movement. Possibly these were ladies of the Amazonian temper' (ibid.: 47). Brown seems to have had a rather poetic view of these early events, for 'these remains of the ancestors of our race witness to the continuity of our civilization and make our English citizenship a nobler possession for ourselves and our descendants' (Vol. I: 23).

There was further debate in the 1920s and 1930s over the nature of the invasions, as well as doubt about the reliability of the historical record (e.g. Wadstein 1927; Zachrisson 1927). On the question of whether migrations or organised invasions were at issue, Myres (1937: 322–3) chose the middle ground, seeing dense areas of organised settlement in the Upper Thames and East Anglia, and more piecemeal settlement in the then almost archaeologically blank areas of Essex and Hertfordshire, where, he thought, the 'scarcity of recognisable Saxon interments implies not only a late date and material poverty, but also a scattered and thinly spread population, which had abandoned its ancestral habits of cremation or sumptuous inhumation because its constituent communities were at first too isolated from one another to resist by weight of numbers the adoption of customs in vogue among the surviving natives'. The year before, Leeds (1936: 29–30) had argued for the potential of cremation cemeteries to map the progress of the settlement, suggesting a series of inroads from Yorkshire to Norfolk, before those into the south-eastern counties where the rite was very scarce. He placed great weight on the large cremation cemeteries of north Germany going out of use at the very time that they begin to appear in Britain (Leeds 1945: 5), suggesting that their replacement by a small number of inhumation graves was indicative of 'poor land-hungry peasants' migrating, and leaving behind the wealthier inhabitants (Leeds 1946: 30). Collingwood & Myres (1936: 342–3), in the same manner, saw the reasons for the migrations as over-crowding on the continent, such that 'it was only a matter of time before the Saxons began to look on Britain no longer as a source merely of plunder and booty, a happy hunting-ground for piracy and slave-raiding, but as offering a more permanent way of escape from the increasing discomfort of their lives at home'. Later, Hawkes (1982: 65) suggested an interesting variation on this 'migration' theme: she suggests that the early fifth-century Britons of Kent were faced with an influx of 'boat people' (again we see here the influence of modern-day events): 'Whole families and communities uprooted by, and fleeing from, the ruin created by the peak of the marine transgression which was flooding their fields and rendering their homelands uninhabitable', and that the Britons settled the newcomers down wherever there was room. She also suggests that as Roman control slackened during the fifth century, 'more and more of their kinsmen were able to join them. By the middle of the century large tracts of eastern and middle England had been taken over by the English' (ibid.).

It was always a matter of some puzzlement for the early Anglo-Saxon archaeologists that some of the earliest classes of artefacts are found in the Upper Thames valley, far from any coastline. E.T. Leeds argued that these 'Saxon' invaders came up the Bedfordshire Ouse and the Icknield way from areas south and west of the Fens, and others had them coming up the Thames itself, while 'those who still pin their faith to the traditional story in the *Anglo-Saxon Chronicle* can only say that if they were really in any sense West

Saxons, they had no business in the year 500 to be settled in the Oxford district at all' (Myres 1937: 321). This highlights the problem of trying to interpret the archaeology within the traditional historical frameworks, and shows how the furnished burial rite has been so intimately linked with the identification of 'Germanic' invaders or settlers. This linkage is still very strong in much present-day archaeological writing about this period, and various articles have shown how interpretations have swung between mass migrations and elite invasion and take-over at various points throughout this century (e.g. Hamerow 1994; Härke 1995). There is some worth in the argument that these vacillations are due to changing socio-political cirumstances (e.g. Härke 1998).

Interesting attitudes to things Germanic, for example, can be seen in certain writings dating from around the time of the Second World War. Kendrick (1938: 61) railed against the material culture of these invaders: 'the long strings of garish nobbly beads, the big fantastically shaped brooches, the exaggerated forms of girdle-hangers, pins, bucket-mounts, and the like, and the sprawling lumpiness of most of the ornamental metalwork, strengthen the total effect of uncouth barbaric craftsmanship that was usually incapable of rising above awkward ostentation and over-elaboration in display'. Leeds (1936: 20) similarly regarded them as 'an impoverished people, a race of pirates', who lived in filthy hovels (ibid.: 26). But Leeds was wrong on this point – his excavations at Sutton Courtenay in Berkshire in the 1920s had uncovered buildings dating to the fifth and sixth centuries, but these were *Grubenhäuser*, now known as sunken-feature buildings, which were raised over a pit in the ground, with this pit often being used for rubbish disposal once the building had gone out of use; it is also likely that these were workshops and not actual dwellings. It may be that ideas about the racial attributes of Anglo-Saxon cemeteries are also mistaken.

Interestingly, Kendrick thought that the fine jewellery found in Kent and other areas, now dated to the later sixth and seventh centuries, actually belonged to Arthurian Britain. He saw it as a 'natural resurgence of barbaric tendencies set free by the withdrawal of the Romans' (1938: 59) and that 'it is, in fact, precisely because of its new stamp, because of the alert invention and vigorous development behind it, that the native inhabitants of the land in which it appears can be regarded as the only people able to have produced it' (ibid.: 60). Such views were characteristic of a time when things Arthurian were gaining in popularity (for example, T.H. White's novels, first published in 1937), perhaps symbolic of an increase in insular patriotism at this time. Stories which emphasised native survival were more conducive to the atmosphere of the period than those which described invasion and conquest.

This is not to say, however, that rejection of migration and invasion as explanatory mechanisms is necessarily related to present-day political concerns, as Härke (1998) suggests. He maintains that critique of his arguments for a 'Germanic' weapon-bearing group of males in early Anglo-Saxon cemeteries who can be distinguished by their superior stature is due to British archaeologists being uncomfortable with accounts of 'their' past which see domination by outside peoples. As has been shown in Chapter Three, however, Härke's arguments as they relate to the skeletal material can be soundly criticised on scientific grounds – it is not always a matter of subjective opinion when one archaeologist's views are questioned.

Dating the conquest

As well as using the material to identify the nature of the conquest, it has also been used, in conjunction with the documentary sources, to try to assign dates to it. Various attempts have been made to set the date earlier than the traditional AD 449/450 – for example Myres' attempts to date some of the urns in the Caistor-by-Norwich cremation cemetery to the early fourth century AD – through comparison with examples from Funen (Denmark) and the Netherlands, using North German chronologies. Hawkes (1974: 412), however, wrote a stinging critique of Myres' dating schemes: 'Nowhere does he discuss or question the validity and comparative value of these systems, and it must be said here that the pots in the German homelands are dated by associated objects, usually native brooches which themselves are datable only by typological means assisted by occasional associations with objects of Roman type.' It was not, however, that Hawkes believed there was no Germanic presence in Britain before AD 450 – in fact, she spent much of her academic career advocating the role of Germanic *foederati* and *laeti* (types of mercenary soldier) in the settlement of Britain.

In what has been described as her seminal paper (Hawkes & Dunning 1961), she argued that a type of late Roman metalwork found in a few late fourth-century cemeteries such as Dyke Hills, Dorchester, was paralleled by contemporary weapon graves in Gaul, which were generally accepted to be the graves of soldiers in the late Roman army (see Halsall 1992 and Welch 1992 for contrasting reviews of this debate). Building on Werner's (1950) argument that the deposition of arms with the dead was a Germanic custom, she argued that these graves were those of German *laeti* who had been settled in parts of Gaul. By extension, the apparently unarmed individual in Dyke Hills (who was buried near a woman with two brooches of 'north Germanic' origin) was a German, too (although it should be noted that Swanton (1973: 41) was convinced that a spearhead was originally present in this grave). This argument is an interesting one, which has been extremely influential. However, it is all built on a rather shaky premise – the assumption that both the metalwork involved and the practice of weapon burial are 'Germanic'.

To deal with weapon burial first: Hawkes & Dunning acknowledged (1961: 8) the argument by de Laet, Dhondt & Nenquin (1952) that the so-called Germanic characteristics of warrior graves were no more than military fashion common to German and Gallo-Roman soldiers serving in the late Roman army. However, on the basis of one site (Furfooz in Belgium, which had a high proportion of warrior graves, but which was located in the bath-house at a Roman fortified site, and contained an old woman who had been decapitated and a locally made pot with 'German' prototypes), they argued that 'we have a group of military settlers whose material culture is almost indistinguishable from that displayed in graves at Vermand and other late Roman cemeteries in north Gaul, and who can be identified as Germans because they left behind them unmistakable traces of their racial customs and beliefs' (Hawkes & Dunning 1961: 9). As the Roman army was known to have recruited its forces from 'barbarian peoples' at the end of the fourth century, and Germanic *laeti* and *foederati* were similarly known to have settled in the same areas as those with the warrior graves, 'we are surely justified in concluding that Werner was correct when he said that the warrior graves were the graves of Germans' (ibid.: 9). No matter that the Dyke Hills burial was possibly unarmed, and that it was not necessarily associated with the female grave: 'he too was a German, one of a detachment of German soldiers settled with their womenfolk in or near the Roman town of Dorchester' (ibid.: 10). Welch (1992: 270) admits that it is not these male burials with their late Roman belt-sets and/or weapons which provide the evidence for Germanic origins. Rather, it is the 'graves of their womenfolk', containing evidence paralleled in Free Germany, which for him provide the crucial link. Again, we come back to the issue of inferring ethnicity from the presence of certain objects in the grave (see Chapter Seven for a critique of this view).

An even more unsteady leap of logic lies behind the designation of this body of metalwork as Germanic. As Hawkes & Dunning acknowledged (1961: 11), the chip-carving technique, the motifs and designs, and even the animal-head terminals of these buckles and belt-plates are classical in origin. However, 'the great mass of the material, with its florid chip-carving and bizarre, stylized, animal figures, is already barbaric in feeling . . . The resultant style has generally been attributed to the influence of Germanic tastes in late Roman provincial art' (ibid.). As the use of these styles is seen on 'Anglo-Saxon' metalwork in the fifth and sixth centuries, the stylistic origins are assumed to be Germanic too, when, in fact, there is no logical reason why they are not purely a late fourth-century innovation in provincial Roman art. Indeed, from quite an early date there has been debate about where the influences which had produced this 'Germanic'-style jewellery had actually arisen from. Kendrick, in his book *Anglo-Saxon Art to AD 900* (1938) argued for the strong influence of provincial Roman motifs on Anglo-Saxon forms of decoration. Lethbridge (1956: 115) strongly agreed, commenting that the development of pagan Anglo-Saxon art was ultimately based on distorted classical patterns and animal ornament. Haseloff (1974: 2) demonstrated this to be the case, showing how the decoration of late fourth-century belt-fittings on the Roman frontiers of the Rhine and Danube, with their decorative edges of crouched animals, formed the basis for the motifs used in Salin Style I.

Despite this, the assumptions made here are commonly applied to many different artefacts of fifth- and sixth-century date when found in eastern Britain – if they are of a non-classical form, or are decorated in a 'barbaric' style, then they are identified as 'Germanic' in origin, even when there is little evidence, as in the case of the late Roman military belt-sets, that they originated outside the empire (see also Halsall 1992). There are, however, several characteristic artefact types which do not have extensive parallels on the other side of the North Sea. As Leeds (1945: 5) noted of small-long brooches: 'They are so much a feature of English Anglo-Saxondom that it is astonishing to find that they are seemingly quite scarce in the districts from which the invaders came.' Finds of such 'Germanic' artefacts are, however, used regardless as evidence for the presence of 'Germanic' settlers in Britain in the fifth and sixth centuries AD. Moreover, differences in the style of this metalwork and pottery were used to try to discern different origins for the various peoples who were said to have settled in Britain.

THE ANGLO-SAXON WAY OF DEATH

Identifying the conquerors (Fig. 6.1)

We have seen how Thomas Wright made an early start on this process in 1852 with *The Celt, the Roman and the Saxon*, where he detailed the differences between the artefacts of Angles, Saxons and Jutes. The accumulation of more evidence over the course of the late nineteenth and early twentieth centuries served to blur these once clear-cut distinctions, however. By 1937 enough evidence had accumulated to allow Myres to question Bede's division of eastern Britain into the regions of the three tribes. He drew attention to the Saxon element in the supposedly Anglian areas of the Fens and areas bordering the Humber, with saucer brooches, equal-armed brooches and Saxon ceramics found in Cambridgeshire (Myres 1937: 325–6), and pottery from the Humber area being more closely paralleled in Frisia (now the Netherlands) than in northern Germany (ibid.: 326). Leeds, in the same way, had noted that Bede's tribal divisions did not stand in the face of the archaeological evidence, with the whole area from Norfolk to the Berkshire Downs, especially the area around Cambridge, standing out in its overlapping and mixed distributions (1945: 78–80). Incidentally, this is the area which he marks out as 'Anglo-Saxon' on his distribution maps (**Fig. 6.2**).

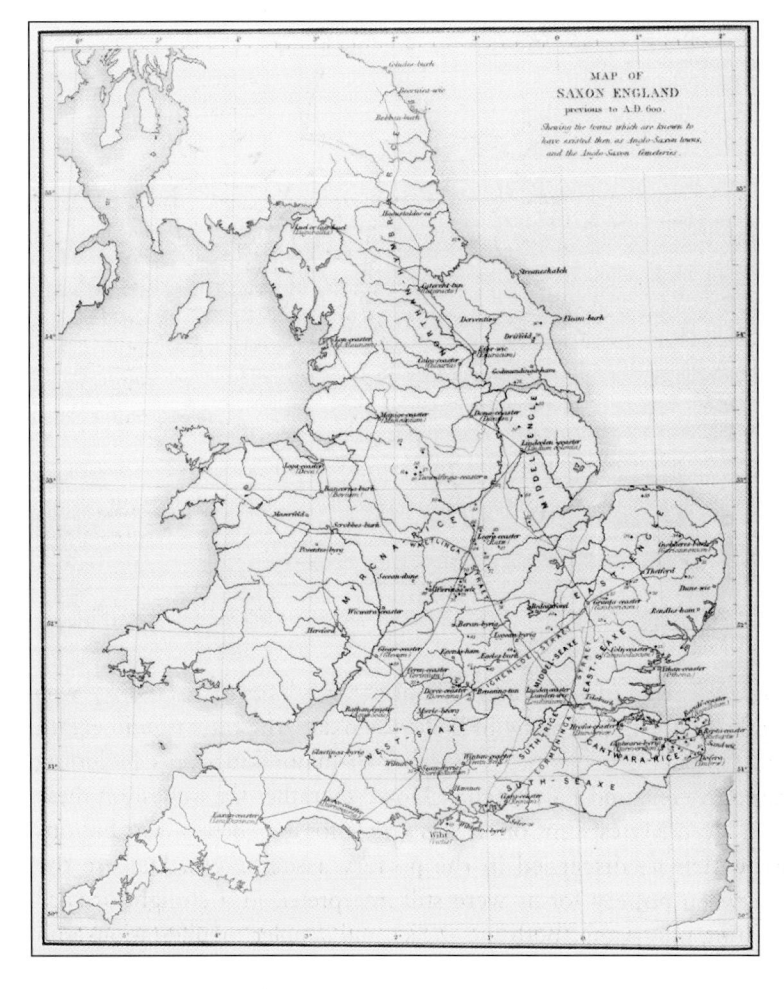

Fig. 6.1. Map of 'Saxon England', showing place-names and locations of then-known cemetery sites (reproduced from Faussett 1856: 110).

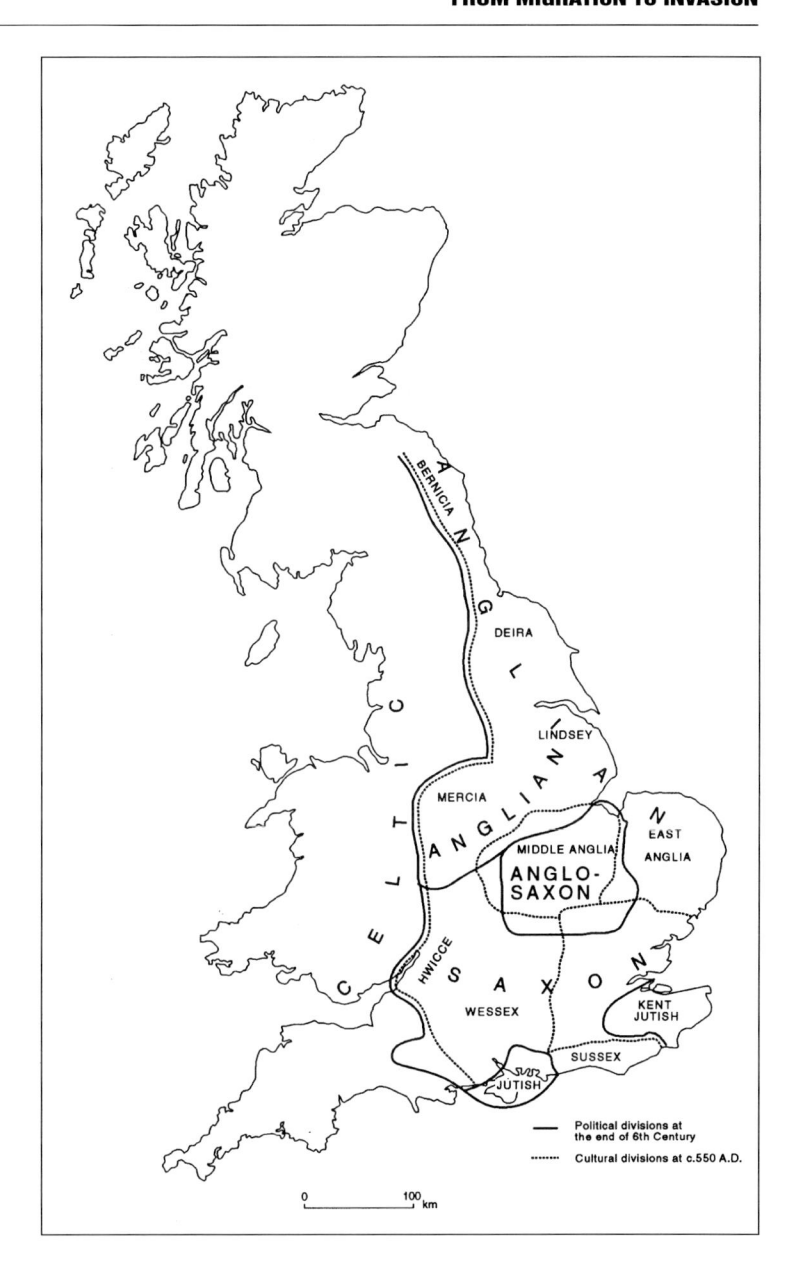

Fig. 6.2. Map of Britain, showing the 'Anglo-Saxon' area as envisaged by Leeds (after Leeds 1913: fig. 4).

Myres (1970: 3) noted that most of the statement in the *Ecclesiastical History* was undoubtedly derived from the political geography of Bede's own day (the early to mid-eighth century AD, when Britain was divided up into a number of major kingdoms including Wessex, Essex, Northumbria, Mercia and East Anglia). However, rather than question these groupings at a fundamental level, Myres went on in this article to 'test' Bede's distributions of peoples against those which he discerned in the pottery assemblages. Despite the ambiguities, similarities between pottery forms were still interpreted in a straightforward manner by Myres as indicating migration: 'Both the earlier and simpler manifestations and the more exuberant developments of the second half of the [fifth] century occur in Britain exactly as they do in Germany. This can only mean that folk who enjoyed this peculiar vogue were pouring into Britain throughout this time and bringing this exotic taste with them. The similarities between the English and the continental examples are too close to permit any other explanation' (Myres 1970: 18). He saw, however, parallels between the material culture of the Saxon areas of the continent, such as pottery urns with 'standing arches' (or *stehende Bogen*) and saucer brooches, and that of supposedly 'Anglian' areas of Britain: 'In the earliest days it would seem that folk of Angle and Saxon, and indeed other, antecedents were establishing themselves indiscriminately over the regions that were later dominated by Anglian regimes' (ibid.: 23). Others sought an explanation for such 'cultural mixing' by suggesting that the incoming tribes were already inextricably mixed before embarking on their migrations to Britain (see, for example, Evison 1965: 6).

Sonia Chadwick Hawkes saw the people of Kent as having a mixed continental origin, with Danish, Frisian, Jutish and Frankish elements all visible in the material culture seen in the fifth- and sixth-century cemeteries such as Bekesbourne, Howletts and Bifrons (Hawkes 1969: 189–90), although she was adamant that the Frankish element was the result of trade rather than migration (ibid.: 191). This built on an idea already put forward by Christopher Hawkes (1956: 96), who painted a clear picture of groups being pushed around northern Europe in the fifth century, with the lack of cremation cemeteries in Jutland suggesting an influx of 'inhuming Danes' from south Sweden, pushing 'Jutes who would not become "Half-Danes" into Frisia, and then into Kent, using archaeology to confirm this view: 'their homeland connexions with both the Angle–Jutish peninsula and the intervening Frisian coast, have been confirmed for us by Myres in his recognition of "Anglo-Frisian" pottery' (ibid.).

Even today, archaeologists are using the same reasoning behind their interpretations of the material. Vera Evison, for example, felt able to state that 'The *saucer brooches* ornamented with five running spirals have been regarded as a reliable indication of the presence of fifth-century Saxons, for they occur in a limited area between the mouths of the Elbe and Weser before the migration, and further developments of the species take place only in England' (Evison 1981: 137). Yet, there are many other artefacts, as has been outlined in earlier chapters, which do not have consistent distributions. Possible explanations for these patterns will be explored in the next chapter.

The fate of the natives

With the attribution of the vast majority of the metalwork and pottery styles to various Germanic tribal influences, in those periods when popular opinion supported considerable 'native' survival in the face of an invasion (rather than mass extermination of the Britons by large numbers of migrants), archaeological attention naturally turned to trying to identify 'British' artefacts and practices in the fifth and sixth centuries.

Belief in a large degree of native survival was seen early in this century. Baldwin Brown (1903: 50–1) thought the native women intermarried with the invaders: 'one would imagine the fair British maiden, with attractions enhanced by a refining touch of Classical culture and perhaps by Christian graces, exercising considerable influence over the minds of the hardy immigrants'. Leeds (1916: 60) was convinced of such survival, for example stating that 'No one, it is presumed, nowadays places explicit belief in the querulous statements of Gildas about the total extermination of the populace. On the contrary, the belief is growing and will grow further still that there was a not inconsiderable survival of the native population in the conquered territory, though for the most part living within the valleys and districts more retired from the main lines of intercommunication.' In his later career, he saw no reason to doubt these early beliefs: 'Hardly anyone credits nowadays the possibility of total extermination . . . In early England, even though it might apply in a large measure to the male portion of the older population, it is certain that many women must have been spared to become the slaves, concubines or wives of the invaders' (Leeds 1945: 4).

There were attempts to identify the traces of these natives. Collingwood & Myres (1936: 449), for example, related the use of inhumation to native survival: 'in the primarily inhuming regions we must allow for a survival of the Britons on a scale sufficient to influence promptly and effectively the burial-customs of their conquerors'. Myres also thought that certain clues, such as the continuation of enamelling techniques, could show the 'extent to which, in different parts of the country, the shattered remnants of the native population merged themselves slowly and painfully in the growing Anglo-Saxon states' (ibid.: 451). Leeds (1936: 3; 1945: 44) thought he could identify 'native work' in the artefacts of the fifth and sixth centuries – hanging bowls, penannular, annular and disc brooches were all seen as indicating the continuing existence of Britons in the Anglo-Saxon settlements.

In later years Myres was still interested in relations between Saxons and native Britons. Looking at pottery assemblages in cremation cemeteries he observed that: 'nearly every series of urns that one examined included one or two specimens that, however barbaric in form or decoration, were, in some way difficult to define, undeniably Romano-British or even "Late Celtic" in feel' (1956: 16). He termed this pottery Romano-Saxon and stated that it 'reflects in varying degrees the survival of the native population in different communities, no doubt mainly in the form of captive women in whose hands the older craftsmanship here and there maintained a faint and flickering continuance' (ibid.: 34). This type of pottery was later shown in fact to be provincial Roman in origin (Gillam 1979; Roberts 1982).

Again, we have the problem of trying to link artistic styles to people's identities. 'British' material culture (in the sense of objects which carry on in production from the fourth century into the fifth) is almost non-existent, therefore 'Britons' are impossible to identify. More recently a few attempts have been made to link certain burial practices to surviving native customs (and therefore surviving natives).

In the areas of Yorkshire and Humberside Faull and Eagles (both 1979) sought to identify the Anglo-Saxon takeover through the archaeological record. Eagles (1979: 46), commenting on the crouched burials from East Yorkshire, suggested that 'Although many of these graves contained Anglo-Saxon objects, it is possible that some of them belonged to British inhabitants, who had intermarried with the Anglo-Saxons.' In the same year Faull (1979: 85) more emphatically stated that crouched burial could be seen as indicative of a degree of survival of native society, for: 'The finds indicate that the descendants of the British population did not have inferior status, but were distributed throughout the society, implying that by the sixth century the two groups had become integrated in these particular areas.' In 1992 Higham concurred with these ideas of Faull and Eagles, but went a step further, adding that: 'where we can distinguish Britons it seems likely that local knowledge of Anglo-Saxon rites was flawed, and that the entire social hierarchy was predominantly British, imperfectly acculturated to Anglo-Saxon ways. Such surely applies among the crouched inhumation cemeteries of East Yorkshire' (1992: 184).

These three authors show considerable similarities in their approaches. The idea of native survival is favourable to all. It was Faull's explicit aim in her doctoral thesis (1979) to look for British survival in Yorkshire, and she saw the study of crouched burial as a way of doing this. Higham, similarly, was proposing the idea of an elite takeover of sub-Roman Britain by small groups of incoming Anglo-Saxons, and thus needed to 'find' evidence for the native population (1992: 235–6). However, closer examination of those cemeteries in East Yorkshire with a high proportion of crouched or tightly flexed burials – at Uncleby (Smith 1912a), Garton Station (Stead 1991, British Museum records), and Garton II (Mortimer 1905) – reveals some interesting features. These cemeteries with a preponderance of crouched burials are of the later period of furnished burial, the seventh and eighth centuries. It seems nonsensical to suggest that such practices can therefore represent 'native' survival, for crouched burial is not the dominant rite in this area in the preceding two centuries. Crouched burial would seem to be a later innovation.

Reliance on the 'straightforward' interpretation of material culture or single practices as directly indicating a person's ethnic origins means that the vast majority of accounts of the early years after the Roman withdrawal are phrased in terms of some variant of the migration or invasion argument. While few would now countenance versions which see the complete takeover of eastern Britain by Germanic migrants, there are a few exceptions (often historians, or those not familiar with the complex archaeological evidence). As late as 1992, Beresford Ellis (1992: 100) was able to say 'we can safely assert that, in the face of Saxon attacks, large sections of the Celtic population were exterminated while others decided to seek homelands in safer areas', while in the same year, Palm & Pind (1992: 51) appear to have been relying on late nineteenth-century works when they wrote:

> The migrants came to this land in a process of peaceful colonization rather than conquest. Great tracts of the land were very thinly populated, and it was possible for the new population to take over empty areas. Besides their manner and customs, the new peoples naturally also brought with them their own jewellery, costume and weapons. Differences in their preferred dress is one of the things which makes it possible to differentiate the various peoples in their archaeological material.

Alternatively, it may be that most of the people buried in Anglo-Saxon cemeteries were descendants of the indigenous population, and we should be asking a different kind of question: why did the people of eastern Britain in the fifth and sixth centuries choose to adopt these rites?

Relating Artefacts to Identities

In all the works cited above the role of material culture is seen as straightforward. The different styles of artefact were thought to directly reflect the mixture of the Germanic settlers who migrated to England in the fifth and sixth centuries (and possibly as early as the fourth in some areas – see Hawkes & Dunning 1961; Evison 1965). As has been seen, the central problem in this debate is how the form and decoration of artefact types is to be related to the identity of the people buried with them. As early as 1956 Tom Lethbridge, an archaeologist who worked mainly in Cambridgeshire, published a paper which touched on the heart of this very issue. In it he stated: 'Leeds, Baldwin Brown and Reginald Smith established their typologies and fixed their dates. Leeds found the continental districts in which certain types of ornaments originated. He distinguished districts in England in which fashions of folk ornament became more or less fixed. One thing, however, eluded this archaeological approach. No one could prove that the wearers of these ornaments were Saxons, or Angles, or Romano-Britons or a mixture of them all' (Lethbridge 1956: 114). He also noted the problem of heirlooms – of goods which had been in use for maybe one, two, even more generations being included as grave-goods: 'Typology is not to be despised, but it must not be regarded as a fool-proof time-scale' (ibid.: 114), illustrating this with a vivid example from his own excavations at Holywell Row, in Suffolk: 'Here a girl, perhaps ten years old, was buried with brooches, girdle-hangers and other things, which were worn or patched at the time of burial. She was provided with festoons of beads much too big for her. She was not buried with her own jewels, but with old and worn-out objects, which probably had not even belonged to her mother. They had been picked out of some old remnants chest. The cracked brooch with its missing garnets, the girdle-hangers roughly patched for the occasion – these may have belonged once to her grandmother or great-aunt' (Lethbridge 1956: 114).

In this short paper, dismissed by his contemporaries, Lethbridge got to the heart of an issue which has only recently come to the forefront in archaeology: how do we relate material culture to the identities of the people wearing or using it? This issue will be discussed in more detail in Chapter Seven, as these rethinkings about culture are proving to be the driving force behind reconceptualisations of the material.

SEVEN

DEVELOPING ALTERNATIVES

The previous chapter has shown how many of the narratives about early Anglo-Saxon cemeteries have their interpretations framed in terms of migrations and/or invasions from various regions of the continent and Scandinavia in the fifth and sixth centuries AD. It was argued that such interpretations are based on too-literal readings of the meagre documentary sources; sources which need to be viewed within their own socio-political contexts before their meanings can be hazarded. It was also suggested that the archaeological evidence itself has been too simplistically 'read-off' within these historical frameworks. The furnished burial rite, especially burial of weapons but also of jewellery, was seen as inherently 'Germanic' with its use denoting the presence in these early cemeteries of immigrants or their descendants.

However, in the last two decades archaeologists and historians have been contributing to a major revision of such interpretations, challenging the uses to which their sources have traditionally been put. This chapter will outline these challenges, before going on to look at some alternative explanations which have been put forward for the changes in burial rites that we see throughout the fifth, sixth, seventh and eighth centuries AD.

DEBATING CULTURE-HISTORY AND RETHINKING ETHNICITY

It is interesting to examine how those 'simplistic' readings of material culture came about, for this tells us a lot about the assumptions which we bring to our material. Actually they rest on a number of different, but inter-connected ideas. These are, firstly, that artefacts are direct indicators of people's ethnic identities – that burial with a brooch which was made in a certain continental district shows that person to have originated from that district; secondly, that those ethnic identities were 'natural' ones, inherited from one's parents and determined by one's origin; and thirdly, that such ethnic identities were all-important, separating 'Anglo-Saxon' from 'Briton', and determining their attitudes towards one another.

The link between artefacts and identities, though a strongly held one in Anglo-Saxon archaeology, is actually open to question. Historians of archaeology have demonstrated very clearly how this link was made from the mid-nineteenth century as a way of interpreting archaeological evidence so that it would fit in with historical debates, which were often framed around the concept of 'races' and origins of nations. Although Darwinism had shown that humans could not have multiple origins, for we are all one species, they were still thought of as belonging to different ancestral stocks, from which various personal and cultural characteristics were inherited (Jones 1997: 43). In the atmosphere of late nineteenth-century nationalism, where 'peoples' and 'nations' were supposed to coincide, there was an interest in tracing back the history and culture of such 'national' groups as far as possible (Olsen & Kobylínski 1991: 9). In addition, language and physical anthropology began to be equated with these groups, such that there arose the expectation that a 'Saxon' would speak a 'Germanic' language, use 'Germanic' material culture and also be of a specific physical type (ibid.). What we have here is the generation of the idea that the world is populated by 'peoples' who have distinctive characteristics, both physical and cultural, and who exist in sharply delineated physical territories. The shadow of nationalism is very clear in this formulation.

This expectation soon became transferred into archaeology in the form of a method which became known as the 'culture-historical' approach. In 1895 the German prehistorian Gustaf Kossinna put forward the idea that archaeology was capable of isolating cultural areas which could be identified with specific ethnic or national units and traced back into prehistory (Malina & Vasícek 1990: 62). In a later development of this idea he argued: 'Sharply defined archaeological culture areas correspond unquestionably with the areas of particular peoples or tribes' (Kossinna 1911: 3, cited in Veit 1989: 37). Although formalised in this way by Kossinna (1911) and later by Childe (1929; 1935), a similar method had actually been used for decades by early historical archaeologists. It was easier for the latter, as the documentary sources (which, as seen in the last chapter, are often not as objective as one might assume) talked of the past as populated by distinct groups of people – the Saxons, Angles and Jutes, for example. As already outlined, early archaeologists such as Roach Smith were thus expecting to be able to discern tribal differences in the material they excavated from cemeteries, and it was natural for them to link the objects they discovered to the tribal differences which the historical sources apparently described. In addition, this has convincingly been argued to be the model which early prehistorians like Childe and Kossinna adopted when they applied their theories to periods without historical sources (Anthony 1990: 896).

In prehistoric archaeology, as well as in Anglo-Saxon archaeology, there thus arose the idea of human history being peopled by groups with clearly identifiable 'cultures' and static boundaries. Change within an area could only be accounted for by events such as contacts, migrations and conquests (Jones 1996: 65; 1997: 12). Even after the damnation of Kossinna following the Second World War (this was after his death, but archaeological evidence had been used, following his method, as propaganda for German expansion into neighbouring countries, on the basis that they had been 'German' in the distant past), culture areas were still seen as expressions of ethnic groups or peoples, and were equated with the tribes first documented historically in a given area (Veit 1989: 39–40). Yet, as outlined in the previous chapter, these early historical sources do not provide us with objective history. For the English, Bede's *Ecclesiastical History* and the *Anglo-Saxon Chronicle* have been shown to be very much products of their own time, rather than an accurate reflection of events which occurred several centuries earlier (Sims-Williams 1983). Much of the debate has thus rested on a circular argument – early archaeologists took historical sources as providing an accurate model of the peopling of the past, and historians have had their interpretations strengthened by archaeological accounts which depict the movements of such 'tribal' groups.

In an attempt to break out of this circle, some historians have been taking a more critical approach to their sources, in terms of what they actually say about the nature of ethnic identification in the early medieval period. Geary (1983: 18), for example, has highlighted the assumptions often used by historians when dealing with early medieval texts (such as that ethnicity would have been recognisable to others, that it would not change except over several generations, and that it was a source of friction within societies), and has demonstrated how such assumptions have coloured readings of the sources. In addition, the contexts in which people or groups were given names in the documentary sources have been re-examined, and the conclusion drawn that groups such as the Franks (James 1988), the Burgundians (Amory 1993) and the Anglo-Saxons (Wormald 1983; Reynolds 1985; Pohl 1997) are as much historical creations as anything – in other words, that documentary records have helped to create that which they purported to describe. The role of the church and its historians seems to have been a major factor in this process (Pohl 1997: 19). It has also been pointed out that many people who are mentioned in early medieval sources are not given any ethnic attribution at all, and it has been suggested that perhaps an ethnic identity was important only for some members of the population, and that such identities were brought into being in connection with certain members of the elite (Amory 1994; Pohl 1997: 23). Moreover, ethnicity cannot be seen as a cause of antagonism between groups, for this is an inadequate explanation in a pre-modern context. Rather, we need to examine the underlying relationships which caused those ethnic identifications to be made – ethnicity was not an inherent aspect of biology, but a constructed identity, which was probably of little importance for the vast majority of the population. Thus the historical basis which provided the foundation for interpretations of both prehistoric and early medieval ethnicity in the past has been shown to be far more illusory than was once thought.

The very idea of the 'concreteness' of ethnicity has also been challenged, mainly by research in sociology and anthropology working with present-day populations. Contemporary observations of how human groups define themselves and others has produced the general consensus that ethnicity is not an objective, biological attribute, which can be independently observed by others. Rather, it is something which is lived and created, a 'self-defining system', which is emphasised in certain situations, but not others (Barth 1969; Epstein 1978; Geary 1983; Jones 1997: 60). The creation of feelings of similarity (to members of one's own group) and difference (from members of others) is important in the construction of such groups (Bentley 1987: 34; Jones 1997: 93). Language, artefacts and everyday practices do not coincide in the expression of neatly bounded groups, although such things can be consciously seized on in the expression of ethnic allegiance (McGuire 1982: 160–1; Jenkins 1997: 76–7; Jones 1997: 95, 125). Thus, ethnicity and ethnic groups do not exist separately from the people involved in them – it is only when a group of individuals see themselves as forming an ethnic group (usually in opposition to others), and act in accordance with that sense of belonging, that an ethnic group can be said to exist (Jones 1997: 84). In this light, ethnic groups are continually imagined (though not imaginary) groups (Jenkins 1997: 77), which can have no fixed boundaries, as they are not solid, bounded categorisations. In addition, ethnicity may only be one aspect of an individual's sense of identity – they may experience an 'ethnic' sense of belonging on various different levels of inclusiveness and exclusiveness (Cohen 1978: 387; Bentley 1987: 36; Jenkins 1997: 85), as well as being subject to social norms regarding their age, gender and status.

While, on an intuitive level, it seems obvious that what we understand to be the 'ethnic identity' of a person can be recognised from their appearance, when such identifications are looked into more closely (especially from our contemporary perspective), ethnicity becomes more complex and harder to identify concretely. What seems 'common-sense' at first sight, in fact rests on a series of assumptions derived from modern western historico-political contexts, where all belong to one nation, sharing a national language and with distinct national differences in ways of dressing and acting (all things which themselves change with time and are not necessarily clear-cut). However, it would be a mistake to back-project the illusion of the inevitability of such contemporary differences onto the identification of difference in the past. As Amory (1993: 3) has argued: 'Ethnic consciousness, so universal and so important in the modern world, is often assumed to have been universal and primary in the past as well, although in the hothouse culture of Late Antiquity, status and religious sect may have been more important defining traits. It is particularly difficult to shed the ancient notion that a group called by a given name maintained itself as a static and self-perpetuating biological community, a race.' This is especially true given that many of the names used for groups were either applied retrospectively or by contemporary outsiders. While individuals may have been ascribed ethnic identities in this period (those promising allegiance to a 'Frankish' leader may have identified themselves, or been identified, as Franks, for example), we cannot rely on the modern-day concept of 'national' ethnicity as a way of explaining identity in the Anglo-Saxon period – it would have been much more fluid, contingent and probably personality-based than this.

Archaeologists, too, have been questioning the methods for the identification of ethnic groups in the past. Some have queried the very existence of ethnic groups as fixed, bounded entities in the past (Shennan 1989: 11–12; Jones 1997: 109). The idea that a 'people' and a language necessarily coincide has been called into doubt (Olsen & Kobylínski 1991: 15–16; Robb 1993; Moore 1994; Zvelebil 1995: 41; Pluciennik 1996), as have correlations between material culture distributions and population groups (Håland 1977; Zvelebil 1995: 40–2). In addition, the nature of those material culture distributions is being discussed more intensively. It has been recognised that the distributions of archaeological types which comprise a 'culture' do not coincide exactly with each other (Shennan 1978: 113; Clarke 1968: 363), and that archaeological distributions comprise an enormous variety of cross-cutting patterns, produced by different factors (Shennan 1989: 13).

Where does this leave us in our attempts to place evidence from Anglo-Saxon cemeteries into a wider context? What, exactly, is it evidence for, given that the reasoning behind seeing it as evidence for Germanic invasion and settlement seems to be based on rather shaky grounds? Lethbridge got to the heart of the matter when he stated (1956: 113): 'Because a large number of ornaments are found in a series of graves and it can be shown that the origin of the style of ornaments lies in some continental district or other, is it any proof that the people in those graves were descended from those in the land in which that style of ornament was formerly common? Of course it is not,' and that, 'Because we speak of a collection of objects as Anglo-Saxon, we must not assume that they indicate the presence of a pure-blooded Teutonic stock in the district in which they were found. They indicate no more than the presence in that district of people with a taste for barbaric ornaments of Teutonic types' (ibid.: 114). The key question is, therefore, how we interpret this material culture.

In recent years, some archaeologists have been focusing on the active role of material culture, pointing out that the objects and artefacts that people use in their day-to-day lives do not directly reflect social conditions, but that they are a crucial part of the way that people conduct their lives (Barrett 1990: 179). Material culture is integral to social life – it helps to mediate relationships between people, by conveying information about them in subtle ways, in the same way that business suits or uniforms can convey status, role or authority today, and set up social expectations of the ways in which people should interact. Like such uniforms, objects do not have inherent meanings, but through their use in specific contexts, they become imbued with significance in the eyes of those who use them, and those who watch them being used (Sørensen 1991: 121). The things that people use are the result of many separate choices, rather than being inevitable aspects of their society (their 'culture'), although of course the range of artefacts which are available to choose from may be limited by a variety of factors such as production, trade and cost (whether a particular artefact is available, and whether one can acquire it).

It is in this context that we need to view the artefacts found through excavation of Anglo-Saxon cemeteries, rather than seeing them as direct indicators of population movement. There is a further complicating factor, too, in that when we deal with cemetery evidence we are not looking at unconscious everyday activity, as we might see on a settlement site, but at an intermittent and deliberately articulated practice. The mourners are the active participants in burial rituals (Barrett 1990: 182), such that burials are not static – there is nothing 'natural' about them. Rather, they are the result of many different culturally situated decisions. A person's identity cannot be 'read off' from the way in which he or she was buried, but the burial itself can shed light on the aspects of the deceased which the mourners thought important to emphasise through the use of material culture and other aspects of the ritual (Lucy 1998: 107).

Rather than making *a priori* assumptions about what the burial rite means, then, a different approach is needed. Through detailed analysis of burials, archaeologists can start to observe the construction, in the context of the burial rite, of gender- and age-based identities using material culture, and how such identities changed over time (see, for example, Pader 1982; Lucy 1998; Stoodley 1997). Examination of assemblages of grave-goods, with associated textiles, can give an in-depth picture of how people of different sex and age were dressed for burial. In terms of the preparation and provisioning of burial costumes, this can indicate how different groups were viewed by the mourners. Such provisioning will not directly reflect the role of the deceased in life, but we can start to see the complex patterning of ideas about death and the dead held by the mourners. Patterning visible on a local or regional level might suggest deliberate reinforcement of local or regional identities by the mourners. However, it is not enough to see local patterning as represented by the presence of a handful of brooches in a handful of cemeteries: if one is arguing for a regional costume (cf. Hines 1994), then it must be a costume, for example the long-sleeved garment suggested by the use of sleeve-clasps (although as seen in Chapter Five this is not found in every cemetery within the region specified by Hines).

Attention to the contexts in which imported artefacts were used have thrown up some interesting patterns. Brugmann (1999: 38) has shown how pottery, brooches, bracteates and Jutish-Kentish square-headed brooches provide the main links between Kent and Jutland in the early phase of cemetery use, yet she points out many instances of unorthodox use of these artefacts, and the very limited selection of continental artefacts employed in Anglo-Saxon fashions at this time. In previous interpretations the very presence of these imported artefacts would have been enough to infer the burial of immigrants. However, such detailed analyses show that something more complex was going on: the deliberate selection of artefacts from a range of available material, and their deliberate inclusion within burials as an integral part of localised burial rites.

Studies of brooch use and burial rite in eastern England have shown considerable freedom in the expression of individual identity, both within graves and between cemeteries (Fisher 1995; Lucy 1998). In her study of applied and cast saucer brooches with running spiral decoration, Dickinson (1991) has, through extremely detailed analysis of the decorative schemes, shown that a number of 'rules' and a sort of vocabulary were in operation, governing the possibilities in which these brooches could be made and, she argues, encouraging invention, leading to a variety of forms. Through this analysis she also identified a 'Primary' series, which represented the earliest English examples, closely based on continental forms (ibid.: 48). This series comprises four brooches, which are intriguingly found in East Anglia, Essex and Kent, well away from the later main distribution of this brooch type in the Upper Thames valley (ibid.: Fig. 6). With regard to the origins of the use of spiral decoration on the continent, she agrees that it was borrowed from late Roman metalwork, especially chip-carved belt equipment, arguing that such decorative schemes had social connotations, being linked with imperial military costume (1991: 62, following Böhme 1974: 24–31). She remarks that the translation of these schemes from male military equipment to female jewellery was an important transition: 'Cast appliqué saucer brooches especially may then have helped to define and discriminate between powerful families within Old Saxony, through their symbolic associations with Roman authority' (Dickinson 1991: 62). The change in their distribution after the adoption of the brooch form in Britain may thus represent a change in this symbolic association (ibid.: 68): 'saucer brooches were the most impressive brooch-form generally available to fasten a peplos-type gown in the Upper Thames region, as well as in much of southern and Midlands England; their role as display items, marking out the higher-status families, may have increased throughout the sixth century' (Dickinson 1993a: 39).

Thus, whereas Leeds (1936: 79) saw the area stretching from the Tyne to north Suffolk as 'culturally one; it is the province of the cruciform brooch in its more developed forms', such interpretations now need a great deal more justification. This is not to say that there was no population movement in the fifth and sixth centuries. This would have been extremely unusual, for Britain, especially eastern Britain, has in all periods of history and prehistory, until very recently, displayed extensive signs of contact across the Channel and the North Sea, evidenced by the movement of goods and ideas. Such movement would have undoubtedly included people moving back and forth. What does have to be rejected, though, is the idea that it was solely population movement which brought about the significant social and cultural changes of the fifth and sixth centuries AD. This is what is meant by rejecting migration as an 'explanatory mechanism' – it does not mean dismissing the idea that people moved, merely the idea that in observing their movement you can account for all subsequent change (contra e.g. Böhme 1986). Moreover, this contact was not all one-way. In the late fifth and early sixth centuries a series of cemeteries ranging from the Somme estuary to the Pas-de-Calais region, in Calvados and the Contentin peninsula in western Normandy, and the site at Herpes in the Charente valley in south-western France, have all been reported as containing objects which were undoubtedly made in southern England (Welch 1991: 263). These finds include button brooches, square-headed small-long brooches and jewelled disc brooches (ibid.: 264–5). Hand-made pottery with an Anglo-Saxon style of decoration also implies contact between these regions and southern England, though interpretations of this contact include immigration, intermarriage and trading contacts (ibid.: 265–6).

As we have seen in previous chapters, the evidence from cemeteries varies widely in geographical and chronological terms – people take the burial rite and make of it something meaningful for themselves; they do not simply adopt it wholesale, or inherit those ways of burial from their predecessors. This process of appropriation and adaptation is what makes burial rites in this period so fascinating to study. A good example of this is Loveluck's (1995) argument about the origins of the tradition of furnished barrow burial which is found in the Peak District in the middle and later decades of the seventh century. Whereas these graves have usually been seen solely as those of an incoming Anglo-Saxon elite establishing control over the native population (Fowler 1955; 138; Ozanne 1963: 47), Loveluck puts forward a convincing case for some of them being the burial places of a native regional elite, trying to maintain their status in the face of external pressures (1995: 85). He shows how some (but not all) seventh-century burials with Anglo-Saxon goods such as gold and garnet jewellery have parallels with earlier traditions in the area, such as the inclusion of quartz pebbles and red antler tines, suggesting an element of continuity. He thus argues for a change in the native burial tradition, in the face of an incoming Anglo-Saxon elite as seen in those barrows which are made of earth, contain only Anglo-Saxon goods and exhibit no native characteristics, such as those at Benty Grange, Cold Eaton and White Low (although we would disagree about the 'Germanic' nature of these). He thus demonstrates how social competition could feasibly lead to changes in tradition, in a later seventh-century context where identities were starting to be defined in terms of allegiance. Likewise, Richards (1992: 135) argues for the earlier cemeteries that 'the form of the burial is a symbol being used to assert the domination of Germanic culture, not the annihilation of the previous inhabitants', and that 'the increasing popularity of weapon burial among the inhabitants of sixth- and seventh-century England may represent the growth of an "Anglo-Saxon invasion" origin-myth as much as an increase in warfare. The myth probably emphasised a shared ethnic past, valiant sea journeys and distinguished ancestors rather than post-Roman colonial vestiges' (ibid.: 147). Are we, as Richards seems to be suggesting, actually seeing here the attempt to create a form of communal identity, through such burial rites; a sort of parallel to what Bede was to attempt two centuries later, when he wrote his *Ecclesiastical History of the English People* at a time when there was no 'English people', but an admixture of small to large polities, all with different origin-myths (Reynolds 1985)?

We cannot any more assume that people moved, on the basis of standard interpretations of history and archaeology. Such things must be demonstrated, by showing a series of links between different areas both in terms of material and, more importantly, in the ways in which that material was used, as proposed by Hills (1999a). Only then, when such links are clearly demonstrated, can migration or population movement be inferred, and even then there is more explaining to do, in terms of how such material spread out to other communities and why they chose to adopt it. Some interesting ideas about why burial rites change in the absence of incomers have now been developed to explain the changes which occur at the end of the sixth century in eastern Britain

Tracing the Conversion

As outlined in Chapter Three, these changes involve the adoption of different burial assemblages, with a shift seen especially in the types of jewellery and weaponry which are buried. Fifth- and sixth-century cemetery sites were often abandoned and new ones founded, often in quite contrasting locations. These later cemeteries employ a range of different practices; they can have 'high-status' burials, often under large barrows and with elaborate grave-goods, as at Sutton Hoo; or they can be 'Final Phase' cemeteries, with their distinctive gold and garnet jewellery and other artefact types, where whole communities seem to have been buried, under small barrows in some areas, such as Kingston Down in Kent. Many of the graves in such cemeteries are unfurnished, and sometimes entire cemeteries are almost entirely lacking in grave-goods (see Geake 1992 for an overview).

The remarkable finds at Sutton Hoo should thus be seen in this context of changing burial practices. This site stands out in its local context. As Hills has said: 'The Sutton Hoo treasure springs unexpectedly out of a rural agricultural society, in a part of the region where there is no very obvious density of population, nor immediate source of wealth. In the context of other burials from early Saxon England, it is even more extraordinary . . . It is difficult to set in its context a phenomenon which has so little in common with its background, and which appears without precedent or successor' (Hills 1983b: 103). In its entirety, it is unique. Yet how many other burials like it have been destroyed through barrow-opening in previous centuries (Wilson 1992b: 12)? It was only sheer chance which led to the sixteenth-century robber-trench missing the central burial chamber.

Various elements of the burial under Sutton Hoo mound 1 are paralleled in various parts of Europe and Scandinavia. The shield seems to be a Swedish import, the helmet appears to be a Scandinavian-inspired imitation of a Roman parade helmet, similar to those at Vendel and Valsgärde in Sweden, and the shoulder-clasps and body armour belong to the same sphere of late antique prestige and display (Webster 1992: 77). Use of a boat for burial is seen at both these Swedish sites, as well as at Snape, not far away in Suffolk. The location of large barrows in isolated groups away from earlier cemeteries is seen at Asthall, Benty Grange and Taplow (ibid.: 77–8). Contacts are also evidenced with the Merovingian world and further east, through the 'Coptic' bowl and other Byzantine bronze and silver vessels (ibid.: 80).

More attention is now placed on the symbolism expressed at Sutton Hoo and sites resembling it. Ostentatious barrow burial in the seventh century is seen as a deliberate statement in the face of the spread of the new Christian religion with its Merovingian overtones (Carver 1992a; van der Noort 1993), while the *Romanitas* represented within a number of the grave-goods is significant at a time of emerging kingdoms (Webster 1992: 78–9), and also of specific concepts of kingship. The arrays of vessels for drinking and feasting seen at these sites – twenty-eight in Sutton Hoo mound 1, and nineteen at Taplow – represent the dead person as a provider of food and shelter for followers (ibid.: 79). Moreover, Carver (1992c: x) sees the burial rite as allegorical: 'the material culture of the graves is thus used, as a common language, to signal political affiliation and allegiance rather than events', such that, 'the East Angles could re-enact and replicate what they imagined to be the cultured pagan Scandinavia, and the regalia of Byzantium, without necessarily having seen either'.

What we have at Sutton Hoo, and maybe at cemeteries of lesser status too, are deliberate statements made by the mourners about a range of different aspects of their society: in their references to warfare, to feasting, to overseas links, they seem to be attempting to tie themselves in with various ideological schemes which are diametrically opposed to the spreading sphere of Christianity which was starting to dominate lowland Britain in the seventh century. Given this interpretation, how should we view the other main type of later burial found – the 'Final Phase' cemetery? Why do these community cemeteries undergo sudden changes at the end of the sixth century, and can this be directly related to this process of conversion?

Although the early excavations in Kent by Faussett and Douglas mainly took place in what we now know to be Final Phase cemeteries, little work was done on the chronologies and typologies of the artefacts until the 1930s (Geake 1997: 1–2). Lethbridge (1931: 82–4) was the first to argue against the predominant view at the time that Christians would have been buried unfurnished with his report on the Burwell (Cambridgeshire) excavations, and his ideas were built upon by Leeds (who had excavated two such cemeteries himself), calling the last chapter of *Early Anglo-Saxon Art and Archaeology* 'The Final Phase' (Geake 1997: 2).

As Geake (1997: 107–8) explains, because the first excavated cemeteries of this nature were Kentish, and they were so well published and illustrated, when archaeologists in the rest of the country came to compare their material with that already published, many artefacts were mistakenly attributed to specifically Kentish origins (based also on historical assumptions about the importance of Kent in the late sixth and seventh centuries owing to its contacts with the Frankish kingdoms). She notes how Leeds, Lethbridge, Meaney and Hawkes all saw the role of Kent as pivotal in the spread of this material, yet her own search for parallels and prototypes for the seventh- and eighth-century English material in the cemetery finds and museum exhibits of the former Frankish empire turned up very few artefactual links between the two areas, with the exception of polychrome disc brooches, the seax, shoe fittings and the triangular buckle (ibid.: 108). Instead, parallels and influences could be seen to originate from a variety of sources, with some new types of artefacts, such as the short necklaces with pendants, work-boxes and double-tongued buckles, having Roman or Byzantine origins (something already suggested by Hyslop in 1963), while others, such as annular brooches, finger-rings and bracelets, were earlier Anglo-Saxon types which carried on in sometimes more classically influenced forms (Geake 1997: 120).

As Hines (1999a: 65) has pointed out, for a long time this transition from migration period to final phase grave-goods has been dated to 'around 600', and it has been very easy to associate this shift with the documented conversion to Christianity which begins in eastern England around this time. However, this equation seems a little too neat. These later sixth- and seventh-century assemblages have been found widely distributed over central, southern and eastern England, although fewer burials than before were furnished with them, with up to half of all burials within each cemetery having no grave-goods (Geake 1992: 84–5; Hyslop 1963; Lethbridge 1931). It has been suggested that these new cemeteries (and they very often are new cemeteries, spatially distinct from those with earlier assemblages) represented increasing polarity of wealth (Arnold 1982a; Geake 1992: 85), for the new assemblages often contained items such as gold or silver necklaces, or inlaid seaxes. It has also been argued that they were symbolic of a larger cultural group, probably with elite affiliations (Geake 1992: 92). Hines (1994: 54) has argued that 'the new dress-style and forms were indeed the uniform of a relatively newly established elite, who allied with one another, for instance by intermarriage, and sustained and imitated one another by means of material exchange'. These changes were occurring at a time when Christianity was becoming steadily more important as a religious, political and economic force, and when increasing social stratification was taking place, which was to culminate in the existence of historically attested kings and kingdoms in the later seventh century.

Geake has pointed out the political consequences of converting to Christianity at this time, for conversion meant throwing one's lot in with Francia, as well as with Rome (Geake 1992: 91; Morris 1983: 46–8). She has therefore suggested that the 'Final Phase' types of burial, still displaying a form of ritual investment, were an alternative to Christian burial rites (1992: 93). They were thus a way of expressing an opposition to Christian ideology – an opposition which, it has been argued, was given a more extreme manifestation in the 'defiant paganism' cemeteries typified, for example, in the burial rites and material culture employed at Sutton Hoo (Carver 1992a: 181).

The cessation of furnished burial can also be seen in this context of kingdom formation. Although sites such as Garton Slack in Yorkshire could be interpreted as early Christian burials, for they largely conformed to later Christian practices, being unfurnished, extended, supine and oriented to west, the situation was probably more complex than this. Halsall (1995) has argued that the decline of the furnished burial custom in Merovingian France reflected the decline in social differences based on age and gender in favour of those based on class, wealth and rank. The grave-goods which lasted for any length of time tended to be those which were least gender-specific (Geake 1992: 92), although those objects with gender-associations tended to be female-linked, and were now deposited with all age groups and not just with adult females (Geake 1997: 128). Recently attention has been drawn to the lack of regulation of the mode or location of burial in the seventh and eighth centuries (Geake 1992: 89; James 1988: 139; Morris 1983: 49–50). There is, in fact, little evidence that western-oriented unfurnished burial was required by the mainstream Christian orthodoxy, although burial rites may have been influenced by Northumbrian burial practices (Geake 1992: 90). Probably more significant, though, was the effect of elite burials, and the shift within the aristocracy to burial within or around churches.

State formation and the origins of kingship have long been recognised as intimately bound up with Christianity (Bassett 1989; Wallace-Hadrill 1975: 181–2; Yorke 1990). Indeed, Carver (1989: 152) stated that: 'The stratification of society appears to be close in time to the arrival of Christianity – probably too close indeed to distinguish cause from effect.' Maybe we should suggest an alteration to James's maxim (1989: 47): as well as kings producing peoples, perhaps Christianity produced kings, at least in the sense recognised by Bede. As James himself has pointed out: 'The clearest connection between England and the Continent in this problem of the origins of kingdoms is not to do with the realities of political power but with the way in which the English kings and their subjects came to regard kingship, as closer contact and eventually Christianity brought them the triple image of Roman emperor, Merovingian king and Hebrew monarch' (James 1989: 52).

The involvement of the elite with the new religion may have had tremendous implications for politics, social relations, economic structures and burial rites. Religious foundations would have presented a huge drain on an area's resources, requiring food, animals and often grants of land, frequently made in perpetuity, for their upkeep (Blair 1988; Geake 1992: 91; John 1960). They would have thus affected the way that society and land were organised. Churches and other religious establishments may also have represented an alternative form of investment to grave-goods (Geake 1992: 92), if grave-goods are seen in the light of ritual destruction or disposal of wealth. Carver (1989: 157) has suggested in a similar vein that the advent of formalised taxation may have led to the decline in grave-goods, with the Christian furnished graves being those of families exempt from tax.

Grave-goods appear to go out of use suddenly in the early decades of the eighth century, and for a while largely unfurnished cemeteries are found (Geake 1997: 135). Possibly the explanation for this development lies in the fact that the grave-goods in these 'unfurnished' cemeteries are no longer being used to signal anything about the deceased's identity, and that such signalling was no longer relevant to the needs of society. If the role of furnished burial really was to advertise certain features of a dead person and perhaps their lineage, then in these later centuries it would have been defunct in two senses. Firstly, there were other, far more effective, ways of advertising (and perhaps gaining) membership of the elite, and these would have been intimately involved with the church. Secondly, if furnished burial was seen as an arena of competition and negotiation between communities and lineages, the formalisation of power structures into an aristocracy meant that, in effect, such competition had ceased, and some segments of society had come out victorious in their battle for power, and were so safely consolidated in their dominant position that they had no further need of burial rites to justify their position (see Geake 1997 and Hines 1996 for similar arguments).

Conclusions

The Anglo-Saxon burial rite has been interpreted in many different ways since the first discovery and recording of these furnished cemeteries over two hundred years ago. There is now little controversy over their broad dating to the fifth to early eighth centuries, although chronologies for specific artefact types can still occasion argument. What does prompt debate are questions about how this material should be interpreted. This chapter and the last have put forward the argument that the dominant frameworks within which interpretation has largely been made were conditioned by specific historical and political circumstances, and that the questions which nineteenth-century archaeologists asked of their material, while appropriate for the time, are no longer relevant to modern-day scholarship. This in itself will occasion controversy – there are many Anglo-Saxon archaeologists who still view the main imperative of the subject as answering questions about Anglian and Saxon invasions and the becoming of the 'English'.

While the English were undoubtedly a product of the first millennium AD, it is argued here that this may have been due at least in part to the scholarship of Bede and others like him – that it is in the writing of 'national' histories that nations can become created. I am very much more doubtful that interpretation of cemetery evidence can tell us of similar processes. What it can give us insight into is much more limited in scope – yet, I think, far more interesting. Cemeteries can tell us, through skeletal data, something of the physical conditions of existence. Through the grave-goods which were buried, they can tell us a variety of things about the production and exchange of artefacts and materials, which might throw some light on social relations in this period. In the symbolism apparent within the burial rite we see something of ideational schemes, and what the mourners thought it was important to emphasise about the dead person, whether it was their age, their gender, their status within the community or a mixture of all of these. Analysis of cemeteries can tell us about attitudes to space and landscape, and studying the history of sites tells us about the sense of permanence felt by those using (and thus maintaining) them.

I am, however, far more circumspect about the ability of cemeteries to tell us very much at all about the 'ethnic' origins of the people buried in them. Too many interpretations have been put forward which see ethnicity as a fixed, inheritable aspect of social identity, which can be simply 'read off' from the grave-goods which were buried with the deceased. Humans are not this straightforward: they are not now, and they would not have been in the past – they would have created their identities in a much more flexible way than this, much as we do today. Denying this to the people living in Britain in the fifth and sixth centuries is to deny a central aspect of humanity, and serves to reduce them to automatons who were unable to change the conditions of their existence. Through detailed analysis of burial assemblages, and the ways in which grave-goods were appropriated from different sources and put to use within the burial rite, we may see inklings of the social construction of those nascent identities which were given tribal names by Bede, but it has to be recognised that these were historical constructions, of new types of identities, rather than the gradual re-emergence of those which had been submerged in the trauma of migration.

In short, these cemeteries can be used to say a great deal about contemporary societies in the fifth, sixth and seventh centuries – indeed, they are one of our most important sources of information, and they link us most directly to the people whom we wish to study. They tell us little of migrations or invasions of people from the continent and Scandinavia. Rather, they take us into a richer and more complex world, where we can encounter both the physical reality of early medieval people, and something of their thoughts and aspirations. They also give indications of networks of influence, which reached across the Channel and the North Sea in the fifth, sixth and seventh centuries. People living in eastern Britain were integrally involved in these networks, which stretched from northern Norway to south-western France, and probably beyond. They came into contact with a range of ideas, brought by merchants, travellers and others, and they selected those that were appropriate for use and deployment within their local contexts. Perhaps the changes in burial rites seen from the fifth century are a result, to a certain extent, of this contact and appropriation of ideas – a process that allows for a certain dynamism in the people involved, rather than one-way traffic from the continent to Britain. The influences certainly continue for many centuries afterwards, and they were present during the Roman period – perhaps it is not the fact that people move across the North Sea and Channel continually that needs explanation, but that previous archaeological explanations have viewed such movements as the root of change, and the sole cause of it, rather than as part of a much longer on-going process of exchange of goods, ideas and people.

The Anglo-Saxon way of death, as practised by the people of eastern Britain from the fifth to the eighth century AD, offers us evidence that we are only just learning to interpret. Many questions remain: why were these burial rites adopted when they were, and why did they change when they did? Why did investment in burial dwindle away in the eighth century? What did the complex variation within a cemetery mean? We have no certain answers as yet. However, now that the cemeteries can be seen for what they are – not innate residues of 'Germanic culture', but expressions of the beliefs and aspirations of intelligent and creative people – the real work of investigation can begin.

BIBLIOGRAPHY

Åberg, N. 1926. *The Anglo-Saxons in England*, Uppsala, Almqvist & Wiksells Boktryckeri

Adams, B. & Jackson, D. 1989. 'The Anglo-Saxon cemetery at Wakerley, Northamptonshire. Excavations by Mr D. Jackson, 1968–9', *Northamptonshire Archaeology* 22, 69–178

Ager, B.M. 1985. 'The smaller variants of the Anglo-Saxon quoit brooch', *Anglo-Saxon Studies in Archaeology and History* 4, 1–58

Akerman, J.Y. 1847. *An Archaeological Index to the Remains of Antiquity in the Celtic, Romano-British and Anglo-Saxon Periods*, London, J.R. Smith

Akerman, J.Y. 1857. 'An account of researches in Anglo-Saxon cemeteries at Filkins, and at Broughton Poggs, Oxon.', *Archaeologia* 37, 140–6

Akerman, J.Y. 1860. 'Report on researches in an Anglo-Saxon cemetery at Long Wittenham, Berkshire, in 1859', *Archaeologia* 38, 327–52

Akerman, J.Y. 1861. 'Report on further researches in an Anglo-Saxon burial ground at Long Wittenham, Berkshire, in the summer of 1860', *Archaeologia* 39, 135–42

Alcock, E. 1992. 'Burials and cemeteries in Scotland', in N. Edwards & A. Lane (eds), *The Early Church in Wales and the West*, Oxford, Oxbow Monograph 16, pp. 125–9

Alcock, L. 1971. *Arthur's Britain: History and Archaeology AD 367–634*, London, Allen Lane, The Penguin Press

Allen, G. 1880. 'Are we Englishmen?', *Fortnightly Review* 28, 472–81

Amory, P. 1993. 'The meaning and purpose of ethnic terminology in the Burgundian Laws', *Early Medieval Europe* 2, 1–28

Amory, P. 1994. 'Names, ethnic identity, and community in fifth- and sixth-century Burgundy', *Viator* 25, 1–30

Anthony, D. 1990. 'Migration in archaeology: the baby and the bathwater', *American Anthropologist* 92, 895–914

Arnold, C.J. 1982a. 'Stress as a stimulus to socio-economic change: England in the seventh century', in C. Renfrew & S. Shennan (eds), *Ranking, Resource and Exchange*, Cambridge, Cambridge University Press, pp. 124–31

Arnold, C.J. 1982b. *The Anglo-Saxon Cemeteries of the Isle of Wight*, London, British Museum Publications

Ashe, G. 1968. *The Quest for Arthur's Britain*, London, Paladin

Austin, W. 1928. 'A Saxon cemetery at Luton, Beds.', *Antiquaries Journal* 8, 177–92

Avent, R. 1975. *Anglo-Saxon Garnet Inlaid Disc and Composite Brooches*, Oxford, British Archaeological Reports, British Series 11

Avent, R. & Evison, V.I. 1982. 'Anglo-Saxon button brooches', *Archaeologia* 107, 77–124

Bakka, E. 1958. *On the Beginnings of Salin's Style I in England*, Bergen, John Griegs Boktrykkeri

Baldwin Brown, G. 1903–15. *The Arts in Early England – Saxon Art and Industry in the Pagan Period*, London, John Murray, vols I–IV

Barfoot, J.F. & Price Williams, D. 1976. 'The Saxon barrow at Gally Hills, Banstead Down, Surrey', *Research Volume of the Surrey Archaeological Society* 3, 59–76

Barrett, J.C. 1990. 'The monumentality of death: the character of early Bronze Age mortuary mounds in southern Britain', *World Archaeology* 22, 179–89

Barth, F. 1969. 'Introduction', in F. Barth (ed.), *Ethnic Groups and Boundaries*, London, Allen & Unwin, pp. 9–38

BIBLIOGRAPHY

Bassett, S. (ed.) 1989. *The Origins of Anglo-Saxon Kingdoms*, Leicester, Leicester University Press

Bateman, T. 1853. 'On early burial-places discovered in the County of Nottingham', *Journal of the British Archaeological Association* 8, 183–92

Bateman, T. 1861. *Ten Years' Diggings in Celtic and Saxon Grave Hills in the Counties of Derby, Stafford and York*, London, J.R. Smith

Bender Jørgensen, L. 1992. *North European Textiles until AD 1000*, Aarhus, Aarhus University Press

Bentley, G. 1987. 'Ethnicity and practice', *Comparative Studies in Society and History* 29, 24–55

Beresford Ellis, P. 1992. *Celt and Saxon: the Struggle for Britain AD 410–937*, London, Constable

Bilikowska, K. 1980. 'The Anglo-Saxon settlement of Bedfordshire', *Bedfordshire Archaeological Journal* 14, 25–38

Bishop, M.W. 1984. 'An Anglian cemetery at Cotgrave, Nottinghamshire', *Transactions of the Thoroton Society of Nottinghamshire* 88, 106

Blair, J. 1988. 'Minster churches in the landscape', in D. Hooke (ed.), *Anglo-Saxon Settlement*, Oxford, Blackwell, pp. 35–58

Blair, J. 1995. 'Anglo-Saxon pagan shrines and their prototypes', *Anglo-Saxon Studies in Archaeology and History* 8, 1–28

Boddington, A. 1987. 'From bones to population: the problem of numbers', in A. Boddington, A. Garland & R. Janaway (eds), *Death, Decay and Reconstruction*, Manchester, Manchester University Press, pp. 180–97

Böhme, H.W. 1974. *Germanische Grabfunde des 4. bis 5. Jahrhunderts zwischen unterer Elbe und Loire*, München, Münchener Beiträge zur Vor- und Frühgeschichte 19

Böhme, H.W. 1986. 'Das Ende der Römerherrschaft in Britannien und die angelsächsische Besiedlung Englands im 5. Jahrhundert', *Jahrbuch des Römische-Germanischen Zentralmuseums Mainz* 33, 469–574

Böhner, K. 1958. *Die Frankischen Altertümer des Trierer Landes, Germanische Denkmäler der Völkerwanderungszeit*, Serie B I, Berlin, Mann

Bond, J.M. 1996. 'Burnt offerings: animal bones in Anglo-Saxon cremations', *World Archaeology* 28, 76–88

Bone, P. 1989. 'The development of Anglo-Saxon swords from the fifth to the eleventh century', in S.C. Hawkes (ed.), *Weapons and Warfare in Anglo-Saxon England*, Oxford, Oxford University Committee for Archaeology Monograph No. 21, pp. 63–70

Bonney, D. 1966. 'Pagan Saxon boundaries and burials in Wiltshire', *Wiltshire Archaeological Magazine* 61, 25–30

Bonney, D. 1972. 'Early boundaries in Wessex', in P.J. Fowler (ed.), *Archaeology and the Landscape*, London, John Baker, pp. 168–86

Bonney, D. 1979. 'Early boundaries and estates in southern England', in P.H. Sawyer (ed.), *English Medieval Settlement*, London, Edward Arnold, pp. 41–51

Boyle, A., Dodd, A., Miles, D. & Mudd, A. 1995. *Two Oxfordshire Anglo-Saxon Cemeteries: Berinsfield and Didcot*, Oxford, Thames Valley Landscapes Monograph No. 8

Boyle, A., Jennings, D., Miles, D. & Palmer, S. 1998. *The Anglo-Saxon Cemetery at Butler's Field, Lechlade, Gloucestershire*, Oxford, Thames Valley Landscapes Monograph No. 10

Bradford, J. & Goodchild, R. 1939. 'Excavations at Frilford, Berks., 1937–8', *Oxoniensia* 4, 1–70

Brenan, J. 1991. *Hanging Bowls and their Contexts: an archaeological survey of their socio-economic significance from the fifth to seventh centuries A.D.*, Oxford, British Archaeological Reports, British Series 220

Briggs, J.J. 1869. 'Notice of a discovery of ancient remains at King's Newton, Derbyshire', *Reliquary* 9, 1–3

Briscoe, T. 1986. 'The use of brooches and other jewellery as dies on pagan Anglo-Saxon pottery', *Medieval Archaeology* 30, 136–42

Brooks, D.A. 1984. 'Gildas' *De Excidio*. Its revolutionary meaning and purpose', *Studia Celtica* 18/19, 1–10

Brooks, D.A. 1994. 'The Theory and Methodology of Classifications of the Fifth and Sixth Centuries A.D. in Anglo-Saxon England with Reference to Great Square-Headed Brooches', Unpublished PhD dissertation, University College, London

Brothwell, D. 1981. *Digging Up Bones* (3rd edn), Oxford, Oxford University Press

Brown, D. 1974. 'So-called "Needle Cases"', *Medieval Archaeology* 18, 151–4

Brown, D. 1976. 'Archaeological evidence for the Anglo-Saxon period', in A. McWhirr (ed.), *Archaeology and History of Cirencester*, Oxford, British Archaeological Reports, British Series 30, pp. 19–45

BIBLIOGRAPHY

Brown, D. 1977. 'Firesteels and pursemounts again', *Bonner Jahrbucher* 177, 451–77

Brown, M.A. 1983. 'Grave orientation: a further view', *Archaeological Journal* 140, 322–8

Brown, P. & Schweizer, F. 1973. 'X-ray fluorescent analysis of Anglo-Saxon jewellery', *Archaeometry* 15, 175–92

Brown, P.D. 1967. 'The Anglo-Saxon cemetery at Harwell, grave 7', *Oxoniensia* 32, 72–4

Browne, T. 1658. *Hydriotaphia, or Urn Buriall, or, A Discourse of the Sepulchrall Urnes lately found in Norfolk . . .*, London (ed. F.L. Huntley Meredith, New York, 1966)

Brownsword, R. & Hines, J. 1993. 'The alloys of a sample of Anglo-Saxon great square-headed brooches', *Antiquaries Journal* 73, 1–10

Bruce-Mitford, R.L.S. 1968. 'Sutton Hoo excavations, 1965–7', *Antiquity* 42, 36–9

Bruce-Mitford, R.L.S. 1975. *The Sutton Hoo Ship-Burial. Volume 1. Excavations, Background, the Ship, Dating and Inventory*, London, British Museum Publications

Bruce-Mitford, R.L.S. 1978. *The Sutton Hoo Ship-Burial. Volume 2. Arms, Armour and Regalia*, London, British Museum Publications

Bruce-Mitford, R.L.S. 1983. *The Sutton Hoo Ship-Burial. Volume 3. Late Roman and Byzantine Silver, Hanging-Bowls, Drinking Vessels, Cauldrons and other Containers, Textiles, the Lyre, Pottery Bottle and other Items*, London, British Museum Publications (ed. A. Care Evans)

Bruce-Mitford, R.L.S. & Harden, D.B. 1956. 'Edward Thurlow Leeds 1877–1955', in D.B. Harden (ed.), *Dark Age Britain. Studies Presented to E.T. Leeds*, London, Methuen, pp. ix–xvi

Brugmann, B. 1999. 'The role of continental artefact-types in sixth-century Kentish chronology', in J. Hines, K. Høilund Nielsen & F. Siegmund (eds), *The Pace of Change. Studies in Early-Medieval Chronology*, Oxford, Oxbow Books, pp. 37–64

Brush, K. 1988. 'Gender and mortuary analysis in pagan Anglo-Saxon archaeology', *Archaeological Review from Cambridge* 7, 76–89

Brush, K. 1993. 'Adorning the Dead: The Social Significance of Early Anglo-Saxon Funerary Dress in England (Fifth to Seventh Centuries AD)', Unpublished PhD dissertation, University of Cambridge

Burgess, B. 1886. 'Opening of a tumulus at Taplow', *Records of Buckinghamshire* 5, 331–5

Burgess, J.T. 1876. 'Saxon remains at Offchurch', *Journal of the British Archaeological Association* 32, 464–7

Burke, E. 1790. *Reflections on the Revolution in France*, London, J. Dodsley

Burrow, J.A. 1981. *A Liberal Descent – Victorian Historians and the English Past*, Cambridge, Cambridge University Press

Bushe-Fox, J.P. 1949. *Fourth Report on the Excavations of the Roman Fort at Richborough, Kent*, London, Society of Antiquaries of London Research Report 16

Butterworth, C.A. & Lobb, S.J. 1992. *Excavations in the Burghfield Area, Berkshire*, Salisbury, Wessex Archaeology Report No. 1

Carnegie, S. & Filmer-Sankey, W. 1993. 'A Saxon "Cremation Pyre" from the Snape Anglo-Saxon Cemetery, Suffolk', *Anglo-Saxon Studies in Archaeology and History* 6, 107–11

Carver, M. 1986. 'Sutton Hoo in context', *Settimane di Studio del Centro Italiano di Studi Sull'Alto Medioevo* 32, 77–117

Carver, M. 1989. 'Kingship and material culture in early Anglo-Saxon East Anglia', in S. Bassett (ed.), *The Origins of Anglo-Saxon Kingdoms*, Leicester, Leicester University Press, pp. 141–58

Carver, M. 1990. 'Pre-Viking traffic in the North Sea', in S. McGrail (ed.), *Maritime Celts, Frisians and Saxons*, London, Council for British Archaeology Research Report 71, pp. 117–25

Carver, M. 1992a. 'Ideology and allegiance in East Anglia', in R. Farrell & C. Neuman de Vegvar (eds), *Sutton Hoo: Fifty Years After*, Hamilton Ohio, American Early Medieval Studies 2, pp. 173–82

Carver, M. 1992b. 'The Anglo-Saxon Cemetery at Sutton Hoo: an interim report', in M. Carver (ed.), *The Age of Sutton Hoo*, Woodbridge, Boydell Press, pp. 343–71

Carver, M. 1992c. 'Preface' in M. Carver (ed.), *The Age of Sutton Hoo*, Woodbridge, Boydell Press, pp. vii–x

Carver, M. 1995. 'Boat-burial in Britain: ancient custom or political symbol?', in O. Crumlin-Pedersen (ed.), *The Ship as Symbol*, Copenhagen, National Museum, pp. 111–23

Carver, M. 1998. *Sutton Hoo. Burial Ground of Kings?*, London, British Museum Press

Chadwick, H.M. 1907. *The Origin of the English Nation*, Cambridge, Cambridge University Press

Chadwick, S. 1958. 'The Anglo-Saxon cemetery at Finglesham, Kent: a reconsideration', *Medieval Archaeology* 2, 1–71

BIBLIOGRAPHY

Chamberlain, A. 1994. *Human Remains*, London, British Museum Press
Childe, V.G. 1929. *The Danube in Prehistory*, Oxford, Clarendon Press
Childe, V.G. 1935. 'Changing methods and aims in prehistory, Presidential Address for 1935', *Proceedings of the Prehistoric Society* 1, 1–15
Churchill, W. 1956. *A History of the English-Speaking Peoples: The Birth of Britain, Vol. I*, London, Cassell & Co.
Clarke, D. 1968. *Analytical Archaeology*, London, Methuen
Clarke, G. 1979. 'The Roman cemetery at Lankhills', *Winchester Studies 3: Pre-Roman and Roman Winchester Part 2*
Clarke, R. 1940. 'Norfolk in the Dark Ages, 400–800 A.D. Part II', *Norfolk Archaeology* 27, 215–49
Clarke, R. 1957. 'Archaeological discoveries in Norfolk, 1949–54', *Norfolk Archaeology* 31, 395–416
Clay, R.C. 1927. 'The barrows on Middle Down, Alvediston', *Wiltshire Archaeological Magazine* 43, 432–7
Cohen, R. 1978. 'Ethnicity: Problem and focus in anthropology', *Annual Review of Anthropology* 7, 379–403
Colgrave, B. & Mynors, R. (eds). 1969. *Bede's Ecclesiastical History of the English People*, Oxford
Colley, L. 1992. *Britons: Forging the Nation 1707–1837*, London, Pimlico
Collingwood, R.G. & Myres, J.N.L. 1936. *Roman Britain and the English Settlements*, Oxford, Clarendon Press
Collins, A. & Collins, F. 1959. 'Excavations on Blewburton Hill, 1953', *Berkshire Archaeological Journal* 57, 52–73
Collis, J. 1983. *Wigber Low, Derbyshire: a Bronze Age and Anglian Burial Site in the White Peak*, Sheffield, Department of Prehistory and Archaeology, University of Sheffield
Cook, A.M. & Dacre, M.W. 1985. *Excavations at Portway, Andover 1973–1975*, Oxford, Oxford University Committee for Archaeology Monograph No. 4
Cox, M. 1996. *Life and Death in Spitalfields 1700 to 1850*, York, Council for British Archaeology
Crabtree, P. 1995. 'The symbolic role of animals in Anglo-Saxon England: Evidence from burials and cremations', in K. Biddick (ed.), *The Symbolic Role of Animals in Archaeology*, MASCA Research Papers in Science and Archaeology Vol. 12, pp. 200–26
Crawford, G. 1983. 'Excavations at Wasperton: 3rd interim report', *West Midlands Archaeology* 26, 15–27
Crawford, S. 1991. 'When do Anglo-Saxon children count?', *Journal of Theoretical Archaeology* 2, 17–24
Crawford, S. 1993. 'Children, death and the afterlife in Anglo-Saxon England', *Anglo-Saxon Studies in Archaeology and History* 6, 83–91
Curtis, L.P. 1968. *Anglo-Saxons and Celts*, New York, New York University Press
Davies, S.M. 1985. 'The excavation of an Anglo-Saxon cemetery (and some prehistoric pits) at Charlton Plantation, near Downton', *Wiltshire Archaeological and Natural History Magazine* 79, 109–54
De Laet, S.J., Dhondt, J. & Nenquin, J. 1952. 'Les *laeti* du Namurois et l'origine de la civilisation mérovingienne', in Anon. (ed.), *Études d'Histoire et d'Archéologie Dédiées à Ferdinand Courtoy*, Namur, Publication Extraordinaire de la Société Archéologique de Namur, pp. 149–72
Detsicas, A.P. 1973. 'Excavations at Eccles, 1972. Eleventh interim report', *Archaeologia Cantiana* 88, 73–80
Detsicas, A.P. 1974. 'Excavations at Eccles, 1973. Twelfth interim report', *Archaeologia Cantiana* 89, 119–34
Dickinson, T. 1974. *Cuddesdon and Dorchester-on-Thames, Oxfordshire: Two early Saxon 'princely' sites in Wessex*, Oxford, British Archaeological Reports, British Series 1
Dickinson, T. 1976. 'The Anglo-Saxon Burial Sites of the Upper Thames Region, and their Bearing on the History of Wessex, circa AD 400–700', Unpublished DPhil dissertation, University of Oxford
Dickinson, T. 1979. 'On the origin and chronology of the early Anglo-Saxon disc brooch', in S.C. Hawkes, D. Brown & J. Campbell (eds), *Anglo-Saxon Studies in Archaeology and History 1*, Oxford, British Archaeological Reports, British Series 72, pp. 39–80
Dickinson, T. 1980. 'The present state of Anglo-Saxon cemetery studies', in P. Rahtz, T. Dickinson & L. Watts (eds), *Anglo-Saxon Cemeteries 1979*, Oxford, British Archaeological Reports, British Series 82, pp. 11–33
Dickinson, T. 1982. 'Fowler's Type G penannular brooches reconsidered', *Medieval Archaeology* 26, 41–68
Dickinson, T. 1991. 'Material culture as social expression: the case of Saxon saucer brooches with running spiral decoration', *Studien zur Sachsenforschung* 7, 39–70
Dickinson, T. 1993a. 'Early Saxon saucer brooches: a preliminary overview', *Anglo-Saxon Studies in Archaeology and History* 6, 11–44

BIBLIOGRAPHY

Dickinson, T. 1993b. 'An Anglo-Saxon "cunning woman" from Bidford-on-Avon', in M. Carver (ed.), *In Search of Cult – Archaeological Investigations in Honour of Philip Rahtz*, Woodbridge, Boydell Press, pp. 45–54

Dickinson, T. & Härke, H. 1992. *Early Anglo-Saxon Shields*, London, Society of Antiquaries

Dickinson, T. & Speake, G. 1992. 'The seventh-century cremation burial in Asthall Barrow, Oxfordshire: a reassessment', in M. Carver (ed.), *The Age of Sutton Hoo*, Woodbridge, Boydell Press, pp. 95–130

Douglas, J. 1793. *Nenia Britannica: or, a Sepulchral History of Great Britain*, London, B. & J. White

Down, A. & Welch, M. 1990. *Chichester Excavations VII: Apple Down and the Mardens*, Chichester, Chichester District Council

Drinkall, G. & Foreman, M. 1998. *The Anglo-Saxon Cemetery at Castledyke South, Barton-on-Humber*, Sheffield, Sheffield Excavation Reports 6, Humber Archaeology Partnership

Dryden, H. 1882. 'Excavation of an ancient burial ground at Marston St Lawrence, Co. Northampton', *Archaeologia* 48, 327–39

Dumville, D. 1977. 'Sub-Roman Britain: history and legend', *History* 62, 173–92

Dunning, G. & Wheeler, M. 1931. 'A barrow at Dunstable, Bedfordshire', *Archaeological Journal* 88, 193–217

Eagles, B.N. 1979. *The Anglo-Saxon Settlement of Humberside*, Oxford, British Archaeological Reports, British Series 68

Ellis Davidson, H. & Webster, L. 1967. 'The Anglo-Saxon burial at Coombe (Woodnesborough), Kent', *Medieval Archaeology* 11, 1–41

Epstein, A.L. 1978. *Ethos and Identity. Three Studies in Ethnicity*, London, Tavistock Publications

Evison, V.I. 1956. 'An Anglo-Saxon cemetery at Holborough, Kent', *Archaeologia Cantiana* 70, 84–141

Evison, V.I. 1961. 'The Saxon objects', in J. Hurst, 'The kitchen area of Northolt Manor, Middlesex', *Medieval Archaeology* 5, pp. 226–30

Evison, V.I. 1963. 'Sugar-loaf shield-bosses', *Antiquaries Journal* 43, 38–96

Evison, V.I. 1965. *The Fifth Century Invasions South of the Thames*, London, Athlone Press

Evison, V.I. 1968. 'Quoit brooch style buckles', *Antiquaries Journal* 48, 231–46

Evison, V.I. 1975. 'Sword rings and beads', *Archaeologia* 105, 303–15

Evison, V.I. 1978. 'Early Anglo-Saxon applied disc brooches, Part I: On the Continent', *Antiquaries Journal* 58, 88–102

Evison, V.I. 1979. *Wheel-Thrown Pottery in Anglo-Saxon Graves*, London, Royal Archaeological Institute

Evison, V.I. 1981. 'Supporting-arm brooches and equal-arm brooches in England', *Studien zur Sachsenforschung* 1, 127–41

Evison, V.I. 1982. 'Anglo-Saxon glass claw beakers', *Archaeologia* 107, 43–76

Evison, V.I. 1983. 'Some distinctive glass vessels of the post-Roman period', *Journal of Glass Studies* 25, 87–93

Evison, V.I. 1987. *Dover: The Buckland Anglo-Saxon Cemetery*, London, Historic Buildings and Monuments Commission Report No. 3

Evison, V.I. 1988. *An Anglo-Saxon Cemetery at Alton, Hampshire*, Hampshire Field Club Monograph No. 4

Evison, V.I. 1994a. *An Anglo-Saxon Cemetery at Great Chesterford, Essex*, London, Council for British Archaeology Research Report No. 91

Evison, V.I. 1994b. 'Anglo-Saxon glass from cremations', in C. Hills, K. Penn & R. Rickett (eds), *The Anglo-Saxon Cemetery at Spong Hill, North Elmham. Part V: Catalogue of Cremations (Nos 2800–3334)*, East Anglian Archaeology 67, pp. 23–30

Evison, V.I. & Hill, P. 1996. *Two Anglo-Saxon Cemeteries at Beckford, Hereford and Worcester*, London, Council for British Archaeology Research Report No. 103

Farley, M. 1992. 'The Cop round barrow at Bledlow, Buckinghamshire: Prehistoric or Saxon?', *Records of Buckinghamshire* 34, 11–13

Farwell, D. & Molleson, T. 1993. *Excavations at Poundbury 1966–80. Volume II: The Cemeteries*, Dorchester, Dorset Natural History and Archaeological Society Monograph Series No. 11

Faull, M.L. 1976. 'The location and relationship of the Sancton Anglo-Saxon cemeteries', *Antiquaries Journal* 56, 227–33

Faull, M.L. 1979. 'British Survival in Anglo-Saxon Yorkshire', Unpublished PhD dissertation, University of Leeds

Faussett, B. 1856. *Inventorium Sepulchrale: an Account of some Antiquities dug up at Gilton, Kingston, Sibertswold, Barfriston, Beakesbourne, Chartham, and Crundale, in the County of Kent, from A.D. 1757 to A.D. 1773*, ed. by C. Roach Smith, London, printed for the subscribers

BIBLIOGRAPHY

Fehring, G. 1991. *The Archaeology of Medieval Germany*, London, Routledge

Fennell, K.R. 1974. 'Pagan Saxon Lincolnshire', *Archaeological Journal* 131, 283–93

Field, N. 1989. 'Archaeology in Lincolnshire and South Humberside, 1988', *Lincolnshire History and Archaeology* 24, 53–61

Field, N. & George, I. 1998. 'Archaeology in Lincolnshire 1998', *Lincolnshire History and Archaeology* 33, 35–46

Filmer-Sankey, W. 1990. 'A new boat burial from the Snape Anglo-Saxon cemetery, Suffolk', in S. McGrail (ed.), *Maritime Celts, Frisians and Saxons*, London, Council for British Archaeology Research Report No. 71, pp. 126–34

Filmer-Sankey, W. 1992. 'Snape Anglo-Saxon cemetery: the current state of knowledge', in M. Carver (ed.), *The Age of Sutton Hoo*, Woodbridge, Boydell Press, pp. 39–51

Fisher, G. 1995. 'Kingdom and community in early Anglo-Saxon eastern England', in L. Anderson Beck (ed.), *Regional Approaches to Mortuary Analysis*, New York, Plenum Press, pp. 147–66

Fitzpatrick, A. 1997. *Archaeological Excavations on the Route of the A27 Westhampnett Bypass, West Sussex, 1992. Volume 2: the Late Iron Age, Romano-British and Anglo-Saxon Cemeteries*, Salisbury, Wessex Archaeology Report No. 12

Flaherty, C. 1999. 'The use of DNA analysis of human skeletal remains in early Anglo-Saxon England to examine sex and kinship', paper presented at the 64th Annual Meeting of the Society for American Archaeology, 26 March 1999, Chicago, Illinois

Ford, W.T. 1996. 'Anglo-Saxon cemeteries along the Avon valley', *Transactions of the Birmingham and Warwickshire Archaeological Society* 100, 59–98

Fowler, E. 1960. 'The origins and development of the penannular brooch in Europe', *Proceedings of the Prehistoric Society* 26, 149–77

Fowler, E. 1963. 'Celtic metalwork of the fifth and sixth centuries A.D.', *Archaeological Journal* 120, 98–159

Fowler, M.J. 1955. 'The Anglian settlement of the Derbyshire–Staffordshire Peak District', *Derbyshire Archaeological Journal* 74, 134–51

Fox, C. & Palmer, W.M. 1926. 'Excavations in the Cambridgeshire Dykes. V. Bran or Heydon Ditch. First Report', *Proceedings of the Cambridge Antiquarian Society* 27, 16–42

Freeman, E.A. 1869. *Old English History for Children*, London, Macmillan

Freeman, E.A. 1872. *The Growth of the English Constitution*, London, Macmillan

Freeman, E.A. 1881. *The Historical Geography of Europe*, London, Macmillan

Freeman, E.A. 1888. *Fifty Years of European History: Teutonic Conquest in Gaul and Britain*, London, Macmillan

Frere, S.S. & St Joseph, J.K. 1974. 'The Roman fortress at Longthorpe', *Britannia* 5, 1–129

Gaimster, M. 1992. 'Scandinavian gold bracteates in England. Money and media in the Dark Ages', *Medieval Archaeology* 36, 1–28

Gale, D. 1989. 'The seax', in S.C. Hawkes (ed.), *Weapons and Warfare in Anglo-Saxon England*, Oxford, Oxford University Committee for Archaeology Monograph No. 21, pp. 71–83

Geake, H. 1992. 'Burial practice in seventh- and eighth-century England', in M. Carver (ed.), *The Age of Sutton Hoo*, Woodbridge, Boydell Press, pp. 83–94

Geake, H. 1994. 'Anglo-Saxon double-tongued buckles', *Medieval Archaeology* 38, 164–6

Geake, H. 1997. *The Use of Grave-Goods in Conversion-Period England, c.600–c.850*, British Archaeological Reports, British Series 261

Geake, H. 1999. 'Invisible kingdoms: the use of grave-goods in seventh-century England', *Anglo-Saxon Studies in Archaeology and History* 10, 203–15

Geary, P.J. 1983. 'Ethnic identity as a situational construct in the early middle ages', *Mitteilungen der Anthropologischen Gesellschaft in Wien* 113, 15–26

Genrich, A. 1981. 'A remarkable inhumation grave from Liebenau, Neinburg, Germany', in V.I. Evison (ed.), *Angles, Saxons and Jutes. Essays presented to J.N.L. Myres*, Oxford, Clarendon Press, pp. 59–71

Gillam, J.P. 1979. 'Romano-Saxon pottery: an alternative explanation', in P.J. Casey (ed.), *The End of Roman Britain: papers arising from a conference, Durham 1978*, Oxford, British Archaeological Reports, British Series 71, pp. 103–18

Goddard, E.H. 1896. 'Notes on objects from a Saxon interment at Basset Down', *Wiltshire Archaeological Magazine* 28, 104–8

Goffart, W. 1988. *The Narrators of Barbarian History (A.D. 550–800)*, Princeton, Princeton University Press

Gooch, G. 1952. *History and Historians in the Nineteenth Century* (2nd edn), London, Longman

Goodier, A. 1984. 'Boundaries in Anglo-Saxon England: a statistical study', *Medieval Archaeology* 28, 1–21

Gowland, R. 1998. 'The Use of Prior Possibilities in Ageing Perinatal Skeletal Remains: Implications for the Evidence of Infanticide in Roman Britain', Unpublished MSc dissertation, Universities of Bradford and Sheffield

Green, B. & Rogerson, A. 1978. *The Anglo-Saxon Cemetery from Bergh Apton, Norfolk*, East Anglian Archaeology 7, Gressenhall, Norfolk Archaeological Unit

Green. B., Milligan, W.F. & West, S.E. 1981. 'The Illington/Lackford workshop', in V.I. Evison (ed.), *Angles, Saxons and Jutes. Essays presented to J.N.L. Myres*, Oxford, Clarendon Press, pp. 187–226

Green, B., Rogerson, A. & White, S.G. 1987. *The Anglo-Saxon Cemetery at Morningthorpe, Norfolk*, East Anglian Archaeology 36, Gressenhall, Norfolk Archaeology Unit

Green, J.R. 1874. *A Short History of the English People*, London, Macmillan

Green, J.R. 1881. *The Making of England*, London, Macmillan

Green, J.R. 1883. *The Conquest of England*, London, Macmillan

Griffith, A.F. 1915. 'An Anglo-Saxon cemetery at Alfriston, Sussex', *Sussex Archaeological Collections* 57, 197–210

Grimes, W.F. 1960. *Excavations on Defence Sites, 1939–1945*, Vol. I, Ministry of Works Archaeological Reports 3, London. HMSO

Guest, E. 1850. *On the Early English Settlements in Southern Britain*, London

Guest, E. 1883. *Origines Celticae (a fragment) and other contributions to the history of Britain*, London, Macmillan

Guido, M. 1999. *The Glass Beads of Anglo-Saxon England c. AD 400–700*, ed. M. Welch, Woodbridge, Boydell Press for Society of Antiquaries

Hagen, R. 1971. 'Anglo-Saxon burials from the vicinity of Biscot Mill, Luton', *Bedfordshire Archaeological Journal* 6, 23–6

Haith, C. 1997. 'Pottery in early Anglo-Saxon England', in I. Freestone & D. Gaimster (eds), *Pottery in the Making. World Ceramic Traditions*, London, British Museum Press, pp. 146–51

Håland, R. 1977. 'Archaeological classification and ethnic groups: A case study from Sudanese Nubia', *Norwegian Archaeological Review*, 10, 1–17

Hale, J.R. 1967. *The Evolution of British Historiography*, London, Macmillan

Halsall, G. 1992. 'The origins of the Reihengräberzivilisation: forty years on', in J. Drinkwater & F. Elton (eds), *Fifth-Century Gaul: A Crisis of Identity?*, Cambridge, Cambridge University Press, pp. 196–207

Halsall, G. 1995. *Settlement and Social Organisation. The Merovingian Region of Metz*, Cambridge, Cambridge University Press

Hamerow, H. 1994. 'Migration theory and the migration period', in B. Vyner (ed.), *Building on the Past*, London, Royal Archaeological Institute, pp. 164–77

Hamerow, H. & Pickin, J. 1995. 'An early Anglo-Saxon cemetery at Andrews Hill, Easington, Co. Durham', *Durham Archaeological Journal* 11: 35–64

Harden, D.B. 1956. 'Glass vessels in Britain and Ireland, AD 400–1000', in D.B. Harden (ed.), *Dark Age Britain – Studies presented to E.T. Leeds*, London, Methuen, pp. 132–61

Harden, D.B. 1972. 'Ancient Glass, III: Post-Roman', *Archaeological Journal* 128, 78–117

Harden, D.B. 1977. 'Anglo-Saxon and later Medieval glass in Britain: some recent developments', *Medieval Archaeology* 21, 1–24

Härke, H. 1989. 'Knives in early Saxon burials: blade length and age at death', *Medieval Archaeology* 33, 144–8

Härke, H. 1990. 'Warrior graves? The background of the Anglo-Saxon weapon burial rite', *Past and Present* 126, 22–43

Härke, H. 1992a. 'Changing symbols in a changing society: the Anglo-Saxon weapon burial rite in the seventh century', in M. Carver (ed.), *The Age of Sutton Hoo*, Woodbridge, Boydell Press, pp. 149–65

Härke, H. 1992b. *Angelsächsische Waffengräber des 5. bis 7. Jahrhunderts*, Cologne and Bonn, Zeitschrift für Archäologie des Mittelalters, Beiheft 6

BIBLIOGRAPHY

Härke, H. 1995. '"The Hun is a methodical chap": reflections on the German tradition of pre- and proto-history', in P.J. Ucko (ed.), *Theory in Archaeology. A World Perspective*, London, Routledge, pp. 46–60

Härke, H. 1998. 'Archaeologists and migrations: a problem of attitude?', *Current Anthropology* 39, 19–45

Harman, M., Molleson, T. & Price, J. 1981. 'Burials, bodies and beheadings in Romano-British and Anglo-Saxon cemeteries', *Bulletin of the British Museum, Natural Hist. Geol.* 35, 145–88

Harrison, G.J. 1997. 'Quoit Brooches: A Reassessment', Unpublished MA thesis, University of Durham

Haseloff, G. 1974. 'Salin's Style I', *Medieval Archaeology* 18, 1–15

Haseloff, G. 1981. *Die Germanische Tierornamentik der Völkerwnderungszeit*, Berlin, De Gruyter

Hawkes, C.F.C. 1956. 'The Jutes of Kent', in D.B. Harden (ed.), *Dark Age Britain – Studies presented to E.T. Leeds*, London, Methuen, pp. 91–111

Hawkes, S.C. 1961. 'The Jutish style A. A study of Germanic animal art in southern England in the fifth century A.D.', *Archaeologia* 98, 29–75

Hawkes, S.C. 1969. 'Early Anglo-Saxon Kent', *Archaeological Journal* 126, 186–92

Hawkes, S.C. 1974. 'Post-Roman and Anglo-Saxon', *Archaeological Journal* 131, 408–20

Hawkes, S.C. 1976. 'Orientation at Finglesham: Sunrise dating of death and burial in an Anglo-Saxon cemetery in east Kent', *Archaeologia Cantiana* 92, 33–51

Hawkes, S.C. 1982. 'Anglo-Saxon Kent c. 425–725', in P. Leach (ed.), *Archaeology in Kent to AD 1500*, London, Council for British Archaeology Research Report No. 48, pp. 64–78

Hawkes, S.C. 1990. 'Bryan Faussett and the Faussett collection: An assessment', in E. Southworth (ed.), *Anglo-Saxon Cemeteries: A Reappraisal*, Stroud, Alan Sutton, pp. 1–24

Hawkes, S.C. & Dunning, G.C. 1961. 'Soldiers and settlers in Britain, fourth to fifth century', *Medieval Archaeology* 5, 297–330

Hawkes, S.C. & Hogarth, A.C. 1974. 'The Anglo-Saxon cemetery at Monkton, Thanet. Report on the rescue excavations of May/June 1971', *Archaeologia Cantiana* 89, 49–90

Hawkes, S.C. & Wells, C. 1975. 'Crime and punishment in an Anglo-Saxon cemetery?', *Antiquity* 49, 118–22

Head, J.F. 1938. 'The excavation of the Cop round barrow, Bledlow', *Records of Buckinghamshire* 13, 313–51

Hedges, J.D. & Buckley, D.G. 1985. 'Anglo-Saxon burials and later features excavated at Orsett, Essex, 1975', *Medieval Archaeology* 29, 1–24

Henslow, J.S. 1847. 'On supposed British cinerary urns found at the village of Kingston, near Derby, in 1844', *Journal of the British Archaeological Association* 2, 60–3

Higham, N. 1992. *Rome, Britain and the Anglo-Saxons*, London, Seaby

Hills, C. 1977a. 'Chamber grave from Spong Hill, North Elmham, Norfolk', *Medieval Archaeology* 21, 167–76

Hills, C. 1977b. *The Anglo-Saxon Cemetery at Spong Hill, North Elmham. Part I*, Norfolk Archaeology 6

Hills, C. 1979. 'The archaeology of Anglo-Saxon England in the pagan period: a review', *Anglo-Saxon England* 8, 297–330

Hills, C. 1980. 'Anglo-Saxon cremation cemeteries, with particular reference to Spong Hill, Norfolk', in P. Rahtz, T. Dickinson & L. Watts (eds), *Anglo-Saxon Cemeteries 1979*, Oxford, British Archaeological Reports, British Series 82, pp. 197–207

Hills, C. 1983a. 'Animal stamps on Anglo-Saxon pottery in East Anglia', *Studien zur Sachsenforschung* 4, 93–110

Hills, C. 1983b. 'Economic and settlement background to Sutton Hoo in eastern England', in J.P. Lamm & H.A. Nordström (eds), *Vendel Period Studies. Transactions of the Boat-Grave Symposium in Stockholm, February 2–3, 1981*, Stockholm, Statens Historiska Museum, pp. 99–104

Hills, C. 1993. 'The Anglo-Saxon settlement of England. The state of research in Britain in the late 1980s', in M. Müller-Wille & R. Schneider (eds), *Augewählte Probleme Europäischer Landnahmen des Früh- und Hochmittelalters*, Sigmaringen, Jan Thorbecke, pp. 303–15

Hills, C. 1999a. 'Did the people of Spong Hill come from Schleswig-Holstein?', *Studien zur Sachsenforschung* 11, 145–54

Hills, C. 1999b. 'Spong Hill and the Adventus Saxonum', in C.E. Karkov, K.M. Wickham-Crowley & B.K. Young (eds), *Spaces of the Living and the Dead: an Archaeological Dialogue*, Oxford, Oxbow for American Early Medieval Studies 3, pp. 15–26

Hills, C. & Penn, K. 1981. *The Anglo-Saxon Cemetery at Spong Hill, North Elmham. Part II*, East Anglian Archaeology 11, Gressenhall, Norfolk Archaeological Unit

Hills, C., Penn, K. & Rickett, R. 1984. *The Anglo-Saxon Cemetery at Spong Hill, North Elmham. Part III: Catalogue of Inhumations*, East Anglian Archaeology 21, Gressenhall, Norfolk Archaeological Unit

Hills, C., Penn, K. & Rickett, R. 1987. *The Anglo-Saxon Cemetery at Spong Hill, North Elmham. Part IV: Catalogue of Cremations*, East Anglian Archaeology 34, Gressenhall, Norfolk Archaeological Unit

Hills, C., Penn, K. and Rickett, R. 1994. *The Anglo-Saxon Cemetery at Spong Hill, North Elmham. Part V: Catalogue of Cremations*, East Anglian Archaeology 67, Gressenhall, Norfolk Archaeological Unit

Hines, J. 1984. *The Scandinavian Character of England in the pre-Viking Period*, Oxford, British Archaeological Reports, British Series 124

Hines, J. 1990. 'Philology, archaeology and the *adventus Saxonum vel Anglorum*', in A. Bammesberger & A. Wollmann (eds), *Britain 400–600: Language and History*, Heidelberg, Carl Winter, pp. 17–36

Hines, J. 1992. 'The seriation and chronology of Anglian English women's graves: a critical assessment', in L. Jørgensen (ed.), *Chronological Studies of Anglo-Saxon England, Lombard Italy and Vendel Period Sweden*, Copenhagen, Arkaeologiske Skrifter No. 5, Institute of Prehistoric and Classical Archaeology, University of Copenhagen, pp. 81–93

Hines, J. 1993. *Clasps, Hektespenner, Agraffen. Anglo-Scandinavian Clasps of Classes A–C of the 3rd to 6th Centuries AD. Typology, Diffusion and Function*, Stockholm, Kungl. Vitterhets Historie och Antikvitets Akadmien

Hines, J. 1994. 'The becoming of the English: identity, material culture and language in early Anglo-Saxon England', *Anglo-Saxon Studies in Archaeology and History* 7, 49–59

Hines, J. 1996. 'Britain after Rome: between multiculturalism and monoculturalism', in P. Graves-Brown, S. Jones & C. Gamble (eds), *Cultural Identity and Archaeology: the Construction of European Communities*, London, Routledge, pp. 256–70

Hines, J. 1997. *A New Corpus of Anglo-Saxon Great Square-Headed Brooches*, Woodbridge, Boydell Press for Society of Antiquaries

Hines, J. 1999a. 'The sixth-century transition in Anglian England: an analysis of female graves from Cambridgeshire', in J. Hines, K. Høilund Nielsen & F. Siegmund (eds), *The Pace of Change. Studies in Early-Medieval Chronology*, Oxford, Oxbow Books, pp. 65–79

Hines, J. 1999b. 'The Anglian migration in British historical research', *Studien zur Sachsenforschung* 11, 155–65

Hirst, S. 1985. *An Anglo-Saxon Cemetery at Sewerby, East Yorkshire*, York University Archaeological Publications No. 4

Hirst, S. 1993. 'Death and the archaeologist', in M. Carver (ed.), *In Search of Cult – Archaeological Investigations in Honour of Philip Rahtz*, Woodbridge, Boydell Press, pp. 41–3

Hobsbawm, E.J. 1990. *Nations and Nationalism since 1780*, Cambridge, Canto

Hogarth, A.C. 1974. 'Structural features in Anglo-Saxon graves', *Archaeological Journal* 130, 104–19

Høilund Nielsen, K. 1997. 'The schism of Anglo-Saxon chronology', in C. Kjeld Jensen & K. Høilund Nielsen (eds), *Burial and Society. The Chronological and Social Analysis of Archaeological Burial Data*, Aarhus, Aarhus University Press, pp. 71–99

Høilund Nielsen, K. 1999. 'Style II and the Anglo-Saxon elite', *Anglo-Saxon Studies in Archaeology and History* 10, 185–202

Hope-Taylor, B. 1977. *Yeavering: An Anglo-British Centre of Early Northumbria*, London, HMSO, Department of the Environment, Archaeological Report No. 7

Housman, H. 1895. 'Exploration of an Anglo-Saxon cemetery in the parish of Castleacre, Norfolk', *Norfolk Archaeology* 12, 100–4

Huggett, J. 1988. 'Imported grave goods and the early Anglo-Saxon economy', *Medieval Archaeology* 32, 63–96

Hume, D. 1762. *History of England*, London, A. Millar

Hunn, A., Lawson, J. & Farley, M. 1994. 'The Anglo-Saxon cemetery at Dinton, Buckinghamshire', *Anglo-Saxon Studies in Archaeology and History* 7, 85–148

Hunter Blair, P. 1977. *An Introduction to Anglo-Saxon England*, Cambridge, Cambridge University Press

Hyslop, M. 1963. 'Two Anglo-Saxon cemeteries at Chamberlains Barn, Leighton Buzzard, Bedfordshire', *Archaeological Journal* 120, 161–200

Işcan, M.Y., Loth, S.R. & Wright, R.K. 1984. 'Metamorphosis at the sternal rib end: a new method to estimate age at death in white males', *American Journal of Physical Anthropology* 65, 147–56

BIBLIOGRAPHY

Işcan, M.Y., Loth, S.R. & Wright, R.K. 1985. 'Age estimation from the rib by phase analysis: white females', *Journal of Forensic Sciences* 30, 853–63

Ivers, R., Busby, P. & Shepherd, N. 1995. *Tattenhoe and Westbury. Two Deserted Medieval Settlements in Milton Keynes*, Aylesbury, Buckinghamshire Archaeological Society Monograph Series No. 8

Jackson, D.A. 1970. 'Fieldwork and excavation in north-eastern Northamptonshire', *Bulletin of the Northamptonshire Federation of Archaeological Societies* 4, 35–48

James, E. 1988. *The Franks*, Oxford, Blackwell

James, E. 1989. 'The origins of barbarian kingdoms: the continental evidence', in S. Bassett (ed.), *The Origins of Anglo-Saxon Kingdoms*, Leicester, Leicester University Press, pp. 40–52

James, H. 1992. 'Early Medieval cemeteries in Wales', in N. Edwards & A. Lane (eds), *The Early Church in Wales and the West*, Oxford, Oxbow Monograph 17, pp. 90–103

Jann, R. 1985. *The Art and Science of Victorian History*, Columbus, Ohio State University Press

Jarvis, E. 1850. 'Account of the discovery of ornaments and remains, supposed to be of Danish origin, in the parish of Caenby, Lincolnshire', *Archaeological Journal* 7, 36–44

Jenkins, R. 1997. *Rethinking Ethnicity: Arguments and Explorations*, London, Sage Publications

Jessup, R.F. 1946. 'An Anglo-Saxon cemetery at Westbere, Kent', *Antiquaries Journal* 26, 11–21

John, E. 1960. *Land Tenure in Early England*, Leicester, Leicester University Press

Jones, S. 1996. 'Discourses of identity in the interpretation of the past', in P. Graves-Brown, S. Jones & C. Gamble (eds), *Cultural Identity and Archaeology: The Construction of European Communities*, London, Routledge, pp. 62–80

Jones, S. 1997. *The Archaeology of Ethnicity*, London, Routledge

Jones, M.U. & Jones, W.T. 1974. 'An early Anglo-Saxon landscape at Mucking', in T. Rowley (ed.), *Anglo-Saxon Settlement and Landscape*, Oxford, British Archaeological Reports, British Series 6, pp. 20–35

Katz, D. & Suchey, J.M. 1986. 'Age determination of the male *os pubis*', *American Journal of Physical Anthropology* 69, 427–35

Kemble, J.M. 1849. *The Saxons in England*, London, Longman

Kemble, J.M. 1856. 'On mortuary urns found at Stade-on-the-Elbe, and other parts of North Germany, now in the museum of the Historical Society of Hanover', *Archaeologia* 36, 270–83

Kemble, J.M. 1863. *Horae Ferales; or Studies in Archaeology of the Northern Nations*, London, Lovell Reeve

Kendrick, T.D. 1934. 'Style in early Anglo-Saxon ornament', *Ipek* 9, 66–76

Kendrick, T.D. 1938. *Anglo-Saxon Art to AD900*, London. Methuen

Kennett, D.H. 1973. 'Seventh-century cemeteries in the Ouse Valley', *Bedfordshire Archaeological Journal* 8, 99–108

Kennett, D.H. 1978. *Anglo-Saxon Pottery*, Aylesbury, Shire Publications

Kenward, J. 1885. 'A first note on the Anglo-Saxon cemetery at Wheatley, Oxfordshire', *Proceedings of the Birmingham Philosophical Society* 4, 179–83

King, R., Barber, A. & Timby, J. 1996. 'Excavations at West Lane, Kemble: an Iron Age, Roman and Saxon burial site and a medieval building', *Transactions of the Bristol and Glos. Archaeological Society* 114, 15–54

Kingsley, C. 1875. 'The Roman and the Teuton', a series of lectures delivered before the University of Cambridge

Kinsley, A.G. 1989. *The Anglo-Saxon Cemetery at Millgate, Newark-on-Trent, Nottinghamshire*, Nottingham, Nottingham Archaeological Monographs 2

Kinsley, A.G. 1993. *Excavations on the Romano-British Settlement and Anglo-Saxon Cemetery at Broughton Lodge, Willoughby-on-the-Wolds, Nottinghamshire 1964–8*, Nottingham, Nottingham Archaeological Monographs 4

Kjeld Jensen, C. & Høilund Nielsen, K. 1997. 'Burial data and correspondence analysis', in C. Kjeld Jensen & K. Høilund Nielsen (eds), *Burial and Society. The Chronological and Social Analysis of Archaeological Burial Data*, Aarhus, Aarhus University Press, pp. 29–61

Knol, E., Prummel, W., Uytterschaut, H., Hoogland, M., Casparie, W., de Langen, D., Kramer, E. & Schelvis, J. 1996. 'The early medieval cemetery of Oosterbeintum (Friesland)', *Palaeohistoria* 37/38, 245–316

Knüsel, C. 1993. 'Pagan charm and the place of anthropological theory', *European Journal of Archaeology* 1, 205–8

Knüsel, C., Janaway, R. & King, S. 1996. 'Death, decay and ritual reconstruction. Archaeological evidence of cadaveric spasm', *Oxford Journal of Archaeology* 15, 121–8

BIBLIOGRAPHY

Kossinna, G. 1911. *Der Herkunft der Germanen: zur Methode der Siedlungsarchäologie*, Würzburg, Kabitsch

Laing, L. & Laing, J. 1979. *Anglo-Saxon England*, London, Routledge & Kegan Paul

Laing, L. & Laing. L. 1996. *Early English Art and Architecture*, Stroud, Sutton Publishing

Lapidge, M. & Dumville, D. 1984. Gildas. New Approaches. Woodbridge. Boydell Press

Lappenberg, J.M. 1845. *A History of England under the Anglo-Saxon Kings* (trans. B. Thorpe), London, J. Murray

Lawson, G. 1978. 'The lyre from grave 22', in B. Green & A. Rogerson, *The Anglo-Saxon Cemetery at Bergh Apton, Norfolk: Catalogue*, East Anglian Archaeology 7, Gressenhall, Norfolk Archaeoloy Unit, pp. 87–97

Layard, N.F. 1907. 'Anglo-Saxon cemetery, Hadleigh Road, Ipswich', *Proceedings of the Suffolk Institute of Archaeology and Natural History* 13, 1–19

Leeds, E.T. 1912. 'The distribution of the Anglo-Saxon saucer brooch in relation to the battle of Bedford, AD 571', *Archaeologia* 63, 159–202

Leeds, E.T. 1913. *The Archaeology of the Anglo-Saxon Settlements*, Oxford, Clarendon Press

Leeds, E.T. 1916. 'On an Anglo-Saxon cemetery at Wheatley, Oxfordshire', *Proceedings of the Society of Antiquaries* 29, 48–63

Leeds, E.T. 1923. 'A Saxon village near Sutton Courtenay, Berks', *Archaeologia* 73, 147–92

Leeds, E.T. 1924. 'An Anglo-Saxon cremation-burial of the seventh century in Asthall Barrow, Oxfordshire', *Antiquaries Journal* 24, 113–26

Leeds, E.T. 1936. *Early Anglo-Saxon Art and Archaeology*, Oxford, Clarendon Press

Leeds, E.T. 1938. 'An Anglo-Saxon cemetery at Wallingford, Berkshire', *Berkshire Archaeological Journal* 42, 93–101

Leeds, E.T. 1939. 'Anglo-Saxon remains', in L.F. Salzman (ed.), *The Victoria History of the County of Oxford, Vol. I*, London, Oxford University Press, pp. 346–72

Leeds, E.T. 1945. 'The distribution of the Angles and Saxons archaeologically considered', *Archaeologia* 91, 1–106

Leeds, E.T. 1946. 'Denmark and early England', *Antiquaries Journal* 26, 22–37

Leeds, E.T. 1949. *A Corpus of Early Anglo-Saxon Great Square-Headed Brooches*, Oxford, Clarendon Press

Leeds, E.T. & Atkinson, R.J. 1944. 'An Anglo-Saxon cemetery at Nassington, Northants.', *Antiquaries Journal* 24, 100–28

Leeds, E.T. & Harden, D.B. 1936. *The Anglo-Saxon Cemetery at Abingdon, Oxford*, Oxford, Ashmolean Museum

Leeds, E.T. & Pocock, M. 1971. 'A survey of Anglo-Saxon cruciform brooches of the florid type', *Medieval Archaeology* 15, 13–36

Leigh, D. 1980. 'Square-Headed Brooches of Sixth Century Kent', Unpublished PhD thesis, University College, Cardiff

Leigh, D. 1985. 'Differential abrasion and brooch wear', *Science and Archaeology* 27, 8–12

Leigh, D. 1990. 'Aspects of early brooch design and production', in E. Southworth (ed.), *Anglo-Saxon Cemeteries: A Reappraisal*, Stroud, Alan Sutton, pp. 107–24

Lennard, R. 1934. 'The character of the Anglo-Saxon conquests: a disputed point', *History* (n.s.) 18, 204–14

Lethbridge, T.C. 1929. 'Recent excavations in the Cambridgeshire Dykes. VI. Bran Ditch, second report', *Proceedings of the Cambridge Antiquarian Society* 30, 78–93

Lethbridge, T.C. 1931. *Recent Excavations in Anglo-Saxon Cemeteries in Cambridgeshire and Suffolk*, Cambridge, Cambridge Antiquarian Society Quarto Publications, New Series III

Lethbridge, T.C. 1933. 'Anglo-Saxon burials at Soham, Cambridgeshire', *Proceedings of the Cambridge Antiquarian Society* 33, 152–63

Lethbridge, T.C. 1936. *A Cemetery at Shudy Camps, Cambridgeshire. Report of the Excavation of a Cemetery of the Christian Anglo-Saxon Period in 1933*, Cambridge Antiquarian Society Publications, Quarto Series, New Series 5

Lethbridge, T.C. 1938. 'Anglo-Saxon remains', in L.F. Salzman (ed.), *The Victoria History of the County of Cambridgeshire and the Isle of Ely, Vol. I*, London, Oxford University Press, pp. 305–34

Lethbridge, T.C. 1951. *A Cemetery at Lackford, Suffolk: report of the excavation of a cemetery of the pagan Anglo-Saxon period in 1947*, Cambridge Antiquarian Society, Quarto Publications, New Series 6

BIBLIOGRAPHY

Lethbridge, T.C. 1956. 'The Anglo-Saxon settlement in eastern England: a reassessment', in D.B. Harden (ed.), *Dark Age Britain – Studies presented to E.T. Leeds*, London, Methuen, pp. 112–22

Lethbridge, T.C. 1958. 'The riddle of the dykes', *Proceedings of the Cambridge Antiquarian Society* 51, 2–5

Lethbridge, T.C. & Carter, H.G. 1928. 'Excavations in the Anglo-Saxon cemetery at Little Wilbraham', *Proceedings of the Cambridge Antiquarian Society* 29, 95–104

Liddle, P. 1981. 'An Anglo-Saxon cemetery at Wanlip, Leicestershire', *Transactions of the Leicestershire Archaeological and Historical Society* 55, 11–21

Liddle, P. & Middleton, S. 1994. 'An Anglo-Saxon cemetery at Wigston Magna, Leicestershire', *Transactions of the Leicestershire Archaeological and Historical Society* 68, 64–86

Lovejoy, C.O., Meindl, R.S., Pryzbeck, T.R. & Mensforth, R.P. 1985. 'Chronological metamorphosis of the auricular surface of the ilium: a new method for the determination of adult skeletal age at death', *American Journal of Physical Anthropology* 68, 15–28

Loveluck, C. 1995. 'Acculturation, migration and exchange: the formation of an Anglo-Saxon society in the English Peak District, 400–700 A.D.', in J. Bintliff & H. Hamerow (eds), *Europe between Late Antiquity and the Middle Ages*, Oxford, British Archaeological Reports, International Series 617, pp. 84–98

Loyn, H.R. 1962. *Anglo-Saxon England and the Norman Conquest*, London, Longman

Lucy, S.J. 1992. 'The significance of mortuary ritual in the political manipulation of the landscape', *Archaeological Review from Cambridge* 11, 93–105

Lucy, S.J. 1997. '"Housewives, warriors and slaves?" Sex and gender in Anglo-Saxon burials', in J. Moore & E. Scott (eds), *Invisible People and Processes: Writing Gender and Childhood into European Archaeology*, Leicester, Leicester University Press, pp. 150–68

Lucy, S.J. 1998. *The Early Anglo-Saxon Cemeteries of East Yorkshire. An Analysis and Reinterpretation*, Oxford, British Archaeological Reports, British Series 272

Lucy, S.J. 2000. 'Early medieval burials in East Yorkshire: reconsidering the evidence', in H. Geake & J. Kenny (eds), *Early Deira: archaeological studies of the East Riding in the fourth to ninth centuries* AD, Oxford, Oxbow Books, pp. 11–18

Lyne, M. 1994. 'The Hassocks cemetery', *Sussex Archaeological Collections* 132, 53–85

MacDougall, H.A. 1982. *Racial Myth in English History – Trojans, Teutons and Anglo-Saxons*, Montreal, Harvest House

MacGregor, A. 1998. 'Antiquity inventoried: Museums and 'national antiquities', in the mid-nineteenth century', in V. Brand (ed.), *The Study of the Past in the Victorian Age*, Oxford, Oxbow Monograph No. 73, pp. 125–37

McGuire, R.H. 1982. 'The study of ethnicity in historical archaeology', *Journal of Anthropological Archaeology* 1, 159–78

McKinley, J. 1994a. *The Anglo-Saxon Cemetery at Spong Hill, North Elmham. Part VIII: The Cremations*, East Anglian Archaeology 69, Gressenhall

McKinley, J. 1994b. 'Bone fragment size in British cremation burials and its implications for pyre technology and ritual', *Journal of Archaeological Science* 21, 339–42

Mackeprang, M.B. 1952. *De Nordiske Guldbrakteater*, Jysk Arkaeologisk Selskabs Skrifter, Bind II

Malim, T. & Hines, J. 1998. *The Anglo-Saxon Cemetery at Edix Hill (Barrington A), Cambridgeshire*, London, Council for British Archaeology Research Report No. 112

Malina, J. & Vasícek, Z. 1990. *Archaeology Yesterday and Today*, Cambridge, Cambridge University Press

Manchester, K. 1981a. 'A leprous skeleton of the 7th century from Eccles, Kent, and the present evidence of leprosy in early Britain', *Journal of Archaeological Science* 8, 205–9

Manchester, K. 1981b. 'Hydrocephalus in an Anglo-Saxon child from Eccles', *Archaeologia Cantiana* 96, 77–82

Manchester, K. 1983. 'Secondary cancer in an Anglo-Saxon female', *Journal of Archaeological Science* 10, 475–82

Manchester, K. & Elmhirst, O. 1982. 'Forensic aspects of an Anglo-Saxon injury', *Ossa* (for 1980), 179–88

Marsden, B. 1974. *The Early Barrow-Diggers*, Aylesbury, Shire Publications

Matthews, C.L. 1962. 'The Anglo-Saxon cemetery at Marina Drive, Dunstable', *Bedfordshire Archaeological Journal* 1, 25–47

Matthews, C.L. & Hawkes, S.C. 1985. 'Early Saxon settlements and burials on Puddlehill, near Dunstable, Bedfordshire', *Anglo-Saxon Studies in Archaeology and History* 4, 59–115

BIBLIOGRAPHY

Mayes, P. & Dean, M. 1976. *An Anglo-Saxon Cemetery at Baston, Lincolnshire*, Sleaford, Occasional Papers in Lincolnshire History and Archaeology 3

Mays, S. 1998. *The Archaeology of Human Bones*, London, Routledge

Meaney, A. 1964. *A Gazetteer of Early Anglo-Saxon Burial Sites*, London, Allen & Unwin

Meaney, A. 1981. *Anglo-Saxon Amulets and Curing Stones*, Oxford, British Archaeological Reports, British Series 96

Meaney, A. & Hawkes, S.C. 1970. *Two Anglo-Saxon Cemeteries at Winnall*, Society for Medieval Archaeology Monograph Series 4

Meindl, R.S., Lovejoy, C.O., Mensforth, R.P. & Walker, R.A. 1985. 'A revised method of age determination using the *os pubis*, with a review and tests of accuracy of other current methods of pubic symphyseal ageing', *American Journal of Physical Anthropology* 68, 29–46

Meyrick, O. 1950. 'A Saxon skeleton in a Roman well', *Wiltshire Archaeological Magazine* 53, 220–2

Miles, A.E.W. 1963. 'The dentition in the assessment of individual age in skeletal remains', in D. Brothwell (ed.), *Dental Anthropology*, Oxford, Pergamon Press, pp. 191–209

Millard, L., Jarman, S. & Hawkes, S.C. 1969. 'Anglo-Saxon burials near the Lord of the Manor, Ramsgate. New light on the site of Ozingell?', *Archaeologia Cantiana* 84, 9–30

Moore, J.H. 1994. 'Putting Anthropology back together again: the ethnogenetic critique of cladistic theory', *American Anthropologist* 96, 925–48

Morris, J. 1962. 'The Anglo-Saxons in Bedfordshire', *Bedfordshire Archaeological Journal* 1, 25–47

Morris, J. 1973. *The Age of Arthur*, Chichester, Weidenfeld & Nicolson

Morris, R.K. 1983. *The Church in British Archaeology*, London, Council for British Archaeology Research Report No. 47

Mortimer, C. 1990. 'Some Aspects of Early Medieval Copper-Alloy Technology, as Illustrated by a Study of the Anglian Cruciform Brooch', Unpublished DPhil thesis, University of Oxford

Mortimer, C. 1999. 'Technical analysis of the cruciform brooch', in U. von Freeden, U. Koch & A. Wieczorek (eds), *Völker an Nord- und Ostsee und die Franken*, Bonn, Rudolf Habelt, pp. 83–9

Mortimer, C. & Stoney, M. 1996. *Decorative Punchmarks on Non-Ferrous Artefacts from Barrington Edix Hill Anglo-Saxon Cemetery 1989–91, Cambridgeshire, in their Regional Context*, Ancient Monuments Laboratory Report 62/96

Mortimer, J.R. 1905. *Forty Years Researches in British and Saxon Burial Mounds of East Yorkshire*, London, A. Brown & Sons

Musty, J. 1969. 'The excavation of two barrows, one of Saxon date, at Ford, Laverstock, near Salisbury, Wiltshire', *Antiquaries Journal* 49, 98–117

Musty, J. & Stratton, J. 1964. 'A Saxon cemetery at Winterbourne Gunner, near Salisbury', *Wiltshire Archaeological Magazine* 59, 86–109

Myres, J.N.L. 1937. 'The present state of the archaeological evidence for the Anglo-Saxon conquest', *History* (n.s.) 21, 317–30

Myres, J.N.L. 1956. 'Romano-Saxon pottery', in D.B. Harden (ed.), *Dark Age Britain – Studies presented to E.T. Leeds*, London, Methuen, pp. 16–39

Myres, J.N.L. 1959. 'Anglo-Saxon pottery of the Pagan period', *Medieval Archaeology* 3, 7–13

Myres, J.N.L. 1969. *Anglo-Saxon Pottery and the Settlement of England*, Oxford, Clarendon Press

Myres, J.N.L. 1970. 'The Angles, the Saxons and the Jutes', *Proceedings of the British Academy* 56, 1–32

Myres, J.N.L. 1977. *A Corpus of Pagan Anglo-Saxon Pottery*, Oxford, Clarendon Press

Myres, J.N.L. & Green, B. 1973. *The Anglo-Saxon Cemeteries of Caistor-by-Norwich and Markshall, Norfolk*, Reports of the Research Committee of the Society of Antiquaries No. 30

Myres, J.N.L. & Southern, W.H. 1973. *The Anglo-Saxon Cremation Cemetery at Sancton, East Yorkshire*, Hull, Hull Museum Publications No. 218

Neville, R.C. 1854. 'Anglo-Saxon cemetery excavated January 1853', *Archaeological Journal* 11, 95–115

Nicholas, T. 1868. *The Pedigree of the English People*, London, Longman

Nielsen, R. 1992. 'Early Anglo-Saxon burials in Croydon', *London Archaeologist* 7, 6–7

O'Connor, T. 1994. 'A horse skeleton from Sutton Hoo, Suffolk, UK', *Archaeozoologia* 8, 29–37

Olsen, B. & Kobyliński, Z. 1991. 'Ethnicity in anthropological and archaeological research: a Norwegian-Polish perspective', *Archaeologia Polona* 29, 5–27

BIBLIOGRAPHY

Owen-Crocker, G. 1986. *Dress in Anglo-Saxon England*, Manchester, Manchester University Press

Ozanne, A. 1963. 'The Peak Dwellers', *Medieval Archaeology* 6/7, 15–52

Pader, E.-J. 1980. 'Material symbolism and social relations in mortuary studies', in P. Rahtz, T. Dickinson & L. Watts (eds), *Anglo-Saxon Cemeteries 1979*, Oxford, British Archaeological Reports, British Series 82, pp. 143–59

Pader, E.-J. 1982. *Symbolism, Social Relations and the Interpretation of Mortuary Remains*, Oxford, British Archaeological Reports, British Series 130

Palm, M. & Pind, J. 1992. 'Anglian English women's graves in the fifth to seventh centuries AD – a chronological analysis', in L. Jørgensen (ed.), *Chronological Studies of Anglo-Saxon England, Lombard Italy and Vendel Period Sweden*, Copenhagen, Arkaeologiske Skrifter No. 5, Institute of Prehistoric and Classical Archaeology, University of Copenhagen, pp. 50–80

Palmer, J.F. 1885. 'The Saxon invasion and its influence on our character as a race', *Transactions of the Royal Historical Society* (n.s.) 2, 173–96

Parfitt, K. & Brugmann, B. 1997. *The Anglo-Saxon Cemetery on Mill Hill, Deal, Kent*, Society for Medieval Archaeology Monograph No. 14

Parker, S., Roberts, C. & Manchester, K. 1986. 'A review of British trepanations with reports on two new cases', *Ossa* 12, 141–57

Parker Pearson, M., van der Noort, R. & Woolf, A. 1993. 'Three men and a boat: Sutton Hoo and the East Saxon kingdom', *Anglo-Saxon England* 22, 27–50

Peake, H. 1906. 'Ancient earthworks', in P.H. Ditchfield & W. Page (eds), *The Victoria History of Berkshire. Volume One*, London, Archibald Constable & Co., pp. 251–84

Peake, H. & Horton, E.A. 1915. 'Saxon graveyard at East Shefford, Berks.', *Journal of the Royal Anthropological Institute* 45, 92–130

Peardon, T.P. 1933. *The Transition in English Historical Writing 1760–1830*, New York, Columbia University Press

Pearson, C.H. 1867. *History of England during the Early and Middle Ages*, London, Bell & Daldy

Penn, K. 1998. *An Anglo-Saxon Cemetery at Oxborough, West Norfolk: Excavations in 1990*, East Anglian Archaeology Occasional Papers No. 5

Perkins, D. 1987. 'The Jutish cemetery at Half Mile Ride, Margate: a reappraisal', *Archaeologia Cantiana* 104, 219–36

Perkins, D. 1991. 'The Jutish cemetery at Sarre revisited. A rescue evaluation', *Archaeologia Cantiana* 109, 139–66

Perkins, D. 1992. 'The Jutish cemetery at Sarre revisited. Part II', *Archaeologia Cantiana* 110, 83–120

Phillips, C.W. 1934. 'The present state of archaeology in Lincolnshire. Part II', *Archaeological Journal* 91, 97–187

Pike, L.O. 1866. *The English and their Origin*, London, Longman, Green & Co.

Pluciennik, M. 1996. 'Genetics, archaeology and the wider world', *Antiquity* 70, 13–14

Pohl, W. 1997. 'Ethnic names and identities in the British Isles: a comparative perspective', in J. Hines (ed.), *The Anglo-Saxons from the Migration Period to the Eighth Century. An Ethnographic Perspective*, Woodbridge, Boydell Press, pp. 7–40

Poulton, R. 1987. 'The former Goblin Works, Leatherhead: Saxons and sinners', *London Archaeologist* 5, 311–17

Powell, A. & Fitzpatrick, A. 1997. 'The Anglo-Saxon cemetery and undated features', in A. Fitzpatrick (ed.), *Archaeological Excavations on the Route of the A27 Westhampnett Bypass, West Sussex, 1992*, Wessex Archaeology Report No. 12

Powlesland, D. 1997a. 'Early Anglo-Saxon settlements, structures, form and layout', in J. Hines (ed.), *The Anglo-Saxons from the Migration Period to the Eighth Century. An Ethnographic Perspective*, Woodbridge, Boydell Press, pp. 101–24

Powlesland, D. 1997b. 'Comment', in J. Hines (ed.), *The Anglo-Saxons from the Migration Period to the Eighth Century. An Ethnographic Perspective*, Woodbridge, Boydell Press, p. 164

Powlesland, D. in press. *West Heslerton: The Anglian Cemetery*

Powlesland, D., Houghton, C. & Hanson, J.H. 1986. 'Excavations at Heslerton, North Yorkshire 1978–82', *Archaeological Journal* 143, 53–173

Prummel, W. 1992. 'Early medieval dog burials among the Germanic tribes', *Helinium* 32, 132–94
Rahtz, P. 1978. 'Grave orientation', *Archaeological Journal* 135, 1–14
Ravn, M. 1998. 'Germanic Social Structure (c. AD200–600). A Methodological Study in the Use of Archaeological and Historical Evidence in Migration Age Europe', Unpublished PhD dissertation, University of Cambridge
Reichstein, J. 1975. *Die Kreuzförmige Fibel*, Neumünster, Karl Wachholtz Verlag
Reynolds, A. 1999. 'Anglo-Saxon Law in the Landscape', Unpublished PhD dissertation, University College, London
Reynolds, N. 1976. 'The structure of Anglo-Saxon graves', *Antiquity* 50, 140–4
Reynolds, N. 1988. 'The rape of the Anglo-Saxon women', *Antiquity* 62, 715–18
Reynolds, S. 1983. 'Medieval *origines Gentium* and the community of the realm', *History* 68, 375–90
Reynolds, S. 1985. 'What do we mean by "Anglo-Saxon" and "Anglo-Saxons"?', *Journal of British Studies* 24, 395–414
Rhodes, M. 1990. 'Faussett rediscovered: Charles Roach Smith, Joseph Mayer and the publication of the *Inventorium Sepulchrale*', in E. Southworth (ed.), *Anglo-Saxon Cemeteries: A Reappraisal*, Stroud, Alan Sutton, pp. 25–64
Richards, J.D. 1987. *The Significance of Form and Decoration of Anglo-Saxon Cremation Urns*, Oxford, British Archaeological Reports, British Series 166
Richards, J.D. 1992. 'Anglo-Saxon symbolism', in M. Carver (ed.), *The Age of Sutton Hoo*, Woodbridge, Boydell Press, pp. 131–47
Rigold, S. 1974. 'Coins found in Anglo-Saxon graves', in J. Casey & R. Reece (eds), *Coins and the Archaeologist*, Oxford, British Archaeological Reports, British Series 4, pp. 201–5
Roach Smith, C. 1850a. 'On fibulae in the museum of the Hon. R.C. Neville FSA', *Journal of the British Archaeological Association* 5, 113–16
Roach Smith, C. 1850b. *Collectanea Antiqua, Etchings and Notices of Ancient Remains, Vol. I*, printed for the subscribers
Roach Smith, C. 1852a. *Collectanea Antiqua, Etchings and Notices of Ancient Remains, Vol. II*, printed for the subscribers
Roach Smith, C. 1852b. 'Notes on Saxon sepulchral remains found at Fairford, Gloucestershire', *Archaeologia* 34, 77–82
Roach Smith, C. 1857. *Collectanea Antiqua, Etchings and Notices of Ancient Remains, Vol. IV*, printed for the subscribers
Roach Smith, C. 1860. 'On Anglo-Saxon remains discovered recently at various places in Kent', *Archaeologia Cantiana* 3, 35–46
Roach Smith, C. 1861. *Collectanea Antiqua, Etchings and Notices of Ancient Remains, Vol. V*, printed for the subscribers
Roach Smith, C. 1868. *Collectanea Antiqua, Etchings and Notices of Ancient Remains, Vol. VI*, printed for the subscribers
Robb, J. 1993. 'A social prehistory of European languages', *Antiquity* 67, 747–60
Roberts, C. & Manchester, K. 1995. *The Archaeology of Disease*, Stroud, Alan Sutton Publishing
Roberts, W.I. 1982. *Romano-Saxon Pottery*, Oxford, British Archaeological Reports, British Series 106
Robinson, B. & Duhig, C. 1993. 'Anglo-Saxon burials at the "Three Kings", Haddenham 1990', *Proceedings of the Cambridge Antiquarian Society* 81, 15–38
Rodwell, K. 1993. 'The cemetery', in M.J. Darling & D. Gurney (eds), *Caistor-on-Sea Excavations by Charles Green, 1951–5*, East Anglian Archaeology 60, Field Archaeology Division, pp. 252–5
Rowlands, M. 1988. 'Repetition and exteriorisation in narratives of historical origins', *Critique of Anthropology* 8, 43–62
Saint John, J.A. 1862. *History of the Four Conquests of England, Vol. I*, London, Smith, Elder & Co.
St J. O'Neil, B. 1948. 'War and archaeology in Britain', *Antiquaries Journal* 28, 20–44
Salin, E. 1904. *Die altgermanische Thierornamentik*, Stockholm, Wahlström & Widstrand
Schnapp, A. 1996. *The Discovery of the Past, The Origins of Archaeology*, London, British Museum Press
Scull, C. 1993. 'Balances and weights from early Anglo-Saxon graves: Implications for the contexts of exchange', *Studien zur Sachsenforschung* 8, 97–102
Scull, C. & Bayliss, A. 1999. 'Radiocarbon dating and Anglo-Saxon graves', in U. von Freeden, U. Kock & A. Wieczorek (eds), *Wölker an Nord- und Ostsee und die Franken*, Bonn, Rudolf Habelt, pp. 39–50

BIBLIOGRAPHY

Shennan, S.J. 1978. 'Archaeological "cultures": an empirical investigation', in I. Hodder (ed.), *The Spatial Organisation of Culture*, London, Routledge, pp. 113–39

Shennan, S.J. 1989. 'Introduction: archaeological approaches to cultural identity', in S.J. Shennan (ed.), *Archaeological Approaches to Cultural Identity*, London, Routledge, pp. 1–32

Shepherd, J. 1979. 'The social identity of the individual in isolated barrows and barrow cemeteries in Anglo-Saxon England', in B.C. Burnham & J. Kingsbury (eds), *Space, Hierarchy and Society. Interdisciplinary Studies in Social Area Analysis*, Oxford, British Archaeological Reports, International Series 59, pp. 47–79

Sherlock, S. & Welch, M. 1992. *An Anglo-Saxon Cemetery at Norton, Cleveland*, London, Council for British Archaeology Research Report 82

Sims-Williams, P. 1983. 'The settlement of England in Bede and the Chronicle', *Anglo-Saxon England* 12, 1–41

Smith, H. 1870. 'Notes on prehistoric burial in Sussex', *Sussex Archaeological Collections* 22, 57–76

Smith, P.S. 1988. 'Early Anglo-Saxon burials from Stafford Road, Brighton, East Sussex', *Sussex Archaeological Collections* 126, 31–51

Smith, R.A. 1901. 'Anglo-Saxon remains', in H.A. Doubleday (ed.), *The Victoria History of the County of Norfolk, Vol. I*, London, Archibald Constable & Co., pp. 325–51

Smith, R.A. 1902. 'Anglo-Saxon remains', in W. Ryland, D. Adkins & R.M. Serjeantson (eds), *The Victoria History of the County of Northampton, Vol. I*, London, Archibald Constable & Co., pp. 223–56

Smith, R.A. 1903. 'Anglo-Saxon remains', in A. Doubleday & W. Page (eds), *The Victoria History of the County of Essex, Vol. I*, London, Archibald Constable &Co., pp. 315–31

Smith, R.A. 1904. 'Anglo-Saxon remains', in A. Doubleday & W. Page (eds), *The Victoria History of the County of Bedford, Vol. I*, London, Archibald Constable & Co., pp. 175–90

Smith, R.A. 1905. 'Anglo-Saxon remains', in W. Page (ed.), *The Victoria History of the County of Buckingham, Vol. I*, London, Archibald Constable & Co., pp. 195–205

Smith, R.A. 1906. 'Anglo-Saxon remains', in P.H. Ditchfield & W. Page (eds), *The Victoria History of the County of Berkshire, Vol. I*, London, Archibald Constable & Co., pp. 229–49

Smith, R.A. 1907. 'Anglo-Saxon remains', in W. Page (ed.), *The Victoria History of the County of Leicester, Vol. I*, London, Archibald Constable & Co., pp. 221–42

Smith, R.A. 1908. 'Anglo-Saxon remains', in W. Page (ed.), *The Victoria History of the County of Kent, Vol. I*, London, Archibald Constable & Co., pp. 339–87

Smith, R.A. 1911. 'Anglo-Saxon remains', in W. Page (ed.), *The Victoria History of the County of Suffolk, Vol. I*, London, Archibald Constable & Co., pp. 325–56

Smith, R.A. 1912a. 'The excavation by Canon Greenwell F.S.A., in 1908, of an Anglo-Saxon cemetery at Uncleby, East Riding of Yorkshire', *Proceedings of the Society of Antiquaries* 24, 146–58

Smith, R.A. 1912b. 'Anglo-Saxon remains', in W. Page (ed.), *The Victoria History of the County of Yorkshire, Vol. II*, London, Archibald Constable & Co., pp. 73–108

Smith, R.A. 1923. *A Guide to the Anglo-Saxon and Foreign Teutonic Antiquities in the Department of British and Medieval Antiquities, British Museum*, London, British Museum Press

Smith, R.J. 1987. *The Gothic Bequest*, Cambridge, Cambridge University Press

Sørensen, M.L.S. 1991. 'The construction of gender through appearance', in D. Walde & N. Willows (eds), *The Archaeology of Gender: Proceedings of the 22nd Chacmool Conference*, Calgary, University of Calgary Archaeological Association, pp. 121–9

Speake, G. 1980. *Anglo-Saxon Animal Art and its Germanic Background*, Oxford, Clarendon Press

Speake, G. 1986. 'Review of J. Hines – The Scandinavian Character of Anglian England in the Pre-Viking Period', *Medieval Archaeology* 30, 203–4

Speake, G. 1989. *A Saxon Bed Burial on Swallowcliffe Down*, London, English Heritage Archaeological Report No. 10

Spurrell, F. 1889. 'Dartford antiquities. Notes on British Roman and Saxon remains there found', *Archaeologia Cantiana* 18, 304–18

Stead, I.M. 1991. *Iron Age Cemeteries in East Yorkshire*, London, English Heritage Archaeological Report No. 22

Stilborg, O. 1992. 'A chronological analysis of Anglo-Saxon men's graves in England', in L. Jørgensen (ed.), *Chronological Studies of Anglo-Saxon England, Lombard Italy and Vendel Period Sweden*, Copenhagen, Arkaeologiske Skrifter No. 5, Institute of Prehistoric and Classical Archaeology, University of Copenhagen, pp. 35–49

Stone, J.F. 1932. 'Saxon interments on Roche Court Down, Winterslow', *Wiltshire Archaeological Magazine* 45, 569–99

Stoodley, N. 1997. 'The Spindle and the Spear: a critical enquiry into the construction and meaning of gender in the early Anglo-Saxon inhumation burial rite', Unpublished PhD dissertation, University of Reading

Stoodley, N. 1999a. 'Burial rites, gender and the creation of kingdoms: the evidence from seventh-century Wessex', *Anglo-Saxon Studies in Archaeology and History* 10, 99–107

Stoodley, N. 1999b. 'Post-migration age structures and age-related grave-goods in Anglo-Saxon cemeteries in England', *Studien zur Sachsenforschung* 11, 187–97

Stoodley, N. forthcoming. 'Multiple burials, multiple meanings? Interpreting the early Anglo-Saxon multiple interment', in S. Lucy & A. Reynolds (eds), *Burial in Early Medieval Britain*

Stubbs, W. 1870. *Select Charters and other illustrations of English Constitutional History from the earliest times to the reign of Edward the First* (9th edn, 1913 revised H.W.C. Davies), Oxford, Clarendon Press

Stubbs, W. 1880. *The Constitutional History of England, Vol. I* (1st edn, 1874–8), Oxford, Clarendon Press

Stubbs, W. 1906. *Lectures on Early English History* (ed. A. Hassall), London, Longman

Sutcliff, R. 1959. *The Lantern Bearers*, Oxford, Oxford University Press

Sutcliff, R. 1979. *The Light Beyond the Forest*, Oxford, Bodley Head

Sutcliff, R. 1981. *The Road to Camlann*, Oxford, Bodley Head

Swanton, M.J. 1973. *The Spearheads of the Anglo-Saxon Settlements*, London, Royal Archaeological Institute

Swanton, M.J. 1974. *A Corpus of Pagan Anglo-Saxon Spear Types*, Oxford, British Archaeological Reports, British Series 7

Taylor, A.J. 1991. 'John Nowell Linton Myres 1902–1989', *Proceedings of the British Academy* 76, 513–27

Thomas, G.W. 1887. 'On excavations in an Anglo-Saxon cemetery at Sleaford, in Lincolnshire', *Archaeologia* 50, 383–406

Thurnham, J. 1867. 'On an Anglo-Saxon fibula in the museum of the Society', *Archaeologia* 41, 479–91

Timby, J. 1993. 'Sancton I Anglo-Saxon cemetery: Excavations carried out between 1976 and 1980', *Archaeological Journal* 150, 243–365

Timby, J. 1995. *The Anglo-Saxon Cemetery at Empingham II, Rutland*, Oxford, Oxbow Monograph 70

Trevelyan, G.M. 1926. *History of England*, London, Longman, Green & Co.

Trollope, E. 1863. 'Saxon burial ground at Baston, Lincolnshire', *Archaeological Journal* 20, 29–31

Trotter, M. & Gleser, G. 1952. 'Estimation of stature from long bones of American whites and negroes', *American Journal of Physical Anthropology* 10, 463–514

Turner, S. 1799–1805. *A History of the Anglo-Saxons*, London, Cadell & Davies

Tyler, S. 1992. 'Anglo-Saxon settlement in the Darent Valley and environs', *Archaeologia Cantiana* 110, 71–81

Tyler, S. 1996. 'Early Saxon Essex AD 400–700', in O. Bedwin (ed.), *The Archaeology of Essex. Proceedings of the Writtle Conference*, Chelmsford, Essex County Council, pp. 108–16

van der Noort, R. 1993. 'The context of early medieval barrows in western Europe', *Antiquity* 67, 66–73

Veit, U. 1989. 'Ethnic concepts in German prehistory: a case study on the relationship between cultural identity and objectivity', in S.J. Shennan (ed.), *Archaeological Approaches to Cultural Identity*, London, Routledge, pp. 35–56

Vierck, H. 1978. 'Trachtenbunde und Trachtgeschichte in der Sachsen-Forschung, ihre Quellen, Ziele und Methoden', in C. Ahrens (ed.), *Sachsen und Angelsachsen*, Hamburg, Ausstellung des Helms-Museums, pp. 21–43

Wadstein, E. 1927. 'On the origin of the English', *Skrifter utgivna av K. Humanistiska Vetenskaps-Samfundet i Uppsala* 24, 5–39

Wallace-Hadrill, J.M. 1975. 'The graves of kings: an historical note on some archaeological evidence', in J.M. Wallace-Hadrill (ed.), *Early Medieval History*, Oxford, Blackwell, pp. 39–59

Warhurst, A. 1955. 'The Jutish cemetery at Lyminge', *Archaeologia Cantiana* 69, 1–40

Webster, L. 1986. 'Anglo-Saxon England AD400–1100', in I. Longworth & J. Cherry (eds), *Archaeology in Britain since 1945 – New Directions*, London, British Museum Press, pp. 119–60

Webster, L. 1992. 'Death's diplomacy: Sutton Hoo in the light of other princely male burials', in R. Farrell & C. Neuman de Vegvar (eds), *Sutton Hoo: Fifty Years After*, American Early Medieval Studies 2, pp. 75–81

Welch, M. 1983. *Early Anglo-Saxon Sussex*, Oxford, British Archaeological Reports, British Series 112

Welch, M. 1986. 'Button brooches, clasp buttons and face masks', *Medieval Archaeology* 30, 142–5

BIBLIOGRAPHY

Welch, M. 1991. 'Contacts across the Channel between the fifth and seventh centuries: a review of the archaeological evidence', *Studien zur Sachsenforschung* 7, 261–9

Welch, M. 1992. 'The archaeological evidence for federate settlement in Britain within the fifth century', in F. Vallet & M. Kazanski (eds), *L'Armée Romaine et les Barbares du IIIe au VIIe siècle*, Saint-Germain-en-Laye, Musée des antiquities nationale, pp. 269–78

Welch, M. 1999. 'Relating Anglo-Saxon chronology to Continental chronologies in the fifth century AD', in U. von Freeden, U. Kock & A. Wieczorek (eds), *Wölker an Nord- und Ostsee und die Franken*, Bonn, Rudolf Habelt, pp. 31–7

Weller, S., Westley, B. and Myres, J.N.L. 1974. 'A late fourth-century cremation from Billericay, Essex', *Antiquaries Journal* 54, 282–85

Wells, C. 1960. 'A study of cremation', *Antiquity* 34, 29–37

Wells, C. 1974. 'Probable trephination of five early Saxon skulls', *Antiquity* 48, 298–302

Werner, J. 1950. 'Zur Entstehung der Reihengräberzivilisation', *Archaeologia Geographica* 1, 23–32

West, S. 1985. *West Stow: The Anglo Saxon Village*, Ipswich, East Anglian Archaeology Report No. 24

West, S. 1988. *The Anglo-Saxon Cemetery at Westgarth Gardens, Bury St Edmunds, Suffolk*, East Anglian Archaeology Report 38, Suffolk County Planning Department

West, S. & Owles, E. 1973. 'Anglo-Saxon cremation burials from Snape', *Proceedings of the Suffolk Institute of Archaeology* 33, 47–57

Wheeler, R.E.M. 1943. *Maiden Castle, Dorset*, Oxford, Reports of the Research Committee of the Society of Antiquaries of London No. 12

White, R. 1990. 'Scrap or substitute: Roman material in Anglo-Saxon graves', in E. Southworth (ed.), *Anglo-Saxon Cemeteries: A Reappraisal*, Stroud, Alan Sutton, pp. 125–52

White, T.H. 1958. *The Once and Future King*, New York, Putnam

Whitelock, D. 1952. *The Beginnings of English Society*, Harmondsworth, Pelican History of England Vol. 2

Whitwell, J.B. 1967. 'Archaeological notes 1966', *Lincolnshire History and Archaeology* 2, 31–54

Wilkinson, L. 1980. 'Problems of analysis and interpretation of skeletal remains', in P. Rahtz, T. Dickinson & L. Watts (eds), *Anglo-Saxon Cemeteries 1979*, Oxford, British Archaeological Reports, British Series 82, pp. 221–31

Williams, H. 1997. 'Ancient landscapes and the dead: the reuse of prehistoric and Roman monuments as early Anglo-Saxon burial sites', *Medieval Archaeology* 41, 1–32

Williams, H. 1998. 'Monuments and the past in early Anglo-Saxon England', *World Archaeology* 30, 90–108

Williams, P.W. 1983. *An Anglo-Saxon Cremation Cemetery at Thurmaston, Leicestershire*, Leicestershire Museums, Art Galleries and Records Service, Archaeological Reports Series No. 8

Willson, J. 1990. 'Rescue excavations on the Anglo-Saxon cemetery at Eastry 1989', *Kent Archaeological Review* 100, 229–31

Wilson, D. 1960. *The Anglo-Saxons*, Harmondsworth, Pelican

Wilson, D. 1992a. *Anglo-Saxon Paganism*, London, Routledge

Wilson, D. 1992b. 'Sutton Hoo – Pros and Cons', in R. Farrell & C. Neuman de Vegvar (eds), *Sutton Hoo: Fifty Years After*, American Early Medieval Studies 2, pp. 5–12

Winterbottom, M. (ed. and trans.) 1978. *Gildas. The Ruin of Britain and other works*, London and Chichester, Phillimore & Co.

Wood, I. 1990. 'The Channel from the 4th to the 7th centuries AD', in S. McGrail (ed.), *Maritime Celts, Frisians and Saxons*, London, Council for British Archaeology Research Report 71, pp. 93–7

Wormald, P. 1983. 'Bede, the *Bretwaldas* and the origins of the *Gens Anglorum*', in P. Wormald (ed.), *Ideal and Reality in Frankish and Anglo-Saxon Society*, Oxford, Blackwell, 1983

Wright, T. 1845. *The Archaeological Album; or, Museum of National Antiquities*, London, Chapman & Hall

Wright, T. 1849. 'Saxon remains found in Gloucestershire', *Journal of the British Archaeological Association* 5, 343–9

Wright, T. 1852. *The Celt, the Roman and the Saxon*, London, Hall

Yorke, B. 1990. *Kings and Kingdoms of Early Anglo-Saxon England*, London, Seaby

Zachrisson, R.E. 1927. 'Romans Kelts and Saxons in Ancient Britain', *Skrifter utgivna av K. Humanistiska Vetenskaps-Samfundet i Uppsala* 24.12, 1–94

Zvelebil, M. 1995. 'At the interface of archaeology, linguistics and genetics: Indo-European dispersals and the agricultural transition in Europe', *Journal of European Archaeology* 3, 33–70

INDEX

Åberg, Nils, 11–13, 18–19, 27, 163
Abingdon (Berks.), 47, 86
Aethelbert, King of Kent, 4
Akerman, J.Y., 9–10
Aldwincle (Northants.), 69
Alfriston (Sussex), 84, 94–5
Alton (Hants.), 3, 73, 78, 86, 119, 130
Alveston Manor (Warks.), 135
amber beads, 42
amethyst beads, 42–3, 135
amulets, 44–7
Anglian material culture, 11, 83–4, 133–5
Anglo-Saxon Chronicle, The, 158, 175–6
animal accessory vessels, 112–13
animal offerings, 63, 80, 90–4, 112–13
animal ornament, 19–21
annular brooches, 37
Apple Down (Sussex), 69, 70, 73, 77, 82, 102, 116, 118–19, 121
applied saucer brooches, 35–6, 135
Arreton Down (Isle of Wight), 146
arrowheads, 47, 51, 87–8
Arthurian literature, 14, 165
Asthall (Beds.), 102, 106, 121, 182
axes, 47, 51, 87–8

bags, 46–7
balance and weights, 60
Baldwin Brown, G., 12
Banstead Common (Surrey), 93
Barrington (Cambs.), 24, 69, 84, 95, 97
barrow burial,
　primary, 4–6, 95, 101, 117–18, 180–2
　secondary, 95, 124–30
Baston (Lincs.), 113–14, 117
beads, 41–3
　amber, 42
　amethyst, 42–3, 135

　crystal, 43
　glass, 41–2
Beakesbourne (Kent), 29
Beckford (Hereford and Worcs.), 69, 151
bed burial, 96–7
Beddington (Surrey), 146
Beddoe, John, 162
Bede, *Ecclesiastical History*, 11, 156–8, 175–6
Bensford Bridge – *see* Churchover
Benty Grange (Derbys.), 4–5, 146, 180, 182
Bergh Apton (Norfolk), 63, 84
Berinsfield (Oxon.), 73, 97, 118
Bidford-on-Avon (Warks.), 77
Bifrons (Kent), 29, 78, 94
Billericay (Essex), 119
bird brooches, 33
Biscot Mill, Luton (Beds.), 97
Bledlow (Bucks.), 146
Blewburton Hill (Berks.), 124
boat burial, 95–6, 181
body position, 78–81
Boss Hall, Ipswich (Suffolk), 102
boundary burial, 148–9
Bowcombe Down (Isle of Wight), 146–8
boxes, 47, 57–8, 135
bracelets, 44
bracteates, 44, 135
Bradstow School, Broadstairs (Kent), 98
Bran Ditch, Fowlmere (Cambs.), 75
Breach Down (Kent), 8, 78
Brettenham (Norfolk), 116
Brighton (Sussex), 85
Brightwell (Suffolk), 117
British Archaeological Association, 8
brooch forms, 27–40, 83–6, 133–5
brooches,
　annular, 37
　applied saucer, 35–6, 135

INDEX

bird, 33
button, 36–7, 135
composite disc, 39–40
cruciform, 27–9, 133–5
disc, 34–5, 135
equal-armed, 33
Frankish, 33
Germanic, 33
keystone garnet disc, 39–40, 135
penannular, 37–8
plated disc, 39–40
quoit, 38
radiate, 33
saucer, 36, 135, 179
small-long, 31–3, 133
square-headed, 29–31, 133
supporting arm, 33
swastika, 37, 40–1, 135
tutulus, 33
Broome (Norfolk), 67
Broomfield (Essex), 101–2
Broughton Lodge, Willoughby-on-the-Wolds (Notts.), 89, 115
Browne, Sir Thomas, 5
bucket pendants, 43
buckets, 57
Buckland Denham (Somerset), 68
buckles, 58
bullae, 44
Burghfield (Berks.), 95, 97
Burn Ground, Hampnett (Glos.), 68, 89, 126
Burwell (Cambs.), 47, 86, 182
Buttermarket, Ipswich (Suffolk), 24, 102
button brooches, 36–7, 135

cabochon pendants, 44
Caenby (Lincs.), 78
Caistor-by-Norwich (Norfolk), 108–10, 113–15, 144, 166
Caistor-on-Sea (Norfolk), 72–3, 95
Canterbury (Kent), 4
Cassington (Oxon.), 47
Castle Acre (Norfolk), 114–15
Castledyke (Humberside), 43, 51–2, 68–70, 72, 80, 82, 85, 87, 90, 94, 128
cauldrons, 55
Cestersover – *see* Churchover
Chadlington (Oxon.), 75

Chadwick Hawkes, Sonia, 13–14, 19, 166–7, 170
Chadwick, H.M., 163
chain-mail, 48, 87
chamber graves, 102
Chartham Down (Kent), 6
Chatham Lines (Kent), 6
Chavenage (Glos.), 106
Cheesecake Hill, Driffield (Yorks.), 80
Chelmorton (Derbys.), 97
Cherry Hinton (Cambs.), 97
Chessell Down (Isle of Wight), 95
Christian burial rites, 1, 181–4
Churchover (Warks.), 121, 124
Cleatham (Lincs.), 115
coin pendants, 43
Cold Easton (Derbys.), 109, 180
combs, 60–1
composite disc brooches, 39–40
Coombe (Kent), 115, 117, 119–21
Coptic bowls, 54
correspondence analysis, 23
costume, 25, 83–90
Cotgrave (Notts.), 82
Cow Lowe (Derbys.), 146
cowry shells, 46, 135
cremation, 1, 4–6, 104–22, 140–4
  pyres, 106
  unurned, 116
  urns, 10, 18, 51–4, 113–15
  with weapons, 4
Cross Barrows, Compton (Berks.), 68
crouched burial, 80, 172
Croydon (Surrey), 118–19
cruciform brooches, 27–9, 133–5
Crundale (Kent), 10, 124
crystal balls (mounted), 45, 135
crystal beads, 43
Cuddesdon (Oxon.), 130
culture-history, 175–6
cylindrical boxes, 47

die, 60
Dinton Folly (Bucks.), 86, 133
disc brooches, 34–5, 135
DNA analysis, 68, 73
dog burials, 90
Dorchester (Oxon.), 130, 149, 166–7

206

INDEX

double burials, 82
Douglas, Revd James, 6, 8, 10
Dover Buckland (Kent), 13, 23, 52, 63, 68, 82, 84, 89, 94–5, 101, 130, 139–40
Downton (Wilts.), 94
draughtsmen, 60, 63, 109
Driffield (Yorks.), 80

ear-rings, 43
East Shefford (Berks.), 74, 102
Eccles (Kent), 69, 126
Elsham (Lincs.), 110, 115–16
Empingham (Rutland), 80, 82, 102, 133
equal-armed brooches, 33
ethnicity and material culture, 166–7, 173–81
Evison, Vera, 13–14
execution cemeteries, 75, 152

Fairford (Oxon.), 9
Farndish (Beds.), 149
Farthingdown (Surrey), 80, 93
Faussett, Revd Bryan, 6, 8, 10, 124
Faversham (Kent), 57, 93, 132
Feering (Essex), 146
Field Dalling (Norfolk), 115
Filkins (Oxon.), 89
Final Phase burial rites, 4–5, 84–5, 181–4
finger-rings, 44
Finglesham (Kent), 13, 29, 84, 98, 128, 151
fire-steels, 60
Five Knolls, Dunstable (Beds.), 75
Fleam Dyke (Cambs.), 128
foederati, 166–7
Folkestone (Kent), 140
food offerings, 63, 92–4, 110
Ford, Laverstock (Wilts.), 92–3
Fordcroft, Orpington (Kent), 124
Foulden (Norfolk), 90
Frankish brooch types, 33
Frankish burial rites, 5, 11
Freeman, E.A., 161–2
Frilford (Beds.), 126, 150
Furfooz (Belgium), 166

Garton II (Yorks.), 128, 172
Garton Slack (Yorks.), 128, 183
Garton Station (Yorks.), 126, 149, 172
Germanic brooch types, 33

Germanic burial rites, 15, 149–50, 166–7
Gildas, *De Excidio*, 155–8
Gilton, Ash (Kent), 6, 10, 28, 94–5
girdle-hangers, 45, 133
Girton (Cambs.), 115, 150
glass beads, 41–2
glass vessels, 57, 135
grave-goods and age, 111
grave-goods and sex/gender, 15, 110–11
grave layout and gender, 132
grave linings/coverings, 97, 101–2
grave markers, 102
grave orientation, 1–2, 130–2
grave robbing, 102
grave structures, 97–102, 118–19
Great Addington (Northants.), 75
Great Casterton (Rutland), 150
Great Chesterford (Essex), 13, 68, 80, 90–4, 101, 126, 139
Greenwich Park (London), 6, 67
Guest, Edwin, 161

Haddenham (Cambs.), 97
Hadleigh Road, Ipswich (Suffolk), 68
Half Mile Ride, Margate (Kent), 95
hanging-bowls, 54
Harwell (Oxon.), 68–9
Haslingfield (Cambs.), 33, 115
Hassocks (Sussex), 150
Hawkes, Christopher, 14
helmets, 47, 51, 87
Helpston (Derbys.), 115
Herpes (France), 180
Highdown (Sussex), 84
historical sources, 155–8, 175–6
Holywell Row (Suffolk), 84, 88, 93, 173
horse burials, 90–2
Horton Kirby (Kent), 81
Howletts (Kent), 29, 132

Illington (Norfolk), 113, 115
Ingram, Revd James, 160
iron tools, 60, 88
Itchen Abbas (Hants.), 150

Kelleythorpe (Yorks.), 130
Kemble (Glos.), 75, 150
Kemble, J.M., 11, 160–1

207

INDEX

Kempston (Beds.), 78, 89, 101, 115, 144
Kendrick, T.D., 165
Kenninghall (Norfolk), 89
Kentish material culture, 11, 85, 182
Kentish pottery, 54
keystone garnet disc brooches, 39–40, 135
kingdom formation, 183–4
Kingsley, Charles, 161–2
King's Newton (Derbys.), 114, 117
Kingston Down (Kent), 6, 82, 181
Kingston-on-Soar (Derbys.), 114
King's Walden (Herts.), 94
Kingthorpe (Yorks.), 94
knives, 58–60
Kossinna, Gustaf, 175

laeti, 166–7
Lakenheath Aerodrome (Suffolk), 89, 92, 116
language and culture, 175
Lappenberg, J.M., 160
Lapwing Hill (Derbys.), 97, 146
Laverstock (Wilts.), 148
Leatherhead, Goblin Works (Surrey), 152
Lechlade, Butler's Field (Glos.), 63, 78, 82, 86, 100, 119, 128, 139
Leeds, E.T., 11–13, 17, 19, 29, 163–5, 171
Leighton Buzzard (Beds.), 97
Letchworth (Herts.), 68
Liebenau (Germany), 106
linked pin suites, 44
Little Chester (Derbys.), 124
Little Wilbraham (Cambs.), 33, 84, 86, 90, 106, 115
'live' burial, 78–80
Longthorpe (Cambs.), 124
Long Wittenham (Berks.), 55–7, 130
Loveden Hill (Lincs.), 75, 90, 101, 108–9, 113–16, 139
Luton (Beds.), 82
Lyminge (Kent), 85, 149
lyres, 63

Maiden Castle (Dorset), 124, 126
Margate (Kent), 102
Marina Drive (Beds.), 86, 94
Markshall (Norfolk), 110, 112
Marston St Lawrence (Northants.), 85, 92, 146
Mayer, Joseph, 9

metal-detecting, 10
metal vessels, 54–5
Mill Hill, Deal (Kent), 72, 77, 84–6, 124
Milton-next-Sittingbourne (Kent), 94
miniature artefacts, 45
Minster Lovell (Oxon.), 90
Mitcham (Surrey), 75
Monkton (Kent), 97
Morningthorpe (Norfolk), 63, 84–5, 99, 102
Mucking (Essex), 65, 97, 110, 154
multiple burial, 80, 82, 107–8
mutilation, 75
Myres, J.N.L., 11, 13, 17–18, 164, 168–71

'native' survival, 170–2
Newark (Notts.), 107–10, 112–15
Newport Pagnell (Bucks.), 130
Norton (Cleveland), 80, 86
Nydam Style decoration, 18

Offchurch (Warks.), 94
Old Walsingham (Norfolk), 5
Oosterbeintum (Netherlands), 90
Orpington (Kent), 133
Orsett (Essex), 47, 99
Osengal (Kent), 86, 95, 101–2
Oxborough (Norfolk), 130

penannular brooches, 37–8
pendants, 43–4
    bucket, 43
    cabochon, 44
    coin, 43
    scutiform, 44
Petersfinger (Hants.), 152
pins, 44
Pitsford (Northants.), 117
plated disc brooches, 39–40
playing counters, 63, 109
Polhill (Kent), 132
Portway (Hants.), 77, 81–2, 89, 93–4, 101–2, 110, 116, 119, 128, 139, 144, 146, 149, 151
pottery stamps, 52–3
pottery vessels, 51–4
Poulton Down (Wilts.), 69
Poundbury (Dorset), 1
'princely' graves, 4, 146–8, 181–2

INDEX

prone burial, 78–80
Puddlehill (Beds.), 68, 95
purse-mounts, 60

quoit brooches, 38
Quoit Brooch Style, 19–20, 38

racial theory, 161–2, 174–6
radiate brooches, 33
Redbourne (Herts.), 5
reuse of existing monuments, 124–30
Richborough Castle (Kent), 149
ring-ditches, 98–101, 119
Roach Smith, Charles, 6, 8–11, 163
Roche Court Down (Wilts.), 93, 97
Rochester (Kent), 95
Roger of Wendover, 5
Roman cemeteries, 1, 166–7
Roman objects, 46–7, 86
Roman-Saxon continuity, 150–1
Roman towns, 2
Roxby (Lincs.), 97, 151
runic symbols, 94–5

St Augustine, 4
St Peter's Broadstairs (Kent), 90, 98–101, 133
Salin Style I animal ornament, 18–19, 20–1, 31
Salin Style II animal ornament, 18–19, 20–1
Sancton (Yorks.), 106, 112–13, 151
Sandy (Beds.), 150
Sarre (Kent), 19, 29, 38, 88, 93–5, 102
saucer brooches, 36, 135, 179
Saxonbury, Lewes (Sussex), 133
Saxon material culture, 11, 83–4, 135
scales and weights, 60, 88
Scandinavian burial rites, 5
scientific dating methods, 24–5
scutiform pendants, 44
seaxes, 51, 87–8, 135
seriation, 22–3
Sewerby (Yorks.), 78–80, 82, 84, 97, 128, 149
Shakenoak (Oxon.), 31
shears, 61, 135
shields/shield bosses, 48–9, 87–8
ship burial, 95–6
Shudy Camps (Cambs.), 97
Sibertswold (Kent), 6, 93

skeletal remains, 65–73, 106–7, 139
skillets, 55
Sleaford (Lincs.), 80, 94, 97, 140
sleeve-clasps, 37, 86, 133–5
small-long brooches, 31–3, 133
Smith, R.A., 12
Snape (Suffolk), 95, 106, 115, 144, 181
Snodland (Kent), 94–5
Soham (Cambs.), 126
Soham Waterworks (Cambs.), 86, 88
South Elkington (Lincs.), 110
spearheads, 48, 87–8
Spitalfields (London), 67
Spong Hill (Norfolk), 23, 54, 94, 99, 102, 104–17, 121–2, 139, 144, 149, 152
spoons, perforated, 45–6
Sporle (Norfolk), 95
Springfield (Essex), 92, 99, 119, 128
square-headed brooches, 29–31, 133
Stifford Clays (Essex), 99, 119
stoup, 55–7
Stowting (Kent), 82, 94
stratigraphy, 21–2
Stretton-on-Fosse (Warks.), 133
Stubbs, William, 161–2
Süderbrarup (Germany), 121
supporting-arm brooches, 33
Sutton Courtenay (Berks.), 128
Sutton Hoo (Suffolk), 4–5, 63, 65, 75, 87, 90–2, 95–6, 101, 115, 128, 148, 181–2
Swaffham (Norfolk), 84
Swallowcliffe Down (Wilts.), 97
swastika brooches, 37, 40–1, 135
sword beads/rings, 47, 50
sword beaters, 60
swords, 50–1, 87–8, 135

Tallington (Lincs.), 86
Taplow (Bucks.), 87, 101–2, 182
teeth (human and animal) as grave-goods, 94
textile analysis, 83
Thornham (Norfolk), 128
Thorpe, Benjamin, 160
Thurmaston (Lincs.), 116
toilet-sets, 61–3
treasure trove legislation, 10
trepanation, 72, 80
Turner, Sharon, 159–60

INDEX

tutulus brooches, 33
typology, 13, 16–21

Uncleby (Yorks.), 80, 82, 172
Updown, Eastry (Kent), 151
unurned cremation, 116

Valsgärde (Sweden), 5, 181
Vendel (Sweden), 5, 181

Wakerley (Northants.), 77, 95
Wallingford (Berks.), 86
Wallud's Bank, Luton (Beds.), 97
Wasperton (Warks.), 84, 150
weapon burial, 1, 3–4, 74, 87–8, 149, 166–7
weapon injuries, 68–9, 88
weaponry, 48–51
weaving batons, 60, 135
Westbere (Kent), 115
Westbury-by-Shenley (Bucks.), 80
Westgarth Gardens (Suffolk), 80, 88

Westhampnett (Sussex), 100, 126
West Heslerton (Yorks.), 3, 67, 72, 73, 77, 89, 92, 95, 126, 130–2, 139, 154
West Stoke (Sussex), 117–18
West Stow (Suffolk), 3, 101, 154
Wheatley (Oxon.), 47, 97
White Low (Derbys.), 180
Wigber Low (Derbys.), 93–4
Wigston Magna (Leics.), 86
window urns, 115
Winnall (Hants.), 13, 86
Winterbourne Gunner (Wilts.), 101
Wolterton (Norfolk), 115
wooden bowls, 57
wooden cups, 57
Woodingdean (Sussex), 95, 97
Worthy Park (Hants.), 70–2, 78
Wright, Thomas, 11, 168
Wylie, William, 9

Yorkshire Antiquarian Club, 9